Schizophrenia

Towards a New Synthesis

Schizophrenia

Towards a New Synthesis

Edited by

J. K. WING

Institute of Psychiatry,
London, England

1978

ACADEMIC PRESS · London

GRUNE & STRATTON · New York

U.K. edition published and distributed by
ACADEMIC PRESS INC. (LONDON) LTD.
24/28 Oval Road
London NW1

United States edition published and distributed by
GRUNE & STRATTON INC.
111 Fifth Avenue
New York, New York 10003

Library of Congress Catalog Card Number: 77-93490
ISBN (Academic Press): 0-12-759450-7
ISBN (Grune & Stratton): 0-8089-1140-6

Printed in Great Britain
by Clark, Doble & Brendon Ltd, Plymouth

Contributors

DOUGLAS BENNETT, *The Bethlem and Mandsley Hospitals, Denmark Hill, London SE5 8AZ, England*

BRIAN COOPER, *Central Institute of Mental Health, University of Heidelberg, 6800 Mannheim 1, West Germany*

CLARE CREER, *Social Services Department, Royal Borouth of Kensington and Chelsea, Town Hall, Hornton Street, London W8, England*

HUGH FREEMAN, *Department of Psychiatry, Hope Hospital, University of Manchester, Salford M6 8HD, England*

LESLIE L. IVERSEN, *MRC Neurochemical Pharmacology Unit, Department of Pharmacology, University of Cambridge, Hills Road, Cambridge CB2 2QD, England*

H. GWYNNE JONES, *Department of Psychology, University of Leeds, Leeds LS2 9JT, England*

JULIAN LEFF, *MRC Social Psychiatry Unit, Institute of Psychiatry, De Crespigny Park, London SE5 8AF, England*

JAMES SHIELDS,† *Institute of Psychiatry, De Crespigny Park, London SE5 8AF, England*

PETFR H. VENABLES, *Department of Psychology, University of York, Heslington, York YO1 5DD, England*

J. K. WING, *MRC Social Psychitary Unit, Institute of Psychiatry, De Crespigny Park, London SE5 8AF, England*

† Deceased.

Preface

The title of this book is not intended to suggest that many of the ideas or facts in it are new; still less that its echoes of the titles of Julian Huxley's and E. O. Wilson's books on evolution imply a similar grandeur of scope and theory. Our aim is much more modest. We have attempted to bring together in one volume up-to-date accounts of the progress made along several quite different lines of development, biological, psychological and social, and to describe the current state of knowledge within each one. The possibility of a "synthesis" derives from two circumstances; first, that several of these lines seem to be converging and, second, that the authors bring to their expositions a common assumption that the truth about schizophrenia is not to be found within one restricted field of knowledge. Each reaches out to other fields. The fact that the authors all recognize the need to restrict theoretical and therapeutic claims to those with a fair degree of empirical support is a further unifying influence. We cannot claim that knowledge of the causes, biology, treatment and management of "the schizophrenias" has reached the level achieved for such contemporary puzzles as diabetes mellitus or migraine (the problems, after all, are immeasurably more difficult), but we do consider that we have demonstrated a degree of advance and even of synthesis that few could reasonably have predicted even a decade ago. By the same token, the gaps where further advance is needed become more obvious when shown in context.

Clearly a book of this kind must have a multiple authorship but this has disadvantages. There is an inevitable unevenness of style though we have tried to keep technological jargon to a minimum and to eliminate vagueness as far as possible. A good deal of repetition has been removed in the editing but some remains, since it was thought valuable for the reader to see certain points being discussed in several different contexts.

Moreover, the authors do not belong to any particular "school" and do not necessarily hold the same opinions about problems of causation and treatment. Much of the repetition will be found in Chapters 1 and 11, where an attempt is made to provide a coherent framework for our present understanding of the nature of schizophrenia and its management. A further disadvantage, inevitable in any monograph on a limited topic, is that the same detailed attention cannot be given to problems that arise out of the relations between schizophrenia and other conditions. For example, the reader will need to consult other monographs and more general textbooks in order to obtain a comprehensive picture of the problems of differential diagnosis, or to compare and contrast the biochemistry of the affective disorders with that of schizophrenia.

Within these limitations we hope that the book will appeal to a fairly wide readership: clinicians of all kinds (psychiatrists, general practitioners, clinical psychologists and social workers), scientists in the relevant fields of biology, psychology and social studies, and possibly others who have been sufficiently intrigued by contemporary controversies to want to explore the subject further. The original aim was to provide a book that would be intelligible and useful to psychiatrists working for their specialist qualifications, and we hope that this too has been achieved.

A word is necessary concerning the use of the term "schizophrenia" in this book. Since much of the material discussed was collected and described by workers who adopted very diverse approaches, it can never be certain that the clinical conditions involved were comparable with each other, although a substantial degree of overlap can often be assumed. It is only recently that the need to include the diagnostic criteria in explicit, and if possible in standard, terms has been recognized. Much sterile controversy over conflicting evidence might have been avoided if it had been adopted earlier. Since to reiterate this fundamental qualification every time it is relevant would be boring in the extreme, the practice has been adopted of putting the term "schizophrenia" in quotes on the first occasion of its use in each chapter (except in Chapter 1, where the qualifications are already very explicit), with a footnote referring the reader to this page. We hope this device will not be found too tedious and that readers will appreciate the necessity for it.

As this book was going to press we learned of the death of James Shields. His chapter provides an example of the eager curiosity, high scholarship and balanced judgement that characterizes all his work. It would be a fitting tribute if some young reader were inspired by this latest account to carry forward the study of psychiatric genetics with the same enthusiasm and scientific integrity.

July 1978   J. K. Wing

Contents

Clinical Concepts of Schizophrenia

I

J. K. Wing

Historical Developments

Controversy concerning the applicability and usefulness of various ways of classifying mental disorders has been going on for centuries, but in a book entitled "Schizophrenia" it is convenient to begin our discussion by considering the ideas current two decades before Kraepelin laid down the system of classification which most psychiatrists now, in one or another adaptation, use. At that time, just over a hundred years ago, there was much the same discussion as now concerning the value of "disease entities". The adherents of one school argued for the concept of a unitary psychosis; pointing out that there is an infinite variety of experience and behaviour, and that to delineate boundaries between named classes is as fruitless as to try to classify the shapes of clouds. The overlap between classes is so extensive as to make classification virtually useless. States of madness dissolved into each other, with or without a temporal sequence. Some proponents of this view held that all mental illness began as melancholia and progressed through paranoia to dementia; others that virtually any sequence could occur. Another school argued that clouds *can* usefully be classified, whatever the appearances to the contrary, and that severe mental disorders classified by syndrome have characteristics—such as aspects of aetiology, pathology, treatment, course and outcome—in common. These approaches, and various intermediate versions of them, are discussed by Karl Jaspers in Chapter 12 of his *General Psychopathology* (1963), and they still preoccupy theoreticians today.

Emil Kraepelin suggested a classification of those severe mental disorders which were not clearly organic in origin (such as senile dementia, Pick's disease, or GPI), dividing them into two large groups: dementia praecox and the manic-depressive disorders. He was drawing upon a wide range of clinical observation and theory, particularly in Germany and France, as well as on his own extensive experience (1919, 1921). The two classes of disorder were said to be recognizable by their characteristic symptoms, and further differentiated because the course was quite different.

Kraepelin's concept of dementia praecox incorporated as subclasses conditions that had been described by Morel, Hecker and Kahlbaum as specific conditions: hebephrenia, catatonia and paranoid deterioration. The common symptoms were auditory hallucinations, delusions, thought disorder based on unusual associations, stereotypies, affective flattening, and lack of interest in the outside world; usually with no signs of organic impairment. Although, as the name suggests, Kraepelin thought that dementia praecox typically occurred in young people and that there was a general tendency towards emotional and intellectual deterioration (not present in manic-depressive disorders), he did recognize and clearly state that onset could occur in later life and that a proportion of patients recovered completely. Another group of cases, in which emotional and intellectual deterioration was less marked, and in which delusions and hallucinations were predominant, he called paraphrenias. The non-hallucinatory delusional disorders he called paranoia.

Eugen Bleuler published his own clinical observations and theories in 1911, building explicitly on Kraepelin's formulation, and emphasizing more than Kraepelin had done that follow-up always revealed "some significant residual symptoms common to all" (Bleuler, 1911). He proposed the name "schizophrenia" to cover all Kraepelin's subtypes as well as paraphrenia. The new name was more convenient, because it has an adjectival form, and was preferable because it did not carry an implication of invariable early onset and inevitable deterioration. Bleuler's "schizophrenia" covered all Kraepelin's subclasses with the addition of paraphrenia. More important than these innovations, Bleuler put forward the view that all the clinical manifestations of schizophrenia could be interpreted in terms of two of Kraepelin's symptoms—emotional flattening and thought disorder (loosening of associations). Other symptoms, such as delusions or hallucinations, could be regarded as secondary or accessory to the more fundamental ones, and could occur in many other types of mental disorder.

Bleuler used the term "autism" to describe a turning away from the external environment into a private world of fantasy which resulted from the combination of the two fundamental symptoms. "The reality of the autistic world may also seem more valid than that of reality itself; the patients then hold their fantasies for real; reality for an illusion" (Bleuler, 1911). The term was also used to refer to mechanisms present in normal people, so that there was a continuum from normality to abnormality (Bleuler, 1919). "The difference between this wider concept of autism and the autism characteristic of schizophrenia is obviously that while the normal person may experience all kinds of wishful 'autistic' thinking, he will also be able to correct the wishful aberrations, at least to himself" (WHO, 1973, p. 19). Kretschmer (1942) pointed out that there could be at least two varieties of severe autism: the "hyper-aesthetic" or Hölderlin type, in which the individual is over-sensitive to the environment and for this reason retreats into an inner fantasy life; and the "anaesthetic" variety, in which there is a simple withdrawal, without much inner experience. A further complication was introduced by Leo Kanner, who adopted the term "autism" as a name for a syndrome observed in small children who showed disturbances of affective contact together with an anxious desire towards the preservation of "sameness" in certain features of the environment (Kanner, 1942). Kanner's syndrome (early infantile autism) has no relationship to schizophrenia (Bosch, 1962, 1970; Rutter, 1972; L. Wing, 1976) but for many years the use of the term "autism" led to a confusion between the two concepts (Wing, 1976). Indeed, the confusion can still be found in current writing (Goldfarb et al., 1976).

Bleuler thus widened the boundaries of Kraepelin's concept, since clinicians could adopt their own threshold between normal and abnormal. He himself diagnosed "schizophrenia" in a number of deviant individuals, such as tramps, convicted offenders, and eccentrics, on the basis of "fundamental" symptoms, although "accessory" phenomena were absent: the so-called "simple" variety of schizophrenia. This was the basis for later subtypes such as sluggish, pseudoneurotic and pseudopsychopathic schizophrenia (Levit, 1977; Hoch and Polatin, 1949; Dunaif and Hoch, 1955).

By contrast, Kurt Schneider (1971) provided a list of symptoms "of the first rank" which, in the absence of epilepsy, intoxication, or other evidence of gross cerebral damage, he regarded as likely to indicate a diagnosis of schizophrenia. They include: hearing one's thoughts spoken aloud, voices talking to each other, voices that comment on one's behaviour, a conviction that external forces are interfering with bodily functions or interfering with or removing or broadcasting thoughts, and the experience that emotions or behaviour or volition are under the control of an external agency. Schneider pointed out that the same experiences are sometimes present in cases where there is a known organic cause. He did not suggest that they must be related to a specific underlying biological abnormality, nor like Langfeldt (1937) did he argue that they carried a specially poor prognosis. Schneider's main concern was to define a syndrome that was particularly useful in differentiating schizophrenia from manic-depressive disorders, but the effect of applying his criteria is, of course, markedly to restrict the clinical concept, by using clearly defined and readily observable criteria. Other delusional and hallucinatory phenomena could occur in schizophrenia but they were common in other psychoses also.

The term "schizo-affective" was introduced by Kasanin (1933) to cover cases with a sudden onset and "marked emotional turmoil". Subsequently, the term has come to be used in a different way, to describe patients who show both schizophrenic and affective (particularly depressive) symptoms.

Recent large-scale international studies of acutely ill patients have done something to clarify the way the term "schizophrenia" is used in different parts of the world. Two in particular, the US–UK Diagnostic Project (Cooper et al., 1972) and the International Pilot Study of Schizophrenia (WHO, 1973), are apposite because of the use of a standard technique of interviewing patients, known as the Present State Examination (PSE), which is based on a detailed glossary of differential definitions of symptoms. It is possible for psychiatrists trained in this technique to achieve a very considerable degree of agreement as to what symptoms are present, irrespective of the culture or language which they share with the patient. A set of rules, embodied in a computer program known as Catego, can be applied to the observed profile of symptoms in order to obtain a reference classification (equivalent under certain circumstances to a diagnosis) against which clinical diagnoses can be compared (Wing et al., 1974).

The following clinical descriptions are based mainly on results from these studies. They will be divided into two groups. The first group contains syndromes* most characteristically seen during acute episodes of schizophrenia, which disappear following treatment or the cessation of stress, although they can become chronic. These are the so-called florid or positive or productive syndromes. The second group contains syndromes more characteristically seen in the chronic state. They in-

---

* The term "syndrome" is used to describe a number of symptoms that are commonly found in association with each other.

clude the syndrome of characteristics associated with social withdrawal, often called "negative" (the clinical poverty syndrome), and the syndrome of schizophrenic thought disorders, which is often negative in the same sense but can occasionally give the appearance of productivity. These syndromes often precede, accompany or follow the more acute variety. Both types can fluctuate in intensity at different stages of the course.

There is no satisfactory terminology for these syndromes, since both types can be acute or chronic, positive or negative. However, the florid types are usually acute and the negative types usually chronic, and so they will be called the acute and the chronic syndromes, for brevity and convenience. Chapter 10 contains some graphic descriptions of both groups, given by relatives who have experienced them at close quarters. The next two sections of this chapter contain a more academic account.

Acute Schizophrenic Syndromes and their Differentiation

THE CENTRAL SYNDROME

In each of the two large international studies, about two-thirds of all patients given a clinical diagnosis of schizophrenia described experiences equivalent to Schneider's first rank symptoms. When symptoms of this central syndrome were present there was a more than 90% probability that the clinical diagnosis would be schizophrenia or paranoid psychosis —295 and 297 in the International Classification of Diseases (WHO, 1974). Since the syndrome occurred only rarely or minimally in other disorders such as mania and depression, its presence was highly discriminating and useful in differential diagnosis (Scharfetter *et al.*, 1976; Wing and Nixon, 1975; Wing *et al.*, 1978). This confirmation of Schneider's criteria in large-scale clinical practice makes it worthwhile to examine them in detail. They include: "loud thoughts", thought echo, thought substitution or insertion, thought broadcast, voices commenting on the patient's thoughts or actions, voices talking to each other, feelings that bodily functions are interfered with by external agents, feelings that the patient's will or emotions or behaviour are taken over and controlled by external agents or forces. Consciousness is clear and no organic impairment is present.

Each of these symptoms has a precise definition and mistakes (particularly false positives) can easily be made if the patient is in an excited state, or does not understand the question, or tends to answer affirmatively to leading questions without giving descriptions based on his or her own experiences. (See definitions given in the glossary to the PSE, Wing *et al.*, 1974.)

For example, the symptom of thought insertion is based on the patient's experience that thoughts which are not his own are introduced into his mind. Depressed patients sometimes say that the Devil is causing them to think evil thoughts, but this is not the symptom. Similarly, manic patients may say that their thoughts are as powerful as the thoughts of the sun; this is not the symptom either. It is fairly common, in several types of psychotic state, for patients to say that their thoughts can be read, but this is not the same as thought insertion. Typically, thought insertion is described by the patient in terms of some causal idea, such as a radio set implanted in the brain, or rays directed from another planet, or telepathy, which explains how the alien thoughts have been inserted. Occasionally, however, the patient reports only the simple experience. Thus there appears to be a continuum between experiences such as "loud thoughts", thought insertion, thought broadcast, auditory hallucinations experienced as within the mind and those experienced as real external events.

The reason that voices "talking about" the patient are specified as coming within the central syndrome, while voices "talking to" the patient are not, is that the latter occur quite frequently in other conditions. In depression, for example, a patient may hear a voice telling him he deserves to die because he has sinned against the Holy Ghost. The mood and content are characteristic of depression. In mania, a patient may hear a voice saying, "You are the King. Go to the Palace." Such hallucinations are usually of single voices, speaking in short sentences, and not persisting over long periods. (Very rarely, two voices may be heard, speaking one or two sentences each, but this should not, in the circumstances, be regarded as diagnostic of schizophrenia.) Voices experienced as speaking to the patient are, of course, very common in schizophrenia, and may persist for very long periods. Some patients report having had such experiences continuously for years on end. If mood and content are taken into account, there is rarely any difficulty in distinguishing which type of hallucination is involved.

Delusions of influence and control are also very common during acute schizophrenic episodes. The patient experiences his will as being replaced by that of some other force or agency. The symptom is often elaborated in various ways: the patient says that someone else's words are coming out using his voice, or that his handwriting is not his own, or that he is a zombie or robot whose every movement is determined by some alien power. When the symptom is elaborated in such ways there is little room for doubt. Quite often, however, in various psychotic states, the patient says he is being influenced or controlled when all he means is that he feels his life is purposeless, or must be left to fate, or that he is not very strong-willed, or that God disposes all human lives. Such statements are not evidence that the symptom is present. Another cause of difficulty arises when a member of a cultural group that believes in possession becomes excited or depressed. An example is given on p. 15.

Each of the symptoms in the central syndrome can be analysed in this way and only when the physician has heard a great many patients in acute psychotic states describe their experiences is it possible to become expert in differential recognition.

One further symptom that is usually regarded as highly discriminating for schizophrenia, if organic conditions are excluded, is the primary or autochthonous delusion. This is a delusion that seems to appear fully formed without any previous experiences such as "loud thoughts" or auditory hallucinations to explain it. A patient who was having a liver puncture became convinced, at the moment that the needle was inserted that he had been "chosen by God". Shortly afterwards, the full clinical syndrome developed. No previous abnormal experiences were elicited, but he did describe a state of unusual puzzlement, beforehand, lasting several hours (see below). Delusions of reference or misidentification sometimes begin, out of the blue, in this way. The patient suddenly attributes an idiosyncratic meaning to a shop-sign, or a car registration number, or a remark heard on television, that is felt to refer to himself, and is experienced with great conviction. Usually such symptoms are accompanied or followed by others in the central syndrome.

When the central syndrome is present, there is almost always a very wide range of other symptoms as well, most of them less discriminatory. The significance of this fact will be considered later.

PERCEPTUAL ABNORMALITIES

All the symptoms in the central syndrome are based on abnormal experiences described, often with great clarity and force, by the patient. Chapman (1966) described in considerable detail perceptual abnormalities experienced by patients, such as objects changing in size or shape or colour, time becoming speeded up or slowed down or earlier events being repeated, sounds becoming louder or softer or purer. The patient may notice a pattern of cracks in the wall standing out sharply. Such experiences are often interpreted in delusional terms or as formed hallucinations of various senses. They are then classifiable elsewhere. Toxic states should, of course, always be considered. Visual hallucinations do occur in schizophrenia but are not highly discriminating in themselves. Somatic hallucinations are often reported in bizarre delusional terms: "My liver has been turned to gold by a ray sent from Mars", may be an explanatory delusion, based on a somatic hallucination. Delusional mood is a common symptom in early acute schizophrenia. The mood is often one of intense but vague puzzlement; familiar surroundings seem strange, people's motivations seem inexplicable, something odd seems to be going on. It is during this mood that first rank experiences, perceptual abnormalities and primary delusions often develop for the first time.

The symptoms of depersonalization and derealization are common in neuroses as well as psychoses and have no diagnostic significance. The terms were, however, used by Langfeldt (1960) in an unusual way (Stengel, 1960), to designate certain delusional experiences and explanations that are characteristic first rank symptoms. It is best to restrict the terms to the common usage (Carpenter and Strauss, 1973; Wing and Nixon, 1975).

OTHER DELUSIONAL SYNDROMES

So far we have been discussing abnormal delusional and perceptual experiences, on the basis of which delusions and hallucinations may be elaborated. Another group of delusions and hallucinations (which can be found in association with the central syndrome) is based on mood. The patient says, for example, that he has ruined himself and his family and deserves severe punishment, when, apart from his depressed mood, no-one else can understand his reaction. Equivalent manic delusions are based on elation. Such mood-based syndromes can occur with the central schizophrenic syndrome as part of the same clinical picture but when they occur as the predominant psychotic symptoms they are diagnosed with the affective psychoses.

However, there is a further group of delusional symptoms that do not form part of the central schizophrenic syndrome and are not based on mood. They are classified according to content: persecutory, reference, grandiose, religious, fantastic, sexual, somatic, and so on. The term "paranoid" is used to cover them all, not only delusions of persecution. Most commonly several varieties occur together.

Occasionally, however, a patient describes only a single over-valued idea—concerning the fidelity of his spouse, the size of his nose, the feeling that people think he smells or that he is homosexual. Such ideas may have "delusional" force, dominating the patient's behaviour and allowing him or her no time to devote to everyday affairs at all. It can therefore become totally disabling. Such "monosymptomatic delusions" are not highly discriminating for any one diagnosis but may be classified in different ways according to the other symptoms present. Sometimes, delusions appear explicable in terms of the social and personal circumstances of the patient. For example, an elderly patient with a poor memory may mislay his wallet and say some member of the family has stolen it. Analogous ideas are sometimes found in deaf people and in the mentally retarded.

When no characteristic delusional or perceptual or affective experiences seem to underlie false beliefs, which are expressed with great conviction when all the evidence contradicts them, it is usual to apply the same word "delusion", though a different word might be less confusing. Such paranoid delusions can reasonably be classified, in the absence of marked mood changes, as one of the paranoid psychoses (297 in the ICD), but some psychiatrists all over the world tend to include them under the schizophrenic psychoses. There is nothing to be lost by keeping such paranoid conditions in a separate class, since this can be combined with others for statistical purposes, but once they are included under a wider label there is no possibility of separating them again. In the International Pilot Study of Schizophrenia, 17% of conditions diagnosed as schizophrenic or paranoid psychoses had no first rank symptoms but did have one of these paranoid syndromes. Most, in fact, were classified as schizophrenic psychoses.

OTHER PSYCHOTIC SYNDROMES

Another small group (6%) of patients diagnosed as schizophrenic or paranoid in the IPSS had none of the syndromes described in the three sections above, but did show abnormalities of behaviour that might be regarded as diagnostic (such as catatonic symptoms), or as indicating a chronic schizophrenic condition. Clearly, if patients talk to themselves persistently, it may be inferred that they hear hallucinatory voices even though they do not describe such experiences. Both the nature of the symptom and its possible cause are often doubtful, however. Other patients receive a diagnosis of schizophrenia solely on the basis of Bleuler's autism; a combination of flattening of affect and thought disorder. As we have seen earlier, these symptoms are difficult to define reliably and specifically. Further discussion will be found under the heading of "the clinical poverty syndrome" below.

Catatonic symptoms occurring in the absence of more typical schizophrenic syndromes should always be considered as possibly belonging to some other condition. The obvious example is the catatonia of encephalitis lethargica, in which all the characteristic symptoms can be seen—automatic obedience, the maintenance of awkward postures, echopraxia, echolalia, negativism, stupor and excitement (Sachs, 1973). It is unwise to diagnose schizophrenia purely on catatonic symptoms.

NEUROTIC SYNDROMES

Many patients with acute schizophrenia describe a full range of neurotic syndromes in addition to delusions and hallucinations. They are often depressed, anxious, tense, worried, irritable, distractible, hypochondriacal, and complain of a variety of aches and pains. These symptoms may precede the more typical onset and thus appear to justify a type of "pseudo-neurotic" schizophrenia, but such a label is pointless once the typical schizophrenic symptoms appear and can be of very little use if applied in anticipation of them; indeed, it can then be harmful.

A typical obsessional disorder may, very rarely, precede the onset of schizophrenia. Occasionally it may be very difficult to differentiate between an obsession and a delusion, but this is also rare.

Chronic Schizophrenic Syndromes

As in the case of the acute syndromes, the adjective is somewhat of a misnomer, since the chronic syndromes can begin and remit suddenly as part of a more florid episode. Fluctuations are quite common. However, by and large, they are chronic. There are two main kinds, each equivalent to one of Bleuler's fundamental characteristics—flattening of affect and loosening of the associations.

THE CLINICAL POVERTY SYNDROME

The first major syndrome is composed of a series of behaviours that tend to cluster together: emotional apathy, slowness of thought and movement, underactivity, lack of drive, poverty of speech, and social withdrawal. This syndrome can be reliably measured, when fairly severe, by means of behaviour scales (Venables, 1957; Wing, 1961; Wing and

Brown, 1970). The intensity of the syndrome gives a measure of social performance, since it is correlated with output on simple industrial tasks (Catterson *et al.*, 1963), with ability to communicate using verbal or non-verbal language, and with indices of central and peripheral arousal (see Chapter 5). The most severely impaired patient conveys little information through facial expression, bodily posture or gait, voice modulation, gesture, or conversation.

There have been decades of investigation into the nature of the underlying deficit. It used to be assumed that it increased inexorably with time, following the first florid attack, hence the use of the term "deterioration". Babcock (1933), for example, thought it began in childhood and could be traced throughout the course, but her conclusions were based on cross-sectional surveys of verbal and performance tests and most subsequent workers disagreed with them (e.g. Kendig and Richmond, 1940; Foulds and Dixon, 1962). One interesting observation, not yet adequately explained, was that the improvement of performance due to practice, which would be expected (by analogy with normal people and even with the severely mentally retarded) to be negatively accelerated, tended in schizophrenia to be slow and linear (O'Connor *et al.*, 1956; O'Connor and Rawnsley, 1959; Wing and Freudenberg, 1961).

Numerous studies have shown that negative impairments can be influenced by the social environment in which the patient is living, although there is often a residual impairment, even in the most satisfactory environment (Brown *et al.*, 1966, Wing *et al.*, 1964; Wing and Brown, 1970; Wing and Freudenberg, 1961; see also Chapters 6, 8, and 9).

Although the clinical poverty syndrome is often chronic, it can increase sharply in severity during an acute attack and improve again as the florid symptoms decrease (Hirsch *et al.*, 1973; Stevens, 1973).

SCHIZOPHRENIC THOUGHT DISORDER

Both Kraepelin and Bleuler pointed to the significance of an underlying disorder of thought hypothesized from the speech and other verbal communications of patient with schizophrenia. Bleuler's term was "loosening of associations", which describes very well the unpredictable turn that a sentence can take. When marked, so that the original sense is lost and the patient seems, in mid-sentence, to move in some completely different direction, it is called "the knight's move". When the symptom has been present for a long time, in severe form, and fragmentary delusions are incorporated, speech may appear entirely incoherent: "We've seen the downfall of the radium crown by the Roman Catholics, whereas when you come to see the drinking side of the business, God saw that Noah, if he lost his reason, he got nobody there to look after them." Sometimes the content of speech is so vague as to produce an impression of complete emptiness, even when quite a lot of words are used. Distortions of words, or the creation of new words (neologisms) may occur, and questions may be answered "past the point". For example: "What's your address?" "It's supposed to be Salisbury near Birmingham."

Minor variants are fairly common, and can be quite amusing to the patient's associates. Occasionally, an impression of creativity may be given, but the crippling effect of schizophrenia on artists like Hölderlin and Nijinsky indicates the commoner result. When the symptom is severe, the patient may be unable to think to any purpose, but go off on to side-tracks so frequently that only relatively routine activities, requiring little new thought, remain unaffected. All forms of communication may be affected: writing and drawing, gestures, and even work. One patient was well able to screw the sides of a box on its base, but he always put in the screws at unusual places and left several out altogether. His explanation was unintelligible to his work supervisor and he could not be employed.

Other kinds of thought disorder occur in depression, mania, obsessional ruminative states, and anxiety states. The term "thought disorder" is not synonymous with schizophrenia.

INTERACTION BETWEEN CLINICAL POVERTY SYNDROME AND THOUGHT DISORDER

Jung (1906) quoted Stransky's experiment, in which normal subjects were asked to speak for a minute or two without paying any attention to what they were saying. The result was not dissimilar to schizophrenic speech disorder. The nature of the chronic psychological deficit in schizophrenia is discussed in Chapter 5, but it would not be unfair to suggest that decades of work have done little more than amplify the clinical descriptions given by Kraepelin and Bleuler. Flattening of affect and thought disorder often go together (Bleuler's "autism"). Part of the apathy and social withdrawal could result from a patient's long experience of failed attempts at communication with others, leading him to give up trying to establish contact, and even to avoiding company altogether. This mechanism (analogous to the adverse secondary reaction of institutionalism; see below) must be quite common. It cannot, however, explain all the slowness or underactivity.

When both chronic impairments are present in severe form, in the absence of somatic conditions, the diagnosis of schizophrenia can be tentatively made on this basis alone. However, there are many other causes, both of communication problems and of social withdrawal. The latter is found in depression, in mental retardation, in childhood global language disorders (particularly early childhood autism), in Asperger's syndrome, in physical handicap, and in some personality dirorders. Care must therefore be taken when marked social withdrawal is the presenting feature but there is no history of a florid schizophrenic episode. The diagnosis of schizophrenia is best not made at all, or regarded as purely speculative.

RELATIONSHIP BETWEEN ACUTE AND CHRONIC SYNDROMES

The nature of the relationship between the florid and the negative schizophrenic syndromes has long been in dispute. When other factors such as course and aetiology are added (to say nothing of modifying factors such as age, sex, intelligence and body build), it is easy to see how different diagnostic schools have developed in various parts of the world.

Considering only the central syndrome and the chronic syndromes, there are three basic groupings:

(a) acute schizophrenia, occurring in limited episodes, with little chronic impairment. Such attacks often occur following precipitation by physical or social factors;

(b) chronic schizophrenia, characterized only by the clinical poverty syndrome and thought disorder, and with no history of acute florid episodes. When severe, and when all other possible diagnoses have been excluded, it is legitimate to hypothesize schizophrenia. When mild it is rarely correct to do so.

(c) combined acute and chronic syndromes, often with some long-term abnormality preceding and following the first florid attack. Some theoreticians have sought to limit the term "schizophrenia" to this group.

If the classification really were as simple as this, i.e. if cases fell easily and identifiably into the three main groups, communication between psychiatrists would be considerably eased. Unfortunately, although the three groups are recognizable clinically, there are plenty of intermediate examples. Before considering classification further, and before tackling the question of diagnosis, we must consider the effect of precipitating and modifying factors.

Precipitating and Modifying Factors

CEREBRAL AND SYSTEMIC DISEASE AND TOXIC FACTORS

There is abundant evidence that acute florid schizophrenic episodes can be precipitated by organic disease or by toxic agents. The best-documented examples are the schizophrenia-like psychoses associated with epilepsy (Slater *et al.*, 1963). Slater did not believe that the combination could be a chance one. As in the case of the more clear-cut precipitation of schizophrenic states by amphetamine, bromide and alcohol, it seemed to be a question of "symptomatic schizophrenia". An association with other somatic diseases, such as porphyria, cerebral tumour, or trauma, and Huntington's chorea, has also been established (Davison and Bagley, 1969). Childbirth is another possible precipitant. In each of these cases, florid schizophrenic symptoms may be completely typical, although accompanied by other symptoms indicating the underlying diagnosis. The implications for biochemical research are discussed in Chapter 4. A possible relationship to cerebral dominance is reviewed by Lishman and McMeekan (1976).

There is some evidence that the chronic negative syndromes are less evident in schizophrenia-like disorders precipitated by such factors. In Slater's series of 69 cases of epilepsy, for example, delusions in clear consciousness occurred in 67, but loss of affective responsiveness in only 28. Acute amphetamine psychosis is also less likely to be followed by chronic impairments (Connell, 1958).

Pasamanick and Lilienfeld (1955) suggested that there were predisposing as well as precipitating factors; in particular, prenatal or perinatal brain damage. The evidence is statistical only, but some confirmation may be derived from the fact that in identical twin pairs discordant for schizophrenia, the schizophrenic co-twin has often had a low birth weight and poor school performance (Kringlen, 1967; Pollin *et al.*, 1966; Tienari, 1963).

SOCIAL AND CULTURAL FACTORS

The considerable evidence that social factors quite frequently precipitate acute attacks of schizophrenia is reviewed in Chapter 6. The three main types of factors are changes in the patient's social environment (Brown and Birley, 1970), overzealous therapy (Stone and Eldred, 1959; Wing *et al.*, 1964) and intrusive relatives (Brown *et al.*, 1972; Vaughn and Leff, 1976). The clinical poverty syndrome is markedly affected by the nature of the social environment, both for better and for worse (Wing and Brown, 1970; Wing and Freudenberg, 1961). It is possible that cultural differences in the onset and course of schizophrenia (Murphy and Raman, 1971; WHO, 1978), if confirmed in more epidemiologically adequate studies, could be due to differences in exposure to factors such as these.

Social factors modifying the clinical picture are also of great importance. Two examples may be taken from the IPSS (WHO, 1973, pp. 275–6). The first patient was a Chinese Taoist priestess living in Taiwan. At the age of 37, she developed a psychotic illness characterized by restlessness, refusal of food, odd behaviour out of character with her occupation and usual mode of life, confused speech and neglect of her personal appearance. Much of her behaviour and speech could, however, be understood as an exaggeration of her ordinary vocational preoccupations. She asked too many poor people to stay in her house, called passers-by "ghosts", said she had been to the sixty-eighth layer of hell, believed that God had taken her soul somewhere and used her body and voice to speak his will. She suspected that she was possessed by her foster-father's spirit, and that she was under a spell cast by the wife of the man she was living with. She was admitted to hospital in a state of complete exhaustion and near-starvation. The diagnosis was not schizophrenia but hysterical psychosis (ICD, 298.1). Only a knowledge of local customs and beliefs enabled the psychiatrist to ask the precise questions that could differentiate these symptoms from those of the central syndrome.

The second patient was an Indian living in a village near Agra. The history was typical of mania: elation, increased libido and appetite, overactivity, grandiose and persecutory ideas. He identified himself with the god, Hunuman, said that Durga lived within his body, and thought that he could do everything in the world.

> The ghost Braham Dev possessed me. He made me do things. He made me break things. He made me sleepless. This ghost abused others through my voice. I had not made proper offerings to this ghost and so he became angry and possessed me. I felt extremely happy from within when I was possessed by this ghost.

The psychiatrist diagnosed mania (ICD, 296.1) and commented that many of the ideas expressed by the patient were culturally specific and quite common in the village.

Other types of social modifying factors are illustrated by a group case history quoted by Gruenberg (1957). A police van delivered four people to a Massachusetts mental hospital. One man, aged 60, was manic. Another was mentally retarded. "A woman was suffering from a psychosis which the hospital was never quite able to classify. A thirteen-

year-old boy in a severely disturbed state was later called hysterical."
The manic member of the quartet was lodging with the family composed of the other three. At the time they were taken to hospital all four
had been jointly engaged in discovering and destroying the devils they
thought were hiding inside the walls and furniture. The boy was supposed to be in communication with his dead sister who, in turn, was in
direct touch with God, who had revealed that the boarder was the
second Messiah. A more recent review, and presentation of socially-
shared psychopathology, is given by Sims and colleagues (1977).

Pathoplastic features are common in psychiatric patients everywhere
in the world. Small subcultural groups with a religious or some other
ideological motivation, small family groups like those described by
Gruenberg and Sims, and patients deriving their attitudes from more
remote contacts with such ideas, often contribute puzzling features to
the clinical picture in individual cases, and psychiatrists need to be
aware of the total social context before reaching a diagnosis. Otherwise,
a diagnosis of schizophrenia will be made more frequently than is justifiable, either on strict clinical grounds, or from the point of view of
treatment.

Other social factors to be taken into account are education and
occupation, discussed in Chapter 2. Leff has also pointed to important
differences in the way affective reactions differ according to cultural
setting.

OTHER MODIFYING FACTORS: AGE, SEX, INTELLIGENCE

Several other factors need to be taken into account because they modify
the clinical picture and may mislead the unwary into making an incorrect diagnosis. Four of the most important are age, sex, intellectual level
and age of onset. The importance of age and sex can be illustrated by
considering the specific inception rates. For example, figures can be
derived from case registers such as those in Camberwell and Salford
representing the number of patients in the specified age and sex group
who first contact psychiatric services (in-patient, day-patient, out-
patient or domiciliary) during a year, and are given a diagnosis of
schizophrenia. These show that, although onset is commoner in the
younger age groups, schizophrenia can begin at any age. Overall, the
inception rates are not very different for men and women. The rates for
young men (up to the age of 34), however, are higher than those for
young women, whereas at ages over 35 the rates are higher in women
(Wing and Fryers, 1976). The explanation may be that women are

more able to cope with the condition and therefore come into contact with services later or, more probably, that the age of onset is generally delayed in women compared with men. If so, the reason is still quite unknown.

A further difference between the sexes is that, at the time of onset, women are more likely to be married than men. This is partly due to the later age of onset in women and partly to the fact that women are more able to carry on their social roles after the onset than are men, due to different social expectations.

The clinical picture of schizophrenia beginning in women after the menopause has long been thought to have characteristic features: great pressure to talk, affective symptoms and a sexual content to the delusions. Kraepelin and others thought this condition should be separately classified (presenile delusional psychosis), but such features can be found at all ages, and in men as well as women, although there does seem to be some relationship to age and sex. Post (1966) has described features characteristic of psychoses developing after the age of 60. He points out that paranoid personality traits and paranoid symptoms are brought out and exaggerated by loneliness, deafness, mild dementia, and belonging to a socially isolated group. Before the onset of severe dementia, some patients "hover for many months near the ill-defined borders between sub-acute and chronic confusion, when their cognitive deficits are still variable and their defects somewhat patchy." However, although uncommon, there is no doubt that schizophrenic and paranoid psychoses can begin for the first time after the age of 60, usually with a florid delusional picture and depressed mood. They respond quite well to the phenothiazines.

In adolescence and young adulthood, these "paraphrenic" features are less noticeable (although full-blown delusional and hallucinatory states are still quite common), and the chronic syndromes tend to be predominant ("hebephrenia"). The turbulence of adolescence, and the relative plasticity of personality, are reflected in the way the symptoms present. Since the subclasses of schizophrenia merge into each other almost imperceptibly it is doubtful how far it is worth preserving the traditional distinction between hebephrenic, catatonic and paranoid varieties, once the pathoplastic effect of age and sex and social factors have been taken into account.

Intellectual level is a further modifying factor. The nature of the psychological deficit in schizophrenia is still unclear (see Chapter 5) but there is no doubt that many patients perform at a lower level than would be expected from their early development, although there does not seem to be much deterioration in this respect after the first attack (Foulds and Dixon, 1962). Several studies have suggested that children who later develop schizophrenia as adults have scored lower on intelligence tests than other children or their own siblings, though the differences are not large and could be due to motivational factors, as maladjustment is also common. Watt and Lubensky (1976), for example, state that boys who later became schizophrenic were negativisitic, egocentric, unpleasant and antisocial, while equivalent girls were quiet, introverted and ego-centric. Hanson *et al.* (1976) described three characteristics which, if present together in childhood, might indicate a very high risk of schizophrenia developing subsequently: poor motor skills, high vari-ability in psychological test results, and "schizoid" behaviour (emo-tionally flat, withdrawn, distractable, passive, irritable and negativistic) when observed at age four *and* at age seven. Only the presence of all three factors together is likely to be predictive according to these authors. Lee Robins (1970) considered that a combination of neurotic and anti-social behaviour during childhood could presage adult schizophrenia but not that a shy, withdrawn personality was predictive.

These conclusions confirm clinical experience that many schizo-phrenic patients present with a history of unusual behaviour reaching back into childhood, although the nature of the abnormality is by no means clear or specific. Most of the work suffers inevitably from methodological deficiencies, one of the commonest, however, being most easily remediable—the lack of good clinical descriptions of the adult psychotic condition. Without these, the diagnosis of "schizo-phrenia" means very little, and the results of the studies cannot be compared or generalized.

Schizophrenic and paranoid psychoses can begin during childhood, usually in the immediately pre-pubertal years. The symptoms are typi-cal except for the obvious pathoplastic effects of age. There should be no confusion with psychoses having an onset in early childhood, usually on the basis of a global language disorder (Ricks and Wing, 1976), since the symptoms of the latter are quite distinct, the children do not develop schizophrenic psychoses in later life, and there is is no increase in the frequency of schizophrenia in first-degree relatives (Kolvin, 1971; L. Wing, 1976). One other possibly confusing condition (in fact, a variant of early childhood autism) is Asperger's syndrome (Asperger, 1944, 1960; van Krevelen, 1971). Like Kanner's syndrome, it has often been misdiagnosed as schizophrenia, and may account for a proportion of the cases labelled as "simple schizophrenia".

High intelligence is sometimes given undue prominence as a concomitant of schizophrenia, probably because of the tragic impact of the condition when it begins abruptly in a young person of great potential achievement. Psychological deficit is then particularly apparent, by contrast with expectation. The problems of habilitation and settlement are very difficult and insufficiently investigated (see Chapter 9).

Diagnosis

DIFFERENTIATION FROM OTHER CONDITIONS

Psychiatric diagnosis is still primarily based on the recognition of clinical syndromes. We have now considered in some detail the differential definition of the most important syndromes considered by psychiatrists throughout the world to be characteristic of schizophrenic and paranoid conditions, and the influence of predisposing, precipitating and modifying factors on the clinical picture. By and large, differential diagnosis follows a hierarchical scheme (Foulds and Bedford, 1975; MacPherson et al., 1977; Wing, 1978; Wing et al., 1974).

In the first place, the presence of an identifiable cerebral pathology, or a systemic disease affecting the central nervous system, takes precedence. Dementia, acute or subacute delirium, Korsakov's psychosis and other dysmnesic syndromes, even when accompanied by schizophrenic or paranoid syndromes, are diagnosed separately. The same is true of established precipitants such as alcohol, amphetamine or bromide.

If no such factors are recognized, the presence of the central syndrome is sufficient for a diagnosis of schizophrenia (ICD, 295). The differential diagnosis depends on the extent to which the individual symptoms can be recognized, independently of such factors as mood (elation or depression) or subcultural "possession" states.

If the central syndrome is not present, the next step in the hierarchy is determined by the presence or absence of non-central paranoid delusional syndromes. Those dependent on mood or subcultural factors are diagnosed separately, leaving a group of paranoid psychoses which are best classified as such (ICD, 297). Many psychiatrists, however, include these too, with the schizophrenic group.

If no delusional or hallucinatory syndromes are present, the presence of other psychotic features provides only a very doubtful basis for diagnosing schizophrenia, unless there is a well-authenicated previous history of a more typical episode. Behaviour suggestive of auditory hallucinations, such as laughing and talking to the self, may be tentatively classified as schizophrenic, but it occurs in other conditions (e.g. following encephalitis lethargica, and in early childhood autism, when it is *not* due to hallucinations) and it is wise to be very cautious about applying the label. The same is true of catatonic symptoms occurring in the absence of more typical symptoms. Recurrent excitement or stupor, with no evidence of the central syndrome or other paranoid syndromes, may or may not be related to schizophrenia. Recurrent episodes of excitement are common in some developing countries (WHO, 1973), and may be given a diagnosis of unspecified schizophrenia (ICD, 295.9), but the connection with more typical syndromes is purely speculative. The clinical poverty syndrome, in the absence of a history of typical schizophrenia, is best classified under personality disorder.

Neurotic syndromes of all kinds are common in schizophrenia, but in the absence of the central or other paranoid syndromes it is never safe to make the diagnosis. If it appears to the clinician that frank schizophrenia might some day develop, it is best to record the prediction separately rather than making it part of the current diagnosis.

SUBCLASSIFICATION

The conventional subgroupings are paranoid or paraphrenic (295.3), schizoaffective (295.7), hebephrenic (295.1) and catatonic (295.2) schizophrenia, paranoia (297.0), and involutional or late paraphrenia (297.1). Less clear-cut groupings include acute (295.4), residual (295.6), simple (295.0) and latent or pseudoneurotic or pseudopsychopathic (295.5) schizophrenia, reactive confusion (298.2) and acute paranoid reaction or *bouffée délirante* (298.3). Readers are referred to the glossary of terms and guide to the eighth revision of the ICD published by the World Health Organisation (WHO, 1974). The definitions are by no means precise, let alone operational, but they do constitute a considerable advance on what went before. Clinicians are urged to try to use the scheme to record their diagnoses, in order to achieve a degree of comparability in international statistics. However, for clinical use, and for research purposes, a simpler and more operational scheme is preferable. Future editions of the ICD may become much more operational (Sartorius, 1976). A possible means of advance is discussed by Spitzer (1977). More global clinical descriptions will be found in clinical textbooks such as Slater and Roth (1969).

THE USE OF THE TERM "SCHIZOPHRENIA"

The reason why it is important to be clear about how the term "schizophrenia" is being used is that the clinician invariably has some theory concerning the nature or treatment or care of the condition so described. Both from the point of view of evaluation of therapies, and from that of testing statements about cause or pathology, it is essential that clinical conditions can be recognized with a fair degree of reliability and that the labels given them should mean much the same thing to psychiatrists throughout the world. No advance is possible without a minimum degree of communicability.

An example of the misuse of the term "schizophrenia" is given by Rosenhan (1973), who described how eight people gained access to psychiatric hospitals in the United States by complaining of disembodied voices saying the words, "empty", "hollow" and "thud". No other symptoms were fabricated but the conspirators answered all questions put to them by psychiatrists on the basis of their personal (presumably non-schizophrenic) experiences. In each case they were admitted to hospital and all but one were diagnosed as schizophrenic. If these facts can be taken at face value (and the nature of the project must throw doubt on them) the first conclusion to be drawn is that the psychiatrists concerned did not know how to make a diagnosis. The second is that they thought, completely erroneously, that all people with "schizophrenia", even of such a minimal degree, should be admitted to hospital and given medication. Whether or not these conclusions can justifiably be drawn from Rosenhan's project, there is little doubt that some psychiatrists do use the term "schizophrenia" very widely, not to say vaguely, and that people diagnosed on the shakiest evidence (e.g. those with none of the most typical syndromes, but showing only a degree of withdrawal and "oddity") can be treated using powerful pharmacological and social methods. Labelling theorists argue that there is, in fact, little more to a diagnosis than this (Scheff, 1966), but that is a gross oversimplification (Wing, 1978). To avoid such elementary errors, it is necessary to be clear, not only about the clinical grounds for the diagnosis, but about the theoretical and practical implications of making it.

Disease Theories of Schizophrenia

There is a great deal of misunderstanding even among physicians, about the use of the term "disease". In practice, there are two main uses: first, to refer to a limited and specific set of disease theories which seem to explain a specified clinical syndrome and to allow predictions concerning aetiology, treatment and prognosis; second, "to any condition which causes, or might usefully cause, an individual to concern himself with his symptoms and to seek help. The term 'illness behaviour' refers to any behaviour relevant to the second, more general, interpretation" (Mechanic, 1968).

A well developed disease theory (or, more usually, set of theories) is based on knowledge of the homeostatic mechanisms that maintain some relevant bodily function, such as blood sugar, within known limits. When specific factors (causes) operate, one or more normal cycle becomes unbalanced, the limits are exceeded, and a clinical syndrome such as diabetes mellitus becomes manifest. The known presence of a lesion, either causing a disruption of homeostasis, or resulting from it, is extremely helpful in diagnosis, but it is not "the disease". The advance of medicine during the past fifty years would have been very limited if the demonstration of a lesion had been the sole criterion against which a diagnosis could be tested.

Such theories are useful for scientific purposes, since testing them may lead to the acquisition of new fundamental knowledge, but they are also of immense clinical importance because they lead to predictions about causes (and therefore, potentially, about methods of prevention), about treatments and methods of care, and about the future course and outcome. The more precisely the clinical syndromes can be identified, the simpler it is to test disease theories put forward to explain them. So far as individual patients are concerned, this testing means the critical evaluation of predictions made from the theories, in order to discover whether they are indeed to help in relieving or preventing disability or suffering. The clinician is then acting as an applied scientist; selecting, testing, and rejecting or tentatively accepting hypotheses to guide his everyday practice.

The fact that the clinician is using disease theories in this way does not mean that he can use no other frame of reference. A crude identification of "the disease model" with "the medical model" has misled many commentators on contemporary medical practice. The medical role requires the doctor to act, upon occasion, as a teacher, psychologist, social worker, pastoral counsellor, or befriender. The "disease model" requires him to recognize that disease theories are not relevant at all to many of the problems presented by patients, and only partially relevant to many others. This is the theoretical basis for the concept of the multidisciplinary team, which can bring a wide range of skills—biological, psychological and social—to bear. But each member of the team needs to know something of the skills of the others and, in particular, the doctor cannot hope to be a good clinician if he sees his role as purely technological. "Any narrow view of a doctor's role, based on the sole function of biological diagnosis, is likely to lead to a stereotyped mislabelling of the medical profession and a thorough misunderstanding of the value of classification" (Wing, 1977).

Innumerable disease theories have been put forward to explain the syndromes of schizophrenia but nearly all have fallen by the wayside after enjoying a period of favour. Most have been partial or fragmentary, purporting perhaps to explain all the clinical phenomena but in fact based upon a limited range of observations and ignoring the rest. What will eventually be needed is a set of linked theories, relating epidemiology, genetics, biochemistry, pathology, psychophysiology and therapeutics, to the development of the specific clinical syndromes we have considered earlier in this chapter. Each of these aspects is considered in detail in subsequent chapters of this book but it must be remembered that much of the work discussed has not been conducted using clinically standardized definitions of schizophrenic syndromes, and that exclusion on the basis of age or precipitating factors often means that the range of "symptomatic schizophrenias" has not been represented. Nevertheless, a broad conclusion can be reached. The aetiology is unknown but there is evidence in favour of some form of genetic transmission in a substantial proportion of cases. Something is known about predisposing factors and a good deal about somatic and social precipitation. Methods of pharmacological treatment are highly effective in suppressing and preventing the acute episodes and part of the more chronic impairment. Biochemical theories, based on the mode of action of the most effective drugs, are now beginning to survive rigorous tests and one of them, the dopamine theory, links a wide range of observations from clinical psychiatry and neurology, pharmacology, biochemistry and pathology.

By comparison with disease theories of diabetes or hypertension this amount of progress is not to be despised but the clinical psychiatrist must always remember that the term "disease" is shorthand for "linked disease theories". He may put forward hypotheses but not reify them. Moreover, it is extremely unlikely that any one set of theories will account for all the syndromes currently classified by psychiatrists within the rubric of "schizophrenic and paranoid psychoses".

By contrast, other theories have received very little testing, perhaps because they are not formulated sufficiently precisely. One apparent alternative is that the functional psychoses are not distinct conditions but represent interactions between a number of personality dimensions, such as neuroticism, extraversion-introversion, and psychoticism, which are normally distributed in the population. For example, emotional flattening, loosening of associations, and perhaps other traits such as tendency to hallucinations, might be regarded as normally distributed factors, with individuals high on one or more being particularly at risk of developing the central schizophrenic syndrome, even in the absence of physical or social precipitants. A multigene hypothesis would fit this formulation. This is simply one way of restating part of the network of disease theories and does not constitute a true alternative.

A more clear-cut alternative is provided by the psychological theories discussed in Chapter 6 but the evidence for them is in inverse ratio to the claims put forward. The radical labelling theory of Scheff (1966) is discussed in detail elsewhere (Wing, 1978). It can only explain "cases" of the Rosenhan type, which ought to be excluded anyway by proper diagnostic assessment.

Social Disablement

THE GOAL OF RESETTLEMENT

Schizophrenia is one of the most disabling psychiatric disorders. In order to give the maximum help to handicapped individuals, it is necessary to assess their problems in much the same way as for people with other types of disability, physical and mental. The goal is to achieve at least the level of social achievement (conventionally measured in terms of domestic life, occupation and leisure activities) that would have been expected of the affected person if schizophrenia had not supervened. This expectation will vary according to culture, class, age, sex, previous attainment, and so on. It cannot be defined *purely* in terms of personal aims since the individual always lives in a social environment and the expectations of others, such as close relatives, neighbours and potential employers, also need to be given weight. The professional helper therefore has to make a very broad social as well as clinical evaluation when assessing which factors are hindering a full resettlement and which might be susceptible to helpful intervention.

INTRINSIC IMPAIRMENTS

Acute schizophrenic episodes are frequently incapacitating because the delusional and hallucinatory experiences are so overwhelming that the patient is no more able to understand their abnormality (i.e. to evaluate them in the context of remembered normal experience) than is someone in delirium. This "loss of insight" is one of the most distressing features to relatives and one of the most difficult to deal with, since it may necessitate compulsory admission to hospital. A degree of insight is often retained, however, and some patients whose symptoms persist, or recur frequently, may eventually come to recognize their nature and learn how to cope with them (see Chapter 11). A combination of relief from precipitating and everyday stresses ("asylum") and active treatment usually results in the fairly rapid remission of acute symptoms, but a liability to further attacks often remains, and this vulnerability must be recognized as a form of "invisible" chronic impairment.

The persistence of chronic symptoms, particularly those associated with emotional flattening and thought disorder, is a further form of impairment, just as handicapping as more familiar and visible physical disabilities.

The social reactivity of these impairments—i.e. the social precipitants of acute relapse and the social factors that contribute to an accumulation of unnecessary extra disablement—have briefly been summarized above and are dealt with in detail in Chapter 6. Pharmacological and psychological aspects of treatment are described in Chapters 7 and 8. Two other types of handicapping factor also need consideration since they may cause just as much social disablement as the clinical impairments so far considered and may impede all efforts at resettlement that do not specifically take them into account.

EXTRINSIC DISADVANTAGES

By analogy with the terminology used in physical medicine, the clinical impairments can be called "intrinsic". This usage is compatible with a variety of theories as to their origin, its main value being to emphasize that some impairments do not go away even when a full range of biological, psychological and social methods of treatment has been tried and the environment is as favourable as can be devised. Another variety of handicapping factor is called "extrinsic", because it has no necessary relationship to the intrinsic type but independently contributes to social disablement. For example, a long experience of poverty, prejudice, low-grade work, unemployment, or lack of family and social support, are handicapping in themselves. An individual born in a large family, living in poor housing conditions, with inadequate schooling, who leaves early to find himself mixing with alienated peers unable to get work, migrates to a large city to compete with other migrants for low-grade housing and jobs, and thus shares the career of the grossly underprivileged with no background of secure social relationships, is socially disabled even without any illness supervening (Leach and Wing, 1978; Wood, 1976). Such people are at higher risk of developing many kinds of illness, both physical and mental.

There has been a long discussion as to whether social disadvantages such as these are likely to cause schizophrenia, or whether the high rates observed under such conditions are due to a pre-existing drift down the social scale (see Chapter 2). The balance of the epidemiological evidence at the moment is in favour of the view that much of the association noted between the onset of schizophrenia and factors such as social class, marital status, migration and social isolation, is due to selection rather than to stress. On the other hand, it is also clear that a disadvantaged background has an adverse effect on the course because of the lack of social support. This is why an attempt to increase the number of assets, by social skills and vocational training, and by personal counselling, is so important.

ADVERSE PERSONAL REACTIONS

The other type of handicapping factor is dependent upon the intrinsic and extrinsic types. Each individual reacts to his or her experience of impairment and social disadvantage in a different way. Just as in the case of physical disability, the response can be determined and constructive, or apathetic, or idiosyncratic and socially unacceptable (Wing, 1966). Someone who suffers a severe coronary thrombosis may be back at work six weeks after recovery as though nothing had happened. Someone else may react to a mild chest pain by becoming a cardiac invalid, even though assured that no serious disease is present. Such "secondary" handicaps to resettlement are dependent, in turn, upon innumerable other factors, including previous personality and experience of illness, the reactions of important others, and the degree of support and help available.

It is sometimes assumed, quite wrongly, that "schizophrenia" imposes a uniform personality and inadequacy upon sufferers. This is a gross error. It is true, however, that severe intrinsic impairments (whatever their nature) impose limitations on activity and social performance that inevitably lead to dependence on others, however constructive and determined the individual response. Blindness, for example, imposes limitations that can only be overcome by the individual if others provide specific help. The most successful adaptation results from cooperation, but that does not depend only on the blind person. In other historical eras than our own, the disabled have not received the help they need.

We do not now always react as helpfully as we might, partly for the same reasons (lack of understanding, selfishness, fear, a deliberate choice of other priorities and goals) but also partly because of a theory that invisible impairments do not "exist". Paradoxically, this theory may have gained ground because of studies of one of the most obvious secondary reactions seen in schizophrenic patients—institutionalism.

Institutionalism is a gradually acquired contentment with life in an institution (including hostels, group homes and day centres) which culminates in the individual no longer wishing or being able to live any other. It is the limiting case of dependence, lesser degrees of which are very common. The environment reflects back to the handicapped person a reflection of his altered status as a human being. He is seen as a patient or client rather than as an employer, father, customer, or companion. His role becomes constricted, replacing many others that he might have been called on to play. However, the process also depends, as we have seen, on factors within the individual. Institutionalism was seen in particularly clear-cut form in old-fashioned mental hospitals, where patients sometimes remained long after the acute symptoms had disappeared and even though their chronic impairments did not warrant such a degree of protection (Wing and Brown, 1970). Many other attitudes and personal habits were affected. The patient lost any ability he might otherwise have retained to play a wide range of social roles: he did not replenish his stock of useful current information (such as how much a postage stamp costs: the accumulation of such ignorance is extremely handicapping); he did not practise travelling on public transport or shopping; he gradually ceased to make plans for the future or simply repeated some vague formula when he was asked about them.

Much of the success of early rehabilitation programmes was achieved by counteracting the adverse effects of institutionalism and it began to be thought by some that all chronic impairment was imposed by the social environment. Unfortunately, this is not true (Catterson et al., 1963; Hewett et al., 1975; Mann and Cree, 1976). Adverse reactions, including dependency, can develop in virtually any social environment, and are dependent on the experience of unemployment, prejudice, poverty, and isolation: all factors likely to cause low self-esteem and lack of confidence.

THE PREVENTION OF SOCIAL DISABLEMENT

These three factors—intrinsic impairments, social disadvantages, and adverse personal reactions—together produce the unique pattern of social disablement seen in any particular individual. A wide variety of biological, psychological and social techniques is necessary in order to diagnose and treat schizophrenia at an early stage, to limit so far as possible the severity of chronic impairments, to prevent the accumulation of unnecessary secondary handicaps, and to help develop the individual's positive assets. The skills of several disciplines are needed. This process of diagnosis, treatment, rehabilitation, counselling, and care, is known as management and Chapters 7 to 11 are concerned with it.

The Course of Schizophrenia

So many different factors have to be specified before we can meaningfully talk about the course of schizophrenia that it is almost impossible to make general statements. Predisposing, precipitating and modifying factors must be taken into account. This does not mean that the concept of course is valueless, only that it can easily be misused. In the first place, we have seen that the symptoms of the central syndrome can occur in acute episodes without any chronic impairments. An acute florid onset, without any previous indication of abnormality, particularly if precipitated by sudden environmental or physical stress, is most likely to be followed by long clear remissions. At the other extreme, an insidious onset, hardly more than an exacerbation of traits that reach back into childhood, and characterized mainly by emotional flattening and thought disorder, with only sufficient acute delusional or hallucinatory symptoms to make the diagnosis clear, is most likely to follow a chronic course. This is why traits such as social withdrawal are so important in the prognosis (Brown et al., 1966; WHO, 1978; Zubin, 1967).

Second, the symptoms present during one attack of schizophrenia are likely to be present in subsequent psychotic attacks (WHO, 1978). These first two generalizations amount to saying that like predicts like. The longer someone has been socially withdrawn, the more likely he is to remain so. The more relapses with specified symptoms have occurred previously, the more likely the same symptoms will be to recur. This does not mean that acute symptoms are good predictors of whether another breakdown will take place and, if so, when. We have seen that quite different predictors are needed for that. Nor can first-rank symptoms be used to predict future social withdrawal, or vice versa.

Third, the hierarchical principle applies during the course. Even when the diagnosis is beyond doubt, because it rests on recurrent episodes of first-rank symptoms, subsequent episodes may be characterized by symptoms lower in the hierarchy; hence the possibility of diagnosing mania, psychotic depression, other forms of depressions, or anxiety state, if only one subsequent episode is taken into account. Minor neurotic symptoms such as worrying are very common throughout the course (Brown *et al.*, 1966; WHO, 1978). Movement "down" the hierarchy is very common. Movement "up" the hierarchy (e.g. the development for the first time of first-rank symptoms in someone who has had a series of manic episodes) is rare.

Finally, the prediction of social disablement requires yet other factors to be taken into account as well, such as extrinsic social disadvantages and adverse personal reactions. Since at least some of the factors that influence the development of social disablement in schizophrenia (as in many other conditions) are modifiable, it is clear that any idea of inevitable clinical deterioration—i.e. deficit remorselessly increasing over time—must be rejected. Everything depends on the combination of impairments, disadvantages and reactions experienced by the individual patient, and this depends, in turn, at least to some extent, on the way he is treated by his environment.

The concept of "natural history" is therefore not very useful for predicting the outcome in individual patients. Even the overall, average, course is difficult to describe because, although there have been several long-term studies, the criteria for diagnosis, and for measuring course and outcome, have not been comparable. For example, if patients who showed only acute, self-limiting conditions were excluded (as being "schizophreniform" rather than schizophrenic), the outcome could clearly be adversely affected. Before the Second World War, outcome was often measured in terms of discharge from hospital, but we know that many people remained in hospital whose symptoms did not really warrant this (Wing and Brown, 1970). The clinical course may therefore have been somewhat better in former days than appears from the literature. Similarly, we know that nowadays, discharge does not always mean that a patient is symptom-free (Brown *et al.*, 1966). More than a century ago, during the era of "moral treatment" the discharge rates were as high as they are now (Bockoven, 1956; Jones, 1972).

Nevertheless, an apparent improvement in prognosis is evident from the follow-up studies that have been published. Kraepelin (1910), for example, thought that about 17% of in-pations treated at his Heidelberg clinic were socially adjusted many years later. Mayer-Gross (1932) followed up 260 schizophrenic patients out of a total of 294 admitted to the same clinic in 1912 and 1913. Sixteen years later, although there had

B*

been a high death rate, 35% had made "social recoveries" outside hospital. This proportion of one-third is approximately the number who were discharged from English and American hospitals during the 1930s after first admission for schizophrenia; the remainder staying in hospital indefinitely (Brown, 1960).

Harris and his colleagues (1956) followed the course of 125 schizophrenic patients admitted to the joint Maudsley and Bethlem Royal Hospital between 1945 and 1950 and found that 45% could be regarded as social recoveries five years later. A further 21% were socially disabled but living out of hospital. More recently, a study of 111 patients first admitted to three British psychiatric hospitals in 1956 showed that 56% had recovered socially five years later while 34% were socially disabled but out of hospital (Brown et al., 1966).

Thus not only the discharge rates but also the "social recovery" rates seem to have improved. The most recent of these studies still found that about one-quarter of schizophrenic patients were severely socially disabled five years after admission and, even if this proportion has dropped somewhat during the past ten years, it is still high enough to demand a great deal of investment in rehabilitation and sheltered environments. The best description of the long-term course by a clinician familiar with a large group of patients over many years is given by Manfred Bleuler (1972).

If all the knowledge we have acquired about the treatment and management of schizophrenia were skilfully applied, if the appropriate range of services were available, and if patients and relatives received realistic advice and counselling, there is little doubt that the course and outcome would be still further improved.

2 | Epidemiology

Brian Cooper

Problems of Definition

Epidemiology has been defined as the study of "the distribution and determinants of disease frequency in man" (MacMahon and Pugh, 1970), or of "the distribution of disease in time and space, and of the factors that influence this distribution" (Lilienfeld, 1957). Some such broad definition, applicable to the study of infectious and non-infectious disease alike, would be acceptable today to most epidemiologists. Moreover, by common consent the term "disease" is used in this context to cover all causes of death or disability, including accidents, suicide, drug abuse and mental disorders.

No correspondingly simple, accepted definition exists for "schizophrenia".* The absence of any established aetiology or pathology for this condition, and the resulting uncertainties of diagnosis, remain a major topic of concern in psychiatry. Less widely recognized is the extent to which these difficulties have discouraged epidemiologists from undertaking research into the subject.

Workers engaged in biological research can to some extent (though never entirely) circumvent the diagnostic problem by selecting for study clinically homogeneous groups of patients, and comparing them with control groups of persons with no definite schizophrenic features. Borderline or doubtful cases are thus deliberately excluded, and differences between index and control groups maximized. The same strategy is not open to the epidemiologist, who by the nature of his work must

* See page viii.

take into account all cases, including those on the borderline, and who can legitimately employ case-control studies only if the comparison groups are known to represent their parent populations (Cooper and Morgan, 1973).

Partial solutions, in terms of improved case definition and firmer operational criteria, have been discussed in the preceding chapter. One must, however, bear in mind that contemporary knowledge of the epidemiology of schizophrenia is based largely on the reported findings of studies undertaken before this advance, few of which would now be accepted as methodologically sound. The conclusions of such studies must therefore be accepted as provisional rather than definitive.

It should be noted that research findings that are too inaccurate for testing aetiological hypotheses may, none the less, prove useful in other contexts. If it is assumed, for example, that the label "schizophrenia" covers a heterogenous group of mental illnesses occurring in early and middle adult life, many of which are seriously handicapping and tend to run a chronic or recurrent course, then total prevalence and incidence rates for a defined population will be of value in estimating the need for specialist services, even though they may not help to identify causal factors.

Frequency of Schizophrenia in the General Population

Data on the prevalence, incidence and distribution of schizophrenia in various countries have been derived from two main types of source: from the records of psychiatric institutions and specialist services ("second hand" data) and from the findings of epidemiological field-surveys ("first hand" data). In contrast to the findings for other diagnostic categories, such as chronic alcoholism, depression and the neuroses, rates for schizophrenic illness obtained from these two sources differ from one another relatively little. Probably, as Ødegaard (1952) has argued, most patients with this condition are admitted to hospital at some stage, so that first admission statistics lag behind, but correspond roughly to, inception rates. This may no longer prove true in the future, as it becomes common practice to treat acute schizophrenia without admission to hospital.

The data collected in psychiatric case-registers (local record-linkage and data-storage systems) are more comprehensive and more reliable than data collected at national or regional level, since they include all out-patient and day-patient contacts, and are subjected to quality checks. The morbidity rates calculated from case-registers are therefore likely to be more accurate than, and to provide a useful supplement to, national rates.

PREVALENCE RATES

The prevalence of a disease is its frequency in the general population, expressed as a rate. Case-register data can be used to estimate prevalence on a given census day (point-prevalence), or within a given time-interval (period-prevalence) or both. Field surveys, because of the time required for case-finding, lend themselves more readily to estimation of period- than of point-prevalence. Whichever type of rate is calculated, the result will depend partly on whether the whole population, or a defined part of it (such as all persons over 15 years), is taken as denominator. Some care must be exercised, therefore, when comparing the findings of different surveys.

Reported one-year prevalence rates from the larger surveys lie mostly in the range 2 to 4 per 1,000 total population. In Table I, which summarizes the findings of fifteen surveys in twelve different countries, the

Table I Survey data on prevalence of schizophrenia (population samples of over 10,000)

Country	Investigator	Year of survey	Population studied	Prevalence per 1,000
S. Korea	Yoo	1956–60	11,974 (rural)	3·8
Chine	Lin	1946–48	19,931 (mixed)	2·1
Japan	National survey	1954	total (census)	2·3
India	Dube	1970	(mixed)	2·2
Iran	Bash and Bash-Liechti	1972	(rural)	2·1
USA	Lemkau	1936	55,129 (urban)	2·9
	Roth and Luton	1938	24,804 (rural)	1·7
Denmark	Strömgren	1935	45,930 (rural)	3·3
	Juel-Nielsen and Strömgren	1962	total (census)	1·5
Germany	Brugger	1929	37,561 (rural)	1·9
England	Wing et al.	1966	175,304 (urban)	3·4
Scotland	Mayer-Gross	1948	56,231 (mixed)	4·2
USSR	Zharikov	1972	175,783 (urban)	5·1[a]
	Krasik	1965	(urban)	3·1
			(rural)	2·6
Bulgaria	Jablensky et al.	1972	140,758 (urban)	2·8

Source: Jablensky and Sartorius (1975).
[a] Per 1,000 aged 16+.

range extends from 1·5 to 4·2 per 1,000 (adjusting the figure of 5·1 given by Zharikov for total population would also give a rate of about 4·0 per 1,000). Pooling the data from the ten studies with known sample size gives a mean prevalence of 3·3 per 1,000.

INCIDENCE OR INCEPTION RATES

The incidence (or inception) of a disease is the frequency of appearance of new cases in the general population, expressed as a rate. Because the onset of schizophrenic illness is often difficult to define clearly, especially in retrospect, incidence rates are usually based on first contacts with schizophrenic services. Reported incidence rates for schizophrenia tend to vary more widely than reported prevalence rates, and on the whole are probably less reliable. Dunham (1965), on the basis of several tudies, estimated a mean rate of 21·8 per 100,000 general population. More recently, however, a number of surveys have yielded much higher rates: 30·6 in Salford, England (Adelstein et al., 1968), 52 in Dublin (Walsh, 1969), 53·6 in Mannheim (Häfner and Reimann, 1970) and 72 in Monroe County, New York State (Babigian, 1975).

Before taking such rates seriously, it is necessary to allow for the effects of different diagnostic concepts and different criteria of what constitutes a new case. We have seen in Chapter 1 that British psychiatrists use a narrower definition of schizophrenia than American or Russian. Kramer (1963) compared age-adjusted first admission rates to public and private mental hospitals in the United States with equivalent rates in England and Wales. The American rate in 1960 was 24·7 per 100,000 total population, compared with 17·4 for England and Wales. Corresponding rates for the major affective psychoses, on the other hand, were 11·0 and 38·5 respectively. More intensive research, using standard techniques of diagnosis, will be needed to define a replicable inception rate for schizophrenia. There is also evidence that more rigorous definition of a "new case" might result in much reduced estimates. The most recent data from two English case-registers allow the calculation of rates of "first-ever contact with psychiatric services" (Wing and Fryers, 1976). For Camberwell (south-east London) and Salford (in the Greater Manchester conurbation), the first-ever inception rates for schizophrenia were only 11 and 14 per 100,000 respectively.

These uncertainties restrict the use of epidemiological data in establishing the treated prognosis of schizophrenia. The prevalence of any illness is basically a function of its incidence and its mean duration

(Kramer, 1969). A period prevalence rate contains two components: one derived from the incidence of new cases during the period, the other from cases that have had their onset beforehand but have persisted, with active symptoms, so that they are still counted as cases at the time of the survey. A comparison between prevalence and incidence rates can thus give some idea of the mean duration of a disease. Because of unreliability in the calculation of both numerator and denominator, estimates of the duration of schizophrenia cannot be made with any confidence. Whereas most of the data cited above tend to suggest an average course of six to seven years, the use of more stringent diagnostic and operational criteria lead to a rather different conclusion. In Camberwell, for example, the first-ever admission rate for 1969–73 was 13·3 per 100,000 total population per annum, compared with a one-day prevalence rate, at the end of that period, of 198 per 100,000 (Wing and Fryers, 1976). These figures correspond to a mean duration of about fifteen years for schizophrenia.

Such estimates must in any event be of limited value for clinical prognosis, since they are based on data for different age-groups and clinical types, which may differ greatly in prognosis; moreover, they are bound to be influenced to some extent by nosocomial factors, such as current admission and discharge policies, and the number of hospital beds available for mental illness. Nevertheless, they serve to illustrate the chronic or recurrent nature of schizophrenia.

Age- and sex-specific rates, as a rule, show peak incidence rates within the range 20–39 years, with a smaller, secondary peak in the over-65 range. Typically onset is earlier among men, whereas women have higher rates in the older age-groups. This broad pattern varies in detail from one survey to another, and is modified by other factors, such as ethnic status.

DISEASE EXPECTANCY (MORBID RISK)

A third type of morbidity index, which has been used a great deal in population genetics, is the *expectancy*, or "lifetime risk", for a disease; that is, the probability (usually expressed as a percentage) that any individual who survives long enough to be exposed during the risk period for a disease will in fact develop that disease. The usual method of calculation in survey research is that of Weinberg, based on the total number of cases and the age-structure of the population (see Chapter 3).

Disease expectancy rates are based on the notion of "lifetime prevalence", or accumulation, of a disease within a population, and are, therefore, most useful in the study of chronic, progressive conditions. Modern concepts of schizophrenia do not conform to this model. Since almost all surveys providing expectancy rates for schizophrenia have been retrospective it is safe to assume that many acute episodes, especially those occurring in early adult life, have gone unreported, and that to this extent the estimated rates have been too low. A further limitation resides in the fact that comparisons between the rates for different populations may be misleading, unless they can be adjusted for differential mortality rates.

Most survey estimates of the expectation of schizophrenia have been something under 1%. Biographical studies of cohorts of persons born on Bornholm Island (Fremming, 1951) and in Iceland (Helgason, 1964) yielded rates of 0·9% and 0·7%, respectively. Pooled data from 19 investigations in six countries provided a mean rate of 0·86% (Zerbin-Rüdin, 1967; Shields and Slater, 1975). In the United States, where schizophrenia is diagnosed more readily than in Europe, the lifetime risk for this condition has been estimated at between 1% and 2% (Yolles and Kramer, 1969), and the latest estimate of risk, based on the Rochester, New York, case-register, is 3%. Apart from the United States, the published findings thus show a substantial measure of agreement, suggesting that the frequency of schizophrenia may be fairly constant in different societies.

Variation in the Frequency of Schizophrenia

Some writers, such as Slater (1968), have argued that this relative constancy of schizophrenic risk from one country to another is difficult to explain other than by a genetic predisposition which is fairly evenly distributed throughout the world. The argument would be more convincing if such a predisposition could be accepted as *the* determinant of schizophrenia. Since, however, as modern twin research has confirmed (see Chapter 3), the occurrence of schizophrenia must be ascribed to an interaction between heredity and environment, a uniform frequency in all cultures would be surprising. It would suggest that biological and environmental risk-factors are evenly distributed all over the world, or, even less likely, that the strength of the two types of factor must be inversely correlated. One can, of course, argue that cultural or other environmental differences account for the observed variation around a genetically determined mean rate, but this hypothesis cannot yet be tested.

Proponents of socio-cultural theories of schizophrenia can point to a number of discrepancies between the published findings, Böök (1953; 1961) found a prevalence rate of 10·8 per 1,000, and an expectancy of 2·9%, in an isolated community in northern Sweden. Eaton and Weil (1955) reported a prevalence of only 1·1 per 1,000 among the Hutterite communities of North America. These two findings represent the extremes of reported frequency of schizophrenia, but each may have been distorted by selective factors.

The north Swedish area studied by Böök was characterized by extreme social isolation. Those who were not prepared to tolerate such conditions might well have moved elsewhere. There was also a very high frequency of cousin marriages. On the other hand, the small and close-knit Hutterite communities might have proved intolerable to those with schizoid tendencies. As we have suggested earlier, studies such as these were carried out before the introduction of standard methods of diagnosis and this introduces further elements of doubt into their interpretation. Murphy (1968), for example, was unable to find any difference in the rate of admission of schizophrenia from the Hutterite areas compared with other areas in Canada's prairie provinces.

High prevalence rates have been estimated for a number of other populations and subgroups, suggesting that their members may carry an increased risk for schizophrenia. A number of reports over the past half-century have pointed to unusually high rates of psychotic illness, including schizophrenia, in Istria and the Croatian littoral, in northwest Yugoslavia (Crocetti et al., 1964; Bedenić et al., 1972). Other groups apparently at an increased risk are the Tamils of southern India and Ceylon, the Southern Irish and the Catholic population of Canada (Murphy, 1968).

A high reported prevalence does not necessarily imply a correspondingly high incidence of disease. Nosocomial factors may be important: in Eire, for instance, treated prevalence rates will tend to be high simply because the country has the highest psychiatric bed ratio in Europe (May, 1976a). Differences in clinical prognosis may also play a part since, given a uniform inception rate, prevalence will vary directly with the proportion of cases which become chronic. The course and outcome of schizophrenic illness, both in Taiwan (Rin and Lin, 1962) and in Mauritius (Murphy and Raman, 1971) appear to be more favourable than in developed industrial societies. Preliminary findings of a two-year follow-up of the International Pilot Study of Schizophrenia seem to indicate that there are differences in the course and outcome of this disorder between the nine participating countries (WHO, 1978). Until the connections between inception rate, clinical prognosis and prevalence of schizophrenia have been more fully explored, any socio-cultural causal hypothesis must be regarded as at best only tentative.

Statistics pertaining to time-trends in the frequency of schizophrenia should also be viewed with some caution because of diagnostic unreliability, and because of the influence of changes in service provision over the years. The evidence, as far as it goes, points to little change in the frequency of schizophrenia during the past century. Goldhamer and Marshall (1953) concluded that age-specific admission rates for this diagnosis had not increased in Massachusetts between 1840 and 1940. Ødegaard (1971) found a constant first admission rate in Norway between 1926 and 1965. Varga (1966), comparing hospitalized psychotic patients in Budapest in 1910 and 1960, found that the proportion diagnosed as schizophrenic had remained constant at about one quarter. Where apparent increases have occurred, as in New York State in the first half of the century (Malzberg, 1963), they have been accompanied by a fall in the rates for other diagnoses, particularly for manic-depressive psychosis, and can be ascribed to changes in diagnostic criteria (Terris, 1965).

Demographic and Social Correlates

Studies of the distribution of illness within defined populations tend to be more reliable than international or intercultural comparisons, because the levels of service provision are more nearly constant, and the diagnostic criteria more uniform. This approach constitutes a logical first step in the identification of high-risk groups within a community, and hence of possible environmental factors. A great many studies have been made of the distribution of schizophrenia in cities and in local populations, and the observed variations in frequency tested against the main demographic and social indices. Most of the significant findings have centred around a group of interlocking social variables, comprising occupational and socio-economic status, social and geographic mobility, type of residential district and extent of family and social contacts.

OCCUPATION AND SOCIAL CLASS

The fact that schizophrenia is concentrated among unskilled workers and members of low-status occupational groups has been repeatedly confirmed, both by local surveys and by national statistical returns (Clark, 1949; Ødegaard, 1956; Brooke, 1957). A pronounced social class difference has been found in incidence and prevalence rates in many countries, regardless of whether social class indices are based simply on occupation (Brooke, 1957; Goldberg and Morrison, 1963), or incorporate other criteria such as educational attainment as well (Hollingshead and Redlich, 1958).

The social class difference was initially thought to be of causal significance, especially as a number of earlier surveys reported that it was also to be found in the corresponding distribution for the schizophrenics' fathers (Tietze et al., 1941; Hollingshead and Redlich, 1958; Clausen and Kohn, 1959). Gradually, however, the weight of the evidence has swung against a causal connection, in favour of the view that the observed difference reflects the course of schizophrenic illness, rather than its origin.

To begin with, the difference is much larger among prevalence than among incidence rates (Dunham, 1965), and can be explained by the accumulation of chronic, unrecovered cases in the lower social strata (Cooper, 1961). Secondly, comparison of the social class distribution of schizophrenic patients at first admission with that of their fathers at about the same age (derived from birth-registration data) showed convincingly that the difference occurs only in the former (Goldberg and Morrison, 1963). More detailed study of a first-admission sample indicated that downward social mobility often precedes the onset of schizophrenic illness, and begins typically at puberty. The affected persons are not socially disadvantaged from birth, but suffer from a form of premorbid handicap which impairs their later school achievement, and puts them at a disadvantage in their work careers. Table II compares the

Table II Social class distribution of male schizophrenic patients and of their male relatives

Social class [a]	Patients [b] %	Fathers %	Brothers %	Paternal grandfathers %	Maternal grandfathers %
I and II	4	29	21	28	20
III	48	48	56	50	51
IV and V	48	23	23	22	29
Total	100	100	100	100	100
No. of persons	44	52	39	46	51
School or student	6	—	3	—	—
Nil, or not known	2	—	4	6	1

Source: Goldberg and Morrison (1963).
[a] Registrar General's occupational classification.
[b] Male schizophrenic patients under 30 years, admitted to one mental hospital, 1958–60 (occupation prior to first admission).

occupational class of the patients with those of their fathers, grandfathers and brothers.

The NIMH "Extended Family" study (Wender *et al.*, 1973) has provided further support for these conclusions, by showing that the mean socio-economic status of schizophrenic patients, who were adopted children, was lower than the corresponding means both for their biological fathers and for their adoptive fathers. On present evidence, it seems probable that the true incidence of schizophrenia is distributed fairly evenly among the different social classes.

MOBILITY AND DISTRICT OF RESIDENCE

The concentration of new cases of schizophrenia (as measured by first-admission rates) in the central zones of large cities, first described by Faris and Dunham (1939), was subsequently confirmed in St Louis (Schroeder, 1942), Worcester, Massachusetts (Gerard and Houston, 1953), Bristol, England (Hare, 1956), Oslo (Sundby and Nyhus, 1963), Detroit (Dunham, 1965), Baltimore (Klee *et al.*, 1967), Dublin (Walsh, 1969) and Mannheim, Germany (Häfner and Reimann, 1970). The Chicago findings were largely replicated in a second survey some thirty years later (Rowitz and Levy, 1968). The explanation of this apparently world-wide phenomenon is still not entirely clear. The "breeder" hypothesis originally put forward by Faris and Dunham—namely, that the social disorganization and anomie typical of the poor, decaying central areas has a pathogenic effect on the more vulnerable inhabitants—has not been substantiated. Later studies indicated that the excess of schizophrenic psychoses in these areas could be explained wholly in terms of persons living alone in cheap hotels and lodging houses, and that the rates for schizophrenia among those living in family groups were evenly distributed throughout cities. These findings suggested that the critical factor was either a downward social "drift" of pre-schizophrenic individuals, accompanied by migration into the cheap rooming-house districts (Gerard and Houston, 1953); or a more active process of "segregation", whereby the pre-schizophrenic individual, even if not declining in social status, tends to seek the anonymity to be found in such districts (Hare, 1956); or, indeed, a combination of both trends.

This general hypothesis would lead one to expect a high rate of mobility among pre-schizophrenic groups; in other words, that schizophrenic patients would be found at first admission to have had relatively frequent changes of address, and to have come from further afield than other newly admitted patients. Most of the published surveys have tended to confirm these predictions.

Higher rates of schizophrenia were found among immigrants than among the native born in New York State (Malzberg and Lee, 1956), in California (Lazarus *et al.*, 1963) and in Ohio (Locke and Duvall, 1964). Adjusting incidence rates for differences in socio-economic status did not remove the differential (Lee, 1963). Dunham (1965), studying two contrasting parts of Detroit, concluded that the excess of schizophrenic illness in the poorer community was due to internal migration. Hare (1956), in Bristol, also found that many schizophrenic patients had moved into the central areas shortly before their admission to hospital.

There have been, however, some discrepant reports. Astrup and Ødegaard (1960), for example, reported that, in Norway, those who migrated from countryside to towns other than the capital, Oslo, appeared to have a lower risk for schizophrenia than those who remained in their native districts. They argued that mobility of this kind was more likely to represent an upward social mobility than a downward drift. Migration to Oslo, however, did follow the more usual pattern. Murphy (1959), who found the rates of schizophrenia in Singapore to be inversely correlated with population mobility, also thought that migration could be positive. Plank (1959) compared schizophrenic patients with a control group of neurotic patients, and found evidence of greater mobility among the latter. These conflicting reports suggest that the association between schizophrenia and population mobility is not unitary but depends upon the balance between upward and downward social mobility that is found in any particular location. It does seem, none the less, that the isolated areas of large cities attract people with schizophrenia and those who will later develop the condition.

SOCIAL RELATIONS AND SOCIAL ISOLATION

A corollary of the "drift" and "segregation" hypotheses is that schizophrenic patients, at the time of first admission, are characterized by social isolation, in that they frequently live alone, have relatively few contacts with relations or friends, and participate in few social activities.

The first of these points—namely, that schizophrenic illness is concentrated among persons who live alone—is well established (Gerard and Houston, 1953; Hare, 1956; Dunham, 1965). The simplest explanation is that schizophrenia is commoner among the single than among the married (Ødegaard, 1946; Malzberg, 1964a). Here, sex appears to have a moderating influence: pre-schizophrenic women marry more often than their male counterparts, and are more often divorced or separated (Farina *et al.*, 1963a; Brown *et al.*, 1966).

To separate the effects of social isolation from those of being unmarried will obviously be no easy task, especially since, in this respect as in many others, schizophrenic patients do not form a homogeneous group. In one study (Farina *et al.*, 1963a), male schizophrenics were divided by means of the Phillips Scale (Phillips, 1953) into groups with good and poor premorbid social adjustment. Those in the first group were mostly married and had many friendships; whereas those in the second group were single and had few friends. The dichotomy was found to be of prognostic significance. It has been shown repeatedly that social adjustment prior to first admission has an important bearing on the clinical outcome. Cooper (1961), for example, found that schizophrenic patients who had been living alone fared much worse, in terms of clinical improvement, rate of discharge and total time spent in hospital, than others who had been living in a family setting.

A more detailed examination of the relationship between social isolation and schizophrenia was carried out in the small city of Hagerstown, Maryland (Kohn and Clausen, 1955; Clausen and Kohn, 1960). Schizophrenic patients, and a normal control group matched for age, sex and social class, were classified, on the basis of biographic interviews, according to their reported social activities and patterns of friendship in early adolescence. Roughly one-third of the schizophrenics were classed as "isolates" or "partial isolates", compared with only 4% of the control subjects. The differences could not be attributed to unequal opportunities for the two groups. Information from family members suggested that the patients classed as i.olates had withdrawn from friendships formed earlier in childhood, as part of a progressive alienation. The non-isolated group (which, it must be emphasized, included a majority of the schizophrenics) had shown no such tendency towards withdrawal in adolescence. Clearly, therefore, isolation could not be regarded as a necessary precursor of schizophrenia.

Information gathered retrospectively, on the premorbid functioning and personality of a mentally sick person, must always be interpreted with caution. This will hold true especially for young schizophrenic patients if, as has often been asserted, their parents must be considered unreliable witnesses. Nevertheless, the Hagerstown findings do conform quite well to the broad pattern delineated by Goldberg and Morrison (1963), Dunham (1965) and other workers: a pattern in which early timidity and shyness, loss of peer relationships in adolescence, poor school performance and early work record, reduction in social status and, finally, migration into a decaying, disorganized urban area, tend to occur as successive stages in the life histories of pre-schizophrenic individuals.

Precipitating Factors

Correlations established by a survey focused on one point in time (the "cross-section" technique) can tell us little about the amount of exposure sick persons have had to a possible risk factor, and little about the extent to which such exposure has actually preceded the onset of illness. The studies already cited have demonstrated how great is the need to supplement survey findings with biographical data, and to establish more firmly the time sequence of events. This need stands out clearly as soon as one comes to consider the role of what is loosely termed "life stress" in the genesis of schizophrenia.

As postulated by Langner and Michael (1963) and other American workers, life stress embraces a wide range of environmental influences which operate cumulatively, during childhood and youth, to produce deformity of the personality, and so to pave the way for subsequent mental disorder. The difficulty in testing this plausible hypothesis lies in the definition of life stress and its objective measurement. In the "Midtown Manhattan Study", frequency and severity of stress were reported greatest in low status groups, whose members also manifested a raised frequency of neurotic symptoms (Srole *et al.*, 1962; Langner and Michael, 1963). More recent studies have emphasized the problems inherent in trying to measure either life stress or "mental health", independently of social class (Dohrenwend and Dohrenwend, 1969).

A similar approach has been used in schizophrenia research where life stress has been formulated in terms of the dynamics of family life, which are held to be linked to social class (Myers and Roberts, 1959). So far, no really convincing evidence has been produced in support of this contention. The better-controlled studies have failed to demonstrate a substantial difference between the family relationships of pre-schizophrenic individuals and those of normal persons from the same social class backgrounds (Kohn, 1969). In a study of low status groups in Puerto Rico (Rogler and Hollingshead, 1965), families with schizophrenic members did not suffer more than others in respect of long-term patterns of adjustment, though they had experienced significantly more stressful events in the year preceding onset of the illness.

In general, the most challenging results to date have come from studies concentrating on the role of life events in the precipitation of acute schizophrenic illness. Evidence of the importance of such events has long been to hand; for example, in the repeated observation that the schizophrenia rates among immigrants vary inversely with the time interval since migration (Malzberg and Lee, 1956; Malzberg, 1964b); or in the very sharp rise in psychosis rates following directly on child-bearing (Pugh et al., 1963; Paffenbarger, 1964). The paucity of systematic research into this aspect of schizophrenia is thus quite striking.

Steinberg and Durell (1968) reviewed the service records of all non-commissioned soldiers in the United States Army, hospitalized for schizophrenia in 1956–60. They found a markedly increased rate in the early months of service, compared with the second year. Early detection of pre-existing chronic cases accounted for only a fraction of the difference, suggesting that there had been a true rise in incidence following entry into the army. The authors ascribed this finding to provocation of schizophrenia, in susceptible persons, by a suddenly increased demand for social adaptation.

A different technique was employed by Brown and Birley (1968), who collected information on life events experienced, in the three-month period before onset of acute symptoms, by 50 newly-admitted schizophrenic patients, and compared the findings with corresponding data for a much larger group of normal controls. The events reported included moving house, starting or losing a job, admission to hospital, birth, marriage or death in the nuclear family, and various forms of domestic crisis. Some events, such as getting engaged to be married, or being promoted at work, were distinctly "positive". They were classified, according to whether or not they could have been controlled or influenced by the patient, as "independent" or "possibly independent". In the three weeks immediately before onset of acute symptoms, 46% of the patients had experienced at least one "independent" event, as compared to an average of only 14% among the controls. During the preceding nine weeks the rate for both patient and control groups had remained fairly steady at 12–14%. In other words, the onset of schizophrenic illness had been preceded by a sharp increase in the frequency of life events of a kind which could not have been brought about by abnormal behaviour on the patients' part.

No differences in age, sex or symptomatology were discovered between the patients whose illness had been preceded by one or more defined life-events, and those with no reported events. However, significantly more of the latter group had stopped taking phenothiazines during the year before acute onset of symptoms. This observation suggested that

both experience of stressful life-events and discontinuation of maintenance therapy had contributed to the occurrence of acute episodes
(Birley and Brown, 1970).

These results were broadly confirmed by a more recent American
study (Jacobs et al., 1974; Jacobs and Myers, 1976), in which newly-
admitted schizophrenic patients were found to have experienced significantly more life-events than normal controls during the preceding six
months, but fewer of certain types of event (especially those involving
some form of loss) than a comparable group of depressed patients.

On the basis of the reported findings, it is possible to estimate the
importance of life events for schizophrenia, in terms of the relative risk
of a new illness in persons who have been exposed to such events, compared with those who have not (Paykel, 1977). The index of "relative
risk" must be defined in relation to the time interval since occurrence of
an event, being highest immediately afterwards and then falling gradually back to the previous level. Table III illustrates the point.

Table III Life events and relative risk of schizophrenia

Authors	Types of event	Time period	Relative risk
Steinberg and Durell (1968)	Entry into US Army	one month	6·2
		six months	2·7
Brown and Birley (1968)	All events	three weeks	6·4
		six months	2·4
Jacobs and Myers (1976);	All events	six months	3·0
Paykel (1977)	Undesirable events	six months	4·5

No published study of life events and schizophrenia has succeeded in
overcoming all the major problems of method. Apart fiom the fact that
all have relied on retrospective data collection, there are unsettled questions concerning the selection of controls and the pooling together of the
first-admission and readmission data. None the less, life-events research
has undoubtedly opened up an important new field of investigation into
schizophrenia. Further evidence concerning precipitating factors is derived from studies in which patients who have long been symptom-free
suddenly develop symptoms of acute schizophrenia following over-
enthusiastic social treatment. Effects of this kind have been reported by
a number of workers (Wing et al., 1964; Stevens, 1973; Goldberg et al.,
1977).

Comparison of the nature and magnitude of life events which precede
onset of schizophrenia, and those preceding onset of depression or

suicidal attempts (Brown and Birley, 1970; Jacobs *et al.*, 1974; Paykel, 1974) suggests that the pathogenic effect of such events is not specific. The question as to why a given type of event leads to schizophrenic illness in some persons, to depression in others, and to a normal adaptive response in the majority, must be taken up in relation to predisposition.

Predisposing Factors

Life-events research illustrates the need to supplement large-scale epidemiological surveys with more intensive methods of data collection, based on fairly small samples. A similar need arises in the investigation of more distant causes. The kind of information available from public records (such as registration of births and deaths) is for the most part only marginally relevant, whereas that which, on theoretical grounds, might be deemed highly relevant (for example, the presence of psychological abnormality in one or both parents) can as a rule be elicited only by means of detailed investigation of individuals and their families. Up to now, no satisfactory method has been devised for linking extensive and intensive methods of enquiry in this field.

The only firmly established predisposing factor of schizophrenia remains that of inheritance, as demonstrated in many twin studies, and more recently, in studies of adoptees. Genetic research on schizophrenia is reviewed in Chapter 3. Although it is now generally accepted that genetic factors are important in the aetiology on schizophrenia, they do not tell the whole story: susceptibility to this condition must be partially environmentally determined.

BIRTH CORRELATES

Extensive survey techniques have been used to test associations between the rate of schizophrenia and such variables as maternal age, birth order in sibships and season of birth. The findings of different studies are somewhat contradictory, and no firm links have yet been established between any birth characteristic and the risk of schizophrenia in later life. There is some indication that, in large sibships, schizophrenia may be commoner among later-born than among earlier-born siblings (Schooler, 1961; Farina *et al.*, 1963b), an association which must be taken in conjunction with the factor of maternal age (Goodman, 1957).

Barry and Barry (1961) found an excess of winter births among schizophrenics, compared with a control population; a subsequent study indicated that the discrepancy could be linked to social class differences
(Barry and Barry, 1964). Seasonal variation in the birth rate of predisposed individuals could be of causal significance (Hare, 1975). The
most obvious explanation of such a trend, restricted to, or more pronounced in, lower social status groups, is some form of dietary deficiency.

PERINATAL COMPLICATIONS

The results of many studies have suggested associations between the rate
of prenatal and paranatal complications, on the one hand, and the
subsequent incidence on neurological and psychological abnormalities,
on the other (MacMahon and Sawa, 1961; Pasamanick, 1961). These
findings aroused speculation that perinatal complications might also act
as risk factors for schizophrenia. The question is difficult to elucidate.
Obstetric histories surveyed in retrospect, even for samples of school-
children—let alone for adults of 30 or 40—must inevitably be lacking in
accuracy and completeness. Moreover, the many intervening variables,
such as ethnic status, social class, age of mother, size of family, etc., will
be difficult—if not impossible—to control. It is thus easy to understand
why, in recent years, attention has become focused on prospective
studies, in which young persons thought to be at increased risk for
schizophrenia are followed up over many years.

So far, the evidence is far from conclusive. Mednick and his co-
workers, using as a sampling frame all children of Danish women hospitalized for schizophrenia, have followed up some 200 such high risk
individuals, together with a matched control group of 100 normal
children (Mednick et al., 1974). Preliminary findings after ten years
indicated that 15 members of the high-risk group had already suffered
a schizophrenic breakdown, and that this subgroup had been characterized by a history of difficult births and perinatal complications
(Mednick et al., 1975). Since it also transpired that the mothers of the
high-risk group who became mentally ill had themselves developed
schizophrenia relatively young, and that early maternal separation had
occurred in excess in this subgroup, the role of perinatal factors could
not be defined. In a longitudinal study of children of schizophrenic
parents and three control groups (Hanson et al., 1976), the former could
be distinguished neither by the perinatal history nor by the presence of
neurological abnormalities. Indeed, the importance of CNS damage or

dysfunction as a risk factor for schizophrenia remains tantalizingly unclear.

FAMILY ENVIRONMENT

Facts and theories about family influence on schizophrenia are not easy to fit into any simple conceptual framework. Brown (1967), in a useful critical review, subsumed the main studies under three headings: structural aspects; quality of family relationships and styles of communication.

There is little evidence that the families of schizophrenic patients have special structural characteristics. Goodman (1957) found a tendency for schizophrenics to have been born to mothers of 30 or over. Hilgard and Newman (1963) noted a small excess of early parental loss among young schizophrenic patients when compared with normal controls. Neither of these findings appears to be specific for schizophrenia. That relating to parental loss could not be confirmed by Oltman and Friedman (1963), who reported no difference in this respect between schizophrenic patients, patients with organic illness and healthy controls. In general, these investigations have been concerned with early predisposing factors of schizophrenia. There is no doubt that the family and household structures of schizophrenic patients prior to first hospital admission do have special features; but these, as we have seen, are determined by the progressive isolation and downward social drift which precede breakdown, and are not of causal significance.

Many enquiries have shown that disturbed interpersonal relationships are common in the families of schizophrenic patients (Gerard and Siegel, 1950; Mishler and Waxler, 1965; Reiss, 1968). Demonstration of such disturbances *ex post facto* is notoriously unreliable as a method of causal research, since the existence of the illness itself, and the grave social consequences to which it gives rise, may be responsible for the observed disturbance of relationships, rather than having been caused by it. Moreover, there is still a lack of hard evidence to show that certain patterns of family relationship, objectively measured, occur more frequently in the families of schizophrenics than among those of alcoholic, depressed or neurotic patients; or, indeed, than in the general population.

The same objections apply with equal force to most of the research linking incidence of schizophrenia with abnormal styles of communication within family groups. These issues are discussed in greater detail in Chapter 6.

Multifactorial and Interactional Theories

The concept of a single, specific disease agent as necessary and sufficient cause, as expressed in the postulates of Henle and Koch, has proved inadequate to the needs of modern causal research in medicine, where increasing use is now being made of multifactorial models. The classical epidemiological triad of agent, host and environment provides a useful base for the construction of this type of model (Susser, 1973). In some hypotheses, an interaction between biological and social factors has been suggested, in order to explain the occurrence of schizophrenia. As yet, none of these hypotheses explain all the reported findings, and none has been subjected to adequate testing. Nevertheless, two will be mentioned briefly, because they give some indication of the way research workers are now thinking about schizophrenia and, consequently, of the probable trends in schizophrenia research in the next few years.

Kohn (1976), an American sociologist, has postulated

> that the constricted conditions of life experienced by people of lower social class position foster conceptions of social reality that are so limited and so rigid as to impair their ability to deal resourcefully with the problematic and the stressful. Although such impairment is unfortunate, it would not in and of itself result in schizophrenia. However, in conjunction with a genetic vulnerability and the experience of great stress, such impairment *could* be disabling and result in schizophrenia.

Kohn's formulation successfully incorporates genetic, early environmental and precipitating factors. Unfortunately, as has already been pointed out, there is no convincing evidence that lower-class conditions of life are conducive to schizophrenia, or, indeed, that schizophrenia actually does occur more frequently among lower-class groups of the population.

Similar objections can be made to the more elaborate causal model proposed by Mednick (1962). According to this theory, schizophrenia represents a highly maladaptive form of avoidance behaviour, shown in the face of environmental stress by persons who, as a result of paranatal brain damage, suffer from specific handicaps. The work of Mednick and his group is discussed in detail in Chapter 5. Here, it is necessary only to emphasize that we still lack the kind of epidemiological data required to establish connections (a) between paranatal complications and the type of functional handicap postulated by Mednick; (b) between the existence of such handicaps and the incidence of schizophrenic illness.

The main heuristic value of this research has been to underline the need for prospective studies, and for clearer definition of the psychophysiological risk factors of schizophrenia.

Conclusion

Throughout this brief review, schizophrenia has been discussed, purely for convenience, as a nosological entity with its own characteristic aetiology, pathology, course and outcome. The assumption is a large one, and there are many psychiatrists today who cannot share it. Two other models are at least equally plausible. In one, the category comprises a loosely associated group of disorders with differing clinical features. In the other, "schizophrenia" is not a disease at all, in the modern sense of the term, but rather a morbid state, analogous to congestive cardiac failure or uraemia, which can result from a number of different pathological processes. In either event, the search for a unitary causal pattern could prove misguided. Garratt (1976) has stated the problem bluntly:

> To the epidemiologist, the traditional psychiatric classification based on signs and symptoms of abnormal mental behaviour seems analogous to the clinical classification in cardiac failure into "right-sided" and "left-sided" failure: the psychiatric equivalent being the schizophrenias and manic-depressive reactions, as described by Bleuler and Kraepelin.

According to this viewpoint, the basic task in psychiatric research is to define a clinico-pathological classification of the major disorders: the equivalent of differentiating rheumatic carditis, coronary-artery disease, etc. If this stage in classification could be reached, it ought then to be possible for research workers using epidemiological techniques to identify the causal factors underlying the pathological entities.

The search for a structural pathology in schizophrenia having proved singularly unrewarding, the best hope of establishing such a classification may well reside in the identification of some biological or psychological "markers" for schizophrenia, representing intermediate stages between the underlying predisposition and its expression as a psychotic illness. Much experimental work has already been done to identify the "primary" handicaps of schizophrenia, in terms of fairly specific psychological impairments (see Chapter 5). The evidence cited above, of a premorbid deterioration in performance and social adjustment, strongly suggests that many pre-schizophrenic individuals suffer from such impairments, long before the appearance of psychotic symptoms. There is still, however, a dearth of information from prospective studies to confirm the point. The demonstration of such abnormalities in person at high-risk for schizophrenia, in the first-degree relatives of schizophrenic patients, or in the patients themselves following clinical recovery, would be highly indicative of one or more types of specific pathology, which would then serve as targets for future epidemiological research.

3 | Genetics

James Shields

The idea has always been with us that heredity can be a cause of mental illness. Since Rüdin's monograph of 1916 there has been a massive amount of genetic investigation into "schizophrenia",* and the results have been interpreted in a variety of ways. Some studies have been primarily genetic: the authors have tried to discover whether, how much and in what manner schizophrenia is inherited. Other authors have used genetic methods in attempts to throw light on broader questions: what causal connections are there between the core group of schizophrenias, strictly defined, and other disorders? To what extent should the schizophrenias, as grouped together clinically by Kraepelin or by Bleuler, be separated into relatively distinct genetic and environmental diseases? Environmental and developmental factors have been investigated, using pairs of identical twins, only one of whom is schizophrenic, or following up high risk groups such as the children of people with schizophrenia.

The first part of this chapter is devoted mainly to studies of the first kind; i.e. to the evidence, accumulated using different methods, for the proposition that the genes an individual has inherited make a significant contribution to the risk of developing schizophrenia. In the second part, some of the current genetic theories are outlined.†

* See p. viii.
† Textbooks, conference reports and other volumes in English relating to genetic aspects of schizophrenia, appearing in the last ten years, include: Rosenthal and Kety, 1968; Rosenthal, 1970; Slater and Cowie, 1971; Erlenmeyer-Kimling, 1972; Gottesman and Shields, 1972; Fieve *et al.*, 1975; and *Schizophrenia Bulletin*, **2**, 3, 1976. It is assumed that the reader will have a knowledge of elementary genetic principles, as set out for example in Roberts (1973) and Carter (1976).

Of course both genes and environment are essential for any kind of development, normal or abnormal, variable or universal. What the genes determine is the capacity to respond to some particular environmental factor in a specific way. Individuals vary so much in their genetic make-up and their environmental experiences that there is rarely any simple and universally accepted answer to questions about the causes of individual differences.

Probably no-one would deny the genetic basis of the form of mental retardation caused by phenylketonuria. This recognizable inborn error of metabolism is inherited as a Mendelian recessive trait. On average, one in four out of a sibship is affected. Nevertheless, interaction with the environment and the possibility of treatment are well established. The condition could easily be regarded as a dietary disease, since a normal, phenylalanine-rich, diet is noxious for the rare homozygous PKU individuals, except for the fact that it is *only* such people who are susceptible.

Schizophrenia is not a disorder like phenylketonuria. Since the time of the earliest studies it has been recognized that "schizophrenia" is not a simple condition with a clear-cut inheritance, like PKU or Huntington's chorea. No simply inherited biochemical error has yet been discovered that will account for even a small proportion of the disorders included within the group of schizophrenias. The evidence for the contribution of genetic factors is mainly epidemiological, depending on the comparison of incidence rates in relevant subgroups of the population, in order to find out how far these rates support or refute a genetic hypothesis. The evidence in support may not satisfy everyone, since causal factors, both genetic and environmental, are many and unidentified. However, over the years it has become increasingly strong and consistent. It has withstood several attempts at refutation. The evidence comes from a combination of family, twin and adoption studies. Each has its limitations, but in combination they rule out alternative purely environmental explanations of family resemblance. Genetic family studies seek to establish whether there is a genuinely increased risk for the relatives of schizophrenics compared with the rate in the general population or in suitable control groups. However, family aggregation might be due to similarities within families in factors such as social deprivation, patterns of child rearing, modes of communication, and so on. The classical comparison of monozygotic (MZ, genetically identical) twins brought up in the same family, with dizygotic (DZ, genetically dissimilar) twins brought up in the same family, seeks to show whether the genes make any difference. This is the same-family-different-genes design. Adoption studies compare groups (e.g. offspring of schizophrenic parentage) that are similar genetically but reared in different environments: the same-genes-different-families design. Such studies can test hypotheses about the interaction of genes and environment.

Methods and Data

GENETIC FAMILY STUDIES

Pedigree studies have so far failed to establish simple Mendelian inheritance—dominant, recessive, or sex-linked—for schizophrenia or any subgroup of schizophrenia. The simplest genetic hypothesis therefore predicts that the frequency of schizophrenia among the relatives of schizophrenic patients will vary with the degree of genetic relatedness. It should be higher in MZ than DZ co-twins; and higher in first degree relatives (parents, full sibs and children), sharing on average half their genes with a schizophrenic proband (index case), than in second degree relatives (half-sibs, uncles and aunts, nephews and nieces, grandparents and grandchildren), who are one step further removed from a schizophrenic proband, and will on average have only 25% of genes in common with him. The rate in second degree relatives should, of course, be higher than that in the general population.

The rate most generally used in genetic studies is neither the prevalence at a given point in time, nor the incidence of new cases in a stated period, but the morbid risk or lifetime expectancy of developing schizophrenia (see Chapter 2). In large representative samples, the lifetime expectancy can be calculated by the life table method (see Slater and Cowie, 1971, Appendices D and E, for this and other methods of calculating rates). In the past, the most frequently used empirical shortcut method has been the Weinberg abridged method. Here the risk period during which the great majority of schizophrenias first occur is customarily taken as between the ages 14–40 or 15–45. The age distribution of the relatives or other population sample studied is taken into account by reducing their total number to the corrected total of risk lives survived (the *Bezugsziffer* or BZ). The number over the age of 40 (or 45) are counted without correction, since, if they are not already schizophrenic, they are not likely to become so, however long they live. The number of those between the ages of 15 and 40 (or 45) are halved, on the assumption that, on average, those included will have survived half the risk period. Those under 15 are omitted altogether. If X is the number in the sample who have been diagnosed schizophrenic, the morbid risk is X/BZ. The Weinberg abridged method is not suitable for MZ twins because of their correlated age of onset, and it is not appropriate if the relatives at risk are mostly bunched together at one or other end of the risk period. In the latter case Strömgren's method can be used which weights the age of each relative according to the proportion of risk survived.

In earlier studies, mostly carried out in the inter-war years by European-trained psychiatrists, the morbid risk for schizophrenia was calculated in some 20 samples of the general population. These included cross-sectional census-type prevalence studies, a few longitudinal incidence studies such as Fremming's (1951) on the Danish island of Bornholm, and studies of the relatives of control probands not selected on account of mental illness. (See Strömgren, 1950, for a critical review.) Despite some variation in findings and high rates in some isolates, many of the morbid risks were around 0·80% or 0·85%, and one of these figures was usually taken as an appropriate estimate of the general population risk for schizophrenia. Since the war slightly higher rates of around 1·0% have been reported. Slater and Cowie (1971) for instance, calculated the cumulative lifetime expectancy of becoming schizophrenic by the age of 65 to be 1·1%, based on first admission rates to mental hospitals in England and Wales, 1952–60.*

Table I shows that the reported morbid risk for the relatives of schizophrenic probands is considerably higher than this. The table is based on the pooled data of all studies reported before 1967, mostly employing European standards of diagnosis. There was, understandably, variation between studies. Thus the rate for sibs, in twelve studies from seven countries, ranged from 4% to 14%. Relatives were not diagnosed in ignorance of the diagnosis of the schizophrenic proband, though when this was done in later studies an increased risk was still found. There are inevitable uncertainties caused by the necessity of making a diagnosis for all relatives, as in some cases the information is not optimal, since the relatives are dead or not available for interview, and medical records, etc. are inadequate. Rates are shown separately for what the investigators called definite schizophrenia (col. (a)), and for definite plus uncertain schizophrenia (col. (b)).

When both parents are schizophrenic, the risk, based on five studies, rises to around 40%. It might be objected that this high risk could be

---

* The writer has calculated the cumulative lifetime risk for schizophrenia to age 55 from first contacts with psychiatric services in Camberwell from Camberwell Register data, supplied by Lorna Wing and Jane Hurry. It was 0·86%. To age 65 the risk was 0·90% (Shields, unpublished).

Table I Morbid risk of schizophrenia for relatives of schizophrenics (after Slater and Cowie, 1971)*

Relationship	Total relatives (age-corrected)	Schizophrenic %	
		(a)	(b)
Parents	7,675	4·4	5·5
Sibs (all)	8,504·5	8·5	10·2
Sibs (neither parent schizophrenic)	7,535	8·2	9·7
Sibs (one parent schizophrenic)	674·5	13·8	17·2
Children	1,226·5	12·3	13·9
Children of mating Schiz. × Schiz.	134	36·6	46·3
Half-sibs	311	3·2	3·5
Uncles and aunts	3,376	2·0	3·6
Nephews and nieces	2,315	2·2	2·6
Grandchildren	713	2·8	3·5

(a) Diagnostically certain cases only.
(b) Also including probable schizophrenics.
* Based on the comprehensive review by Zerbin-Rüdin (1967).

due to the extremely chaotic environment provided by such parents. However, in what must be an equally chaotic environment—that in which one parent is schizophrenic and the other psychopathic—the risk for the sib of the schizophrenic was found to be no higher than 15%.

The low figure for parents can to a large extent be explained by the fact that typical early onset schizophrenic patients are unlikely to become parents. Essen-Möller (1955) has shown that, when allowance is made for the age reached by the parents when they enter the studies, their risk corresponds closely with that for sibs and children. It has regularly been found that, when a parent is affected, it is more often the mother than the father, and this has sometimes been used to support a psychogenic causation. However, the observation is in keeping with the fact that women marry earlier than men and tend to become schizophrenic later than men and so have more time in which to have a family. Men with schizophrenia, when they do have children, are generally found to have as high a proportion of similarly-affected offspring as do women with schizophrenia.

The somewhat higher morbidity rate for the children of schizophrenic patients compared with their sibs suggested in the table is not confirmed in later studies. Manfred Bleuler (1972), for instance, reports rates (inclusive of probable schizophrenia) of 9·4% for children and 9·9% for sibs. It is of interest, however, that the Newcastle-on-Tyne study by Stephens et al. (1975), and a Swedish study by Larson and Nyman

(1970), support the earlier studies in finding the risks for sibs to be close to 10%.

It can be seen in Table I that the average rates for different kinds of second degree relatives—very different in their shared environments—vary between 2·0% and 3·6%. In Bleuler's study, the risk for all second degree relatives is 3·4%, including probable schizophrenia, again in good agreement with the earlier studies.

There is a reasonable amount of agreement among studies using European standards of diagnosis that the morbid risk for children with both parents affected may be around 40%, for first degree relatives around 10%, and for second degree realtives around 3%. Some recent studies, however, sometimes with the diagnosis of relatives made blindly, report rates either much lower or much higher. For example, Winokur et al. (1974), claiming the use of defined research criteria, in their "Iowa 500" study, found the morbid risk for first degree relatives of patients with hebephrenic schizophrenia to be only 2·75%. Kety et al. (1975) employed a wide concept of schizophrenia, including pseudo-neurotic and latent varieties, and reported a 22·2% prevalence (not age-corrected) of definite or uncertain schizophrenia among the paternal half-sibs (second degree relatives) of adoptees with schizophrenia.

The earlier work of the Munich school, on which much of the data of Table I is based, usually failed to find any significant increase of affective psychosis in the families of schizophrenics or of schizophrenia in the families of manic depressives. Ødegaard (1963, 1972), however, finds a considerable overlap but emphasizes the significant degree of diagnostic resemblance between psychotic first degree relatives which still remains. Reed et al. (1973) found little diagnostic resemblance within families. The degree of overlap found may well depend on the adequacy of the clinical material and the diagnostic criteria applied. Many clinicians have noted the occurrence of personality features and abnormalities in the relatives of schizophrenics which have been characterized as schizoid, but these are even more difficult to assess reliably than schizophrenia itself. Descriptions of their nature and estimates of their frequency have varied widely. Shields et al. (1975) discuss some of the problems of the schizoid as a trait for genetic analysis.

Earlier attempts to compare the schizophrenic subtypes failed to show that any of them were genetically distinct diseases. The risk for schizophrenia of any type was increased for the relatives of probands of each type, though there was a tendency in some studies towards family resemblance in respect of hebephrenic and catatonic subtypes. Furthermore these severe cases—the hebephrenics and catatonics—tended to have a higher proportion of schizophrenic relatives than later onset paranoid cases and other schizophrenics of better prognosis (see Shields, 1968). Similarly, several studies have shown a mixture of severe and mild cases within a family, suggesting that attempts to make any rigid genetic dichotomy based on prognosis would seem to be premature (Gottesman and Shields, 1976). We shall refer to the problem of heterogeneity in schizophrenia later.

Many of the non-organic childhood schizophrenic-like psychoses with onset after the age of five are probably related to adult schizophrenia genetically, but not those of earlier onset such as infantile autism (Kolvin *et al.*, 1971).

TWIN STUDIES

Despite the uncertainties, the family studies support the hypothesis that genetic factors are implicated in the aetiology of schizophrenia, but they do not entirely rule out the alternative hypothesis of shared family environment. To disprove the genetic hypothesis one would have to show that groups who differ in their genetic resemblance such as MZ, and DZ twins, do not differ in their rates of schizophrenia when exposed to the same family environment. It would be hard to find persons with more similar environments than same-sexed twins. There have been 11 more or less systematic comparisons of the MZ and DZ co-twins of schizophrenics from seven countries comprising over 1,300 pairs. In all but one study the MZ concordance rate (i.e. both twins schizophrenic) was considerably higher—usually about three times higher—than the DZ concordance rate. On the face of it, the shared family environment hypothesis, at least in the form in which it is put forward to account for the results of the genetic family studies, fails to find support, while the hypothesis that the genes make a difference in schizophrenia is strongly confirmed.

However, there are theoretical and methodological criticisms of twin studies to be answered, and apparent inconsistencies to be explained before this conclusion can be confidently accepted. One of the objections hinges on the biological and psychological peculiarities of being born and brought up as a twin. Could the hazards of twinship account for the high concordance rate, particularly in MZ pairs? To test this objection, one needs to see whether there is an excess of twins, and in particular of MZ twins, who suffer from schizophrenia compared with singletons. This has not been found in either the earlier or the recent studies.

The twin method assumes that one can reliably distinguish MZ from

DZ pairs. The possibility of error can be exaggerated. Pairs in which the twins are frequently mistaken for one another in childhood are generally found to have identical blood groups, and pairs who from their appearance are thought to be dizygotic are generally found to have different blood groups. If errors in zygosity determination occurred at random they would lead to an underestimate of the importance of genetic factors. However, it has been argued that errors do not occur at random. In cases of doubt, an investigator might be inclined to say that a pair of twins discordant for schizophrenia were DZ when they were really MZ, or he might use looser standards for diagnosing schizophrenia in the case of co-twins of schizophrenics known to be MZ; but in Kallmann's (1946) study there was no evidence that he changed diagnoses to schizophrenia any more frequently in MZ than in DZ pairs (Shields *et al.*, 1967). In the Maudsley twin study (Gottesman and Shields, 1972) zygosity and psychiatric disorder were diagnosed independently in an attempt to avoid diagnostic contamination. The histories of all the twins were diagnosed by a group of psychiatrists in ignorance of the zygosity of the pair and of whether the other twin had a diagnosis of schizophrenia. All diagnosticians confirmed the higher concordance for psychosis in the MZ pairs.

One of the main dangers in the twin studies is that of biased sampling, usually in favour of monozygotic and concordant pairs, which is almost certain to occur if one relies on single published case reports or on pairs that the investigator has been told about because they are "interesting". For fifty years (since Luxenburger, 1928) much effort has gone into attempts to obtain as complete samples as possible, for example by matching national twin registers and registers of hospitalized schizophrenics, or by enquiring systematically of every patient on admission whether he is a twin. Some earlier studies may have been less successful in this than others.

Perhaps the most frequent objection raised against the drawing of conclusions from twin studies is the argument that, although both kinds of twins are reared in the same family at the same time, the environments of MZ twins are in some respects more similar than those of DZs. They may be more often dressed alike. They may select more similar environments for themselves, for example choosing the same friends; or they may be exposed to more similar environments, partly for genetic reasons, e.g. being in the same class at school on account of their similarity in intelligence. They may be more closely attached and influence each other more. Such factors may be more relevant to resemblance in some characteristics than in others. When attempts have been made to evaluate the influence of such micro-environmental factors on personality resemblance and mental illness, it has often been shown to be minimal or non-existent. When parents were mistaken as to whether their twins were identical or not, resemblance tended to accord with the actual rather than the assigned zygosity (Freedman, 1968; Scarr, 1968). Those twins who were most closely attached to one another were not found to be more alike in personality than those who were less closely attached (Shields, 1954). And MZ twins reared apart, by different parents and without the opportunity of influencing one another, still tended to show extensive personality resemblance (Shields, 1962). This indicates that such resemblance is not dependent on similarities of the within-family environment of a kind which are greater for MZ than DZ pairs. Twins do not have to be brought up together to be alike.

There have been 26 or 27 MZ pairs reported as having been reared apart, where at least one of them was schizophrenic. Many are not described in detail. Several were not separated until relatively late. Others were reunited at some time or other. Many were brought up in generally unfavourable circumstances. They do not make a suitable group for estimating the "true" concordance rate for schizophrenia in twins, if there were such a thing. But the fact that in about two-thirds of these pairs both twins had schizophrenia or a schizophrenic-like disorder confirms the point with regard to schizophrenia. Further support comes from the adoption studies.

The reported MZ concordance rates for different studies show an embarrassingly wide range, from 0% in the first report of a study of 16 pairs from Finland (Tienari, 1963) to 86% in the largest series of 174 pairs from New York State mental hospitals (Kallmann, 1946). Kallmann's high rate is over-corrected for age by the Weinberg method. The uncorrected rate was 69%, or 59% if only definite cases were counted. The sample was largely based on severe chronic cases, and in several studies such schizophrenics are found to have a higher proportion of affected co-twins than more mildly affected cases. There are many ways in which twin concordance rates can legitimately be presented (Allen *et al.*, 1967; Gottesman and Shields, 1972, Chapter 9). Some of the variation between studies is due to small sample sizes.

Table II shows plain, uncorrected pairwise rates for the earlier studies. It includes doubtfully schizophrenic co-twins as concordant. In the case of Essen-Möller's small Swedish study any twin who on follow-up had a mental illness with schizophrenic features was included. At the time of his original report (1941) none of the seven certain and four

c*

Table II Concordance in the earlier schizophrenic twin series (after Gottesman and Shields, 1966)

Investigator	Date	MZ pairs		SS DZ pairs	
		Total pairs	Concordant %	Total pairs	Concordant %
Luxenburger	1928	19	58	13	0
Rosanoff et al.	1934	41	61	53	13
Essen-Moller	1941	11	64	27	15
Kallmann	1946	174	69	296	11
Slater	1953	37	65	58	14
Inouye	1961	55	60	11	18

doubtful schizophrenic probands had a co-twin with a strictly diagnosed schizophrenic psychosis. Inouye's study came from Japan. The weighted means of the six studies are 65% for MZ and 14% for DZ pairs.

The recent western studies, making use of population registers or based on consecutive admissions to hospitals catering for more varying types of illness, usually report lower concordance rates, and the investigators generally find it necessary to report a range in order to do justice to their data. Some of the apparent discrepancies among recent studies become less marked when an attempt is made to apply similar diagnostic standards to each, and when concordance is calculated according to the proband method. The latter expresses the percentage with schizophrenia found among the co-twins of independently ascertained schizophrenics. Such a rate is acknowledged as more appropriate for genetic analysis than the simple pairwise rate (i.e. proportion of all pairs where both twins are affected), and it corresponds to the kind of rates reported for other relatives. Not all the rates in earlier studies could be expressed probandwise.

Table III shows our summary of recent twin studies (Gottesman and Shields, 1976). The table first shows the range of pairwise concordance reported by the investigators themselves at various times, and then our attempt to answer the question how many schizophrenic or very probably schizophrenic probands had twins with schizophrenia or a schizophrenic-like functional psychosis—a criterion which corresponds to the consensus diagnosis of six diagnosticians in our Maudsley twin study, and which discriminated MZ and DZ concordance rates more successfully than attempts to apply very broad or very strict diagnostic criteria to the histories.

This is not the place for a detailed survey of the studies (cf. Gottesman

Table III Concordance in the recent schizophrenic twin series, 1963–73 (after Gottesman and Shields, 1976)

Pairs	Kringlen (Norway)	Fischer (Denmark)	Tienari (Finland)	Pollin et al. (USA)	Gottesman and Shields (UK)
MONOZYGOTIC					
Pairwise range (reported by investigator)	25–38%	24–48%	0·30%	14–27%	49–50%
Number of pairs (used for consensus)	55	21	17	99	22
Probandwise concordance (our consensus)	45%	56%	35%	43%	53%
DIZYGOTIC (same sex)					
Pairwise range (reported by investigator)	4–10%	10–19%	5–14%	4–8%	9–19%
Number of pairs (used for consensus)	90	41	20	125	33
Probandwise concordance (our consensus)	15%	26%	13%	9%	12%

and Shields, 1972; Shields and Gottesman, 1972). It will be noted that on further investigation in Finland, Tienari (1968, 1971) no longer reports zero concordance, though his MZ rate remains low. The studies by Kringlen (1967) and Fischer (1973), from Norway and Denmark respectively, matched national twin and psychiatric registers in certain years to ascertain their schizophrenic probands, and supplemented this with extensive personal investigation. The Gottesman and Shields series was based on all admissions to the Maudsley hospital in London between 1948 and 1964. The study by Pollin's group (Pollin et al., 1969; Allen et al., 1972; Cohen et al., 1972) is based, using records only, on all twins known to the US Veterans Association. Both twins had to have been called up to serve in the armed forces in a period spanning the Second World War and the Korean war (1941–55), and so were selected for health. The figures reported for Tienari and Pollin et al. are less secure than the others in the table. The rates shown are uncorrected for age, and may therefore underestimate the morbid risk. The samples have mostly been followed up for several years, however, so little correction may be required.

If forced to make a best estimate of the average morbid risk for twins of schizophrenics, it would probably be wisest to rely on the recent studies. Rates of approximately 50% for MZ pairs and 17% for DZ pairs may not be far from the mark.

The main point is that several methodologically careful, well documented, population based twin studies agree in finding that genetically identical pairs are very considerably more alike in respect of schizophrenia than genetically dissimilar pairs, and that the difference is unlikely, to any appreciable extent, to be due to sampling or diagnostic bias or to the greater environmental similarity of the MZ pairs. They confirm that the genes make a difference.

The fact that only about half the MZ pairs are concordant equally confirms that the genes do not make all the difference. Environmental factors of some kind, predisposing or precipitating, are highly critical for the development of schizophrenia, in interaction with the genetic constitution. Stresses or life events which bring about the onset of schizophrenia in some people may be innocuous or even beneficial for others.

Identical twins discordant for schizophrenia. Many attempts have been made through the retrospective study of discordant pairs of MZ twins to throw light on the most likely environmental contributors. The results have been less successful than might have been hoped. The concomitants of discordance can be of many different kinds. In some pairs, a history of drug addiction or organic illness in the schizophrenic twin only, might suggest a "symptomatic schizophrenia" in which genetic factors played little or no part. In many pairs, however, various differences in premorbid personality distinguish the affected from the unaffected twin. In some studies (e.g. Pollin and Stabenau, 1968; Mosher *et al.*, 1971) personality differences, relationship with the parents, relations between the twins and minor differences in birth weight are so closely intercorrelated that it is not possible to sort out their separate effects. In identical pairs, normal and abnormal, one twin is frequently said to take the lead in social relationships, and a common feature throughout all the studies of discordant schizophrenic pairs is for the future schizophrenic to have been regarded as the more submissive. If the submissive twin tends to be more emotionally involved with his parents and also more criticized by them, the findings would be consistent with those of Brown *et al.* (1972), who showed that emotional over-involvement with close relatives, especially if these relatives are critical, is a kind of stress liable to cause schizophrenics to relapse (see Chapter 6). It is also consistent with other psychological theories about the development of schizophrenia. The close association with birth weight differences, sometimes of only a few grammes, found in Pollin and Stabenau's NIMH sample, based on an appeal to psychiatrists, is not confirmed in the more representative series of twins, and is not the strongest piece of evidence that obstetric complications may contribute to the liability to schizophrenia. McNeil and Kaij (1977) review this topic extensively and produce evidence of their own from Sweden that "process schizophrenics", but not "schizophrenic-like psychotics", have a significant increase of obstetric complications in their own births compared with matched controls.

Discordant pairs can also be studied to search for an inherited characterological or biochemical factor relevant to schizophrenia. The scatter of subtest scores on the WAIS intelligence test has been reported to be high in schizophrenics in general. Rosenthal and Van Dyke (1970) found it to be high, both in the schizophrenic and in the normal members of 11 discordant MZ pairs. Again using the Pollin sample, Wyatt et al. (1973) found that index and co-twins both had low levels of monoamine oxidase (MAO) activity in their blood platelets, which was thought to be a characteristic of chronic schizophrenics in general. The association with schizophrenia has not been confirmed in England (Brockington et al., 1976) or in Israel (Belmaker et al., 1976). Though MAO activity may be under some genetic control, it would be premature to regard it as a specific genetic marker for schizophrenia. The approach is a useful one, however, and the MAO hypothesis has been productive. Buchsbaum et al. (1976) are following up young normal subjects, low and high in MAO activity, with interesting results. The low-MAO compared with the high-MAO subjects had a higher rate of psychiatric hospitalization, suicides or attempts, and problems with the law. There were no schizophrenics among those hospitalized. The families of the low-MAO subjects also showed a higher rate of similar problems, especially attempted and completed suicide.

Like the discordant twin studies, the prospective "high-risk" studies of the children of schizophrenics also seek to identify environmental and inherited factors in the development of schizophrenia, with the ultimate aim of prevention. The genetic aspects of these studies have been discussed by Shields (1977).*

ADOPTION STUDIES

Studies using foster children and adoptees, where an individual does not receive his genes and his upbringing from the same parents, provide

* For further references see Garmezy (1974), Erlenmeyer-Kimling (1975) and Hanson et al. (1976). *Genetics, Environment and Psychopathology* (ed. Mednick et al., 1974) includes several of the earlier papers from the largely psychophysiologically oriented high-risk studies of schizophrenia by Mednick and Schulsinger, referred to in Chapter 5.

other approaches for disentangling genetic and environmental influences. Heston (1966) followed up the adopted-away children of chronic schizophrenic mothers, removed from their mothers within three days of birth and brought up in a variety of environmental circumstances but not by members of the mothers' family, and compared with a control group of nonpsychotic parentage, matched for type of rearing. The schizophrenic mothers from state hospitals in Oregon would probably have been diagnosed schizophrenic by most European psychiatrists. In Table IV it can be seen that schizophrenia was found only in the offspring of schizophrenic index cases. It occurred as frequently as might be expected in non-adopted children of chronic schizophrenics. There was also an excess of other disorders in the children of the schizophrenic mothers. Heston considered that most of those diagnosed as psychopathic might earlier have been called schizoid psychopaths.

Table IV Psychiatric disorders in foster-home reared children (data of Heston, 1966)

	Experimental group (Mother chronic schiz.)	Controls
Number studied	47	50
Mean age (years)	35·8	36·3
Schizophrenia	5	—
Mental deficiency, IQ < 70	4	—
Sociopathic personality	9	2
Neurotic personality disorder	13	7

Rosenthal and his colleagues (Rosenthal *et al.*, 1968; Rosenthal, 1972) have confirmed that the children of schizophrenic parents still suffer an excess of schizophrenic disorders, even when adopted away. In the latest report of this part of the adoption studies of schizophrenia carried out in Denmark by the US–Danish team of Rosenthal, Kety, Wender and Schulsinger (Wender *et al.*, 1974), 69 offspring of persons diagnosed by the team as schizophrenic, including "borderline or latent" schizophrenia, have been studied. There were 18·8% considered "probable borderline" or more severe, compared with 10·3% of 107 adoptees whose biological parents were not schizophrenic. The wide concept of schizophrenia employed in these studies makes it impossible to compare the rates with those in most other studies.

In the design employed by Heston and by Rosenthal, the children of schizophrenic parents are reared by normal (or at any rate non-

schizophrenic) foster-parents; in other words,they are "cross-fostered".*
The other cross-fostered group consists of children of normals reared by
schizophrenic parents. Wender *et al.* (1974) were able to study 28 such
cross-fostered offspring and found they suffered no more often from
what they call the "hard" spectrum of schizophrenic disorders (probable "borderline" or more severe) than did a control group. The
approach permits the comparison of four groups—offspring of schizophrenic and of non-schizophrenic parents, reared by persons with and
without a diagnosis of schizophrenia.

Those papers from the US–Danish team of which Kety is the first
author employ a different design. They start by identifying adoptees with
schizophrenia and compare the rate of disorders in their biological and
adoptive families, and in those of matched non-schizophrenic adoptees
—again, a 2 × 2 design. Table V presents the findings in the Kety *et al.*

Table V Families of adoptees: interim findings in the US–Danish adoption study
(data of Kety *et al.*, 1975, interview study, after Gottesman and Shields,
1976)

Relatives	Number	% Schiz. incl. ?latent schiz.
Biological parents of schizophrenic adoptees	66	12·1
Biological parents of control adoptees	65	6·2
Adoptive parents of schizophrenic adoptees	63	1·6
Adoptive parents of control adoptees	68	4·4
Biological half-sibs of schizophrenic adoptees	104	19·2
Full and half-sibs of control adoptees; adoptive sibs of schizophrenics and controls	143	6·3

(1975) interview study, also at the level of the "hard spectrum". It is
based on the families of 33 schizophrenic adoptees and controls from
Copenhagen. It is now being extended to the whole of Denmark.
Schizophrenia-related disorders occurred most frequently in the biological relatives of the schizophrenic adoptees. Other points to emerge,
not indicated in the table, are:

(1) Schizoid and inadequate personality, originally hypothesized as
    part of the schizophrenia spectrum, does not significantly distin-
    guish the biological relatives of schizophrenics in the Kety studies.

(2) Adoptees with "acute schizophrenias" had few schizophrenic rela-

---

* Higgins (1976) employed a similar design when he compared fostered and non-fostered
offspring of schizophrenic parents. He found no greater prevalence of psychotic or other
disorders in the latter group.

tives. Although the number of acute cases was small, the authors inclined to the view that acute schizophrenia is a non-genetic disorder.

(3) Adoptees with "chronic schizophrenia" have relatives with a higher prevalence of chronic schizophrenia than do adoptees with "latent schizophrenia".

(4) Age at separation from the biological mother did not influence the results.

(5) Intra-uterine environment and other maternal factors do not account for the findings, since the paternal half-sibs, who do not come from the same womb as the affected adoptee, had the highest rates of schizophrenia—13% definite, 22% including uncertain schizophrenia.

Gottesman and Shields (1976) have commented on the high prevalence rates in half-sibs, which are difficult to account for. They suggested that the high half-sib rates might partly be due to the fact that this is an adoption study. Parents of schizophrenics whose children are placed for adoption may not be typical of the parents of schizophrenics in general. They may well have a high rate of assortative mating for psychiatric and social problems. For both genetic and environmental reasons their children other than the adoptee (i.e. the half-sibs) might be at increased risk for personality disorder and, if so affected, at risk for being diagnosed as "uncertain latent schizophrenia", given a wide concept of schizophrenia and a mental set focused on detecting possible spectrum disorders. Admittedly this interpretation is speculative.

As indicated earlier (p. 55), adoption studies are best suited for investigating environmental hypotheses, either on their own or in interaction with genetic factors. They permit the comparison of outcomes in groups, similar genetically, under different conditions of rearing—own home, institution, foster or adoptive homes of various kinds, etc.—and in this way can reveal or exclude specific environmental factors as being of general importance. They cannot rule out genetic factors. Accepting the evidence from the twin and family studies that genetic factors make a difference, but not all the difference, to the risk of developing schizophrenia, one would hope that adoption-type studies might succeed in identifying environments that would reduce the risk for the genetically predisposed children of schizophrenics, perhaps even to zero. (It is also conceivable that some environments might be worse for such children than being brought up by their own parents.) A few attempts have been made using this approach, usually with negative results. Heston and Denney (1968) showed that permanent institutional rearing was no more often associated with the occurrence of schizophrenia in the off-spring of schizophrenics than being reared mostly in a non-institutional foster family environment. Wender *et al.* (1973) found no support for the hypothesis that rearing in a low social class environment was impor-tant for the development of schizophrenia in adoptees. Rosenthal *et al.* (1975) rated statements about parent–child relationships made in the course of lengthy psychiatric interviews with the 258 members of cross-fostered and control groups. The subjects were mostly in their early thirties when seen. Relationships had been more strained in the groups reared by a schizophrenic parent (biological or adoptive) than in the others, but there was only a moderate correlation between disturbed parent–child relations and the general psychopathology ratings, account-ing for little of the variance of the latter.

The adoption studies support the genetic hypothesis in that they show that a shared environment does not account for the familial aggre-gation of cases, and that factors such as the presence of schizophrenia or related illness in the family are ruled out as major environmental causes. Perhaps one of the more plausible hypotheses before the adoption studies came along was that the genes did make a difference but that persons with schizophrenic genes also tended to provide schizophrenogenic environments, making it impossible to sort out the relative importance of genes and environment in the transmission of the disorder. The term "schizophrenogenic" is ill defined but is usually assumed by those who use it to characterize the parents of schizophrenics. Such characteristics would have to occur much less frequently in other groups of parents if "schizophrenogenicity" were a major cause of schizophrenia. Though some adoptees may be ill-suited to their adoptive homes, there is no reason to suppose that adoptive parents, a group partially selected for mental health and environmental stability, are as schizophrenogenic as the biological parents of schizophrenics who have produced a schizo-phrenic child.

Clearly the adoption studies do not rule out environmental factors—even family environmental factors—in the complex aetiology of schizo-phrenia, but such factors would appear not to be specific to the parents of schizophrenics. They could be very common in the population but interact unfavourably with a high risk genetic predisposition to schizo-phrenia.

The family, twin and adoption studies present consistent support for the hypothesis that genetic as well as environmental factors are involved in the aetiology of schizophrenia. They refute different purely environ-mental objections. If this point of view is accepted, it means one can turn with greater confidence to genetically oriented family studies on clinical or biological lines. There is disagreement, however, about how much weight should be given to the evidence from twin and adoption studies respectively (*Schizophrenia Bulletin*, 1976). There are a few who would claim that nothing could be said one way or the other about the existence of genetic factors until the first reports of the US–Danish adoption studies appeared in *The Transmission of Schizophrenia* (Rosenthal and Kety, 1968). Against this it can be pointed out that the two approaches are directed to different complementary questions. It is the combined evidence that gives the genetic hypothesis its strength. So far there have been more twin studies, many of them better documented as regards case histories than the adoption studies. Schizophrenic twins may be more representative of schizophrenia than schizophrenics whose children are placed for adoption, or adoptees who become schizophrenic. The results of the US–Danish adoption studies are difficult to interpret because their diagnoses are not comparable with those in other studies. One of their major achievements may lie in breaking new ground in their exploration of ideas about the old problem of disorders related to schizophrenia.

Genetic Theories

Having presented the arguments for genetic factors, we must now discuss views about how the disorder is inherited. There are three main theories. In their crudest form, the first is that schizophrenia consists of several quite separate diseases, some of them genetic, others environmental in origin—the distinct heterogeneity model. The second is that all people with "true idiopathic" schizophrenia possess the same abnormal gene—the monogenic or Single Major Locus model. The third is that schizophrenia is caused by the combination of a large number of genes of minor effect, together with many environmental influences—the polygenic or multifactorial model. In practice the theories are modified by their proponents and to some extent overlap, making it difficult to test them decisively. Almost everyone recognizes that all cases of schizophrenia are not exactly the same genetically, that both genetic and environmental factors play a part, and that greater weight must be given to some causal factors than to others. The differences of opinion are largely a matter of emphasis.

Before discussing each model in more detail, we shall compare them briefly. Figure 1 represents a simple version of each. The number of separate genetic entities and the proportion of sporadic environmental cases on the distinct heterogeneity model are entirely conjectural. It is, however, generally agreed that at least a few schizophrenic-like conditions occur on the basis of some other disease, environmental or genetic. For most purposes such "symptomatic" schizophrenias should be considered separately from the rest. There is no convincing evidence that the various clinical forms of schizophrenia are separate genetic entities.

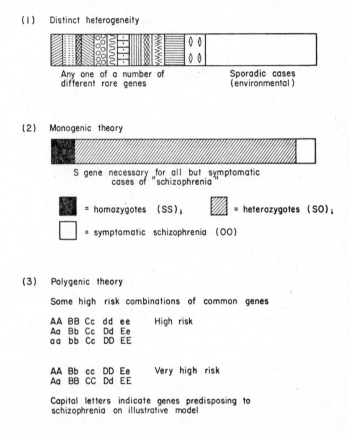

Fig. 1. Hypothetical genetic constitutions of persons with schizophrenic syndromes according to some simple versions of the three main theories. All allow for genetic differences among the schizophrenias.

Monogenic theory in its simplest form—that the same gene is necessary though not sufficient for *all* schizophrenic syndromes—can be regarded as having been refuted by one of the chief proponents of single gene inheritance. Slater *et al.* (1963) showed that typical schizophrenic symptomatology with first-rank symptoms can occur as a consequence of temporal lobe epilepsy. In its modified form it allows ample scope for environmental influences and for other contributory genetic factors, i.e. polygenic influences. Only a minority of people with the SO genetic constitution (heterozygotes) develop the disorder. The model is a relatively simple one and difficult to refute. However, very different estimates have recently been made of the frequency of the S gene, the rate of manifestation in the heterozygote, and the proportion of typical schizophrenic syndromes that are symptomatic rather than idiopathic. Some critics find the low manifestation rate unconvincing, since the major effect of the hypothetical gene has not been detected; nor is there yet convincing evidence of the selective advantage for heterozygotic gene carriers which the theory requires to account for the low fertility in schizophrenia.

According to the polygenic or multifactorial model, schizophrenia ensues once an accumulation of genetic and environmental predisposing factors (the "liability") reaches a threshold level. Most schizophrenic patients will have no close relatives with schizophrenia. When analysed by methods of quantitative genetics, liability to schizophrenia appears to be under a high degree of genetic control. Risk for schizophrenia varies with the degree of genetic predisposition, and vulnerability to environmental stressors varies among those at increased risk. It is therefore pre-eminently what has been termed a "diathesis-stress" theory. A high mutation rate or selective advantage is not required to compensate for the low fertility of schizophrenics. Figure 1 illustrates the point that persons at increased risk for schizophrenia are far from uniform genetically on this model. For the sake of simplicity, it is assumed in the illustration that any five or more schizophrenia-predisposing or capital letter genes at polymorphic loci* A–E place an individual at risk of developing schizophrenia in response to environmental stress. Three of the 51 five-gene possibilities are shown, and one each of the six- and eight-gene combinations. Persons with six or more capital letter genes would be even more highly at risk than those with only five.

CHOOSING BETWEEN THE THREE TYPES OF THEORY

Various methods have been suggested for testing the relative merits of distinct heterogeneity, monogenic models and polygenic models, but the

---

* Polymorphic loci are points on a chromosome where the genes can (and not infrequently do) take more than one form, here designated A or a, B or b, etc. The alternative forms are termed alleles. A person inherits two genes at each locus, one from each parent. Depending on his parents' genes, he could be AA, Aa, or aa.

results are ambiguous. The following findings, for which there is moderately good evidence, might seem to fit more naturally into the polygenic than the monogenic framework:

(1) The excess of mental disorders, other than schizophrenia itself, in the families of schizophrenic subjects.

(2) The increased risk of further cases in the family with (a) increasing severity of disorder in the proband, and (b) the greater number of other relatives already affected.*

(3) The sharpness of the fall in the average risk for relatives, from 10% for first degree to about $2\frac{1}{2}$% or $3\frac{1}{2}$% for second degree, relatives.

(4) The fact that, hitherto, no recognized monogenic disorder has been discovered that is as frequent as schizophrenia.

However, some of the same predictions arise from flexible monogenic theories, modified by polygenes. The extent to which multiple cases of schizophrenia occur on one side of the family only, rather than on both, according to Slater's (1966) computational model, supports the dominant monogenic rather than the polygenic hypothesis, at least if a narrow concept is used in deciding which relatives to count as affected (McCabe *et al.*, 1972); and similarly the lengthy Icelandic pedigrees described by Karlsson also run counter to the simple polygenic theory (Slater, 1972). But these findings are also consistent with several different dominant genes (distinct heterogeneity) and even with a modified "weighted" version of polygenic inheritance.

Some of the above observations could also be accounted for by aetiological heterogeneity, for example the supposed lower risk for relatives of "paranoid" compared with "nuclear" schizophrenics. The paranoid states might not be just a milder form of the same illness with fewer genes (polygenic hypothesis), or greater resistance (monogenic), but might include a sizeable proportion of illnesses with non-genetic causes.

The monogenic theory of Slater and Cowie (1971) and the polygenic theory of Gottesman and Shields (1972, 1973) predict the observed risks for relatives equally well. Nearly all geneticists go out of their way to stress the difficulty of discriminating between the different modes of inheritance (Smith, 1971b). This is not surprising in view of the unreliability of methods of diagnosis and sub-diagnosis, the fact that each of the three theories takes several forms, and, above all, the tendency of some versions of any one theory to look rather like some versions of either of the other two theories. It should, however, be noted that other common chronic disorders, such as diabetes, have also generated a diversity

---

* Ødegaard's (1972) findings as regards (b) have, however, not been replicated by Essen-Möller (1977).

of genetic theories, without giving rise to suggestions that no hereditary
element is involved at all.

The schematic "mixed model" diagram shown in Fig. 2 indicates one
version of how the genetics of schizophrenia may turn out, incorporating
aspects of the three simple models, although it is an unsatisfactory model
from the point of view of testable predictions. The relative size of the
groups is at present conjectural; knowledge will have to await further
developments. As illustrated, there is certainly both heterogeneity and
polygenic influence, and one particular locus may well play a major
part in a sizeable proportion of cases. If there are schizophrenic syndromes for which rare genes, in single or double dose, are mainly
responsible, the interacting environmental factors could be single and
specific, like diet (normal diet) in PKU, or like idiosyncratic drug interactions in psychoses associated with acute intermittent porphyria. In the
multifactorial cases—polygenic, with or without the common specific
gene—the predisposing or precipitating environmental characters may
themselves be multiple. Moreover, the "polygenes alone" group may
well shade into the "primary environmental" group (such as schizophrenic-like psychoses with temporal lobe epilepsy, alcoholic hallu-
cinosis, some "psychogenic" psychoses?), in that persons with only an
average concentration of the schizophrenia-predisposing polygenes may
be affected, but those with a low concentration of such polygenes may
be spared.

In further describing the three types of model and the lines of research
they suggest, mention will be made of how they account for the maintenance of schizophrenia in the population on a genetic basis in view of

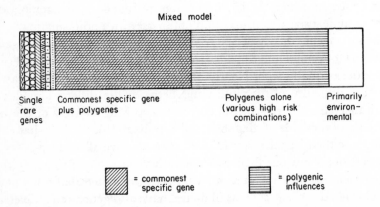

Fig. 2. Conjectural genetic constitutions of persons with schizophrenic syndromes.
Mixed, overlapping version of the three models of Fig. 1.

the reduced fertility of schizophrenic patients. At least until recently, their fertility was only about 70% of average, being lower in males than females and accounted for largely by a low marriage rate (Stevens, 1969; Gottesman and Erlenmeyer-Kimling, 1971).

DISTINCT HETEROGENEITY THEORIES

Blindness and deafness are conditions of which there are many different rare genetic varieties, typically conforming to simple Mendelian inheritance, and together accounting for a significant proportion of cases. Other cases are of environmental origin, leaving a residue of disorders with complex or obscure aetiology. A clinical condition such as retinitis pigmentosa can have different modes of inheritance. Severe mental retardation is very heterogeneous in this sense. Recognized inborn errors of metabolism of many distinct kinds probably account for some 4% of cases, Down's syndrome for some 25%, and unrecognized sex-linked recessives for a further proportion (Davison, 1973), while perhaps 25% may be identifiable as due to specific environmental causes such as maternal rubella, birth damage or meningitis; the remainder are at present of uncertain aetiology (see Shields, 1973).

The proponents of distinct heterogeneity suggest that a substantial proportion of schizophrenias have single major causes of various kinds, many of them genetic. For the latter, the genes would be sufficient—or sufficient with the appropriate environmental releasing stimulus—to produce schizophrenia. Individually the genes would be rare, and it is unlikely that a schizophrenic would have more than one of them. To fit the family data, inheritance might frequently be dominant. The mutation rate for each of the rare genes would not have to be unreasonably high to balance the loss of genes from the gene pool caused by reduced fertility (Erlenmeyer-Kimling and Paradowski, 1966).

It is generally accepted that some conditions with schizophrenic-like symptoms have major causes different from those of the bulk of schizophrenias, but these conditions are usually pulled out of the schizophrenic syndrome. Davison and Bagley (1969) and Davison (1976) have reviewed the subject of these symptomatic schizophrenias and the lessons that might be learned from them. Some, such as schizophrenias following temporal lobe epilepsy, alcohol addiction, and (probably) amphetamine addition, can occur in persons with no more than an average genetic predisposition to schizophrenia, no raised incidence of schizophrenia in the family being detected. They are sometimes termed phenocopies. In genetic biochemical disorders such as Wilson's disease and acute intermittent porphyria and other genetic diseases such as Huntington's chorea, the patient may occasionally develop schizo-phrenic-like, paranoid or confusional symptoms, but these "genocopies" would also not normally be counted among the schizophrenias.

Among the bulk of schizophrenics not so identified there has so far been no convincing evidence in favour of the distinct genetic hetero-geneity theory, in the sense of different single genes. There are not sufficient families showing typical Mendelian patterns of inheritance, or clinical types breeding true enough.

Familial resemblance in Kraepelinian subtype is also difficult to detect. It was not found by Tsuang et al. (1974), though in some earlier studies it was thought to exist to a moderate extent, suggesting a genetic influence on subtype. Resemblance is particularly marked in concordant MZ twins (Kringlen, 1967). This, however, does not lead to the conclu-sion that hebephrenic, catatonic and paranoid schizophrenia are separ-ate genetic diseases. The resemblance is probably due to the fact that MZ twins are alike in all their genes as well as in any that are specific for schizophrenia.

In a series of hypotheses Winokur's group (e.g. McCabe et al., 1971; Winokur et al., 1974; Tsuang, 1975) have suggested that the schizo-phrenias should be divided into separate genetic entities according to subtype and outcome: (1) pure poor-prognosis paranoid, in which the prevalence of schizophrenia in the family is low but runs true to type; (2) hebephrenia, in which the rate in relatives is higher and affected relatives suffer from hebephrenic or sometimes paranoid schizophrenia; (3) good-prognosis schizophrenias (schizo-affective, good-prognosis paranoid and others) which are thought likely to belong to one of the various types of primary affective disorder; and possibly others. At present there is little substantiating evidence (*British Medical Journal*, 1974).

Psychoses with mixed schizophrenic and affective symptoms, with an acute onset, rapid resolution, and frequent recurrence, have given rise to controversy. Angst (1966) found a schizophrenia rate of 7% in the sibs of his "mixed" psychotics. Perris (1974), in agreement with Leon-hard, thinks that "cycloid psychosis"—which others might term schizo-affective psychosis—is a disorder in its own right with a marked and specific heredity; and it may be noted that in Inouye's (1963) twin study "relapsing schizophrenia", which may correspond to cycloid psychosis, had the highest MZ concordance rate (86%). Clayton et al. (1968), however, would group the schizo-affectives with the affective disorders on genetic grounds. McCabe (1975) investigated the Danish diagnosis of "reactive psychosis" and found a raised rate of reactive psychosis in the families of his probands. Many of the parents had had affective disorders, but no relationship to schizophrenia was found. Rosenthal and Kety (1968), as we have seen, consider that the "acute schizophrenias", which include the schizo-affectives, are largely non-genetic in aetiology, but their cases were not recurrent.

Apart from the consideration of different diagnostic criteria in the above studies, it would not be altogether surprising if the acute, good-prognosis schizo-affectives turned out to have several different aetiologies, some being related to schizophrenia and others not. Since they have only relatively recently been introduced into the group of schizophrenias, one might expect some to be likely candidates for exclusion on further consideration, rather on the last in, first out principle. Heterogeneity may also apply to other borderline conditions found to excess in the relatives of schizophrenics, and for this reason sometimes hypothesized as being part of a spectrum of schizophrenic disorders. Alcoholism and suicide, for example, have a raised incidence in schizophrenics' families in some studies. Some cases might have an aetiology related to schizophrenia. No-one, however, would suggest that all alcoholism and suicide has such an aetiology. The independent occurrence of two disorders, e.g. schizophrenia and personality disorder, or schizophrenia and low intelligence, is a possibility to be borne in mind when trying to account for other disorders in schizophrenics' families (Fowler and Tsuang, 1975). We have already drawn attention to the need to take the spouse of the schizophrenic into consideration.

To test the distinct heterogeneity hypothesis of the "splitters" and the homogeneous spectrum hypothesis of the "lumpers", the multiple threshold multifactorial model of Reich *et al.* (1975) offers some theoretical possibility. A three-threshold theory might, for example, propose that soft spectrum disorders (schizoid personality), hard spectrum disorders (e.g. pseudoneurotic schizophrenia) and disorders characterized by the central schizophrenic syndrome (e.g. CATEGO S) were stepwise manifestations of increasing amounts of the same aetiological factors. The test requires reliable estimates of the rate of the three types of disorder in the general population and in the relatives of each type—a tall order at present.

The investigation of separate pedigrees (segregation analysis), instead of pooling data from many families, is a method which has the theoretical possibility of discovering whether schizophrenics can be divided in any sharp way into high-risk familial cases and non-familial sporadic cases. Proponents of heterogeneity might argue this method had not yet been sufficiently explored. It has proved fruitful in other conditions, such as the myotrophies. The opposite approach might also identify genetic heterogeneity: the biological investigation of heavily loaded families, containing more than one schizophrenic, could discover major causes of the syndrome, such as different rare biochemical abnormalities.

MONOGENIC THEORIES

The simplest genetic hypothesis is that the essential cause is a gene at a chromosomal locus where the genes can take one of two possible forms or alleles, ignoring the possibility of further alleles at the same locus. We shall call these variants "S" (predisposing to schizophrenia) and "O" (the normal, non-S form). An individual will inherit one or other of these genes from each parent. The possible genotypes at the locus are therefore OO, SS and SO (heterozygotes). Their relative frequency in the population will depend on the "gene frequency"—the proportion of S genes in the gene pool at that locus. Since schizophrenia is not a simple autosomal dominant trait (all SOs, as well as SSs, affected) or recessive (only SSs, and no SOs, affected), inheritance is assumed to be intermediate, with a lower manifestation rate of schizophrenia in the heterozygous SO than in the rarer homozygous SS genotype.

Böök (1953) proposed such a theory to account for the inheritance of schizophrenia, often of a catatonic type, found in the far north of Sweden. Slater (1958) extended it to apply more generally, and found an excellent fit with Kallmann's and Elsässer's data on the first degree relatives of schizophrenics and the offspring of two schizophrenic parents. He developed his theory further, in Slater and Cowie (1971), using pooled data from the literature, including that on second degree relatives (see Table I). Assuming the expectation of schizophrenia in the population to be 0·85%, predictions from the theory fitted the empirical data best when the S gene frequency was 3%. This gave a 100% manifestation rate for SS, but such individuals would account for only 10% of all schizophrenics. Ninety per cent of schizophrenics would be SO, and for SOs the manifestation rate was calculated to be only 13%. The normal OO homozygote was considered not to be at risk for schizophrenia other than the symptomatic varieties. These will probably be recognized as such, or if not, may be very rare, using strict standards of diagnosis. The low manifestation rate in heterozygotes points to the influence of other factors, genetic and environmental, which modify the chance of becoming affected. As we have already seen, modifying polygenes have also been thought to influence the form of schizophrenia. There is therefore a considerable degree of heterogeneity within the seemingly unitary monogenic model: three genotypes, with different risks, and non-specific polygenic and environmental influence playing an important role in the majority of schizophrenics, the heterozygotes.

Other geneticists, including Elston and Campbell (1970), Kidd and Cavalli-Sforza (1973), Kidd (1975) and Matthysse and Kidd (1976), have fitted monogenic models to the data. Their estimates of gene frequency, manifestation rate in heterozygotes, and so on, differ quite widely. Gene frequency has been estimated to be as high as 10% (Kidd, 1975), and manifestation in SOs to be as low as 6% or 7% (Elston and Campbell, 1970). Matthysse and Kidd (1976) assume the morbid risk for schizophrenia to be 0·87% in the general population and 10·4% in the sibs and children of schizophrenics. Their monogenic or Single Major Locus (SML) model fits the data reasonably well with S-gene frequencies ranging between 0·3% and 2·2%, but the observed rates in MZ twins and in the children of two schizophrenics are high for the model. The upper and lower gene frequencies gives very different estimates of the other parameters. For example, the authors calculate that, if the S gene frequency were 0·3%, all SS homozygotes would be affected; if it were 2·2%, only 38·9%. The SML model considers the possibility of schizophrenia occurring in persons without the S gene. Depending on the gene frequency, the percentage of OO schizophrenics among all schizophrenics lies between almost zero and 61%! Such cases need not all be purely environmental phenocopies, as has been implied; the combined effect of many genes at other loci could play a part, i.e. some cases might be polygenic.

Apart from the inconsistent results of different mathematical models applied to similar data, the low manifestation rates calculated for a hypothetical S gene have been a stumbling block for many readers of the genetic literature. Some of them seem to consider that genetic factors, if they exist at all, must be fully manifest and uninfluenced by other factors. However, when a recognized major genetic factor can be shown to be highly relevant to the risk for developing a disease, it may well be that only a small proportion of those who carry it are affected. The HLA (Histocompatability Leucocyte Antigen) complex, which consists of closely linked gene loci with multiple alleles, contributes significantly to disease susceptibility. Ninety per cent of sufferers from ankylosing spondylitis are of the HLA type B27, compared with only 7% of controls. The disease in its severe form is rare and will be expected to occur in only 1% or 2% of all B27 males and as few as 0·25% of females (Bodmer,

1976). B27 nevertheless remains a major immunological cause of ankylosing spondylitis and the other rheumatic diseases with which it is
associated. This example is not intended to imply that immunological
responses are of major significance in schizophrenia—there is little evidence so far—but to suggest that low manifestation rates may not be as
implausible as they might at first sight seem.

Admittedly, low *ad hoc* manifestation rates are less convincing than
high ones would be. The monogenic theories suggest the search for an
identifiable, simply inherited biochemical factor or, failing that, a biological or psychological trait that is more closely dependent on what is
inherited in schizophrenia than the psychosis itself. Such a trait would
enable most heterozygotes to be recognized. Thought disorder as
measured by an object sorting test was once considered a possibility by
McConaghy (1959) on account of findings in the parents of schizophrenics, before this test was taken up, equally inconclusively, by Lidz
and Wynne as providing evidence for parental communication deviance
being an environmental cause of schizophrenia (see Hirsch and Leff,
1975). Kallmann (1950) considered that heterozygotes for the S gene
tended to be schizoid personalities and the homozygotes schizophrenics.
Heston (1970) noted that in most studies about 50% of the first degree
relatives of schizophrenics had some psychiatric abnormality. This, of
course, is the proportion predicted for a fully penetrant dominant gene.
If all such conditions were considered together as "schizoid disease"—
even though many might not resemble schizophrenia clinically—one
might have a trait, Heston thought, that was simply inherited without
one having to invoke a low manifestation rate. Heston has subsequently
modified his theory (Shields *et al.*, 1975). The kinds of condition which it
is necessary to include among relatives before a 50% rate of affection is
achieved is too wide for the concept to be useful. There will be too many
false positives in the general population. Kay *et al.* (1975) found that
schizoid and other personality disorders were more significantly diagnosed in schizophrenics' relatives than in controls, but the observed
risks did not fit well with Heston's major gene model.

In the early days of psychiatric genetics the hypothesis of necessary
genes at each of two, or even three, loci was put forward to explain the
inheritance of schizophrenia when a simple one-gene hypothesis did not
fit. More recently, Karlsson (1968) put forward a two-locus theory—a
dominant gene for the psychosis and a common recessive gene for the
personality in which it develops. Personality variation is regarded as
occurring on a polygenic basis, and the theory of non-specific modifying

genes and environmental factors is generally thought to be more parsimonious and realistic than invoking a hypothetical second gene. Karlsson (1973) has subsequently abandoned his two-gene for a one-gene theory, similar to Slater's. His findings of an association between schizophrenia and giftedness or creativity in Icelandic pedigrees have not found much support, though Heston had the impression that the normal foster children of schizophrenic parentage were more varied in their interests and abilities than the controls. Juda (1953) found that famous German artists, but not other men of acknowledged genius, had a somewhat raised incidence of schizophrenia in their families. Zerbin-Rüdin (1965) found no raised risk of schizophrenia in the most gifted university entrants or in their first degree relatives.

Monogenic theory has greater difficulty than heterogeneity and polygenic theories in accounting for the continued prevalence of schizophrenia. To compensate for the loss of genes caused by the reduced fertility of schizophrenics, the rate at which the normal allele mutates spontaneously to the S allele would have to be too high to be credible. It has therefore been proposed, notably by Huxley et al. (1964), that heterozygotes, when not themselves affected, are at a selective advantage. By reason of a factor such as increased resistance to infection, relatively more heterozygotes than normal homozygotes should survive and have a family; the relatives of schizophrenics might be expected to have more children than controls. So far there has been little support for the hypothesis, but it is also difficult to refute. Three recent studies, Lindelius (1970) and Larson and Nyman (1973) from Sweden, and Buck et al. (1975) from Canada, failed to detect any evidence of increased fertility or lowered mortality in schizophrenics' families. If there is, or was in the past, a selective advantage in favour of the relatives of schizophrenics, it could be a small one and difficult to detect. It has been suggested that much of any selective advantage in heterozygotes would occur in families with no immediate relatives who are schizophrenic (Kidd, 1975)—but how to find them?—or in the families of paranoid rather than chronic nuclear schizophrenics (Larson and Nyman, 1973). Carter and Watts (1971), in a small study in this country based on general practice, claim a diminished incidence of virus infections in the relatives of schizophrenics. Resistance to viruses that used to be killers in infancy, when mortality is highest, might be the most promising lead for those following this line of thought. On the other hand, some workers suspect that virus infections of some kinds might be a partial cause of schizophrenia (see Richter, 1976).

POLYGENIC THEORIES

In polygenic or multifactorial inheritance of a disorder, many different genes contribute together to its development. They are mostly fairly common and not in themselves pathological. No one gene is necessary. The combination of genes will vary from case to case, and some affected persons will have more of the predisposing genes than others. Though on the simplest model the effects of the genes are purely additive, allowance may have to be made for dominance and interaction. Some of the genes may have more effect than others, or influence a particular facet of the condition. There will therefore be a great deal of genetic diversity within an affected population. Polygenic influences are likely to consist of the more remote and indirect effects of genes: like the branches of a tree, rather than the trunk, the condition will be sensitive to environmental influences.

The theory assumes that the multiple genetic and environmental factors that contribute to aetiology will result in a more or less normally distributed genetic-cum-environmental "liability" to the disease. Once a threshold of liability is passed an individual becomes affected. The prevalence defines the proportion of the population above the threshold at a particular time. Most affected individuals will have normal, sub-threshold parents. Methods are available (Falconer, 1965; Smith, 1971a; and others) for estimating how much of the population distribution of total liability is determined by genetic variation, i.e. the heritability.

Though polygenic inheritance of schizophrenia had been considered as a possibility before, the theory was not easy to test until the threshold model became available. Previously, quantitative genetic analysis had been applied mainly to quantitative traits such as stature and IQ. The threshold model treats the predisposition as quantitative but the disease (schizophrenia, diabetes, duodenal ulcer, or whatever) as present or absent. There may, however, be sub-threshold manifestations of one kind or another in persons whose liability approaches the threshold.

The risk for relatives will depend on the frequency of the condition in the population. The rarer it is, the lower the proportion of relatives whose liability will exceed the threshold. Cleft lip (with or without cleft palate) has a frequency at birth of about one in 1,000. The frequency in sibs is only 4%, but this is 40 times the population prevalence. The MZ twin concordance rate is about 40%. Such data are consistent with a high degree of genetic determination. As Carter (1976) has shown, many congenital abnormalities conform to the principles of polygenic threshold inheritance.

Gottesman and Shields (1967, 1972) were the first to apply the threshold model to schizophrenia and found it fitted as well as any other.
One of the criticisms of the model is that heritability estimates from
family data assume that resemblance between relatives is not significantly influenced by shared family environment. Separate calculations are
therefore desirable, from both kinds of twin and from different first and
second degree relatives. These calculations take into account the schizophrenia risk for the relatives, the closeness of the genetic relationship,
and the general population risk for schizophrenia. Assuming the latter
to be 1%, these gave similar estimates of heritability of about 85%. The
consistency of the estimates from relatives differing in the extent and kind
of environment shared with a schizophrenic is impressive and reflects
the conclusion already drawn from family, twin and adoption studies
concerning the validity of the evidence in favour of genetic factors. It is
important to stress that a high heritability does not imply that curative
or preventive measures will be ineffective; but to discover these, one will
probably have to look outside the range of environments experienced by
the untreated population.

Matthysse and Kidd (1976) put forward a multifactorial (polygenic)
model for schizophrenia, and it might seem to fit the data at least as
accurately as their SML model, since the rates for MZ twins and the
children of two schizophrenics were in better agreement with the theory.
Their view of how risk for schizophrenia would, on this model, vary with
degree of genetic predisposition (Fig. 3) also illustrates the varied vulnerability to environmental stresses among those at increased risk.
Furthermore it helps to explain how high heritabilities can be reconciled
with comparatively low concordance rates in MZ twins—a frequent
stumbling block. Suppose the normal curve of genetic vulnerability to

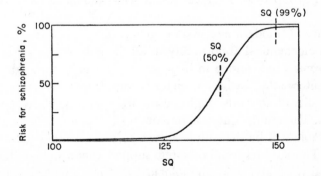

Fig. 3. Risk function for multifactorial model. (From Matthysse and Kidd, 1976.)

be scaled, like IQ, to a mean of 100 and a standard deviation of 15. The risk for schizophrenia will vary, like the "risk" for graduating from college for persons of different IQ. Given the population frequency of schizophrenia, Matthysse and Kidd calculated the risk to be near zero for SQs (schizophrenia quotients) well below 100. It would be 1% for SQ 126. An individual with an SQ of 137 would have a 50% risk, and someone of SQ 148 a 99% risk of becoming schizophrenic. Of all actual schizophrenics it was calculated that 9% would have an SQ of 148 or higher, in other words would be more or less destined to develop the condition in an ordinary environment. The majority of schizophrenics, not so highly at risk, would be sensitive to environmental stresses and "life events" which over time could tip their total liability over the threshold, precipitating a schizophrenic illness. But even severe and multiple stresses would not be expected to result in schizophrenia in someone with an average or low SQ. Since the mean SQ of schizophrenics is 137, it is not surprising that a representative sample of schizophrenic twins should have an MZ concordance rate of 50%.

The problem of how the polygenes maintain themselves in the population is not so acute as with monogenic inheritance. If many genes are implicated the trait will be relatively insensitive to the reduced fertility of psychotics. It is only those few individuals who have unfortunately inherited too many of the predisposing genes who become schizophrenic. In most combinations the genes will not result in reduced fertility. Any loss of genes caused by schizophrenia could well be very slight and offset by a compensating reduction in fertility sustained by carriers of the non-schizophrenic alleles at the same loci, when the latter occur in combinations which influence other polygenic disorders where fertility is also reduced (Edwards, 1972). We may note that the blood group A gene has a minor predisposing influence on cancer of the stomach, while the blood group O gene is associated with duodenal ulcer (Roberts, 1965).

Evidence for moderate or marked genetic factors does not necessarily suggest a biochemical abnormality. If all the polygenes contributing to schizophrenia are assumed to be of very minor effect individually, the study of intervening variables, such as arousal, cognitive abnormalities or personality dimensions, might be a more promising if less spectacular approach. Though the question remains open, it is unlikely that any one such variable will be the simple answer to what is inherited in schizophrenia. There is no special reason to suppose that a style of thinking, a perceptual anomaly, or a physiological response latency, will be any more simply or highly inherited than schizophrenia itself. Some such traits, however, might be correlated with liability and be under some degree of genetic control; and some might be amenable to reduction by environmental means. By way of analogy, blood pressure, cholesterol level and smoking habits, together with sex and age, allow the risk for coronary heart disease to be predicted, according to Khosla *et al.* (1977). It may be difficult to single out a principal contributing factor.

Some of the varieties of polygenic theory may be mentioned. They range from "strong" to "weak". Gottesman and Shields (1972), who propose a relatively strong theory, believe that a large part of the genetic variance may be controlled by a small number of genes relatively specific for schizophrenia, raising the possibility that biological investigation will eventually identify some of the major factors. In so far as the principal genes are rare variants or differ in their effects, this version will overlap with a modified distinct heterogeneity theory.

Eysenck (1972) sees schizophrenia as one of the more extreme manifestations of the personality dimension, "psychoticism", which is independent of "extraversion" and "neuroticism", and under a considerable degree of polygenic control. This would imply, rather surprisingly, that the personalities of persons vulnerable to schizophrenia, manic-depression and other psychoses are largely similar, perhaps resembling those of psychopaths and criminals, who have also been found to score high on psychoticism. To account for the form of the psychosis, Eysenck envisages the further influence of specific genes.

Farley (1976) sees all psychosis as arising from polygenic variation in many social skills and other behaviours of adaptive value. In states of hyper-arousal, individuals at the extremes of the distribution would be liable to display inappropriate, psychotic forms of behaviour, including schizophrenia.

Manfred Bleuler (1972) takes a less unitary view of abnormal behaviour. He acknowledges the importance of hereditary factors in schizophrenia. Since he holds that many genes, not in themselves abnormal, provide the genetic basis, Bleuler's theory fits more closely into the polygenic than into either of the other two frameworks. But it is a theory which denies specificity: of two alleles at a locus, neither can be said to predispose to schizophrenia more than the other—it is entirely a matter of disharmonious interaction with other genes. Since it rules out additive effects, the theory is difficult to test. But in this extreme form it seems that the interaction theory would not predict the transmission of schizophrenia from parent to child.

Kringlen (1967, 1976) holds that inheritance in schizophrenia is weak and polygenic. The genes to some extent influence vulnerability to

D

mental disorder in general. He regards schizophrenia as a way of life, even if an extreme one. Social factors are mainly responsible for the form the illness takes and should be the focus of research. The view is difficult to reconcile with the evidence.

For complex disorders such as schizophrenia, the multifactorial model may be a useful, if temporary, analytic tool during a period of relative ignorance (Curnow and Smith, 1975). The main task as with the other theories, is to identify some of the contributing aetiological factors.

SUMMARY OF THEORIES

The genetic theories we have discussed represent different ways of looking at the data, and it is useful to keep the principles of each one distinct. They are hypotheses about what accounts genetically for the majority of the schizophrenic psychoses: (i) various rare genes, (ii) one particular gene, or (iii) a combination of relatively common genes. The difficulties of choosing between them have been emphasized. Whichever theory is preferred, the tasks ahead are much the same. For the time being, we have to accept a degree of uncertainty concerning the unity or diversity of the schizophrenias, and the manner in which the majority of cases are inherited. Advances in other fields may well be decisive.

Conclusion

In view of the imprecision of some of the data, and the lack as yet of any link between clinical and biochemical genetics in schizophrenia, it is not surprising that the findings presented in this chapter have been subjected to such a diversity of interpretation. There are still a few people—not only anti-psychiatrists, or those wedded to an extreme psychodynamic viewpoint—who do not accept that genes play any part in schizophrenia, but they have to explain the following facts.

(1) No environmental circumstances have been identified that predict even a moderately raised incidence of schizophrenia in persons who have no close relative with the condition.

(2) The closer an individual is related to someone with schizophrenia, the higher the risk of developing the condition.

(3) Genetically identical, or monozygotic, pairs of twins are three times more often concordant for schizophrenia than genetically dissimilar, or dizygotic, pairs; even though twins are usually exposed to the same family and cultural environment. The MZ co-twin of a schizo-

phrenic is about 50 times more likely to be affected than a member of the general population.

(4) MZ twins do not have to be brought up together in an extremely similar environment for them to be alike.

(5) Someone who is a twin is not more likely to be schizophrenic than someone who is not.

(6) Children of schizophrenics who are adopted, while still young, by unrelated persons who are not schizophrenic, still have an increased risk for schizophrenia.

(7) Adoptive relatives of affected adoptees do not have a raised rate of schizophrenic disorders, but their biological relatives do. The latter finding is not accounted for by shared prenatal environment, since it holds for the paternal half-sibs.

(8) Children of normal parents, cross-fostered into a home where an adoptive parent has a schizophrenic disorder, do not themselves have a raised rate of schizophrenia.

(9) Schizophrenia, narrowly defined, occurs in people of widely different cultures. The low social status of schizophrenics on admission can best be accounted for by the downward social drift of the patient.

The far from perfect concordance in MZ twins shows that environmental factors are important for persons at genetic risk for schizophrenia. Since the nature of the critical genetic and environmental factors is not known, uncertainty remains about the range, heterogeneity and mode of genetic transmission of the schizophrenic disorders. Advances in biological and social psychiatry will eventually lead to progress in understanding the interaction between genes and environment. Meanwhile, any attempt to explain schizophrenia that ignores the genetic dimension is bound to be inadequate; it will hamper progress and be to the detriment of patients and their relatives.

Biochemical and
4 Pharmacological Studies:
The Dopamine Hypothesis

Leslie L. Iversen

Biochemical Studies

INTRODUCTION

The idea that madness may be associated with a chemical imbalance in the brain is not new. The founding father of modern neurochemistry, Thudichum (1884), had already voiced this view:

> When the normal composition of the brain shall be known to the uttermost item, then pathology can begin to search for abnormal compounds or derangements of quantities. . . . In short it is probable that by the aid of chemistry many derangements of the brain and mind, which are at present obscure, will become accurately definable and amenable to precise treatment, and what is now an object of anxious empiricism will be one for the proud exercise of exact science.

Bleuler (1911), in his classic description of the "schizophrenias",* expressed the view that madness might be the result of a metabolic disorder.

In the last twenty-five years biochemical and pharmacological research in schizophrenia was given a great stimulus by the discovery that certain drugs can cause hallucinations and other disruptions of normal mental functions, akin to those seen in schizophrenia, and that other drugs have remarkable effects in mitigating some of the cardinal features of schizophrenic psychoses. The discovery of hallucinogenic drugs, such as mescaline, bufotenine and lysergic acid diethylamide (LSD), prompted

* See p. vii.

a search for possibly similar endogenous "psychotomimetic" chemicals in schizophrenic patients; a quest which has so far proved singularly unrewarding. If research into schizophrenia has proved to be "the graveyard of neuropathology" (Plum, 1972), it is also littered with the skeletons of biochemical hypotheses which have failed to stand the test of time. The subject has been well reviewed elsewhere (Kety, 1959a,b, 1967; Richter, 1970, 1976; Wyatt et al., 1971; Boulton, 1971; Ridges, 1973; Matthyse and Lipinski, 1975; Smythies, 1976; Baldessarini, 1977). This review will concentrate on a limited number of topics in biochemical research and will deal at some length with clues that have emerged quite recently from studies of the mode of action of drugs used to treat schizophrenia.

The concept that schizophrenia may be associated with the abnormal production of a "toxic metabolite" has dominated much of the biochemical research in this area, perhaps because of its disarming naïvety and the prospect of a rapid breakthrough if the chemical identity of the hypothetical toxic material could be discovered. It may be that this line of approach is now exhausted, either because the postulated abnormal chemical does not exist, or because we have such a poor understanding of brain chemistry that we have not yet discovereed the appropriate group of brain chemicals to study. In any event, at the moment it seems that more progress is being made through a different approach; one which seeks to understand the mode of action in the brain of drugs that are known to be of value in treating the symptoms of acute schizophrenia. It is hypothesized that such understanding might offer useful clues to the biochemical basis of the disease.

The fact that drugs can effectively reverse some of the symptoms of schizophrenia in itself provides considerable impetus to further research, since it suggests that a modifiable chemical abnormality exists in the brains of people with the disease. Recent improvements in standardized techniques for the diagnosis of schizophrenia, and in our understanding of the genetic factors that underlie the disease encourage the further investigation of biochemical hypotheses. Many biochemical studies of schizophrenia have suffered from the confusion arising from a lack of agreement on diagnostic definitions. Many studies have been poorly controlled in other respects as well. The importance of using great care in diagnosis, and in controlling for extraneous factors, such as institutionalization, diet, and drug treatment, is sadly emphasized by a long series of unreplicated results (Kety, 1959a, 1967). Nevertheless, a number of useful hypotheses has been put forward, each of which deserves further examination.

THE TRANS-METHYLATION HYPOTHESIS

The Hypothesis

The trans-methylation hypothesis, first proposed by Osmond *et al.* (1952) has generated a great deal of interest. It was based on the fact that the chemical structure of the hallucinogenic drug mescaline (Fig. 1) bears some resemblance to naturally occurring catecholamines, such as dopamine and noradrenaline, which function as neurotransmitter substances in the brain. It was suggested that schizophrenia might be related to overactivity in one of the processes of trans-methylation of these amines, leading to an excessive production of toxic by-products. This hypothesis was later extended to encompass the possible formation of other methylated hallucinogenic compounds, such as the indolamines bufotenin and N-dimethyltryptamine (Fig. 2).

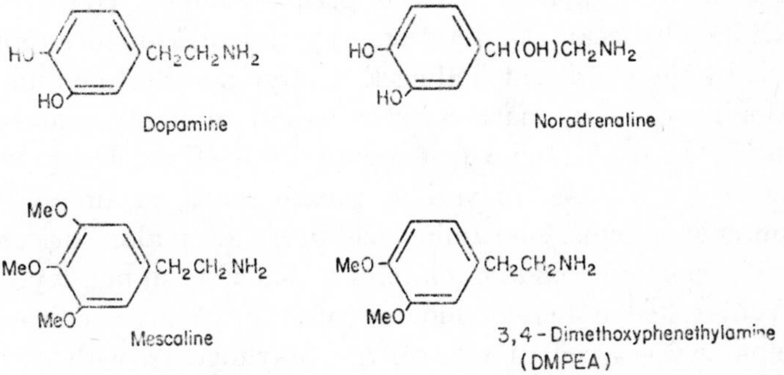

Fig. 1. Catecholamines and some methoxylated derivatives

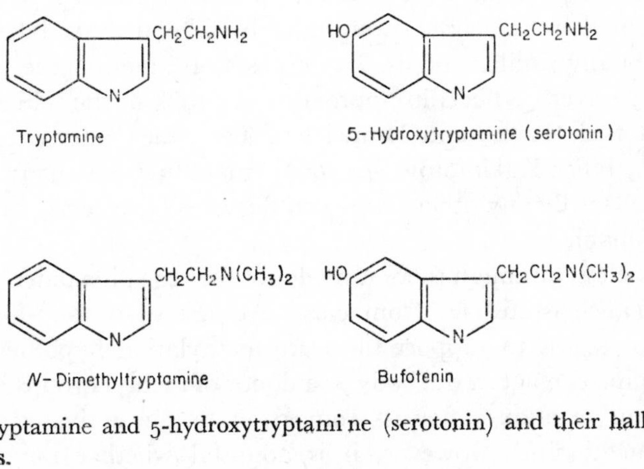

Fig. 2. Tryptamine and 5-hydroxytryptamine (serotonin) and their hallucinogenic derivatives.

An important weakness of this hypothesis is that the phenomena induced by hallucinogenic drugs such as mescaline or LSD differ in important ways from schizophrenia, so that the drugs do not represent a very accurate model. The major symptoms produced by such drugs are disorders of perception, with visual rather than auditory hallucinations predominating. There is little evidence that chronic syndromes such as abnormality of thought and affect are induced by hallucinogenic drugs (Hollister, 1962; Snyder, 1973a). Moreover, schizophrenics receiving such drugs report that the drug-induced experience is quite unlike the spontaneous psychosis (Chloden et al., 1955). This is in contrast to the amphetamines, which mimic more precisely some aspects of acute schizophrenia in normal subjects and which exacerbate the psychotic symptoms of schizophrenics (see p. 101).

The Methionine Effect

The trans-methylation hypothesis has persisted and played such a dominant role largely because of the strong experimental support apparently lent to it by the consistent finding that large doses of the amino acid L-methionine cause a marked exacerbation in many schizophrenic patients. Pollin et al. (1961) first reported this effect. They tested the sequelae of large doses, in various combinations, of amino acids in schizophrenic patients. The amino acids were given alone or combined with the monoamine oxidase inhibitor iproniazid (50 mg/day). Of the amino acids tested, only L-methionine caused any marked effects. When L-methionine was given, at a dose of 20 g/day together with iproniazid, four of the nine patients tested showed marked clinical changes. These consisted of an increased flood of associations, anxiety, increased tension and sometimes panic, and increased motor activity. This procedure was later repeated by the same group, and by several other laboratories, with essentially similar results. Large doses of L-methionine produced temporary adverse affects in approximately 40% of the schizophrenic patients tested (Brune and Himwich, 1962a; Alexander et al., 1963; Park et al., 1965; Kakimoto et al., 1967; Ananath et al., 1970; Antun et al., 1971). Hardly any other finding in this area of research has proved to be so reliable.

Nevertheless, although there is no doubt that the phenomenon exists, its significance is still far from clear. At first sight the effect of L-methionine seems to support the trans-methylation hypothesis, since L-methionine can act in the body as a donor of methyl groups for many methylation reactions after its conversion to the activated form S-adenosylmethionine. However, it is doubtful whether L-methionine loading can, in fact, increase the rate of methylation of biogenic amines (Baldessarini, 1975). An even more difficult question is whether the effects of methionine in schizophrenic patients really represent a worsening of the pre-existing psychosis or merely "a toxic delirium superimposed upon chronic schizophrenia" (Pollin *et al.*, 1961).

Pink Spots and Red Herrings

An extraordinary breakthrough appeared to have been achieved when Friedhoff and van Winkle (1962a) reported the occurrence of a compound in schizophrenic urine which gave a pink spot on paper chromatograms when these were treated first with ninhydri-pyridine and then with Ehrlich's reagent. The compound was detected in 15 of 19 urine samples from schizophrenic patients and in none of 14 normals. Furthermore, Friedhoff and van Winkle (1962b) also claimed to have identified the "pink spot" as 3,4-dimethoxphenylethylamine (Fig. 1), a compound which represents a doubly methylated derivative of the naturally occurring neurotransmitter dopamine and might thus represent the "toxic metabolite" predicted by the trans-methylation hypothesis. Things had never looked better for the trans-methylation hypothesis, and a considerable research effort was initiated around the world on the basis of these findings. Alas, the outcome of this was a profusion of pink spots, red faces and hopeless confusion. Although some groups appeared to substantiate the finding, others were unable to repeat it. Bourdillon *et al.* (1965), for example, in a very large scale survey, reported that "pink spot" could be detected in 66 of 179 urine samples from schizophrenic patients, whereas only one positive result was obtained from 369 samples from normal volunteers or general hospital in-patients. On the other hand, several other groups were unable to repeat these findings, and when more sensitive and precise analytical techniques were applied it became clear that the "pink spot" was not a single compound but a mixture of several different urinary amines, all possessing similar chromatographic properties and giving the same colour reaction. 3,4-Dimethoxyphenylethylamine proved to be only a minor component of this mixture; it was not hallucinogenic in man; and most probably its presence in urine is accounted for not as a product of the metabolism of dopamine in the brain but from dietary sources or from the bacterial metabolism of dietary amines in the gut (for reviews see Boulton, 1971; Ridges, 1973; Baldessarini, 1975).

A further complication, which might explain why a "pink spot" reaction was detected so frequently in urine samples from schizophrenic patients and not in normals was the finding that certain metabolites of

D*

the drug chlorpromazine could also give rise to a "pink spot" on chromatograms (Steinberg and Robinson, 1968; Boulton, 1971). Since chlorpromazine is so widely used in the treatment of schizophrenia, and since urinary metabolites of the drug continue to be excreted for many weeks even in "drug-free" patients (Curry, 1976) the possibility that these may have contributed as artifacts to the "pink spot" seems very real.

Indolamines

The trans-methylation hypothesis has survived, in spite of these vicissitudes. The compounds on which the modern version of this hypothesis has focused are N-methylated indolamines, notably N-dimethyltryptamine (Fig. 2). This substance, and the related compound bufotenin, is a hallucinogen of the mescaline–LSD type (Szara, 1961). It can be formed in small amounts in animal brain when radioactively labelled tryptamine is injected into CSF (cerebrospinal fluid), and it can be formed from tryptamine in small amounts by sequential methylation of the nitrogen catalysed by an indolamine-N-methyl transferase enzyme using S-adenosylmethionine as methyl donor (Saavedra and Axelrod, 1972a). This enzyme is present in abundance in rabbit lung (Axelrod, 1961, 1962), and to a lesser extent in animal and human brain and other tissues (Mandell and Morgan, 1971; Saavedra *et al.*, 1973). The enzyme forms much larger amounts of the monomethylated substance N-methyl tryptamine than of the N-dimethylated product. Reports that this and other methylated indolamines might be formed by enzymes utilizing N-methyltetrahydrofolic acid instead of S-adenosylmethionine as the methyl donor have now largely been discounted as experimental artifacts (Banerjee and Snyder, 1973; Hsu and Mandell, 1973; Laduron *et al.*, 1974). Such reactions occur *in vitro* only as a result of the condensation of tryptamines with formaldehyde liberated by the breakdown of the folic acid cofactor, and the products are not N-methylated indolamines but tetrahydro-β-carbolines (see Baldessarini, 1975 and Fuller, 1976, for reviews).

Tryptamine occurs in small amounts in animal brain (Saavedra and Axelrod, 1972b; Snodgrass and Horn, 1973), and it is a normal constituent of urine, although the origin of the urinary amine is probably largely from the diet or from the metabolism of dietary tryptophan by the gut flora. Tryptamine concentrations have been reported to be elevated in the urine of schizophrenic patients (Brune and Himwich, 1962b; Himwich, 1970).

Although there has been controversy concerning the identification of bufotenin (Fig. 2) as a normal constituent of human body fluids (see Boulton, 1971), there is little doubt that N-dimethyltryptamine can occur in urine, and it is probably present in small amounts in blood and CSF (Smythies, 1976). Because of the lack of a suitably sensitive and specific method for measuring this compound, however, the results on body fluids remain uncertain, although—because of the larger quantities involved—the results from urinary analyses are probably more reliable. Narasimhachari et al. (1971, 1972a) claimed that there was a specific relationship between the urinary excretion of N-dimethyltryptamine and schizophrenia, and others have detected this substance in urine samples from a significant proportion of schizophrenic patients (Kanabus et al., 1973; Bidder et al., 1974; Oon et al., 1975). On the other hand, Carpenter et al. (1975) found no difference in the frequency with which N-dimethyltryptamine was detected in the urine of schizophrenic and normal subjects. Rodnight et al. (1977) using a carefully diagnosed patient population detected urinary N-dimethyltryptamine in 20 of 42 schizophrenics, while a positive result was obtained in only one of 20 normals. On the other hand, in the same study the amine was also detected in a significant proportion of patients with non-schizophrenic psychoses. It seems clear that this line of research is worth pursuing, and that clarification of the importance of N-dimethyltryptamine will only come when improved analytical methods allow precise measurements to be made of the amounts of this amine excreted in urine and present in body fluids and post-mortem tissue specimens from normal and schizophrenic populations. N-dimethyltryptamine remains a plausible candidate as a "toxic metabolite" in schizophrenia; it can be formed enzymically in mammalian tissues and it is pharmacologically active as a hallucinogen.

Furthermore, Wyatt et al. (1973b) showed that an enzyme is present in human blood platelets which can N-methylate both tryptamine and N-methyltryptamine, using S-adenosylmethionine as cofactor. The activity of this indolamine-N-methyl transferase was reported to be significantly higher in schizophrenic than in normal subjects. The same authors were unable to confirm the observation of Narasimhachari et al. (1972b) that indolamine-N-methyl transferase activity could be detected in schizophrenic but not in normal serum.

Vitamins and Epilepsy

Reports of improvement in schizophrenic patients treated with "megavitamin" or orthomolecular therapy in the form of large doses of nicotinamide (Hoffer et al., 1957) appeared to be consistent with the trans-methylation hypothesis. Nicotinic acid or nicotinamide given in large amounts was postulated to act as a methyl acceptor, thus neutralizing the postulated excessive methylating capacity in schizophrenia, a biochemical hypothesis that was later proved to be incorrect (Baldessarini, 1975). Moreover, many subsequent investigations have indicated that the beneficial effects of nicotinamide in schizophrenia are illusory (Ban and Lehmann, 1975), and few would agree with Hoffer (1973): "If all the vitamin B3 were removed from our food everyone would become psychotic within one year."

There is, however, current interest in another vitamin, folic acid. Folic acid is an essential dietary component for the synthesis of the various tetrahydrofolate cofactors, involved in the addition or removal of one carbon fragment in various metabolic pathways. 5-Methyltetrahydrofolate, for example, is an essential cofactor for the regeneration of methionine from homocysteine after transfer of the methyl group of methionine in various trans-methylation reactions (Fig. 3).

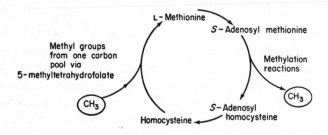

Fig. 3. Role of folic acid in biological methylation reactions.

Reynolds (1968) reviewed the evidence that schizophrenia and epilepsy are relatively mutually exclusive diseases. This revives earlier rationalizations of the value of convulsive therapy in the treatment of psychosis, suggesting that epileptics, by virtue of their convulsions, may have a built in protection against schizophrenia. Reynolds (1968) suggested that a schizophrenia-like psychosis can be precipitated in epileptic patients by anti-convulsant drug therapy. Since many anti-convulsants appear to act as folic acid antagonists, this observation in turn might suggest that schizophrenia is related to a defect in folic acid metabolism. This idea appeared to receive substantial support from the report of Freeman et al. (1975) of a mentally retarded child with a schizophrenia-like psychosis who suffered from an unusual form of homocystinuria, associated with an inability to synthesize 5-methyltetrahydrofolate in whom treatment with folic acid relieved the psychotic symptoms. However, it is doubtful whether this patient would be diagnosed as "schizophrenic" by internationally accepted criteria (Reynolds, 1975) and the therapeutic value of folic acid therapy in schizophrenia, if any, remains to be clarified. The notion that schizophrenia might be associated with a *deficiency* of 5-methyltetralydrofolate, and thus possibly with a defective synthesis of methionine and methyl donor, in any case seems to be exactly the opposite of that predicted by the trans-methylation hypothesis, which would suggest an *excessive* methylation capacity rather than a deficiency. There is little doubt that defects in folic acid metabolism can, if sufficiently severe, lead to mental deterioration of various types, including dementia and psychosis, but the value of these phenomena as models for schizophrenia seems very dubious. Furthermore, the notion that schizophrenia and epilepsy are mutually exclusive is contradicted by the work of Slater *et al.* (1963), who pointed out that schizophrenia symptoms occur relatively commonly in patients with temporal lobe epilepsy.

OTHER BIOCHEMICAL STUDIES

Blood Factors

There have been numerous attempts to detect abnormal components in schizophrenic serum, and an extensive and confusing literature exists. The conclusions from such studies, however, are clearly negative: no reproducible identified abnormalities have been found, (for reviews see Kety, 1967; Wyatt *et al.*, 1971; Ridges, 1973; Matthysse and Lipinski, 1975; Baldessarini, 1977).

Wheat Gluten

Dohan (1966) and Dohan *et al.* (1969) suggested that there might be a connection between a genetic predisposition to coeliac disease and schizophrenia. This hypothesis was based on epidemiological data which suggested that there was a higher incidence of schizophrenia in those countries where wheat and cereal products constitute a major part of the diet, and on the reportedly beneficial effects of maintaining schizophrenic patients on a gluten-free diet. A recent report by Singh and Kay (1976) appeared to support this hypothesis. They claimed that the administration of wheat gluten to schizophrenic patients on a gluten-free diet, with constant neuroleptic drug therapy, led to an exacerbation of symptoms. However, the validity of the statistical analysis used by Singh and Kay (1976) and other features of their experimental design have been criticized (Levy and Weinreb, 1976; Smith, 1976).

Platelet Monoamine Oxidase

Murphy and Wyatt (1972) reported that monoamine oxidase activity, using tryptamine as substrate, was significantly lower in blood platelets from 33 schizophrenic patients than in a comparable control group. They extended these findings in a most interesting study (Wyatt *et al.*, 1973a) in which they examined blood platelet monoamine oxidase activity from 13 sets of monozygotic twins discordant for schizophrenia and from 23 controls. The monoamine oxidase activity of both schizophrenic and non-schizophrenic twins was significantly lower than normal, and it was highly correlated between twins. Although it might appear that a reliable biochemical genetic correlate for schizophrenia had been discovered this does not seem to be the case. Murphy and Weiss (1972) reported that platelet monoamine oxidase was also reduced in manic-depressive psychosis. Furthermore, although some studies have confirmed the finding of reduced monoamine oxidase activity in the platelets of patients with schizophrenia (Meltzer and Stahl, 1974; Nies *et al.*, 1973), as so often happens in this area of research, several other laboratories were unable to repeat the original finding (Friedman *et al.*, 1974; Shaskan and Becker, 1975; Owen *et al.*, 1976). Schildkraut *et al.* (1976) suggested that the finding of reduced platelet monoamine oxidase may apply only to a subgroup of schizophrenic patients in which paranoid symptoms and delusions are prominent. Buchsbaum *et al.* (1976) measured platelet monoamine oxidase in 375 college students and reported that those with the lowest 10% of enzyme activities had more frequent psychiatric abnormalities and family histories of such disorders than the highest 10%. They suggested that low platelet monoamine oxidase activity may constitute a "biochemical high-risk paradigm" for predisposition to various psychiatric disorders, including schizophrenia and affective illnesses. These findings, although of considerable interest, are of doubtful value either in identifying a genetic marker for schizophrenia or in furthering our understanding of its biochemical aetiology.

The possibility that low monoamine oxidase activity might facilitate the accumulation of psychotomimetic amines that are normally degraded rapidly by this enzyme is at first sight an intriguing one. The indolamine N-dimethyltryptamine, for example, is rapidly inactivated by monoamine oxidase, and the reportedly high frequency of excretion of this substance in schizophrenics might be related to a reduced rate of degradation of the amine. Sandler and Reynolds (1976) similarly proposed that β-phenylethylamine might accumulate in schizophrenic tissues because of the reported deficiency of monoamine oxidase activity.

On the other hand, biochemical examination of post-mortem brain tissue has failed to reveal any deficiency in monoamine oxidase activity in schizophrenics (Utena *et al.*, 1968; Schwartz *et al.*, 1974a,b). Furthermore, the chronic administration of monoamine oxidase inhibitors to depressed patients is *not* associated with the high frequency of schizophrenia-like psychosis that might be predicted from these hypotheses.

Dopamine-β-Hydroxylase

Wise and Stein (1973) and Wise *et al.* (1974) reported that there was a highly significant reduction in the activity of the noradrenaline synthesizing enzyme dopamine-β-hydroxylase in post-mortem brain tissue from 18 schizophrenic patients compared with 12 controls. Enzyme activity was significantly reduced in all brain areas examined, with less than 50% of normal activity in hippocampus and approximately a 40% reduction in the diencephalon. Although the diagnostic criteria used were not precise, the authors paid careful attention to many of the factors that can influence post-mortem enzyme stability and appeared to have established an important biochemical defect in schizophrenic brain. They suggested that schizophrenia was associated with a defect in noradrenergic pathways involved in "reward" systems in CNS. To date only one other study has been reported which attempted to replicate these findings, and in this no significant reduction was found in dopamine-β-hydroxylase in nine schizophrenic post-mortem brain samples (Wyatt *et al.*, 1975).

Pharmacological Studies: The Dopamine Hypothesis

INTRODUCTION

In the past decade a new approach to schizophrenia research has emerged, which is based not on the search for a hypothetical "toxic metabolite", but on the clues obtained from our knowledge of the pharmacotherapy of schizophrenic illnesses. In particular two lines of research have converged to point to the critical role played by the CNS transmitter dopamine in the schizophrenia syndrome. One line has concerned the effects of amphetamines, which can induce a schizophrenia-like syndrome in normal people and can exacerbate schizophrenic psychosis; the other has emerged from studies of the phenothiazines and other drugs used in the treatment of schizophrenia. In both cases the drugs appear to act through effects on dopaminergic mechanisms,

From this has emerged the "dopamine hypothesis", which proposes that schizophrenia may be associated with an excessive function of dopaminergic pathways in CNS. This hypothesis, and the supporting evidence, has been the subject of several recent reviews (Snyder, 1973a; Matthysse, 1973; Snyder *et al.*, 1974a; Matthysse and Kety, 1974; Crow *et al.*, 1976; van Praag, 1977; Baldessarini, 1977).

DOPAMINE NEURONES IN CNS

The existence of dopamine as a neurotransmitter in mammalian CNS is a relatively recent discovery. The development of a sensitive assay technique, and the finding that dopamine was present, without substantial amounts of noradrenaline, in certain areas of brain—notably the basal ganglia (Carlsson, 1959) was followed rapidly by the important discovery by Ehringer and Hornykiewicz (1960) that dopamine is severely reduced in basal ganglia tissue obtained post-mortem from patients with Parkinson's disease. Application of the newly developed fluorescence histochemical techniques for visualizing catecholamine neurones then allowed a precise mapping of the distribution of dopaminergic neurones in CNS (Ungerstedt, 1971; Lindvall and Bjorklund, 1974). The results of these studies (Fig. 4) show that dopamine neurones are present in a

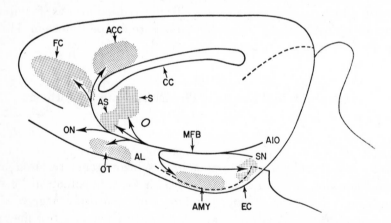

Fig. 4. Diagrammatic representation of distribution of dopamine neurones in rat brain. Fibre pathways (solid black lines) originate from dopamine neurone cell bodies in substantia nigra (SN) and ventromedial tegmentum (A10) and project in medial forebrain bundle (MFB) to striatum (S), nucleus accumbens septii (AS), olfactory tubercle (OT), frontal cortex (FC), anterior cingulate cortex (ACC), entorhinal cortex (EC) and amygdala (AMY). From Lindvall, O. and Bjorklund, A. to be published in *Handbook of Psychopharmacology* (Eds L. L. Iversen, S. D. Iversen and S. H. Snyder), Vol. 9. Plenum, New York.

fairly circumscribed distribution in mammalian brain. A major neuronal system originates from cell bodies in the pars compacta of the substantia nigra in the midbrain and innervates the various regions of neostriatum (caudate nucleus, putamen, globus pallidus). This so-called "nigro-striatal" dopamine pathway accounts for approximately 75% of whole brain dopamine in most mammals. Another collection of dopamine neurones, with cell bodies placed more medially in the ventral tegmentum of the midbrain at the level of the substantia nigra, projects rostrally to innervate various parts of the mesolimbic system, including nucleus accumbens septi and other septal nuclei, olfactory tubercle, medial frontal cortex, cingulate cortex and entorhinal cortex of the temporal lobe. Short-axoned dopamine neurones are also found as local interneurones in the olfactory bulb, in the amacrine cell population of retina, and at the base of the hypothalamus in a tubero-infundibular pathway in which dopamine is thought to play a neuroendocrine role, acting possibly as an inhibitory factor to control the release of prolactin from the anterior pituitary gland.

In their biochemical and pharmacological properties dopaminergic neurones, although similar in many respects to other catecholamine-containing neurones, have quite distinct characteristics. They lack the enzyme dopamine-β-hydroxylase and they possess an active uptake system for dopamine which, unlike the uptake systems in noradrenaline or 5-hydroxytryptamine neurones, is not potently inhibited by tricyclic antidepressant drugs (Iversen, 1975a). Similarly, target cells which respond to dopamine do so by means of specific dopamine receptors which are pharmacologically different from conventional α or β adrenoceptors for noradrenaline and adrenaline. Dopamine receptors are potently stimulated by the drug apomorphine, and not affected by conventional adrenoceptor agonists such as phenylephrine or isoprenaline. Amphetamine and related compounds such as methylphenidate appear to be particularly effective in releasing endogenous dopamine from dopaminergic neurones.

AMPHETAMINES

Amphetamine Psychosis

Connell (1958), in a now classic monograph, was the first to suggest that amphetamine psychosis is a not infrequent phenomenon in habitual users of large doses of the drug, and from his careful clinical study of 42 such patients he asserted that the clinical features of this state were "indistinguishable from acute or chronic paranoid schizophrenia".

There seems to be general agreement that amphetamine psychosis provides a more accurate drug-induced "model schizophrenia" than other
toxic substances (Snyder, 1973b). Numerous patients with amphetamine psychosis have been mis-diagnosed as paranoid schizophrenics,
and the similarity also extends to drug treatment, since drugs such as
the phenothiazines which are used in the treatment of schizophrenia are
also uniquely effective antidotes for amphetamine-induced psychosis.
Amphetamine psychosis is often associated with paranoid delusions,
stereotyped compulsive behaviour and auditory and visual hallucinations both occur with approximately equal frequency. Unlike schizophrenia, however, amphetamine psychosis is also frequently associated
with tactile and olfactory hallucinations, thought disorder is rare, agitation and motor overactivity are common, and patients display brisk
emotional reactions and anxiety, rather than a blunted affect.

Amphetamine psychosis appears to be directly related to the drug and
not to secondary factors associated with repeated drug usage, such as
sleep deprivation. This conclusion has emerged clearly from studies in
which amphetamine psychosis was induced in volunteer subjects.
Griffith et al. (1972) found that psychosis could be produced consistently
in such subjects within 1-4 days after initiation of repeated doses of
amphetamine. Angrist and his colleagues (for review see Angrist et al.,
1974) performed similar experiments with an even more aggressive
dosage schedule (50 mg d-amphetamine each hour) and obtained similar results even more rapidly. Davis (1974) and his colleagues also
observed that a small dose of the amphetamine-like stimulant methylphenidate (0·5 mg/kg) precipitated an acute exacerbation in 22 schizophrenic patients. The same dose of drug given to normal subjects
produced a mild euphoria but no psychosis. d-Amphetamine was
shown to cause a similar exacerbation of symptoms in schizophrenic
patients, and the pharmacologically less active isomer l-amphetamine
was considerably less effective. Similar findings with methylphenidate in
schizophrenic patients have been reported (Janowsky et al., 1977).

Thus amphetamines can reliably induce a condition in normal subjects which is remarkably similar to, though not identical to, paranoid
schizophrenia. These phenomena clearly represent very important
pharmacological clues for schizophrenia research.

A somewhat similar series of results have been obtained with L-DOPA,
an amino acid which enters the brain and is converted to dopamine.
Angrist et al. (1973) reported that L-DOPA, at doses of 3–6 g/day, led
to behavioural worsening in a group of ten schizophrenic patients; in
most cases there was an exacerbation of their psychotic symptoms.

Actions of Amphetamines in Animals

Amphetamines have numerous effects in animals, they suppress appetite, stimulate locomotor activity and various other behaviours, and in high doses they cause a bizarre form of stereotyped behaviour in which the animal constantly repeats selected items from its behavioural repertoire in an apparently meaningless fashion. In small laboratory animals such as the rat this stereotyped behaviour takes the form of repeated sniffing, head movements, rearing and compulsive gnawing. Randrup and his colleagues in Denmark (for review see Randrup and Munkvad, 1974) first suggested that the stereotyped behaviour in response to amphetamine might represent an animal model for amphetamine psychosis and schizophrenia in man. They were also the first to suggest that this action of amphetamine depended critically upon an interaction of the drug with dopaminergic mechanisms in the brain. This hypothesis is now widely accepted. The stereotyped behaviour induced by amphetamine, and by the dopamine-like drug apomorphine, is selectively blocked by small doses of phenothiazines or other drugs that are effective in treating schizophrenia; indeed the ability of a drug to block amphetamine- or apomorphine-induced stereotypy in animals has become a standard screening test of proven predictive value for developing new drugs of this type (Janssen *et al.*, 1967). Furthermore, amphetamines are known to be able to release dopamine from dopaminergic neurones, and the behavioural effects of amphetamine can be completely prevented by treating animals with compounds such as α-methyltyrosine which inhibit the synthesis of endogenous catecholamones in brain. The micro-injection of 6-hydroxydopamine, a selective neurotoxin for catecholamine neurones, into discrete dopamine-containing nuclei in brain has permitted an even more direct demonstration of the importance of dopaminergic neurones in mediating the actions of amphetamine. Creese and Iversen (1974; 1975), for example, found that in animals in which brain dopamine terminals had been almost completely destroyed by 6-hydroxydopamine treatment, both the locomotor hyperactivity and stereotypy responses to amphetamine were abolished. Kelly *et al.* (1975) subsequently found that more selective lesions of the dopamine terminals in the striatum reduced the stereotypy response to amphetamine without affecting the hyperactivity, whereas lesions of the dopamine terminals in the nucleus accumbens (Fig. 4) prevented the hyperactivity response without affecting stereotyped behaviour. Brain noradrenaline did not appear to be required for either amphetamine response. Many other studies have supported the conclusion that three behavioural responses to amphetamine are mediated by a release of dopamine in the brain, and that different dopaminergic pathways control different aspects of the drug-induced behaviour (for review see Iversen, 1977). This conclusion is reinforced by the fact that drugs such as apomorphine which act directly to mimic the actions of dopamine at dopamine receptors in CNS will also produce similar effects on animal behaviour, notably the induction of stereotypy.

ANTI-SCHIZOPHRENIC DRUGS

Chemical Classes

The discovery that certain drugs (neuroleptics) were able to exert beneficial effects on the fundamental psychotic symptoms in schizophrenic patients (Davis, 1965; Klein and Davis, 1969), has had a major impact on the treatment of the disorder, and has stimulated a considerable body of basic pharmacological research in the search for an understanding of their mechanisms of action. The first compound to be discovered, chlorpromazine (Table I), was derived from phenothiazines, which were originally developed for their anti-histamine properties. Large numbers of phenothiazines have now been tested, and many effective drugs in this series have been introduced for the treatment of schizophrenia. Some of these, such as fluphenazine and trifluoperazine, are considerably more potent than chlorpromazine, others such as thioridazine are effective antipsychotic drugs while inducing only a low incidence of undesirable Parkinson-like side effects. All of the effective compounds, however, have certain structural features in common. They possess, for example, a halogen or sulphur substituent at position 2 in the phenothiazine ring, and a side chain with a basic nitrogen separated by 3-carbon atoms from the ring (Zirkle and Kaiser, 1970; Janssen, 1976; Pletscher and Kyburg, 1976). Several other chemical classes of effective anti-schizophrenic drugs have since been discovered; all these are also neuroleptic, i.e. they induce extrapyramidal toxicity. Some are closely related to the phenothiazines, such as the thioxanthenes (Fig. 5). These include some very potent drugs such as flupenthixol, and are of considerable research interest because each drug in this series exists in geometric chemical isomers, the *cis* and *trans* forms, relative to the position of the side chain and halogen substituents at the carbon–carbon double bond by which the side chain is attached to the heterocyclic ring. The different isomers of these drugs possess markedly different pharmacological properties. In all examples so far examined the *cis* isomer is very much more potent in standard animal tests for neuroleptic activity than the *trans* isomer. This difference is particularly marked for the

Table I Selected phenothiazine derivatives

Nonproprietary name	X	R	Antipsychotic dose range [a] (mg/day)
Promethazine	H	$CH_2CH(CH_3)N(CH_3)_2$	—
Diethazine	H	$(CH_2)_2N(C_2H_5)_2$	—
Promazine	H	$(CH_2)_3N(CH_3)_2$	200–1000
Chlorpromazine	Cl	$(CH_2)_3N(CH_3)_2$	400–1600
Thioridazine	SCH_3	$(CH_2)_2$ ⟨N–CH₃ piperidine⟩	400–1600
Triflupromazine	CF_3	$(CH_2)_3N(CH_3)_2$	75–300
Prochlorperazine	Cl	$(CH_2)_3N$ ⟨NCH₃⟩	30–200
Trifluoperazine	CF_3	$(CH_2)_3N$ ⟨NCH₃⟩	6–30
Perphenazine	Cl	$(CH_2)_3N$ ⟨N(CH₂)₂OH⟩	12–64
Fluphenazine	CF_3	$(CH_2)_3N$ ⟨N(CH₂)₂OH⟩	2–20

[a] For adult hospitalized severly disturbed patients

compound flupenthixol (Fig. 5) in which virtually all of the neuroleptic activity resides in the *cis* isomer, α-flupenthixol, and almost no detectable activity is seen in β-flupenthixol, the *trans* isomer. This has recently been confirmed in a clinical trial of the two forms of flupenthixol, which demonstrated that all of the anti-schizophrenic activity of the drug resides in α-flupenthixol (Johnstone *et al.*, 1978). A similar phenomenon is seen with the novel optically-active compound butaclamol, in which all of the neuroleptic activity in animal tests is possessed by the (+)-enantiomer, and none by the stereoisomer (−)-butaclamol (Bruderlein *et al.*, 1975) (Fig. 6). Another important chemical class of neuroleptics has been developed based on the butyrophenone structure, and this has led to the development of some very potent anti-schizo-

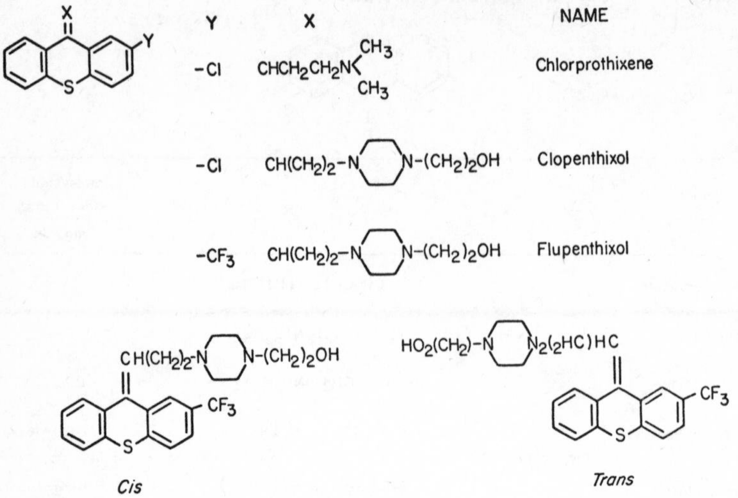

Fig. 5. Structures of some thioxanthenes and the *cis* (α) and *trans* (β) isomers of flupenthixol.

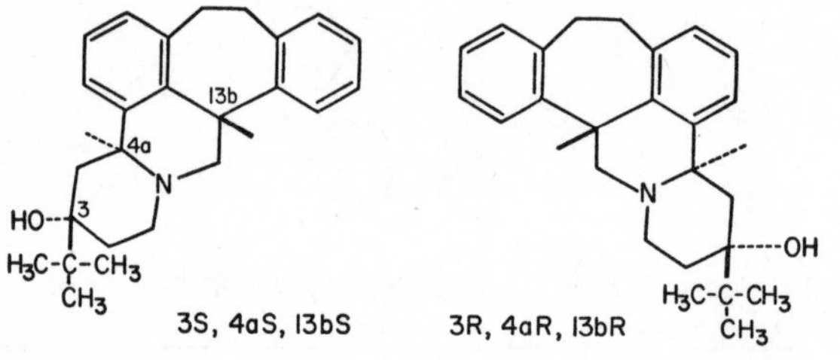

Fig. 6. The stereoisomers of butaclamol; all of the pharmacological activity resides in the (+) 3S, 4aS, 13bS form.

phrenic compounds such as haloperidol, spiroperidol and their di-phenylbutylpiperidine analogues such as pimozide (Fig. 7). Any pharmacological hypothesis which seeks to explain the actions of anti-schizophrenic drugs by a single common mechanism must, therefore, be reconciled with this wealth of structure-activity data. For example, any effect which is produced equally by the different isomers of flupenthixol or butaclamol cannot explain the neuroleptic and antipsychotic activity of these compounds.

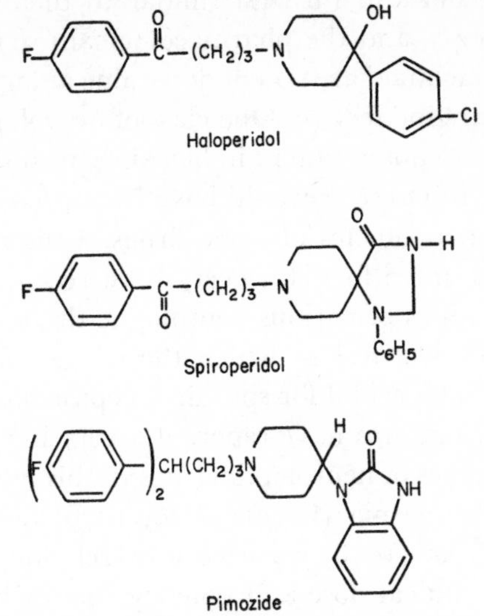

Fig. 7. Structures of the butyrophenones haloperidol and spiroperidol and the related neuroleptic drug pimozide.

Dopamine Receptor Blocking Actions

There is now considerable evidence to suggest that a common pharmacological mechanism shared by all anti-schizophrenic drugs is their ability to act as antagonists at CNS dopamine receptors. This conclusion stems from several different lines of research. Thus, there is a very good correlation between the ability of neuroleptic drugs of various chemical classes to block the behavioural effects of amphetamine and apomorphine in animal tests and the relative clinical potencies of the same drugs in treating schizophrenia (Janssen et al., 1967). As described above, there is convincing evidence that such behavioural effects are mediated through dopaminergic mechanisms. More direct tests of the "dopamine hypothesis" for the mode of action of neuroleptic drugs have become possible in the last few years as the result of the development of in vitro biochemical tests that permit a quantitative assessment of drug effects on CNS dopamine receptor sites. One such system depends on the discovery that dopamine receptors in dopamine-rich areas of brain are coupled to the enzyme adenylate cyclase (Kebabian et al., 1972). Thus, dopamine when added to a homogenate of such a brain area in vitro causes a specific stimulation of cyclic AMP formation, and this response can be antagonized by all anti-schizophrenic drugs (for reviews see Iversen, 1975b; Greengard, 1976). The various phenothiazines display relative potencies in this test similar to their potencies as anti-schizophrenic agents, and the pharmacologically active isomers of flupenthixol and butaclamol are potent dopamine antagonists, whereas the inactive isomers are ineffective. One class of neuroleptics, however, the butyrophenones, are not as potent in blocking the dopamine-stimulated adenylate cyclase response as would have been predicted from the high *in vivo* and clinical potencies of these drugs, a discrepancy which has still not been accounted for. However, more recent experiments have measured the affinities of various neuroleptic drugs at CNS dopamine receptors in an *in vitro* test in which the drugs compete with radioactively labelled haloperidol for specific receptor binding sites in brain homogenates. Two groups have reported a very impressive correlation between the potencies of neuroleptic drugs in this test and their clinical potencies in schizophrenia (Creese *et al.*, 1976; Seeman *et al.*, 1976) (Fig. 8). Creese *et al.* (1976) reported a correlation coefficient of 0·87 between average clinical dose and potency against binding of labelled haloperidol for a series of 22 drugs.

Seeman *et al.* (1976) obtained similar results and found that the absolute concentrations of haloperidol or chlorpromazine required to prevent the binding of labelled haloperidol to receptor binding sites were very similar to the free concentrations of these drugs in plasma from schizophrenic patients. These drug concentrations being approximately 1×10^{-9}M for haloperidol and 30×10^{-9} M for chlorpromazine. Leysen *et al.* (1977) reported similar results with the related compound ³H-spiroperidol. Specific receptor binding of labelled drugs in these studies was defined as that which could be displaced by non-radioactive (+)-butaclamol but not by the inactive isomer (−)-butaclamol, so this test fulfils the stereospecificity criterion described on p. 106 above.

Further evidence that neuroleptics act as dopamine antagonists both in animals and in man has been provided by recent studies of the effects of these substances on the secretion of the pituitary hormone prolactin. With improved radioimmunoassay techniques, plasma concentrations of this hormone have been shown to respond to pharmacological manipulation of dopaminergic mechanisms (Frantz and Sachar, 1976). Dopamine-like drugs such as L-DOPA and apomorphine inhibit the secretion of pituitary prolactin, whereas neuroleptics cause an increase in circulating levels of prolactin, presumably by blocking a tonic inhibitory neuroendocrine control mechanism in which dopamine released from nerve terminals in the median eminence acts directly or indirectly as a "prolactin inhibitory factor". Clemens *et al.* (1974) and Langer *et al.* (1977) found that there was a good correlation between the doses of

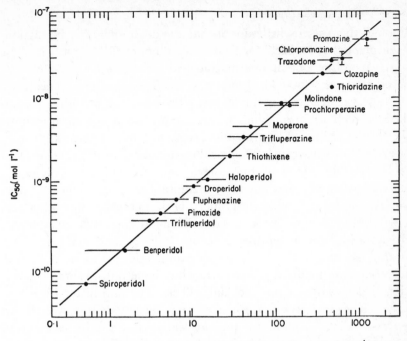

Fig. 8. Comparison of the clinical potencies of neuroleptic drugs, measured as average daily dose in treating schizophrenia with potencies of the same drugs in displacing ³H-haloperidol from dopamine receptor binding sites *in vitro* (IC_{50} = concentration of drug required to displace 50% of specific haloperidol binding). (From Seeman *et al.*, 1976.)

neuroleptic drugs needed to elicit the prolactin response, and the clinical doses of the same drugs when used to treat schizophrenia. Indeed, measurements of plasma prolactin may prove to be of value in psychiatry as a clinical indicator of dopamine receptor blockade.

These findings strongly support the conclusion that the neurological and possibly also the antipsychotic properties of the neuroleptics can be attributed to their dopamine-blocking properties, and this in turn suggests many further questions. Which of the dopamine systems in brain is crucial for the antipsychotic effect? If blockade of dopamine receptors in the brain is crucial for the antipsychotic effect, are Parkinsonian side-effects an inevitable consequence of the effective drug treatment of schizophrenia? Does the mode of action of neuroleptic drugs as dopamine antagonists tell us anything about the biochemical nature of the disease?

Other Pharmacological Properties

Although there seems little doubt that the dopamine-blocking actions of neuroleptics are critical for their antipsychotic effects, many of these drugs have other potent pharmacological actions. For example, most neuroleptics are potent local anaesthetics (Seeman, 1972). This property, however, is shared by many related compounds, including phenothiazines such as promazine, which have little or no antipsychotic effects. The ability of neuroleptic drugs, because of their high lipid solubility, to concentrate in biological membranes, however, means that at relatively high concentrations they disrupt a multitude of biological functions which are dependent on membrane systems. Hence the biochemical literature is filled with reports of the actions of phenothiazines on membrane transport processes or mitochondrial energy metabolism.

In addition many neuroleptic drugs have quite specific receptor blocking actions, other than on dopaminergic mechanisms. Many phenothiazines, including chlorpormazine, have anti-histamine properties, and α-adrenoceptor blocking effects. The anti-histamine properties of drugs such as chlorpromazine may be a contributory factor to the reports that schizophrenic patients show reduced skin responses to histamine (Smythies, 1976), since these studies did not adequately control for concomitant drug therapy.

Peroutka *et al.* (1977) recently surveyed the α-adrenoceptor blocking potencies of several neuroleptic drugs, and suggested that a relationship exists between clinical sedative and hypotensive side-effects of these drugs and their central α-receptor potency. More precisely, the ratio of α-adrenergic to dopaminergic receptor affinities may predict the severity or incidence of such side-effects.

Another property of neuroleptics which may be of clinical importance is the ability of some drugs to act as antagonists at acetylcholine receptors of the muscarine category. Miller and Hiley (1974) and Snyder *et al.* (1974b) using receptor labelling techniques measured the antimuscarinic potencies of a number of neuroleptic drugs in brain (Table II) and found that there was a wide range of activity, from drugs such as fluphenazine or haloperidol which were only weak anticholinergics, to drugs such as thioridazine and clozapine in which the antimuscarinic potencies were comparable to, or even greater than, the antidopaminergic potencies. The interesting correlation which appeared to emerge from these studies was that neuroleptic drugs such as clozapine and thioridazine, which combine antimuscarinic and antidopaminergic properties, are clinically those which cause the lowest incidence of Parkinsonian side-effects. This is pharmacologically plausible, since it is

Table II Comparison of anticholinergic and antidopaminergic properties of neuroleptics

| Drug | Dissociation constant for binding to receptor sites—M | | Ratio of cholinergic: dopaminergic potency[a] |
	Muscarinic	Dopaminergic	
Atropine	$5 \cdot 2 \times 10^{-10}$	—	—
Benztropine	$1 \cdot 3 \times 10^{-9}$	$> 1 \times 10^{-4}$	$> 75,000 \cdot 0$
Ethopropazine	$1 \cdot 0 \times 10^{-8}$	—	—
Thioridazine	$2 \cdot 5 \times 10^{-8}$	$1 \cdot 3 \times 10^{-7}$	$5 \cdot 2$
Clozapine	$5 \cdot 5 \times 10^{-8}$	$1 \cdot 7 \times 10^{-7}$	$3 \cdot 1$
Chlorpromazine	$3 \cdot 5 \times 10^{-7}$	$4 \cdot 8 \times 10^{-9}$	$0 \cdot 14$
Pimozide	$1 \cdot 6 \times 10^{-7}$	$1 \cdot 4 \times 10^{-7}$	$0 \cdot 87$
α-Flupenthixol	$2 \cdot 2 \times 10^{-6}$	$1 \cdot 0 \times 10^{-9}$	$0 \cdot 0005$
Trifluoperazine	$4 \cdot 0 \times 10^{-6}$	$1 \cdot 9 \times 10^{-8}$	$0 \cdot 005$
Spiroperidol	$1 \cdot 2 \times 10^{-5}$	$9 \cdot 5 \times 10^{-8}$	$0 \cdot 008$

Data from Iversen *et al.* (1976).
[a] Ratio of cholinergic: dopaminergic potency indicates how many times more potent a compound is as an anticholinergic than a dopamine antagonist.

well known that the function of the basal ganglia in controlling extrapyramidal motor functions involves a mutual balance between cholinergic and dopaminergic systems. The administration of anticholinergic drugs as an adjunct to neuroleptic therapy is a common clinical practice to reduce Parkinsonian side-effects. These findings can also explain why drugs such as thioridazine have yielded "false negative" results in various animal behaviour or biochemical tests which measure the ability of drugs to antagonize dopaminergic function in the basal ganglia (Crow *et al.*, 1976). The implication, therefore, is that since thioridazine and clozapine are clinically effective as antipsychotics, this action cannot be localized within the nigrostriatal dopamine system, but must be on some other non-striatal dopaminergic pathway. This conclusion is also supported by the neurophysiological results of Bunney and Aghajanian (1976) who found that the ability of drugs to cause an increase in the rate of firing of dopamine cells in the substantia nigra correlated with their extrapyramidal side-effects, whereas the ability of these drugs to alter the firing rate of dopamine cells in the ventral tegmentum (the A10 cell group projecting to mesolimbic areas, Fig. 4) was a much better indicator of antipsychotic effects. Thus, the question of determining the anatomical locus of the actions of antipsychotic drugs on brain dopamine systems does seem to be potentially answerable, and attention is currently focused on dopamine pathways within the mesolimbic nuclei or "limbic" areas of cerebral cortex. Biochemical studies of the properties of dopamine receptors in these various non-striatal areas of brain suggest that there are no obvious differences in drug specificity between dopamine receptors in different brain areas (Burt *et al.*, 1976).

Finally, one other property of some neuroleptics is their ability to act as 5-hydroxytryptamine (serotonin) antagonists. Enna *et al.* (1976), for example, tested the isomeric forms of butaclamol and flupenthixol for their ability to interact with various transmitter and drug receptors in brain. They were able to show no stereospecific interactions of these substance with β-adrenoceptors, GABA, glycine, acetylcholine or opiate receptors but the pharmacologically active forms (+)-butaclamol and α-flupenthixol did prove to be much more potent than their inactive isomers in their interactions with 5-hydroxytryptamine binding sites. Although this property is not likely to be crucial for antipsychotic actions, since it is not shared by all neuroleptics, it may nevertheless be worthy of further investigation. The anti-serotonin actions of some neuroleptics may contribute importantly to their overall profiles. In this respect it is interesting to note that Green and Grahame-Smith (1976a) found that the drug *l*-propranolol appears to act as a central 5-hydroxytryptamine antagonist in animals, and this drug—which completely lacks any dopamine blocking actions—has been reported to have beneficial effects in the treatment of schizophrenia (Yorkston *et al.*, 1974, 1977). Furthermore, there is direct evidence that *l*-propranolol interacts with high affinity at CNS 5-HT receptors *in vitro* (Middlemiss *et al.*, 1977).

Prospects for Drug Development

Drugs used in the treatment of schizophrenia have a wide variety of pharmacological activities, in addition to their dopamine-blocking effects. This is no surprise to the neuropharmacologist who is accustomed to discovering that drugs have multiple sites of action. It may be of importance, however, in determining the overall pharmacological profile for each individual neuroleptic drug. There are features of the actions of these drugs in clinical use, such as their sedative and appetite enhancing properties which are not necessarily related to dopamine receptor blockade. The undesirable side-effects caused by neuroleptics on extrapyramidal function can apparently be neutralized by combining the right set of pharmacological properties. Similarly in future one might imagine the rational design of neuroleptics with various combinations of pharmacological actions to achieve desired clinical goals.

The dopamine hypothesis suggests that the development of new drugs will be made much easier, since simple screening tests for antidopamine properties now exist. However, new compounds discovered in this way will, of course, be likely to behave very similarly to those already in existence. Indeed it might be argued that the widespread adoption by the drug industry of animal screening tests which depend on interference with dopamine-mediated extrapyramidal functions explains why the present generation of antipsychotics all seem to act by a common pharmacological mechanism. The prospect of discovering a completely novel pharmacological mechanism that would be as effective seems more remote, and will probably have to rely more on serendipity than rational drug design. Investigations of the pharmacology and anatomical distribution of pathways in the brain which control or interact with dopaminergic neurones offer one obvious avenue for further research.

Meanwhile pharmaceutical developments, with the advent of new preparations of existing drugs in the form of long-lasting depot injections (such as fluphenazine and flupenthixol), and the introduction of new drugs with long lasting actions after oral dosage (such as penfluridol) are likely to have an important impact on the drug treatment of schizophrenia (see Chapter 7).

THE DOPAMINE HYPOTHESIS OF SCHIZOPHRENIA

Introduction

The "dopamine hypothesis" has two quite distinct meanings. On the one hand it refers to the hypothesis that anti-schizophrenic drugs act by virtue of their dopamine receptor blocking effects—and in this sense the hypothesis now seems to be firmly established. In a second sense, however, the implications of these pharmacological findings are taken to imply that schizophrenia itself may be a dopamine disorder, in which there is excessive activity or perhaps unusually high responsiveness to dopamine in one or more of the dopaminergic neuronal pathways in the brain. The logical soundness of this inference, however, can be questioned. For example, as Vogt (1974) points out, it was known that anticholinergic drugs were effective in treating Parkinson's disease long before we understood the true nature of this disorder as a dopamine-deficiency disease. The fact that anticholinergic drugs are effective therapeutically did not in fact mean that there was any abnormality in cholinergic mechanisms in the brain, but merely that cholinergic influences were in a state of imbalance with the normally opposing influences of dopaminergic systems in the basal ganglia. Similarly, the finding that neuroleptic drugs act as dopamine antagonists does *not* necessarily imply that any abnormality exists in dopaminergic mechanisms in the schizophrenic brain, although this is, of course, still one possibility.

Lack of Evidence for Dopaminergic Hyperactivity

The evidence available already indicates that there is no generalized hyperactivity of dopaminergic neurones in schizophrenics. Thus, measurements of the rate of accumulation of the dopamine metabolite homovanillic acid in lumbar CSF after treatment with probenicid have failed to show abnormally high rates of dopamine turnover in drug-free schizophrenic patients (Bowers, 1974; Post et al., 1975). Indeed the rate of accumulation of homovanillic acid in CSF was found by both groups to be lower than normal, and Post et al. (1975) reported an inverse relation between dopamine turnover estimated in this way and severity of the illness. As expected, however, there is an increased accumulation of homovanillic acid in CSF, at least during the initial period of treatment with anti-schizophrenic drugs (van Praag, 1977). Measurements of plasma prolactin in drug-free schizophrenic patients have also failed to show any abnormalities, indicating that there is no impairment in the function of the tubero-infundibular dopamine system (Meltzer et al., 1974; Crow et al., 1976).

A further indication that schizophrenia might not always be associated with a dopamine abnormality comes from the finding of Crow et al. (1976) that schizophrenia and Parkinson's disease can co-exist in a small number of patients.

On the other hand none of this evidence rules out the possibility that there may be excessive activity or unusual responsiveness in a restricted part of the dopaminergic pathways in brain; for example, in the cerebral cortex, which would not contribute significantly to CSF levels of homovanillic acid (which probably largely reflect the activity of the nigrostriatal system), and which might be affected less severely in Parkinson's disease. The direct test of the "dopamine hypothesis" will probably come from the results of biochemical measurements of dopamine and related biochemical measurements of dopamine and related biochemical systems in various areas of post-mortem brain from schizophrenic patients, work which is now in progress in several laboratories.

The idea that dopaminergic malfunction may be restricted to only certain brain areas in schizophrenia will not be an easy one to test. If true, however, it might help to explain why the "model psychoses" produced by large doses of amphetamine or L-DOPA (see p. 101) above are not exactly similar to schizophrenia. These drugs will, of course, flood all parts of the brain with excess dopamine, and thus cause a generalized dopaminergic overactivity syndrome and release other amines as well. The agitation and increased motor activity seen with amphetamine and L-DOPA might, for example, be explained in this way. On the other hand, it is equally possible that there is no direct malfunction in any portion of the dopamine system in the schizophrenic brain, but instead there is an abnormality in some other neurochemical system which normally counteracts the actions of dopamine—an imbalance which might also be anatomically restricted to a particular brain region. Thus, for example, the recent finding that the morphine-like peptide β-endorphin can, like neuroleptic drugs, cause catalepsy when injected into the rat brain has led to the speculation that endogenous brain peptides of this class might represent naturally occurring protective agents against psychosis, and that schizophrenia might be associated with a deficiency of such peptides (Jacquet and Marks, 1976). There are, of course, many other possibilities. Green and Grahame-Smith (1976b) and Smythies (1976) have suggested that an imbalance may exist between dopamine and 5-hydroxytryptamine systems in schizophrenia. The behavioural effects of excessive stimulation of serotonin systems in brain seem to be mediated through dopaminergic mechanisms (Green and Grahame-Smith, 1976b). There is even a possible link here between the trans-methylation and dopamine hypotheses. The postulated psychotomimetic indolamines could act indirectly to stimulate dopaminergic mechanisms.

All this, however, is highly speculative, although the ideas should be amenable to experimental test. In this sense research on biochemical and pharmacological factors in schizophrenia is now healthier than it has been for a very long time. Real progress has been made in a rational understanding of the actions of antipsychotic drugs, and this new knowledge has given fresh impetus for further research.

Conclusion

There has still not been any definite identification of a biochemical abnormality in schizophrenia. It is perhaps worth considering whether the quest for such a metabolic defect is meaningful, and how it would improve our understanding of the disease if one were to be discovered. That the search is meaningful seems beyond doubt; the major disturbances of brain function which must underlie schizophrenic psychoses must be associated with biochemical rather than neuropathological abnormalities. This is true whether or not schizophrenia is a unitary disease entity, or a collection of different subgroups.

The question of what we will understand if a metabolic abnormality can be identified, is much more difficult to answer. The identification of a specific biochemical disturbance might help to explain the nature of the brain malfunction which underlies the symptoms of the disease, but we would still not understand how this biochemical abnormality came about. How is it that twins with identical genetic composition show a concordance of only about 50% for the disease? What are the mechanisms by which environmental and social factors interact with genetic predisposition to cause schizophrenia, or to lead to a relapse in those successfully treated for this condition? It would certainly be naïve to suppose that a metabolic defect could be regarded as "the cause" of schizophrenia. On the other hand, we can regard neurobiological research as a most promising means of unravelling these complexities and look forward, with some confidence, to further progress.

5 | Cognitive Disorder

Peter H. Venables

Introduction

By ancient tradition "mental life" falls into three subdivisions: cognition, affection and conation. Many people think of "schizophrenia"* as a disorder having its main dysfunction in the cognitive field, in contrast, for example, to mania and depression, which are classified as "affective disorders".

The definition of cognition, however, is broad, and probably no-one would wish to be strict in pigeon-holing certain aspects of behaviour as wholly cognitive, with the idea that emotional or motivational elements cannot enter into consideration. Neisser (1967) suggests,

> the term "cognition" refers to all the processes by which the sensory input is transformed, reduced, elaborated, stored, recovered and used. It is concerned with these processes even when they operate in the absence of relevant stimulation as in images and hallucinations.

Neisser's view of cognition thus covers the processes of sensation, perception, memory and thinking—and probably also motor response. While recognizing thought disorder as one of the primary symptoms of schizophrenia, traditional psychiatric doctrine following Kraepelin and Bleuler did not recognize sensory disturbance as a feature of schizophrenia, and one of the characteristics of the disease was said to be a "clear sensorium". With the introduction of the techniques of the experimental psychologist into clinical investigation it has become appar-

* See p. viii.

E

ent that abnormalities of sensory processes can be found in schizophrenia at quite fundamental levels, and that the characteristic thought disorder is more a dysfunction of the processes of attention and perception, on the integrity of which ordered thought must depend.

In a classic paper, Hunt and Cofer (1944) introduced the term "psychological deficit" to encompass the inefficiencies of cognitive function found in psychotic states. The use of this term is operational. It was employed because it had none of the causative implications of the terms "dementia", "deterioration" or "regression", that had previously been used. "Deficit" implies only that the patient functions at a level of efficiency below that expected by comparison with his peers or with his own past performance. Hunt and Cofer put forward the general view that deficit is seen to a greater extent the more complex the function involved. Thus they too provide little evidence to suggest deficits at a basic sensory level although they indicate that they are apparent in, for instance, choice reaction performance. Twenty-one years later, in an anniversary paper with the title *Psychological deficit in schizophrenia*, Lang and Buss (1965), after reviewing the wide range of studies that had become available by that time, suggested that "the disturbance that appears in all studies of deficit concerns the initiation of responses to selected stimuli and the inhibition of inappropriate responses". These authors suggested that schizophrenic deficit lies in an inability to select appropriate responses. Later, however, they quoted with approval the statement of Hernandez-Péon *et al.* (1956) that "attention involves the selective awareness of certain sensory messages with the simultaneous suppression of others" and stated that "the data on schizophrenic deficit are consistent with the hypothesis that such sensory inhibition centres are defective". They are thus also willing to approve the idea that deficit involves defective functioning of a sensory filtering system. A further point of view, held by many authors, is that there is in schizophrenia a fundamental slowness of processing of sensory input and its translation to output and action.

Cognitive disorders in schizophrenia may be apparent at input, output or in central processing stages and at all levels from simple to complex.

Subjective Experience of Disorder

To give a flavour of the subjective reports of patients concerning their cognitive disorders it is useful to provide some of the material which has been reported on their experiences.

In relation to the inadequate filtering of sensory input:

Everything seems to grip my attention although I am not particularly interested in anything. I am speaking to you just now but I can hear noises going on next door and in the corridor. I find it difficult to shut these out and it makes it more difficult for me to concentrate on what I am saying to you. (McGhie and Chapman, 1961) (Patient 23)

So the mind must have a filter which functions without our conscious thought, sorting stimuli and allowing only those which are relevant to the situation to disturb consciousness . . . What happened to me was a breakdown in the filter and a hodge-podge of unrelated stimuli were distracting me from things which should have had my undivided attention. (Norma MacDonald, 1960)

In relation to changes in sensory experience:

My senses were sharpened, sounds were more intense and I could see with great clarity, everything seemed very clear to me. Even my sense of taste seemed more acute. (Bowers and Freedman, 1966) (Case 6)

Colours seem to be brighter now, almost as if they are luminous. (McGhie and Chapman, 1961) (Patient 17)

Because of the awareness of percepts that are not normally attended to, patients report having to move slowly and that once-automatic actions are no longer automatic. Disturbance of proprioception and vestibular function may also be evident:

I don't like moving fast . . . If I carried on I wouldn't be aware of things as they really are. I would just be aware of the sound and the noise and the movements. Everything would be a jumbled mass. I have found that I can stop this by going completely still and motionless. (McGhie and Chapman, 1961) (Patient 14)

I have to do everything step by step, nothing is automatic now. Everything has to be considered. (McGhie and Chapman, 1961) (Patient 3)

In addition to inadequate filtering of sensory input, whether from distance receptors or from somatic sensation, schizophrenic patients report an inability to deal appropriately with internally generated material:

My trouble is that I've got too many thoughts. You might think of something, say that ashtray, and just think, oh yes that's for putting my cigarette in, but I would think of it and then I would think of a dozen different things connected with it at the same time. (McGhie and Chapman, 1961) (Patient 20)

My mind's away. I have lost control. There are too many things coming into my head at once and I can't sort them out. (McGhie and Chapman, 1961) (Patient 21)

These subjective reports provide some of the bases for a more detailed examination of dysfunctions. This will be undertaken in a sequential fashion from input to output and from simple to complex, bearing in mind that such an ordering accords with convenience rather than reality.

Sensory Disturbances (Audition and Vision)

In patients whose cooperation and motivation are in doubt, the measurement of sensory performance is a difficult procedure. In many early studies, sensory and non-sensory factors were not distinguished and the results produced were of dubious value. Nevertheless, as these early studies were often on non-medicated patients, it would be unwise to dismiss them out of hand, since they provide material now difficult to replicate.

One method of examining sensory effects is to see how far there are differences in speed of response to different sensory stimuli. A very early study by Wells and Kelley (1922) showed that response to a sound stimulus was slower than that to a light stimulus in a group of dementia praecox patients. However, as reaction time varies with stimulus intensity it is not a straightforward matter to make statements that indicate that responses to auditory stimuli are impaired with respect to visual stimuli unless a range of stimulus values is used.

A later pair of studies, still dealing with unmedicated patients, was carried out by Venables and Tizard (1956, 1958). Reaction times to auditory and visual stimuli over a range of stimulus intensities were measured in groups of non-paranoid chronic schizophrenic patients. Over all stimulus intensities, except the highest used in each modality, reaction times to auditory stimuli were longer than those to visual stimuli. This is a reversal of the pattern universally found in normal subjects where reaction times to sound stimuli are always (for comparable intensities of stimulation) faster than those to visual stimuli. An extension of these studies by Venables and O'Connor (1959) showed that the modality reversal effect was true for non-paranoid and for paranoid schizophrenic patients who expressed their delusions incoherently, but was not found in intact monosymptomatic paranoid patients who performed in a similar fashion to normals.

These studies suggest a disturbance of function in the auditory modality in schizophrenia which can be examined more directly by the measurement of auditory thresholds. Early studies, by L. E. Travis (1924) and R. C. Travis (1926), showed that schizophrenic patients had higher auditory thresholds than normal during states of "reverie".

However, others, such as Ludwig *et al.* (1962), found no differences between the auditory thresholds of schizophrenic patients and normals. These studies may well have been contaminated by the intrusion of non-sensory factors such as lack of motivation and differences in cautiousness in the application of criteria for the presence and absence of stimuli. Using a forced choice technique not so open to criticism of this kind, Emmerich and Levine (1970) provided data suggesting an 8 dB loss in auditory sensitivity in comparison with normals. In a parallel study Levine and Whitney (1970) show that chronic schizophrenic patients not only have a higher auditory threshold than normals but also a lower threshold for reports of unpleasantness of a high intensity tone (70 dB for schizophrenic patients as compared to 81 dB for normals). The suggestion from these data is that schizophrenic patients function over a narrower range of stimulus intensities than normals. Bruder *et al.* (1975), also using a forced choice technique and very careful diagnostic techniques to identify schizophrenic patients, report no differences from normal in their patients' ability to detect transient clicks.

A further point of experimental detail that it is important to recognize in studies of this kind is the excessive reaction of schizophrenic patients to the first occasion of testing and the liability of dysfunctions in response to occur as a result of long periods of testing. Thus, it is not impossible that the loss in sensitivity shown by Emmerich and Levine (1970) mentioned above is in part due to the length of the forced choice procedure employed.

The frequency of auditory stimulation used in this study was 400 Hz, an aspect which is important in relation to work reported by Gruzelier and Hammond (1976) in which absolute auditory thresholds were measured over a range of auditory frequencies on two occasions. These workers used a fairly short procedure and reported that "schizophrenics had superior hearing at low frequencies up to 1,000 and 2,000 Hz" and that it was the right ear which showed the lowest threshold on the first occasion of testing but this lateral difference disappeared on the second occasion of testing. No simple statement is therefore possible about the sensitivity of the auditory system in schizophrenia; some attempt at a more comprehensive statement will be made later when further studies have been considered.

Simple studies of visual thresholds in schizophrenic patients do not appear to have been made. The data of Venables and Tizard (1956) and Venables and O'Connor (1959) using reaction time procedures do, however, make possible two statements. The first is that for moderate stimulus intensities, employed for instance by Venables and O'Connor, the use of the visual modality appears to elicit less dysfunction than the auditory modality. On the other hand, Venables and Tizard showed that with high levels of visual stimulation, chronic non-paranoid un-medicated patients showed a "paradoxical" lengthening of reaction time which was taken to indicate the operation of transmarginal protective inhibition (Pavlov, 1927). These data suggest that schizophrenic patients exhibit the characteristics of persons with "weak" nervous systems, in Pavlovian terms. The characteristics of such a system, are that it is more sensitive than the "strong"; i.e., it responds at a level nearer to maximum at lower intensities and shows a decrease in response at high intensities. This decrease is the "paradoxical" effect described above. A more fully explored idea, parallel to the Pavlovian "weak–strong" nervous system dichotomy, is that of "reduction-augmentation", first introduced by Petrie (1960), but studied at greater length using brain event related potential techniques by Buchsbaum and Silverman (1968; Buchsbaum, 1976).

Before dealing with these, however, another set of investigations needs to be examined. These are studies not so much of simple sensory sensitivity but of the detection of sensory signals against a noise background.

Deficits in Signal Detection (Audition and Vision)

A standard paradigm of these types of experiment is that periods of noise (either auditory or visual) are presented, and in some of these periods a signal is present that the subject has to detect. "Signal" and "noise" are experimental terms; signal is a form of stimulation defined by the experimenter as "wanted" or relevant, and noise is stimulation which is "unwanted" or irrelevant. Thus, while it is usual for the "signal" to be some pure sinusoidal tone and the "noise" to be white noise, from the point of view of the experiment it would be perfectly feasible to have the subject detect a white noise "signal" against the background of a pure tone "noise". The data are described in terms of d', a measure of signal detectability indicating the sensitivity of the subject, and β, the degree of cautiousness with which the subject makes his judgement about the presence or absence of the stimulus.

Rappaport et al. (1972) describe a study of this kind in which differences in auditory signal detection between paranoid and non-paranoid schizophrenics were examined both while taking and while not taking phenothiazine medication. A group of non-schizophrenic subjects was also tested. In this experiment the signals were 1,000 Hz tones that had to be detected against a background of continuous white noise. Six signal-noise ratios were employed. The results were as follows: in comparison with normals the d' values of paranoid patients indicated that they detected signals less accurately and it was shown that they were more cautious in reaching decisions; non-paranoid schizophrenic patients detected signals less accurately under easy signal/noise conditions but as well as normals under difficult conditions.

In this and another similar experiment by Rappaport *et al.* (1971) it was shown that the effect of phenothiazine medication was different in paranoid and non-paranoid schizophrenic patients. With increasing phenothiazine dosage signal detection performance worsened among non-paranoid and improved among paranoid patients. The authors suggest that these results may be related to two quite different basic mechanisms. It is thought that the paranoid patient scans his environment widely (using the word "scan" here not only in the visual sense) and because of this he appears to have a primary difficulty in focusing attention and is "wide open" to extraneous stimuli. Medication is reported to reduce the range of environmental stimuli to which the paranoid schizophrenic patient responds. It is suggested that the non-paranoid patient, particularly in the acute stage, is incapacitated by his hypersensitivity to low and moderate intensities of stimulation and by an attenuated response to very strong stimuli. This view is a restatement by Western authors of the theoretical stance described earlier, derived originally from Pavlovian ideas. Phenothiazines are reported to reduce these abnormalities.

A visual analogue of the auditory "signal in noise" study was carried out by Stilson and Kopell (1964) and Stilson *et al.* (1966). The task involved the detection of easily identifiable shapes in the presence of a random dot visual noise signal. Although schizophrenic patients did not differ in their performance from normals in the detection of shapes without the interfering noise signal, they performed significantly worse when interference was present. In these studies the schizophrenic patients were taking phenothiazines. Rappaport *et al.* (1971, 1972) showed that medication affects the detection of auditory signals. Kopell and Wittner (1968) investigated the role of phenothiazines in the detection of visual signals. In a population which contained only one paranoid schizophrenic patient (for whom chlorpromazine had a beneficial effect on auditory signal detection), chlorpromazine worsened detection of visual signals in noise in dose-related fashion. The result is thus analogous to that obtained with auditory signals.

The data reviewed in this section clearly suggest impairment in schizophrenic patients under conditions in which they have to detect a signal against a noisy background. Recent data, while offering general support for this suggestion, indicate that it may not be true for all schizophrenic patients. Gruzelier and Venables (1972) have shown, on the basis of the skin conductance orienting response, that chronic schizophrenic patients may be divided into those who orient to stimuli but show impaired habituation (responders) and those who do not orient (non-responders). Subsequently, Patterson and Venables (unpublished) demonstrated that it is possible to identify a third group of patients (fast habituators) who, while showing normal orienting responses to the first stimulus presented, do not show any further responsivity. We also showed that, while the performance of "responder" and "non-responder" patients on a signal detection task is significantly worse than normal, that of the patients who show fast habituation is not significantly different from normal, and indeed some show better than normal performance.

Sensory Disturbance (Proprioception, Cutaneous Sensation and Vestibular Dysfunction)

Meehl (1962), in his seminal paper "Schizotaxia, Schizotypy, Schizophrenia", reviewed the literature on vestibular dysfunction in schizophrenia and agreed with Hoskins (1946) that a defect in the vestibular system is one of the few fairly clear-cut biological findings in work on schizophrenia. Reviews by Holzman (1968) and Ornitz (1970) supporting this position provided considerable breadth of material suggesting diminished reactivity in schizophrenia with respect to vestibular functions which control balance and adjustments of posture. Thus, for instance, early studies by Freeman and Rodnick (1942) showed that schizophrenic patients exhibit *less* unsteadiness after rotation than do normals, and three decades later Myers *et al.* (1973), using electronystagmographic techniques, provide similar evidence of dysfunction following rotation. The same authors used caloric stimulation to elicit vestibular activity and confirmed the findings of Angyal and Blackman (1940) and Angyal and Sherman (1942) that there is a deficit in vestibular function in schizophrenia.

These experimental data are in accord with patients' comments reported by Chapman (1966); for example,

> When I start walking fast I get a fast series of pictures in front of me. Everything seems to change and revolve around me. Something goes wrong with my eyes and I've got to stop and stand still.

It is suggested that this impairment of vestibular activity may be one of the factors that underlie the disturbances of body image and feelings of depersonalization often found at the onset of schizophrenia. Allied disturbances that might account for such feelings might be in the areas of proprioception and cutaneous sensation.

Rosenbaum *et al.* (1959) reported impaired weight discrimination in schizophrenic patients. In a follow-up study, however, Rosenbaum *et al.* (1965) showed that with heavy weights, discrimination was not impaired although they confirmed the earlier findings of dysfunction with light weights. Testing the alternatives that deficient performance on a weight discrimination task with light weights might be due either to (a) insufficient intensity of proprioceptive feedback to cue behaviour, or to (b) impaired proprioceptive memory, Retzler and Rosenbaum (1974) concluded that proprioceptive deficit is caused by inadequate sensory input.

In a further extension of investigations into bodily sensation, Broekma and Rosenbaum (1975) examined cutaneous sensitivity in schizophrenic patients and normals by the use of a two point aesthesiometer, and also investigated the extent to which muscle tension induced by squeezing a hand dynanometer had influence on cutaneous sensitivity. As a group, schizophrenic patients show impaired sensitivity, but within the group this is least marked in relatively intact paranoid patients while severely disturbed non-paranoid patients show considerable deficit. The schizophrenic–normal difference in cutaneouss senitivity is greater when tested on the leg than on the hand or face. The authors suggested that the smaller innervation of the leg compared with the hand or face means that a smaller signal is transmitted from that source and consequently the results of this study parallel those of weight discrimination where deficit is shown in lifting light but not heavy weights.

Data from these studies appear to indicate inferior sensitivity to low intensity bodily sensations in schizophrenic patients while the data in the case of the distance sensations, audition and vision, although by no means definitive, suggest that patients are probably hypersensitive to weak stimulation.

Two Psychophysiological Investigations of Sensory Dysfunction

AUGMENTATION–REDUCTION

At the end of the third section the Pavlovian notion of "strength of the nervous system" was introduced and the analogy drawn between it and

E*

the more recent concept of "augmentation–reduction". The idea under-lying this concept is that there are individual differences in ability to modify the intensity of a perception: "reducers" decrease the effect of intensity of strong stimulation while "augmenters" show an increase in perception with increase in objective intensity of stimulation. The origi-nal measurements of this dimension of stimulus intensity modulation were made by Petrie (1960) using the kinaesthetic figural after-effect of Köhler and Dinnerstein (1947). This difficult and very subjective tech-nique has been replaced by the more satisfactory procedure of measure-ment of event related potentials (ERP) to stimuli ranging in intensity. Event related potentials are measured by the summation of epochs of EEG activity typically measured from a vertex electrode. The aspect of the waveform that reflects augmentation–reduction is (in the case of visual stimulation) the P_{100}–N_{140} component (P_{100} being the positive waveform with a latency of 100 milliseconds, and N_{140} the negative waveform with a latency of 140 ms). This component can be considered to be fairly early in cortical processing stages and not to reflect modula-tion of activity in sensory pathways.

The findings of studies using this technique are that acute schizo-phrenic patients show evidence of being "reducers" in contrast to normal subjects (or patients with bipolar affective disorders) who tend to show augmenting tendencies.

The question that needs to be asked in relation to the review in earlier sections is:

Is the ERP reducing found in the acute schizophrenic patient merely indicative of his disorganization at high stimulus intensity levels, or could it be a protective homeostatic mechanism providing control of sensory input? (Landau *et al.*, 1975)

Silverman *et al.* (1969), in a study comparing sensory thresholds and ERP augmentation–reduction, showed that reducers evidenced low sensory thresholds. Landau *et al.* (1975) provided evidence that those acute schizophrenic patients who reduced most when tested after three weeks in hospital tended to show the greatest recovery at 16 weeks. They suggested that reducing may be a back-up system that some schizophrenic patients are able to rely on for sensory overload protection when basic faults in the ascending reticular activating system appear. The existence of such fundamental breakdown has been suggested by Mirsky (1969) and Venables (1967). In relation to genetic theories of schizophrenia it is important to note that twin studies provide herit-ability estimates of the P_{100}–N_{140} component ranging from 0·52 to 0·68 (Buchsbaum, 1975).

DISTURBANCES IN SMOOTH PURSUIT EYE MOVEMENTS

In an earlier section defects in vestibular and proprioceptive function were described. Deficits in neuromuscular control were evident from the studies reviewed. The fine regulation of neuromuscular activity is particularly important in pursuit eye movements and it was to be expected that deficits in eye tracking might be found in schizophrenia. Holzman *et al.* (1973) reported a study in which they found that a significant number of schizophrenic patients, when following a swinging pendulum, showed patterns of smooth pursuit eye tracking that differed markedly from those shown by normals and by non-schizophrenic patients. Their technique involved the electrooculographic recording of eye position while following ten cycles of a swinging pendulum. Normal subjects produced patterns that showed smooth sinusoidal form. Schizophrenic patients, on the other hand, showed the imposition of fast saccadic movements on the smooth pursuit waveform and "velocity arrests" where tracking temporarily comes to a halt. In later studies Holzman *et al.* (1974, 1976) showed that eye tracking dysfunction is present in about 70% of schizophrenic subjects and about 45% of first degree relatives. They suggested that that eye tracking behaviour might be used as a genetic marker in studies of schizophrenic aetiology. However, studies by Shagass *et al.* (1974), while generally confirming the work of Holzman and his colleagues, suggest that poor eye tracking performance is not specific to schizophrenia, since it can be demonstrated in patients with diagnoses of affective psychosis. Holzman *et al.* (1974) provided data to suggest that thought disordered patients have poorer levels of eye tracking than those without thought disorder. If, as seems reasonable, thought disorder is not confined to particular sub-diagnostic categories of schizophrenia, then the results of Shagass *et al.* (1974), which show no difference in eye tracking in different sub-diagnostic groups of schizophrenic patients, are not inconsistent with the Holzman results.

Although the early results of Holzman are stated as "probably referable not only to motivational and attentional factors but also to oculomotor involvement" (Holzman *et al.*, 1973), evidence on the extent of involvement of attentional factors was absent until investigated by Shagass *et al.* (1976) and Holzman *et al.* (1976). These studies suggest that although tracking is improved under conditions which, by requiring the subjects to read numbers on the bob, demand attention to the pendulum target, the differences between patients and non-patients is not abolished by this procedure. These studies confirm work using different techniques, indicating impaired performance in tasks requiring neuromuscular integration. They also suggest that disturbances of attention interact with more basic defects in the production of poor performance. In the context of this chapter what is of interest is the association of poor performance with schizophrenic thought disorder. Also, in relation to data which will be reviewed later suggesting that aspects of thought disorder are found in the relatives of schizophrenic patients, the finding of poor eye tracking in relatives is suggestive.

Attention

The material quoted in the second section provides a background suggesting an impairment of attention in schizophrenia. Payne, in his work on overinclusive thinking in schizophrenia, suggested that a disorder of a primary attentional process underlies schizophrenic thought disorder: "this overinclusive thinking results from the breakdown of some central 'filter' mechanism (or 'set') which normally screens out irrelevant thoughts to allow the efficient processing of relevant data" (Payne and Caird, 1967). Payne is here talking about the screening out of irrelevant thoughts; the impairment of attention may, however, also be referred to activities earlier in the cognitive process. Venables (1964) stated that,

> the acute (and possibly the reactive and the paranoid) patient is chacterised by an inability to restrict the range of his attention so that he is flooded by sensory impressions from all quarters. Items of all kinds have equal importance and the meaningfulness of the external world tends to be lost. . . . The figure–ground relationship which allows a picture to convey information is destroyed equally by making the picture nearly all figure or nearly all ground.

A similar view is expressed by Lehmann (1966) who suggests that schizophrenics have a "primary, possibly constitutional susceptibility to be subject to the impact of a higher number of discrete sensory stimuli per time unit of experience than most other pathological and non-pathological individuals". Two points particularly arise from this statement of Lehmann's. The first, in relation to "non-pathological individuals", he takes up himself:

> If he is capable of coping with this greater than average influx of discrete sensory stimuli he might perform at a better than average level, but when the extraordinary sensitivity of his receptive apparatus is not matched by an equally extraordinary performance of his central processing apparatus than his integration breaks down and he may become psychotic.

In this instance Lehmann is referring (in the case of persons who are

able to cope with the wide range of sensory input) to creative individuals
—who, according to Dellas and Gaier (1970), "deployed their attention
more widely, were more aware and receptive and retained more prior to
stimulus experience in usable form, tending not to screen out the
irrelevant". Hasenfus and Magaro (1976) have recently reviewed the
relationship between creativity and schizophrenia. Dykes and McGhie
(1976) have provided experimental data to show that acute schizophrenic patients respond to certain tests in a similar way to highly
creative people, and quite differently from non-creative normals.

The second interesting idea put forward by Lehmann is that an inability to filter signals from the environment may be constitutional. One
possible model for this has been suggested by Venables (1973, 1975).
The basis for this model can be directly illustrated from a statement by
Douglas (1967) in which he says, "The amygdaloid system makes stimuli
more figural while the hippocampal system converts figure into ground."
This statement should be placed alongside that already quoted from
Venables (1964) suggesting a disturbance of attentional process by the
distortion of figure–ground relationships.

Other data are relevant to a hypothetical link between attentional
dysfunction and limbic system involvement. Pribram and his colleagues
(Bagshaw et al., 1965; Kimble et al., 1965) have shown that lesions of the
amygdala produce a state of electrodermal non-responsivity while lesions
of the hippocampus, on the contrary, produce a state of hyper-respon-
sivity with lack of habituation. Animals with this latter lesion also show
the fast recovery of the skin conductance response which appears typical
of hyper-responding adult schizophrenics (e.g. Gruzelier and Venables,
1972) and of children in the premorbid state who will later show
schizophrenic breakdown with a predominance of Schneider's first rank
symptoms (Mednick et al., 1977). In the fourth section the findings of
Gruzelier and Venables (1972) were described showing that a large
proportion of the adult schizophrenic population in hospital fell either
into non-responding or responding-non-habituating classes and consequently showed very similar electrodermal activity to monkeys with
lesions of the amygdala or hippocampus. Thus the sort of physiological
disturbance which has been suggested on the basis of theoretical notions
to underlie schizophrenic attentional disturbance can be shown to produce almost identical distortions of electrodermal responding in man
and animals. It should also be noted that in patients exhibiting hyper-
responsivity (i.e. a condition of orientation with impaired habituation)
this is accompanied by concomitant high levels of arousal indicated by
electrodermal activity, heart rate, systolic blood pressure and finger

temperature, while non-responsivity is accompanied by low levels of these same variables. Thus there is a tendency for patients to occupy extreme points on dimensions of arousal level and arousability.

Although it appears paradoxical to suggest that opposite extremes of physiological functioning can produce a similar behavioural abnormality, both extremes may have the effect that sensory input from the environment is viewed as all figure or all ground. Either way, the meaningfulness of the external world would become distorted.

One of the results of amygdaloid lesions is the development of symptoms of the Kluver-Bucy (1939) syndrome. One symptom which is also produced by more restricted amydalectomy (Goddard, 1964) is that of continuous behavioural orienting, a tendency to behave as though "forced" to react to objects, events and changes in the environmental stimuli (Kluver and Bucy, 1939). Koepke and Pribram (1966) have suggested that this continuous behavioural orientation, and also the lack of autonomic orientation seen in amygdalectomized monkeys results from amygdalectomy eliminating the process whereby a sensory impression is registered and retained in a neural modelling system (Sokolov, 1963). Stimuli are thus always seen as new and worthy of behavioural orientation. Lack of electrodermal activity in this instance is taken to be an indicator of lack of registration. On the other hand, the other extreme of limbic imbalance—hippocampectomy—produces an organism incapable of exercising adequately the hippocampal function known as "gating", the function of the hippocampus is postulated, i.e. the exclusion of patterns of stimuli from attention through a process of efferent control of sensory reception (Douglas and Pribram, 1966).

Thus both forms of imbalance have a similar behavioural effect at a gross level, although they may possibly be identified by particular experimental procedures.

An influential model for research on attentional processes in schizophrenia has been that of Broen (1968). This model uses the concept, derived from learning theory, of a lowered "reaction potential ceiling" (Broen and Storms, 1961) in schizophrenia. When more than one tendency to respond is evoked in a given situation, the probability of the dominant response is normally an increasing function of the differences in response strengths of dominant and competing responses. However, if there is a maximum value which response strengths may reach (the reaction potential ceiling), then as all responses, both dominant and competing, increase in strength they will be limited by this ceiling and their differences will decrease and hence the probability of the dominant response occurring will decrease.

This model is a parallel in terms of *response* selection to that discussed earlier in this section based on notions of stimulus selection.

The maintenance of "figure" in response selection is concerned with the maintenance of the hierarchy of responsivity, in which the dominant response has a markedly higher value than its competitors. This hierarchy may be distorted either because the strengths of all responses are more or less similar due to low levels of drive (an equivalent of all stimuli becoming ground), or in states of high arousal where all responses are near to maximum (an equivalent of all stimuli becoming figure). If this maximum level is lowered, owing to a lowered response ceiling as postulated by Broen to occur in schizophrenia, then this distortion of normal hierarchy is more readily achieved.

Although there are close parallels between "stimulus filtering" and "response selection" theories of attention/processing dysfunction in schizophrenia, they are in many ways competing models. However, it should perhaps be borne in mind that most theories of stimulus filtering, or control of stimulus input, contain notions of the *efferent* control of receptors, thus perhaps it is no longer wise to insist on the maintenance of clear stimulus–response distinctions in this area.

The most complete review of the present "state of the art" in sorting out response determined and stimulus determined models of schizophrenic attention defect is given by Helmsley (1975). His analysis is based on Broadbent's views (1970, 1971) on the distinction between stimulus and response factors determining systematic selection of information. Selection is necessary because of the existence of a limited capacity channel for dealing with information. Filtering of the stimulus input is a probabilistic function; the filter does not act in an all or none fashion but contains biases, so that some sources are attentuated while others receive maximum weight. The result of the filtering process, the "evidence", is linked to "category states" by further biasing rules. These rules are similar to those of response bias and the response selection process is termed "pigeon-holing". Pigeon-holing, or response selection, is required, for instance, in naming the letters rather than the numbers in a display containing both. Clearly, early filtering cannot occur, since the information has to be analysed to determine whether a letter or a number is present before further selection takes place.

At the moment, as Helmsley states, no firm conclusion can be drawn as to whether a response or stimulus selection model is the correct one to adopt an explanatory feature for schizophrenic dysfunction—in part because it is not inconceivable that both systems may show deficits, and in part because most work on attention in schizophrenia has not been designed to attempt to draw a clear distinction between stimulus and response models.

Other theories of attentional dysfunction in schizophrenia need, however, to be considered. On the whole, these are not discrepant with what has been said so far but involve elaborations of the processes involved.

Silverman (1964, 1967) describes three factors in attentional processing: these are (i) stimulus intensity control, (ii) scanning control, and (iii) sensory input processing—ideational gating. The first of these has already been discussed on p. 125 and is the process otherwise called "augmentation–reduction" which is concerned with the extent to which the intensity parameters of external stimuli are maintained within the organism. It is discussed by Silverman as an "intensiveness" dimension. The second "scanning control", is more of an "extensiveness" dimension. Although not specifically relating this scanning control to eye movements, Silverman draws experimental support largely from data on eye movements, which suggest that non-paranoid schizophrenic patients scan their environment less than normal while the opposite is true of paranoid patients.

The third dimension introduced by Silverman, "sensory input processing—ideational gating", has already been dealt with in part. The notion is that "non-paranoid and poor-premorbid" schizophrenic patients attend more than is normal to the sensory attributes of perceptual-ideational inputs and less than is normal to the connotative attributes (Silverman, 1967). The first part of this statement is clearly akin to what has been said earlier about the schizophrenic patients' apparent inability to filter stimuli. The second part, however, is somewhat controversial and relies on rather sparse data. It is, for instance, particularly concerned with the schizophrenic patients' apparent lack of ability to select input on the basis of its affective qualities. Thus Silverman quotes unpublished data to the effect that heart rate deceleration, the orienting response usually given to low intensity light and sound stimuli, occurred in patients with "process" schizophrenia when shown pictures suggesting hostility and dependency. Akin to these data are those from Lobstein (1974), indicating a tendency for chronic non-paranoid schizophrenic patients to show an orienting type heart rate deceleration to intense sounds that elicited a defensive response in normals.

Venables (1964) reviewing data available at that time suggested that one defensive type of attentional stance which might be adopted by chronic schizophrenic patients was that of narrowing of attention. Data from normal subjects, e.g. Easterbrook (1959), suggested that as arousal increased so attention was narrowed to more central aspects of stimulus displays. Subsequent work by Hockey (1970a,b) showed that increased arousal narrowed attention to those items in a stimulus ensemble that had the highest probability of occurrence.

Data from Venables and Wing (1962) showed that those chronic schizophrenic patients who are the most withdrawn also have the highest level of arousal. This would suggest that such patients would also have the most narrowed range of attention. McGhie *et al.* (1965) provide data confirming earlier work (Chapman and McGhie, 1962) which suggested that chronic schizophrenic patients are abnormally distractible, but this seems to contradict the notion that their attention is narrowed.

Broen (1966, 1968), however, suggested a way of reconciling these apparently disparate findings. He suggested that the chronic patient narrows his range of *observation* and thus restricts the number of stimuli actually received. However within the stimuli that are actually observed the range of attention is broad. In stimulus filtering model terms, filtering is deficient; and in response selection terms, the response hierarchy is flat. The idea of a narrowed range of observation is directly equivalent to Silverman's notion of a restricted range of scanning in chronic non-paranoid patients and thus the ideas are initially supportive.

A further variation on model building in this area is that of Yates (1966). Both McGhie and his colleagues (e.g. McGhie, 1970), and Yates, draw on Broadbent's earlier (1958) theory of a limited single channel processor to explain results. If we conceive of a single channel capable of processing only a limited amount of information per unit of time, McGhie suggests that schizophrenic deficit lies in the inability to screen out relevant from irrelevant information with the result that the single channel easily becomes overloaded. Yates' theory differs from McGhie's by suggesting that the "abnormally slow rate at which information in the primary channel is processed" is at the heart of schizophrenic deficit. Because of the slow rate of processing, information has to be diverted to a short-term memory store that can retain information only for a limited time and hence information is lost.

Thus several explanations of deficits in schizophrenic attentional and processing systems have been put forward. At the moment the data do not enable clear distinctions to be drawn between the claims of the different models.

Thought Disorder

One of the aspects of disordered thinking in schizophrenia which has received most attention is that of "overinclusiveness".

Although originally formulated by Bleuler (1911), work on this concept probably received greatest impetus from Cameron (e.g. 1938) who defined the disorder as "the inability to conserve conceptual boundaries with the result that there is an incorporation of irrelevant ideas". The parallel of this notion to the attention defects, shown by the breakdown of a hypothesized filter system, has already been discussed in the previous section where Payne's work was described.

One test used by Payne (e.g. 1962) to measure overinclusiveness is the object classification test originally introduced by Goldstein and Scheerer (1941) as a measure of "concreteness" of thinking. This test involves sorting twelve small objects (four triangles, four circles and four squares), which vary in weight, colour, thickness and type of material. The patient is asked to sort the objects in as many ways as he can. Whereas normal subjects tend to sort the objects into the ten intended categories, schizophrenic patients make use of more unusual sorting schemes, using, for example, groupings based on scratches on the objects or shadows cast by them.

Another test derived from Goldstein and Scheerer (1941), used by Payne and his colleagues and also by Lovibond (1954), is the object sorting test. One of a series of objects is selected by the experimenter and the patient is asked to pick, from a set of objects before him, all those that might be grouped with the selected object. The number of objects so selected by schizophrenic patients tends to be greater than that selected by normals.

Another type of material used to examine overinclusion is the card sorting test of Chapman (1958). This test requires subjects to sort cards bearing the names of common objects, according to guide cards which illustrate the correct concept, an associated but inappropriate concept, and an irrelevant concept.

Broen (1968) differentiates the processes involved in such overinclusion tests along the lines suggested in the previous section, namely that one appears to involve response selection while the other emphasizes the stimulus filtering aspect of the process.

Harrow et al. (1972) also differentiate the processes involved and label Payne's indices those of "behavioural overinclusion". Also using the object sorting test, they derived a filter measure of "conceptual overinclusion", and they also distinguish "stimulus overinclusion" (which is the deficit in input filtering outlined in the previous section).

While it was originally held that overinclusion was a feature of all schizophrenic patients, later work has shown that this is a feature of patients in the acute phase and that chronic schizophrenic patients "are no more overinclusive than normals" (Payne, 1962).

Other work, e.g. Rosman *et al.* (1964) and McConaghy and Clancy (1968), has shown that overinclusive (or allusive) thinking is shown among parents of schizophrenic patients, but that it is also found in a group of "normal" university students and their parents. In following up this work Harrow and Quinlan (1977) suggested that "disordered thinking fits along a continuum of normal thinking and thought disorders are not a discrete entity standing apart from other aspects of thinking". In this work Harrow and Quinlan used the object sorting test and the Rohrschach Test. They discuss whether the disordered thinking shown by these tests is the same as "thought disorder" used as a psychiatric symptom and suggest that the two usages of the term are similar. If they are correct, then clearly some ideas about thought disorder as a symptom which differentiates schizophrenic patients from normal persons need to be reconsidered.

Schizophrenic Language

In considering the relationship of language and thought, Maher (1972) uses the analogy of a typist typing from a script. Inaccuracies in the final copy may be due to faulty typing or to a faulty script. In the case of schizophrenic language, Maher suggests that the patient might be correctly reporting disordered thoughts, but equally might be incorrectly reporting undisturbed thoughts.

Pavy (1968) has pointed out that most work on schizophrenic language has been carried out prior to or without regard to recent work in linguistics. Thus the work on word association, and to a lesser extent that on the information content and communicability of schizophrenic speech, is probably of more relevance to other aspects of cognitive performance than to speech itself.

Schizophrenic patients give higher numbers of uncommon associations to word association tests, but Pavy (1968) suggests that while schizophrenic responses are different from normal,

no consistent pattern of response has been established for the schizophrenic population. These findings are frequently interpreted in terms of a deficit of attention which affects the discrimination of the stimulus and permits the intrusion of irrelevant stimuli.

Bull and Venables (1974) have shown that schizophrenic patients are much more affected than normals in their ability to report the content of passages of speech, which have been altered by cutting out the high frequency sounds to make them less understandable. Thus Pavy's suggestion of difficulties of discrimination seem appropriate.

Several studies have been carried out to investigate the role of contextual constraints and speech perception in schizophrenia. The general outcome appears to be that schizophrenic patients appear less constrained by the overall context of a passage of speech and more influenced by individual words or sections. Using the "cloze" procedure in which, for instance, every fifth word in a passage is deleted and the subjects have to guess the missing words schizophrenic patients tend to be able to guess fewer words than normals. Errors in such a procedure were interpreted by Williams (1966) as indicating that schizophrenic patients associate to the single preceding word rather than to the context of the sentence.

This interpretation is in line with the "immediacy" hypothesis of Salzinger *et al.* (1970) stated as the tendency for schizophrenic behaviour to be controlled by those stimuli that are most immediate in the environment. It is also in accord with the earlier notions of Shakow (1962), whose concept of "segmental set" suggests that schizophrenic patients are unable to maintain contextual set over sufficiently long periods to be able to be influenced by events outside the immediate temporal environment.

While there is a lot of evidence suggesting semantic disturbance in schizophrenia there is little evidence for a deterioration of the structure of language. However, the probes into the latter area have probably not been sufficiently penetrating for firm statements to be made.

Summary

In the introduction it was suggested that deficits in the more complex cognitive processes were probably due to disturbances of attention and perception rather than of thought itself. The data reviewed here support that view. However, in spite of a very considerable body of research, it is still not possible to reach definite conclusions concerning the nature of schizophrenic thought and speech disorders. Such advance as there has been, has consisted in a refinement of the early clinical descriptions (see Chapter 1 and the second section of this chapter), and in methods of quantification.

This being so, research effort in future should perhaps be concentrated more on physiological abnormalities, which are really "primary", rather than on further explanations of cognitive phenomena.

Acknowledgements

This paper was prepared while in receipt of Grant No. G.974/375C from the Medical Research Council, Grant No. MH27777 from the US Public Health Service and Grant No. 6883/I5 from the Wellcome Trust.

6 | Social and Psychological Causes of the Acute Attack

Julian Leff

The work discussed in Chapter 3 has suggested that the contribution of genes to the eventual development of "schizophrenia"* is approximately 50%. Whatever the size of the proportion, it is clear that environmental factors play a substantial part in aetiology. Some of these, as we have seen, are likely to be somatic in nature. Others are psychological or social. In this chapter, we shall be concerned principally with claims that features of the social environment predispose towards a later attack of schizophrenia or precipitate an acute breakdown. A great deal of work, both theoretical and experimental, has accumulated. The theoretical work has been largely based on clinical insights derived from experience of therapy with the families of schizophrenic patients. Part of the experimental work has been carried out in order to test the major theories and part has represented the endeavours of individual research workers following their own hunches. On the whole, the important theories have been inadequately tested. Much of the experimental work has not stemmed from a coherent line of argument and has employed idiosyncratic rather than replicable methods.

We will consider here the major theories in the field—those of Bateson, Lidz, Wynne and Singer, and Laing; the work that has been undertaken to test these theories; and other studies which throw light on family influences on the aetiology of schizophrenia.

* See p. viii.

Major Theories of the Family as a Cause of Schizophrenia

One of the authors who largely commented on this problem was Hajdu-Gaines (1940) who reported data from the psychoanalysis of four female schizophrenic patients. He found a common combination of "cold, rigorous, sadistically aggressive" mother and "soft, indifferent, passive" father. He related the patients' schizophrenic illnesses to the lack of what he considered to be "real parents" in their childhood. This view was taken further by Fromm-Reichman (1948) who coined the term "schizophrenogenic mother". The phrase caught on and has become part of the well-worn currency of psychiatric parlance, despite its imprecision. The criticism of vagueness cannot however be levelled at the double-bind theory of Gregory Bateson.

BATESON'S DOUBLE-BIND THEORY

This theory is concerned with ambiguity of communication between family members and can be stated simply in the form of logical propositions. Bateson and his colleagues (Bateson *et al.*, 1956; Haley, 1959a,b, 1960; Weakland, 1960; Watzlawick *et al.*, 1968) have specified five necessary ingredients of a double-bind situation:

    (1) two or more persons involved;

    (2) a repeated experience;

    (3) a primary negative injunction;

    (4) a secondary injunction conflicting with the first at a more abstract level, and like the first enforced by punishment or signals which threaten survival;

    (5) a tertiary negative injunction prohibiting the victim from escaping from the situation.

In addition the contradictory nature of the commands is denied and the child is not allowed to point out the contradiction. An example should make it easier to recognize double-bind situations: the parent says to the child, "You have the choice of doing A or B. You must not do A. You must not do B. You must make a choice between the two. If you make the wrong choice you will be punished."

Haley (1959b) makes a distinction between contradictions which occur within the same level of discourse (for example, the mother tells the child he may go out but at the same time forbids it) and those which are incongruent at different levels. Examples of the latter are contradictions occurring between the verbal message and what is communicated by the tone of voice or by gesture. Contradictions can emanate from one individual or may develop between individuals with respect to a third person who is the object of the communication. The mother is usually seen as the key figure in these kinds of families. She sets the pattern of communication by imposing the rules, but at the same time further confuses the issue by denying her part in the rule-making.

Central to this theory of the aetiology of schizophrenia is a re-definition of the nature of schizophrenia as a specific pattern of communication rather than an illness of the mind (Watzlawick *et al.*, 1968). The patient is visualized as caught in an intolerable situation from which the only escape is to make ambiguous or meaningless responses in order to prevent the other person from understanding, and administering punishment. These obscure responses, then, constitute the symptoms of schizophrenia.

Evidence for Bateson's Theory

Despite the clear description of the double-bind situation, it is apparently not at all easy to identify such situations in everyday life. Ringuette and Kennedy (1966) used letters written by parents to their children in hospital in order to assess the ability of observers to recognize double-bind statements. Twenty of the letters were from the parents of schizophrenic patients and twenty from the parents of non-schizophrenic residents in a state hospital. A further twenty normal volunteers were asked to write letters as if to their children in a state hospital. The letters were assessed by five groups of judges who were unaware to which groups the writers belonged. The assessors comprised a group of experts on the double-bind concept, a group of first year psychiatric residents trained in the double-bind, experienced psychiatrists trained in the double-bind, untrained psychiatrists, and naïve lay people. The inter-rater agreement between the judges was very low, reaching only 0·19 in the group of experts, which included Bateson, Watzlawick and other pioneers of the double-bind hypothesis. Apart from the poor agreement between the experts on what constitutes a double-bind communication, none of the groups of judges was able to distinguish between the parents of schizophrenics and non-schizophrenics on the basis of the letters. These findings constitute a serious blow to the double-bind hypothesis, though this is somewhat weakened by the argument that written communication is very different from speech, and that a letter involves an emotional distancing between the writer and reader that might tone down or even eliminate double-bind type of statements.

A study that investigated the presence of communication problems in verbal interaction was that by Haley (1968). He set groups of parents the task of giving instructions over a microphone to groups of children.* The parental pair had to instruct their child to select from 24 Japanese playing cards the eight that the parents had in front of them and to arrange them in the same order. In the first part of the experiment groups of parents of normal children, of schizophrenic children, and of children with neurosis or behaviour disturbance, instructed their own children in the task. The normal and neurotic children did equally well, placing over 80% of the cards correctly. The schizophrenic children managed only a 45% accuracy, which is significantly lower than the other two groups. In the next part of the experiment the children were allowed to talk back to the parents to clarify the instructions. All groups improved in their accuracy, but the schizophrenic group improved most, because there was more room for improvement. These findings could be interpreted as being due to confused instructions from the parents of the schizophrenic children, difficulties on the part of the schizophrenic children in understanding their parents, or a combination of the two. Haley investigated this by getting the parents of normals and the parents of schizophrenic children to instruct normal children who were strangers to them. The children responded equally well to both groups of parents, suggesting that the main problem affecting communication in the families of schizophrenics lies in the patients rather than the parents. This is not entirely proven because Haley did not investigate the fourth logical combination, namely schizophrenic children responding to normal parents. In the absence of this experiment, the possibility cannot be ruled out that there is an interactional effect between schizophrenic children and their parents. It is conceivable that parents of schizophrenic children emit only double-bind messages in the heightened emotional interaction with their own children. In the more neutral interaction with unfamiliar children, their communication may appear normal.

Several other investigations have tested limited aspects of the double-bind hypothesis, but Haley's study is the most valid test of the theory and cannot be said to support it. Taking the relevant studies as a whole, it can be concluded that not only are double-bind messages difficult to recognize even for experts, but that they are not confined to the parents of schizophrenic patients.

---

* The term "child" here defines the relationship and not the age. The "children" in Haley's study were all adolescent or adult.

LIDZ'S THEORY

Theodore Lidz and his colleagues at Yale made an intensive study of the families of 17 schizophrenic patients. Fourteen of the families belonged to social classes 1 and 2 and were able to afford in-patient psycho-analytic treatment for the sick member extending over several years. The other three families were lower middle class and in these cases the patients were not hospitalized. Not only is there a strong selective bias operating but no control group was studied. A team of psychiatrists, social workers and others interviewed the family members repeatedly over months or years and also obtained information from people outside the family. From their psychoanalytically oriented investigations, these workers identified two types of family structure which they considered to be causal in the emergence of schizophrenia. One type is called "marital skew", in which one parent yields to the abnormalities and eccentricities of the other, which then dominate the family, so that no conflict is apparent (Lidz et al., 1957). Skewed relationships were found to predominate among the parents of male patients. In such families the mother tended to be the dominant figure, while the father was passive and provided a poor male model for the children. These mothers turned to their sons for the emotional satisfaction the husbands were unable to provide. The other type is called "marital schism" and refers to mar-riages characterized by conflict between the partners, whose personality problems lead them to pursue their own needs while ignoring each other's. The schismatic family is one of divided loyalties, in which each parent competes for the childrens' support and affection in order to en-list allies in the battle with the other parent. Lidz found this type of family to be associated with schizophrenia in the female child.

In both kinds of families the usual distinctions between the genera-tions are not observed, the normal parental cooperation does not occur, and family members act outside their usual roles. This is postulated to arouse anxiety about incestuous feelings and behaviour. As with the double-bind hypothesis, Lidz and his group reformulate schizophrenia, in this instance as learned inappropriate behaviour. The behaviour is seen as a learned response to the fact that the parents behave inappro-priately for their sex and age with respect to each other and to the child. In this distorted family milieu, facts are being altered constantly to suit emotionally determined needs. Lidz's formulation can be viewed as a mixture of role theory and communication theory with the emphasis on the former.

Evidence for Lidz's Theory

The small number of families studied by Lidz and his group and the absence of matched controls render it impossible to test his theory scientifically on his own data. However, scientific studies involving the testing of aspects of Lidz's theory have been conducted. Ferreira and Winter carried out a series of careful studies using social interaction techniques to compare triadic interactions in families with a schizophrenic member with interactions in other families (Ferreira, 1963; Ferreira and Winter, 1965; Ferreira *et al.*, 1966; Winter and Ferreira, 1967). They studied families with a schizophrenic offspring, families with normal offspring, and families in which one member, usually the offspring, had a non-schizophrenic psychiatric condition. They found that the amount of agreement on a questionnaire between mother, father and offspring was significantly less in families containing someone with a psychiatric disorder than in the other families. Agreement was also significantly lower in families containing a schizophrenic member than in the other families with a member with some other psychiatric condition. The father's choice of an answer was found to predominate over the mother's, and the mother's choice over the child's, in all families studied. This is evidence against Lidz's theory of abnormal dominance patterns in the families with a schizophrenic member. In another study involving a different task, the agreement between family members was greater in the "normal" families, but was no worse in families containing a schizophrenic member than in the other two groups. Furthermore there was no better agreement between mother and child than between father and child. This finding goes against theories of mother–child collusion as a characteristic feature of families of schizophrenics.

Another excellent study was designed by Sharan (1965) to test some of Lidz's hypotheses. He studied 12 families with a schizophrenic son and 12 with a schizophrenic daughter, each group of families containing six healthy siblings of the same sex and six of the opposite sex to the schizophrenic member. Each family member completed a questionnaire, following which the parents formed triads with the ill child and then with the healthy child and re-did the questionnaire, using an alternative form on each occasion. The sessions were tape-recorded and scored for "dominance" according to which parent's individual answer most often became the family group decision. "Support" was assessed by comparing the number of supportive and non-supportive remarks directed by one member towards another.

Sharan tested Lidz's claim (**Lidz** *et al.*, 1957, 1958) that the chronic conflict existing in the families with a schizophrenic member interferes with their solving of problems. If this were true and has bearing on why one sibling has schizophrenia and not the other, then the parents should be less supportive of the patient than of a well sibling. He found no consistent differences between parental support of patients compared with siblings.

He also tested the concepts of role-reversal and breakdown of the sex generation boundaries that are central to Lidz's theory. It follows from Lidz's formulation that the patient and the dominant parent should be of the opposite sex. Sharan found no evidence for this, as the father's individual response appeared as the group response more often than the mother's regardless of the sex of the child or whether the patient or the well sibling was present. It also follows that the opposite-sexed parent should have a more mutually supportive relationship with the patient than the same-sexed parent. This received equivocal confirmation: the fathers of female patients were more supportive than the mothers, as predicted, and were also more supportive than the fathers of male patients. Unfortunately, no comparison was made to ascertain whether the fathers of female patients treated the well sibling with less support, as full confirmation of the hypothesis would require.

In conclusion, these studies, and others with less scientific rigour, gave no support to predictions derived from Lidz's theory. Where abnormalities of the kind described by Lidz have been identified in the families of schizophrenic patients, identical abnormalities have also appeared in control groups of families containing a member suffering from some other, or no psychiatric condition. Hence what Lidz and his group have derived from their uncontrolled in-depth investigation of a handful of families is not specific to schizophrenia.

WYNNE'S THEORY

Wynne and his colleagues (1958) studied intensively four families with a schizophrenic member, all being admitted to an in-patient unit. They noticed that there was a strong investment by family members in maintaining the idea or feeling of mutuality—the reciprocal fulfilment of expectations—even though the observers judged mutuality to be, in fact, absent. Wynne coined the term "pseudomutuality" for this situation, in which despite surface appearances, communication is disjointed and fragmented, and irrational shifts in the focus of attention prevent real continuity of interaction. Wynne places strong emphasis on the ability of the members of normal families to share a common focus of attention. He describes the disordered communication of the parents of schizophrenics as lying along a bipolar continuum with amorphous thinking at one end and disjointed thinking at the other. These two styles of communication, amorphous and fragmented, are assumed to be characteristic of the family as a whole, not just of one parent. They are seen as influencing the cognitive development of the offspring, so that the different varieties of schizophrenic thought disorder directly reflect the amorphous-fragmented dimension of family communication.

Underlying these failures to communicate are feelings of meaninglessness, pointlessness, and emptiness, and these feelings are transmitted to the offspring. Within these families role structures are either rigid and stereotyped or loosely and ambiguously structured. Family members are expected to stick firmly to their roles so that the developing child experiences no sense of his own identity apart from his predetermined role. The child brought up in such a family reaches a crisis at adolescence when he has to try to fit in to the wider world, using the unrealistic patterns of thought he has learned in his family. It can be seen that, like Lidz, Wynne uses a mixture of role theory and communication theory, but whereas Lidz's emphasis is on role, Wynne's is on communication.

Evidence for Wynne's Theory

Wynne and Singer went to great trouble to develop a test of the communication aspect of their theory. They adapted the standard Rorschach test for this purpose, using it not to explore the subject's fantasies but to generate a sample of speech. From the study of transcripts of the speech of parents of schizophrenics, they developed in an empirical way a number of categories of deviant communication. Subsequently Singer and Wynne (1966a) published a detailed manual which sets out 41 categories of communication defects and deviances for scoring transcripts from verbatim or recorded sessions of Rorschach testing. Examples of the categories used are "Inconsistent References", "Nihilistic Remarks", and "Words or Phrases Used Oddly". Some of the categories are less well defined than others resulting in a degree of overlap between certain categories. Each example of deviant communication found in a transcript is identified, some of them scoring for more than one category. The scores are added up giving a total Deviance Score for each subject. Wynne and Singer tested a large number of parents with this technique and found they were able to discriminate very reliably between the three groups of parents: those of schizophrenic adults, neurotic adults, and adults with no psychiatric disorder (Singer and Wynne, 1966b). Of the parental pairs, 78% were correctly classified according to the diagnostic group of their offspring (Wynne, 1967). Comparing parents by sex, the fathers of schizophrenics offspring had significantly higher scores than the fathers of neurotic or normal off-spring, but the mothers did not differ significantly from mothers with neurotic offspring. The scores of neurotic individuals as a group always fell between the scores of schizophrenics and normals. It is curious that it was possible to distinguish the parents of neurotics from the parents of normal offspring using a test that was designed to pick up features associated with schizophrenia. However, putting this objection to one side, the results stand out from the whole body of work on the parents of schizophrenics as being remarkable.

For this reason Hirsch and Leff (1971, 1975) attempted to replicate these findings using samples of English patients suffering from schizo-phrenia and neurotic conditions. They were able to reproduce the scor-ing procedure reliably and did in fact find that the Deviance Scores of the parents of schizophrenic adults were significantly higher than those of the parents of neurotic adults. As with one of Wynne and Singer's main samples (Singer and Wynne, 1966b) it was the *fathers* of schizo-phrenic and neurotic subjects who had significantly different scores, and not the mothers. However, the overlap in Deviance Scores between the two English groups was much more extensive than in the American samples: 40% of the parents of schizophrenic offspring scored below the median and 40% of the parents of neurotic offspring scored above the median. Hirsch and Leff explained their much less impressive results on the basis of American–British differences in the diagnosis of schizophrenia (see Chapter 1), and of differences in the methods of collecting the samples. Whereas the English samples represented a con-secutive series of admissions fulfilling the criteria for the study, Wynne and Singer's families were referred to them from a wide area because of their known interest in deviant communication. Hence these families were probably selected because they were already identified as showing relevant types of problem.

A further methodological criticism has been levelled at Wynne and Singer's work. Hirsch and Leff argued that it was possible that the more subjects spoke, the more communication deviances they were likely to produce. Hence differences in Deviance Score might merely reflect differences in verbosity. They examined this possibility by counting the number of words spoken by their subjects. They found a high correlation between verbosity and Deviance Score, confirming their supposition. The mothers of their patients were equally verbose, but fathers with schizophrenic offspring spoke significantly more than the fathers of neurotic offspring. When this difference in verbosity was allowed for statistically, the significant difference between the fathers' Deviance Scores disappeared. Thus it appears that a complicated method of scoring peculiar communication may in effect be achieving no more than a simple count of the number of words spoken. The excessive verbosity of the fathers of schizophrenic adults still remains to be explained, but it is likely to represent a much less specific characteristic than Wynne and Singer's theory of deviant communication leads us to expect.

LAING'S THEORY

In his first book, Ronald Laing (1960) describes people of schizoid personality perceptively and in great detail and admits of no clear dividing line between schizoid personality and schizophrenia. Two assumptions are derived from this; that any schizoid person can become schizophrenic given a certain degree of stress, and that an understanding of the schizoid personality can be used to explain the speech and behaviour of people with schizophrenia. Laing contends that the content of psychotic experience should not be dismissed as irrational and that "delusions contain existential truth".

Although Laing and Esterson (1964) emphasize that schizophrenia should not be viewed as an illness, they concentrate on people who clearly have experienced the central syndromes. They do not consider the individual schizophrenic patient as manifesting symptoms in isolation; the whole family, or even society at large, is sick. The pressures of a sick society are exerted through the family, one of its prime institutions, and result in one family member being selected to bear its burdens. Siegler et al. (1969) have attempted to dissect out the models of schizophrenia that Laing employs in his writings. They describe the above formulation as a "conspiratorial" model in which schizophrenia is conceptualized as a label pinned to certain individuals as a consequence of a social process. This process involves the rejection by society of the experience of some of its members and the categorization of this experience as schizophrenia. As part of this view, the psychiatrist is seen as one of society's agents of control. In contrast to this sociological model, Laing also employs a "psycho-analytic" model, the essential features being that the source of the schizophrenic individuals' difficulties lies in his disturbed family relationships, and that treatment should consist of a special kind of corrective relationship between two people, patient and therapist. Siegler et al. identify a third, "psychedelic" model. From this point of view the schizophrenic person is seen as struggling to achieve autonomy in the face of parental demands that he behave according to their wishes. He only achieves some measure of autonomy by becoming "ill". Schizophrenia is then "a natural way of healing our appalling state of alienation called normality". As such, it is valued as a therapeutic experience through which the patient needs to be guided. Medical treatment of schizophrenia, aimed at cutting short episodes of symptoms, is therefore anti-therapeutic.

From the mixture of existential philosophy, clinical insights and mutually contradictory models one finds in Laing's writings, a number of testable hypotheses can be derived. However, no scientific studies designed to validate Laing's theory have yet been published.

Overview of Family Theories

We are now in a position to make some general comments about tests of the major theories concerning the role of the family in the aetiology of schizophrenia. Not all the following points apply to each theory.

(1) Theories are formulated at a high level of complexity, and are intended to be complete explanations of the origin of schizophrenia. As a result it is difficult to derive predictions from them that are easily testable at a practical level. Where testable statements have been extracted from the theoretical formulations, it has usually been the task of workers other than the original theorists.

(2) The theories fail to explain why the patient falls ill and a sibling remains well under similarly adverse conditions.

(3) The various formulations of the schizophrenic process put forward as part of these theories correspond in many ways to the theorists' different descriptions of patterns of family structure and interaction. In other words, it appears as if the theorists' views of schizophrenia have been determined by their theories of family pathology, rather than vice versa.

(4) The experimental work suffers from a lack of data on normal families, and on the families of people with psychiatric conditions other than schizophrenia.

(5) Studies have often omitted the precaution of blind interviewing. Interviewers and raters should be ignorant of the offspring's diagnosis in any comparison between families containing schizophrenic and non-schizophrenic members.

(6) Comparison between studies is hampered by the lack of agreed

F

definitions of terms such as "role" and "dominance". Each investigator
starts from scratch in devising measures of these fundamental terms,
with the result that no two investigators ever seem to measure the same
aspects of family interaction.

(7) The vast majority of studies are cross-sectional; that is they involve studying the family at a point in time after the patient has
developed schizophrenia. This has a number of important implications.
First, it faces the experimenter with the problem of reconstructing the
past. He is interested in such things as the early mother–child relationship but it is difficult even to get an accurate dating from parents of
observable events such as the child's milestones of development. It is
vastly more difficult to reconstruct an emotional atmosphere. The
attempt to remember the past is affected by the fact that a child has
contracted a serious illness. This may impel the parents to exaggerate
trivial details in the hope of establishing a cause. Alternatively a guilty
sense of responsibility for the child's condition, which is very common,
may lead the parents to normalize their account of the past. Either way
such accounts will tend to suffer from retrospective falsification. This
problem can be avoided by concentrating entirely on current attitudes
and behaviour, as indeed most of the research on families with a schizophrenic member has done. But this involves the research worker in
another dilemma; that of cause and effect. Even if the investigator can
demonstrate convincingly that parents of offspring with schizophrenia
have some characteristic that is not shared by other parents, this does
not by any means prove a causal link between that characteristic and
the origin of the schizophrenia. It could be a response by the parents to
the development of schizophrenia in their child, or even to the appearance of some early harbinger of the frank illness. Alternatively it could
be an expression of the genetic constitution that is shared by schizophrenic patients and their relatives. This latter explanation implies, of
course, that there is no direct causal link between parental characteristics and schizophrenia in the offspring (see Chapter 2). It is likely that
the actual mechanism involves a mixture of genetic and environmental
factors, but this is impossible to work out in a cross-sectional study.

Alternatives to Cross-sectional Studies

An alternative method is to conduct a longitudinal study, starting with
a cohort of children at birth, recording the characteristics of family
communication and interaction as they develop, and finally identifying

schizophrenia as it appears in some of the subjects. The subjects who eventually develop the illness can then be compared with those who remain healthy, in terms of all the features measured in the course of the study. There are two practical drawbacks to this strategy. One is that since the lifetime risk for schizophrenia in the general population is only about 1%, it is necessary to start with a very large cohort of subjects in order to collect a reasonable number of eventual schizophrenic patients. One strategy that has been employed to overcome this disadvantage, is to select a cohort of individuals with a high risk of developing schizophrenia. A few such studies are already under way, the most common risk factor chosen being the genetic one. Thus if the cohort is formed from children who have one schizophrenic parent, the risk of developing schizophrenia is ten times that in the general population so that the size of the cohort need only be one tenth of a normal risk cohort. Another way of defining a high risk cohort is in terms of particular psychophysiological responses of the children (Mednick and Schulsinger, 1968). No definitive results have yet been obtained from these longitudinal studies because they will not yield a substantial number of schizophrenic individuals until the subjects have at least reached their mid-twenties. This brings us to the second drawback. By the time such studies reach maturity the measures employed are likely to look very crude and outdated. Most of them will probably have been replaced by more sophisticated methods of assessment. There is no way round this problem other than to ensure that the measures employed in longitudinal studies have been thoroughly tested in pilot studies.

There is another way of achieving the time-span of a longitudinal study without having to wait decades for the results. That is to use records compiled on children many years ago and to follow up the children as adults. This has been done using Child Guidance Clinic records and school records. The material from Child Guidance Clinics was studied by O'Neal and Robins (1958) and Waring and Ricks (1965). They followed up a large number of children, some of whom were seen in the clinics as long ago as 40 years prior to the study. Having identified those who were subsequently hospitalized for schizophrenia, they then matched them with control children who were not subsequently admitted to a mental hospital.

The main findings from these studies were that the parents of the vulnerable children, who later developed schizophrenia, more often showed longstanding conflict and emotional withdrawal than the parents of the control children. Prolonged overdependence of the vulnerable children on their mothers also distinguished them from the control children. In terms of behaviour, the vulnerable children more often showed pathological lying, physical aggression, eating disorders, phobias, tics and mannerisms. It must be remembered, however, that this sample was obtained from a Child Guidance Clinic and that the majority of people who develop schizophrenia would not have been referred to such a clinic as children.

One way of avoiding this selection bias is to use school records, as Watt *et al.* (1970) did. Of course school records are not compiled with the same degree of psychological expertise as Child Guidance Clinic records, and Watt *et al.* found fewer distinguishing features between pre-schizophrenic children and control children. In fact it was only among boys that any differentiation could be made. Pre-schizophrenic boys were found to be less emotionally stable than their peers and showed more irritable, mischievous and antisocial behaviour. There is a clear similarity here between the findings from the two kinds of records. Furthermore they confirm certain propositions that Hirsch and Leff (1975) felt were reasonably well supported by evidence from cross-sectional studies. These are that the parents with schizophrenic offspring show more conflict than the parents of offspring with other psychiatric conditions, and that mothers of schizophrenic offspring show more concern and protectiveness than mothers of normals. However, as Hirsch and Leff pointed out, these propositions could equally well be explained on the basis of a common genetic endowment in schizophrenic individuals and their parents, as a result of parental influences inducing schizophrenia in the offspring, or even as due to the stress of bringing up a child who manifests certain pre-schizophrenic abnormalities. It is not possible to resolve this issue until the prospective longitudinal studies come to fruition. Meanwhile a considerable body of knowledge has been built up by studies which do not attempt to tease out the aetiology of schizophrenia, but instead are focused on the course of the illness once it has appeared.

Social and Psychological Influences on the Course of Schizophrenia

SOCIAL DEPRIVATION

The effect that the social environment might have on the course of schizophrenia was first suggested by the study of long-stay patients in institutions. The earlier work was descriptive rather than scientific and encompassed institutional effects on a whole range of patients and non-patients. Major contributions were made by sociologists such as Goffman (1961) and Etzioni (1961), who provided theoretical models of institutions which could be used to analyse the structure and functions of psychiatric hospitals. Goffman pointed out that an institution could be run for the benefit of the staff or of the clients, and that most institutions lean towards the former. The aims in such a staff-oriented institution can be understood in terms of an efficiency model, in other words how efficiently can the organization be run, rather than how may the clients' needs best be met. This results in quite subtle forms of control of the patients' activities. For example Sommer (1969) studied the arrangement of chairs in an old women's ward, and found they were all placed in lines against the walls. He tried arranging them in small circles throughout the ward but found that the staff kept placing them back in lines. This was in order to facilitate the passage of food trolleys, medicine trolleys, and cleaning materials, with a complete disregard of the patients' need to communicate with each other. A rigid social hierarchy often exists in such institutions, the patients being at the bottom of it and hence having little opportunity to communicate with the staff. Another aspect of the efficiency model is that management practices are inflexible from one day to the next and from one inmate to another. The inmates are treated as a group before, during, and after any specific activity, so that individualism is suppressed. This is also a consequence of the erstwhile common practice of denying residents any personal possessions, including clothes.

Goffman emphasized that custodial psychiatric hospitals are total institutions which control all aspects of the individual's life, work, leisure, physical and social needs. A common result is that the inmate's initiative and will to do anything for himself are progressively undermined. Added to this was the relative inaccessibility of the old style psychiatric institutions to members of the public, by virtue both of their distance from the towns and the restriction of visiting hours. Thus inmates were often denied any contact with the outside world, so that life went on inside the institution in an unchanging routine oblivious to major upheavals in the country as a whole. Brown (1950a) showed that schizophrenic patients who were visited during the first two months after admission in 1950 had a much greater chance of leaving hospital than those who were not. The prospect of never being able to leave must have added to the discouragement of any initiative, and indeed Wing and Brown (1961) showed that the longer a patient remained in hospital the less likely he was to want to leave.

The net effect of these practices in custodial psychiatric institutions was to subject the patients to sensory and social deprivation and to suppress any initiative. The end result of this process appeared to be apathetic, inert residents showing little or no spontaneous speech or activity. But this effect was not specific to schizophrenia; patients with other diagnoses could be reduced to a similar state, and it was also shown by normal people as a response to imprisonment in concentration camps. Nor is it confined to institutions, as the same end state has been encountered in schizophrenic patients living at home who have never been hospitalized. A study by Wing and Brown (1970) identified the crucial aspects of the environment which are associated with "institutionalism". They studied samples of long-stay schizophrenic women in three mental hospitals, which exhibited marked differences in their social environments. They measured a variety of indices of social deprivation, including the number of personal possessions owned by the patients, the amount of contact with the world outside, the restrictiveness of ward regimes, and the amount of time spent by the patients doing absolutely nothing. The ranking of the three hospitals was the same on all the measures, the last measure being particularly revealing. The patients spent twice as long doing absolutely nothing in the most deprived hospital as in the least deprived. Certain symptoms of schizophrenia measured in these chronic patients proved to be associated with the social atmosphere of the hospital. Blunting of affect, poverty of speech, and social withdrawal were all rated much more highly in the most deprived hospital than in the least.

The samples of patients were followed up for eight years, during which time the social environments of the three hospitals varied according to administrative changes. It was found that social improvement was accompanied by clinical improvement and social deterioration by an increase in clinical poverty. There is a suggestion from this study and from others that schizophrenic patients are particularly sensitive to changes in their social environment. For example, Leff and Vaughn (1972) in a study of patients living in the community but out of contact with the services, found that schizophrenic patients showed much more social impairment than manic-depressive patients. The results of Wing and Brown's study also suggest that the clinical poverty syndrome can be improved by environmental changes. A study of the effect of rehabilitation (Wing and Freudenberg, 1961) confirmed this. A group of chronic schizophrenic patients given active encouragement and supervision in a workshop produced a rapid improvement in output. This was reflected in a decrease in fidgeting and wandering about, and in sitting motionless and staring into space. However these improvements in behaviour were restricted to the workshop environment and did not generalize to other settings such as the ward. Furthermore, once active supervision was withdrawn, output immediately fell to its former level. These findings indicate the necessity for sustained changes in the social environment in order to combat the clinical poverty syndrome in schizophrenia. This is true of all social environments where schizophrenic patients are living. Brown and his colleagues (1966) found that severely handicapped patients living at home were just as likely to spend long periods of time doing absolutely nothing as equivalent patients living in hospital.

Attempts to rehabilitate schizophrenic patients have revealed another aspect of the reactivity of this disease to the social environment. Wing *et al.* (1964) noted that out of 45 moderately disabled patients starting a rehabilitation course, six relapsed in the first week. They suffered a return of delusions and hallucinations that had not been present for years. This suggested that it was possible to overstimulate a chronic schizophrenic patient and to produce a relapse thereby. It seemed as though these patients could only operate successfully between narrow limits of social stimulation, an excess producing a relapse of schizophrenia, whereas a paucity resulted in the clinical poverty syndrome. The dangers of excessive social stimulation have been studied by Brown and his colleagues in relation to life events and to the emotional atmosphere in the patient's home.

LIFE EVENTS

Brown and Birley (1968; Birley and Brown, 1970) compared the occurrence of life events in a group of patients suffering a relapse or first onset of schizophrenia with their occurrence in a control group of normal people. They enquired about events which could be dated to a definite point in time and which usually involved actual or threatened danger or important fulfilments or disappointments. They made a distinction between independent events which were outside the control of the subject, and possibly independent events, which were not so clearly out of his control but which seemed unlikely to be produced by unusual behaviour of the subject himself. The engagement of the subject's sister would rate as an independent event, whereas the subject's own engagement would be counted as a possibly independent one. Brown and Birley found that over a three-month period the proportion of normal people experiencing events of either kind remained constant. By contrast in a group of schizophrenic patients the proportion experiencing a life event rose dramatically in the three weeks before relapse or first onset of their illness. In fact about 60% of patients experienced an independent or possibly independent event during this period. It is worth noting that the events preceding schizophrenic episodes are mixed in nature, some being apparently pleasant, others apparently unpleasant. This contrasts with the situation regarding depression, in which episodes are preceded by events of a distinctly unpleasant nature, usually involving an actual or threatened loss (Brown *et al.*, 1975). Depression appears to be precipitated by events with a particular symbolic meaning to the patient, whereas the events preceding schizophrenic episodes seem to have a more general effect in facing the patient with some abrupt change in his social environment.

EXPRESSED EMOTION OF THE RELATIVE

Apart from the sudden changes represented by life events, more enduring qualities of the social environment have been linked with episodes of schizophrenia. The work began with the follow-up of 156 long-stay male schizophrenic patients who were discharged from hospital (Brown *et al.*, 1958; Brown, 1959b). It was found that the risk of readmission was related to the type of living group to which the patient returned on discharge. This was confirmed in a later follow-up study of 300 schizophrenic patients who were interviewed five years after their key admission (Brown *et al.*, 1966). A key informant was also interviewed and was asked about the patient's behaviour during the final six months of the follow-up period. Severely disturbed behaviour was reported for 30% of patients living with a spouse or parents compared with only 11% of those living alone. This finding could be due to the nature of the informant, people living with the patient being more aware of disturbed behaviour than those living apart. However the groups showed a similar disparity in respect of a more objective criterion, readmission. Half of the patients living with spouse or parents were readmitted at least once in the final three years of the follow-up period compared with 30% of those living alone. These findings are suggestive of a link between relapse of a schizophrenic illness and the atmosphere generated by people close to the patient.

Brown suspected that it was the emotional atmosphere that was important and started to develop methods of measuring this objectively. The first measures developed were of dominant behaviour, hostility, and a global assessment of emotion (Brown *et al.*, 1962). Further work produced a more refined instrument which could be used to measure critical comments, hostility, warmth and emotional over-involvement (Brown and Rutter, 1966; Rutter and Brown, 1966). The ratings were made from interviews with relatives in which standard questions were asked about the patient's behaviour and symptoms and the quality of interpersonal relationships. The interviews were conducted shortly after the patient's admission to hospital with a first attack or relapse of schizophrenia. A high inter-rater reliability was achieved on the above measures both in live interviews and from tape-recordings. Critical comments are rated on the basis of content and tone of voice. For example, a statement made in a matter of fact way that the patient lay in bed all day would not be sufficient to rate as a critical comment. Only if it was uttered in a critical tone of voice would it be rated as such. The total number of critical comments made during the interview is recorded. Hostility involves not just a critical remark about behaviour but either a generalization of criticism or a rejection of the patient as a person. For example, "She is stupid in everything she does". Warmth is judged mainly from tone of voice and is rated on a six-point scale. Emotional over-involvement refers to unusually marked concern about the patient and is rated on the basis of feelings expressed in the interview itself and of behaviour reported outside it. It includes obvious and constant anxiety about minor matters such as the patient's diet and the time he comes home in the evening as well as markedly protective attitudes.

These measures were included in a follow-up study of 101 schizophrenic patients (Brown *et al.*, 1972). The progress of these patients, all of whom lived with relatives, was followed for nine months after discharge from hospital to determine the proportion relapsing with a recurrence of schizophrenic symptoms. Relapse defined in this way is not necessarily coincident with readmission. Relapse was found to be significantly associated with three of the measures of expressed emotion: critical comments, hostility and emotional over-involvement. There was no direct relationship with warmth. In fact hostility rarely occurred in the absence of critical comments, so added little to the predictive value of the measures of expressed emotion. On the basis of the scores on critical comments (seven or more), marked over-involvement, and hostility, families were assigned to high or low expressed emotion (EE) groups. The relapse rate of patients from high EE homes was 58% compared to 16% from low EE homes ($p < 0.001$).

This association can be explained in two ways. It is possible that the emotional atmosphere prevailing in high EE homes affects the schizophrenic patient adversely. Alternatively it could be that the more disturbed the patient's behaviour, the more likely are the relatives to

F*

respond with criticism, hostility and over-involvement and the more likely the patient is to relapse. In this interpretation there is no direct causal link between expressed emotion and relapse. Brown *et al.* (1972) distinguished between these alternative hypotheses by controlling for previous work impairment and behavioural disturbance. When they did this, the statistical association between EE and relapse was not much reduced. On the other hand, when EE was controlled for, the association between impairment/disturbance and relapse almost disappeared. These findings support a direct link between relative's expressed emotion and relapse of schizophrenia in the patient. There was no difference in respect to these results between patients living with parents and those living with spouses.

Two-thirds of the patients took one of the major tranquillizing drugs for most of the follow-up period. For patients living in low EE homes there was very little difference in relapse rates whether they took drugs or not. Patients living in high EE homes derived some benefit from drugs, but the difference in relapse rates did not quite reach statistical significance.

Another variable examined in this study was the amount of social contact patients made with their relatives. It is reasonable to suppose that reducing social contact in a high EE home might diminish the harmful effects. At the time of the follow-up interview a time budget of a typical week was constructed. A distinction was made between patients who spent more than 35 hours per week in face-to-face contact with their relatives and those who spent less than that time together. It was found that the amount of contact made no difference for patients living with low EE families but a very significant one for those in high EE homes.

These findings seemed of such theoretical and practical importance for the study of schizophrenia that it was considered essential to attempt to replicate them. This has now been done (Vaughn and Leff, 1976a) in a project which not only repeated the earlier study but extended it to include a comparison group of patients suffering from depressive neurosis. These patients were included to determine whether the susceptibility to the emotional environment demonstrated in schizophrenic patients is peculiar to this diagnostic group or is shared by other psychiatric patients. The techniques of the earlier study were mastered and adopted wholesale with one exception, the family interview, a shortened version of which was used (Vaughn and Leff, 1976b). Ratings of expressed emotion were made from the abbreviated interview in exactly the same way as Brown and his colleagues had made them from the original interview.

Among the 37 schizophrenic families studied by Vaughn and Leff, the mean number of critical remarks did not differ significantly between parents (7·0) and spouse (11·9). In no case was hostility found in the absence of high criticism so it was not used in assigning relatives to the high EE group. Emotional over-involvement was found in several parents but in no spouse. In the 1972 study, a threshold of seven critical comments was used to divide the families into high and low EE groups of roughly equal size. Using this same cut-off point, and including relatives who showed marked emotional over-involvement in the high EE group, a significant difference in relapse rates was obtained. However, a close inspection of the data revealed that a cut-off point of six critical remarks gave a better separation in terms of relapse rates. In view of the arbitrary nature of the original cut-off point, it was considered justifiable to make an adjustment of this kind.

Using the lower criticism threshold, 21 families were assigned to the high EE group and 16 to the low EE group. Ten patients from high EE homes relapsed (48%) compared with one from a low EE home (6%). As in the 1972 study, there was a significant association between high EE and relapse (Fisher's exact test, $p = 0.007$). Vaughn and Leff were also concerned with the issue raised by Brown and his colleagues of whether the patients' disturbed behaviour mediated the link between relatives' EE and relapse of schizophrenia. They investigated this in a different way by constructing a correlation matrix of all the factors possibly linked to relapse, and then carrying out a stepwise regression analysis. The matrix showed that relatives' EE was more closely related ($r = 0.45$) than any other factor considered, including lack of preventive drug treatment ($r = 0.39$). When behaviour disturbance (based on total score) was partialled out, the correlation between EE and relapse was actually raised ($r = 0.52$). This is conclusive evidence that for schizophrenic patients the relationship between EE and relapse is independent of behaviour disturbance. No clinical variable measured, nor any feature of the psychiatric history added anything to the value of the index of expressed emotion for predicting relapse. This is in accord with the findings of the 1972 study.

Two other factors found to be of prognostic importance in the 1972 study were examined, maintenance therapy with phenothiazines and amount of face-to-face contact with relatives. A rather more stringent criterion was applied to drug taking than that used by Brown *et al.* A patient was only counted as being on regular maintenance therapy if he or she had taken drugs continuously for at least eight of the nine months follow-up period. Maybe for this reason a significantly lower relapse

rate was found for those on drugs, both in the total group of schizophrenics and in those from high EE homes, whereas a similar trend
failed to reach significance in the 1972 study. No protective effect of
drugs could be demonstrated in the low EE group. Face-to-face contact
was estimated from a time budget as in the earlier study and showed
exactly the same pattern. Low face-to-face contact had no effect in the
low EE group but was associated with a significantly lower relapse rate
in the high EE group.

Because of the similarity in design, methodology and findings it was
considered valid to pool the data from the two studies. This produced a
total group of 128 schizophrenic patients, allowing a more detailed
analysis of the outcome of subgroups. In particular, Vaughn and Leff
were interested in the ways in which the variables with prognostic
significance—relatives' EE, maintenance therapy, and face-to-face contact—might be additive. This analysis is presented in Fig. 1.

It is evident from the relapse rates that patients in high EE homes who
spend much time with their relatives and are not protected by maintenance therapy (subgroup 6) have a very poor outcome. The relapse
rates drop considerably if one of the two protective factors is operating

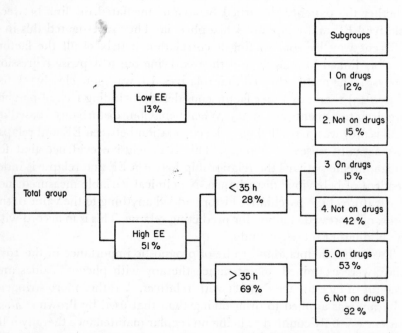

Fig. 1. Nine-month relapse rates of total group of 128 schizophrenic patients. Low
EE = 71 patients; high EE = 57 patients.

(subgroups 4, 5). The prognosis is best of all, however, for patients living in high EE homes but protected both by reduced contact and by maintenance therapy. For this group of patients (subgroup 3), the relapse rate drops to 15%, a rate significantly lower than that of patients with neither protective mechanisms operating ($p < 0.001$), and as low as that of patients from low EE homes (subgroups 1, 2).

The relapse rates in the 6 subgroups in Fig. 1 provide valuable information about the preventive role of maintenance therapy. It is clear from the relapse rates in subgroups 1 and 2 that drugs make no difference for patients living in low EE homes. They are effective, however, in reducing the relapse rate in patients from high EE homes, especially in patients who spend less than 35 hours per week with their relatives. Maintenance therapy and reduced face-to-face contact evidently exert an additive effect in protecting patients in high EE homes against relapse. This finding has important implications both for the practical management of schizophrenia and for a theoretical understanding of the condition. The practical considerations will be discussed first.

Practical Implications

Once the patient at high risk of relapse has been identified the question arises of what preventive measures should be adopted. Clearly every effort should be made to ensure that the patient receives regular phenothiazine medication. This will certainly reduce the relapse rate but will not completely neutralize the effect of the emotional environment (see Fig. 1). In addition attempts should be made to increase the social distance between patient and relatives. A number of approaches seem possible.

The most drastic and effective measure might seem to be to remove the patient from his home altogether and place him in a hostel, group home or other accommodation. Such action might well be unacceptable to patient and relatives and, without their active collaboration, would make matters worse. If the patient is to remain at home but is unemployed then a solution would be to find a job or a place in a Day Centre or Day Hospital. However some schizophrenic individuals are incapable of open employment and may even be unsuitable for sheltered work, or at least unwilling to attend daily. Vaughn and Leff found that even a patient in full employment could be in high face-to-face contact (more than 35 hours per week) with the relatives. For these reasons it may be necessary to work with patient and relative in order to alter their pattern of social interaction. Here one might anticipate encountering resistance from one and probably both partners. It is no accident that some schizophrenic patients are in intimate social contact with their relatives despite the apparently harmful effects of this. The tightness of this bond, particularly when the relative is an over-involved parent, is another feature of its pathological nature and it can prove very difficult to modify.

So far, only means of increasing the social distance between the patient and relative have been considered. It could be argued that this is a relatively superficial approach and that one really needs to tackle the relative's critical or over-involved attitude directly. This is an even more daunting prospect as very little is known about the effect of therapeutic intervention on such attitudes. In a further analysis of her material, Vaughn examined the detailed content of relatives' critical comments. She found that less than a third of all critical remarks concerned behaviour which was related to the patient's symptoms, despite the severe behaviour disturbance and work impairment shown by many patients in the months preceding admission to hospital. The majority of critical remarks were about long-standing personality traits of the patient, and reflected a poor relationship between patient and relative prior to the onset of the illness episode. The same grievances, usually to do with lack of communication and the amount of affection, warmth and interest shown by the patient, came up again and again.

It is reasonable to suppose that poor relationships of long standing are more difficult to alter than adverse reactions to acute symptoms of illness. However, behavioural techniques have recently been applied in these situations and offer some hope of influencing even psychotic behaviour (Liberman et al., 1974). It would seem advisable that any programme set up to prevent relapse in schizophrenia should include the whole range of available techniques, such as family therapy, case work and behaviour modification. These could be employed either separately or in combination in an experimental framework which would enable the most effective approach to be identified. There have been previous attempts to do this (e.g. Goldberg et al., in press) but their goal has been a general one, to normalize the patients' behaviour. The aims of a programme based on the studies of expressed emotion would be very specific: to reduce critical and over-involved attitudes in relatives, and to modify the patients' behaviour that stimulates these. Such a programme is currently under way.

Theoretical Considerations

From a theoretical point of view the work on life events and relatives' expressed emotion raises fundamental questions about the nature of social reactivity in schizophrenia. One of the questions Vaughn and Leff's study was designed to answer was whether the sensitivity to the emotional atmosphere of the home is specific to schizophrenic patients. Unfortunately a complete answer cannot be given because it was impossible to match the relatives of the two diagnostic groups by type of household. Whereas there was a preponderance of parental households in the schizophrenic group, only one of the 30 households containing a depressed patient was parental. With one exception the remainder of the depressives' households were marital. This seems to be partly because a depressed patient is much more likely than a schizophrenic patient to leave the parental home and marry, and partly appears to be due to a link between depression and loss of parents. As emotional over-involvement is virtually confined to parents, the role of this factor in the two diagnostic groups could not be compared. However the part played by critical comments could be examined in both groups and here there was an evident difference. When the same cut-off point of six comments which was used in the schizophrenic group, was applied to the depressive group there was no difference in relapse rates between high and low EE households. However when the cut-off point was lowered to two critical remarks a significant difference in relapse rates emerged; 67% in the high criticism homes and 22% in the low criticism homes. This indicates that the depressed patients in the sample were even more vulnerable to the effects of relatives' criticism than the schizophrenics. Furthermore the amount of face-to-face contact between depressed patients and their relatives did not relate to relapse patterns. Hence reactivity to critical relatives is not specific to schizophrenia but the threshold for relapse appears to be. The protective effect of reduced social contact also seems to be specific to schizophrenia.

There is a similarity between these findings and the results from the work on life events discussed above. Reactivity to life events is also not specific to schizophrenia, but the nature of life events that precipitate episodes of schizophrenia is different from those preceding episodes of depression.

The reactivity of schizophrenic patients both to understimulating and to overstimulating environments has been explained in terms of the concept of arousal. There is evidence from past studies (Venables and Wing, 1962) that arousal levels may be abnormally high in socially withdrawn, chronic schizophrenics, and this has recently been augmented by a study of more acute patients from Vaughn and Leff's sample. Measures of arousal, such as the Galvanic Skin Response and the pulse rate, were made on these schizophrenic patients in their own homes (Tarrier *et al.*, to be published). Recording went on for 15 minutes with the patient and experimenter alone, and then for a further 15 minutes after the key relative was asked to enter the room. The level of expressed emotion of the relative had already been measured several years earlier by Vaughn and Leff, but was not known to the research worker carrying out the psychophysiological measurements. A control group of normal people and their relatives was tested in exactly the same way.

The normal controls reacted to the experimental procedure by a rise in the number of spontaneous fluctuations of the GSR per minute. This is an indication of increased arousal. During the 30 minutes of recording, spontaneous fluctuations showed a smooth reduction to a lower level, interrupted briefly by a short-lived increase when the relative entered the room. Both groups of schizophrenic patients started off the experiment at a much higher level of spontaneous fluctuations than the control group. They remained at this high level throughout the first 15 minutes of the recording, being indistinguishable from each other and showing no signs of adaptation to the arousing situation. The entry of the relative was marked by an increase in spontaneous fluctuations which was significantly greater in the high EE than in the low EE group. Following this the high EE patients continued to show no sign of adaptation, the level of spontaneous fluctuations being just as high at the end of 30 minutes as it was at the beginning. By contrast, the low EE group showed a rapid reduction in the level of spontaneous fluctuations immediately following the entry of the relative. The level dropped sharply and almost reached the low level of the normal controls by the end of the 30 minutes recording. It is of interest that none of these differences between patients from high EE and low EE homes were detectable when they were tested in the laboratory.

This work suggests that the concept of physiological arousal is of use in understanding the social reactivity in schizophrenic patients. Further studies need to be done to determine whether these kind of responses to relatives in the home are specific to schizophrenia or can be found in other psychiatric conditions. Even in the absence of this knowledge, the work described is of importance in identifying psychophysiological measures in the patients which vary in parallel with psychological measures in their relatives. Since the psychophysiological indices were measured some years after the psychological ones, the assumption is confirmed that Expressed Emotion rated in an interview at the time of the patient's admission represents some enduring characteristic of the emotional atmosphere generated by the relative over long periods of time.

Furthermore the sensitivity of the psychophysiological measure to the schizophrenic patient's social environment provides the research worker with the ability to rapidly monitor attempts to change the environment. This is of great importance in the evaluation of therapeutic intervention in the social environment of the schizophrenic patient.

Pharmacological Treatment and Management

7

Hugh Freeman

Drugs Used in Schizophrenia

The publication, in 1952, of the results of a trial in Paris demonstrating a really effective method of suppressing the symptoms of "schizophrenia"* must rank as one of the major medical advances of the century (Delay *et al.*, 1952). No consideration of the treatment and management of schizophrenia can ignore the fact that the course and outcome is markedly influenced by sensible prescription and supervision of medication. The outcome was not totally bleak before the introduction of the phenothiazines and it is not entirely satisfactory now, but medication does greatly mitigate the distress and suffering caused by schizophrenia. Other chapters deal with the interaction between social and pharmacological aspects of treatment. We are concerned here with the specifics of the drugs themselves; their advantages and disadvantages and the problems in administration.

Cawley (1967) describes how the first real pharmacological treatment for schizophrenia, other than mere sedation, was insulin, which was introduced as a specific method in the early 1930s by Sakel in Vienna. It had been a serendipitous finding that hypoglycaemic shock seemed to calm the excitement of morphine withdrawal and from this basis, equally good results were claimed with psychotic excitement, including that of schizophrenia. Before long, it was maintained that insulin had a biologically curative effect on the schizophrenic process (at least in some patients) and special insulin units sprang up in progressive mental hos-

* See p. viii.

pitals throughout the world. Both staff and patients there formed an élite in the generally stagnant culture of asylums at that time and follow-up results seemed to confirm the value of insulin as a specific treatment. It should be remembered that the only alternatives then were ECT (from the early 1940s) and—for a handful of wealthy patients —psychoanalysis.

When enthusiasm for insulin coma was still at its height, Bourne (1953), rather like the small boy in "The Emperor's New Clothes", asked whether there was really a specific pharmacological action involved, or whether the whole thing was not founded on a myth. In a now classic experiment, Ackner *et al.* (1957) showed that comas induced by barbiturates and resolved by amphetamine produced results as good as those obtained by hypoglycaemic comas. In fact, the genuine therapeutic effects of the regime all came from social and psychological factors: the high morale of the doctors and nurses (related to their selection and clearly identified roles), the mystique of a complex and possibly dangerous procedure, the shared experience of patients (who were also selected) and their improvement in bodily well-being, together with a general expectation that schizophrenia could now be successfully treated. This is a phenomenon constantly rediscovered in medicine, particularly in connection with chronic and previously incurable diseases.

Though some psychiatrists vigorously defended insulin coma, in which they had invested much time and enthusiasm, the whole movement melted away even more rapidly than it had grown up. As a reaction to this, there could well have been a return to therapeutic nihilism, but fortunately, drugs which had undoubted therapeutic action on both disturbed behaviour and abnormal psychic experiences, without causing unconsciousness, had already become available. These were described as tranquillizers or neuroleptics. The first was reserpine, the active principle of which was derived from rauwolfia serpentina, which had been used for centuries in Asia to treat mental disorders. The actions of reserpine are similar to those of the later, synthetic tranquillizers, but with relatively many drawbacks; it is slow to act and even slower to be eliminated from body tissues, so that its effect tends to be cumulative. It is liable to produce marked hypotension (having also been one of the first anti-hypertensive drugs) as well as severe depression and a range of other possible side-effects. For some time, it was thought that certain schizophrenic patients who did not do well with the newer tranquillizers might respond better to reserpine, but it now appears that it has no consistent advantages over other drugs.

The present era of neuroleptics really began with the discovery of the phenothiazines. The first of these—promethazine—was primarily an anti-histamine drug, but with sedative and other properties. Chemical manipulation resulted, in 1950, in the synthesis of chlorpromazine which was found to have a very significant tranquillizing action in disturbed psychotic patients. It also has an anti-emetic action, autonomic effects (though only mildly anticholinergic), a central depressing action on body temperature and is a potentiator of the activities of other drugs, e.g. barbiturates, alcohol, narcotic analgesics and lithium. Since its clinical début in 1952, a large number of related compounds have become available for use, though in spite of massive investigation, there is still no reliable evidence that antipsychotic activity varies between them, when used in equivalent dosage.

However, this does not mean they have no clinical differences. The group of compounds with a piperazine side-chain (fluphenazine, perphenazine, trifluoperazine, prochlorperazine) are relatively more potent per unit weight and have less sedative and autonomic action; on the other hand, they produce a much higher incidence of extrapyramidal side-effects. Thioridazine (with a piperidine side-chain, unlike the aliphatic side-chain of chlorpromazine) has few side-effects and very little risk of hypersensitivity, but a greater tendency to cause pigmentary retinopathy. As with most conditions for which a large number of broadly similar drugs are available, it is best for the clinician to become very familiar with a small number and preferably those which have been in use long enough for their disadvantages to have emerged.

After the phenothiazines, the next important development in major tranquillizers was the introduction of the butyrophenones, but of these, only haloperidol is in common clinical use. Although chemically different from the phenothiazines, its pharmacological profile is very similar to that of the piperazine subgroup, with a strong tendency to cause extrapyramidal side-effects. Haloperidol's one unique advantage is that it can be used intravenously for very rapid action, whereas phenothiazines are too irritant to be used intravenously.

Another group, with more prolonged action, are the diphenylbutyl piperidines; pimozide is the most important of these and, whilst of much pharmacological interest, has not yet clearly established its role clinically. It has the advantages that it can be given in a single daily dose for the maintenance therapy of schizophrenia and does not have marked side-effects; a special efficacy has also been claimed in the treatment of monosymptomatic psychoses (Riding and Monroe, 1975) but this has yet to be confirmed. It is unsuitable for acute illnesses and probably for patients with a tendency to aggression; more systematic evaluation is awaited (Pinder *et al.*, 1976). The other compounds in this group are fluspirilene and penfluridol; both can be used as maintenance treatment on a weekly basis (the latter by mouth) but they have no particular advantages over the phenothiazines.

Finally, there are the thioxanthenes, of which the only significant drug is flupenthixol (to be discussed below as a depot preparation) and clozapine, a dibenzodiazepine, which is an effective tranquillizer and free from extrapyramidal side-effects, but at present under suspicion of causing agranulocytosis (Idanpaan-Heikkila *et al.*, 1975). An intriguing footnote to this discussion is the report by Yorkston *et al.* (1974) that propanalol, in higher doses than is usual for cardiovascular disease, may produce remarkable symptomatic improvement in some schizophrenic patients, who have not responded adequately to the usual neuroleptics. In a controlled trial against placebo (Yorkston *et al.*, 1977) patients with chronic schizophrenia whose florid symptoms had not remitted with major tranquillizers showed significantly more improvement when propanalol was added. In animals, propanalol is concentrated in the grey matter of the brain and it may act as a stabilizer of central processes of emotion and information. It also re-establishes a normal sequence of skin-conducting orienting responses, which are usually abnormal in schizophrenics and are rarely corrected by phenothiazines. If further work substantiates this claim, it should be of great theoretical interest in the biochemical study of schizophrenia.

In spite of this wealth of pharmacological choice, all major tranquillizers have a broad similarity of action on the abnormal manifestations of schizophrenia, whether these are excited and disturbed behaviour, or delusions, hallucinations and thought disorder. It has become something of a clinical cliché that one should find "the right drug for the right patient", but review of the literature leads to the disappointing conclusion that the only way of doing this is by trial and error. After lengthy research, Goldberg *et al.* (1972) stated that "no system is yet available, either from empirical research or accumulated clinical experience, to enable matching of particular phenothiazines with particular schizophrenic patients in terms of their symptom profiles". Similarly, Gardos *et al.* (1973) conclude that level of dosage is more important for different types of schizophrenic patient, than choice of the actual compound. They warn against frequent changes of drugs, allowing none to build up to an adequate concentration in the body, and resulting in what Freyhan has called "psychopharmacological roulette".

It is to Freyhan (1959) that we also owe the very useful approach of "target symptoms", i.e. focusing on the patient's symptoms in order of clinical importance and seeking maximum benefit for each, over an adequate length of time and in adequate dosage, with the drug that seems most appropriate for it. In view of the tremendous uncertainties that still remain in treating schizophrenia, this seems the most practical view to take. It should be remembered, though, as a general rule, that more benefit is likely to be seen from neuroleptics in respect of the positive or productive symptoms of schizophrenia (excitement, delusions, hallucinations) than with such negative features as apathy, inertia or social withdrawal.

Assessing Efficacy

The "Insulin Myth" should provide a constant warning of the dangers both of evaluating the efficacy of any therapeutic method from uncontrolled observations and of the difficulty of separating specific from non-specific influences in improvement. Nevertheless, it would be unreasonable to ignore a quarter-century's clinical experience amongst psychiatrists all over the world and the general consensus of this— increasing, rather than diminishing in strength with the passage of time —is that neuroleptics are highly effective for most cases of schizophrenia, though to varying extents in different patients. It is also relevant that standards of clinical practice in psychiatry have much improved in most countries during this period, but greater skill and sophistication have certainly led to no lessening in the use of major tranquillizers, except by a very small number of doctors who dogmatically reject the value of any such form of medication.

Adequate clinical trials have been carried out for most of the neuroleptics in current use. Kennedy (1975) has summarized the more important evidence, which involves not only double-blind trials against placebo—such as that of the US National Institute of Mental Health (1964)—but also less specific studies, showing a decrease in mental hospital populations following the introduction of tranquillizers (Brill and Patton, 1962). The latter, although often dramatic, has to be interpreted with caution since, in the first place, changes in the populations of institutions may not reflect genuine changes in the morbidity of the group being studied. (For instance, discharged patients might simply be readmitted to some other institution, where their residence was not recorded.) Secondly, there is evidence from investigations such as that of Smith et al. (1965) at Colorado State Hospital that the use of tranquillizing drugs per se is unlikely to have much effect on the size of a hospital population, unless followed by changes in administrative policy and organization. This highlights the inevitable interaction of pharmacological and social effects, which is a recurrent theme throughout the present book. Thirdly, it is clear that large numbers of patients were resident, not because of the severity of their current symptoms, but because of "institutionalism" (Wing and Brown, 1970) and finally, many patients were discharged while still handicapped because of the view that the hospital was the wrong environment for them. However, when allowance has been made for all such considerations, it cannot be disputed that neuroleptics have been an essential factor, from the time of their introduction, for the reduced hospitalization of schizophrenic patients in many countries.

Some of the problems of assessing the value of preventive medication are discussed on p. 177.

Side-effects

All drugs have unwanted effects, in addition to their therapeutic actions, and neuroleptics are no exception; however, considering their great potential benefits, the side-effects of drugs used in schizophrenia are well within acceptable limits if prescribing is careful. This section will deal only with the actions of phenothiazines, since other neuroleptics are very similar in their side-effects.

Extrapyramidal symptoms occur with all major tranquillizers. In fact, many European workers, such as Haase and Janssen (1965) have maintained that some evidence of extrapyramidal action is an essential indication that the drug is at an effective level for treatment. This view is based more on faith than on firm evidence, particularly as patients show marked personal differences in their sensitivity to such effects. A study by Simpson and Angus (1970) showed no consistent relationship between severe extrapyramidal side-effects and therapeutic response (see also Chapter 4).

The three main kinds of extrapyramidal symptoms are akathisia, parkinsonism and dystonia; these appear in the short term and are related to dosage. Akathisia consists of motor restlessness and agitation, which the patient cannot control and may cause him to pace up and down, fidget or rock repetitively; it is distressing to varying degrees and occurs particularly with phenothiazines of the piperazine group. Parkinsonism may show the same picture as the idiopathic form, e.g. stiffness, tremor, shuffling gait and dribbling. Dystonia (or dyskinesia) consists of distressing involuntary muscle spasms, particularly affecting the head and neck, but sometimes the trunk or limbs; oculogyric crises may also occur and even opisthotonos. According to Ayd (1961) dystonia is commoner in men and in younger patients.

Of increasing significance recently is a fourth type of disturbance—tardive dyskinesia—first described in connection with phenothiazines by Hunter *et al.* in 1964. This differs from the others in occurring only after a long spell of continuous medication and not resolving quickly when the drug is withdrawn. It consists mainly of involuntary movements of the head and tongue, affecting speech, posture and sometimes breathing; surprisingly enough, it does not seem to cause subjective distress. It is due to a persistent change in the action of striatal dopamine receptors and Marsden (1976) states that this disturbance probably occurs in up to 40% of patients treated for long periods with neuroleptics, though such a figure would probably not be generally accepted. The movements remain in about half the cases where medication is stopped, though improvement may gradually occur over as long as 18 months. The risk of tardive dyskinesia seems to be higher over the age of 50, where there has been any form of brain damage and where phenothiazines of the piperazine subgroup have been used in high dosage for a long time.

Phenothiazines also affect the autonomic nervous system, having an anti-adrenergic action, particularly in the case of the piperidine subgroup. There may be cardiac dysrhythmias and postural hypotension, which can even proceed to circulatory collapse; patients likely to be affected should be warned to get up slowly after lying down. In men, ejaculation may be impaired—an effect sometimes used in the treatment of premature ejaculation. There may also be atropine-like effects, e.g. dry mouth, difficulty in micturition, blurred vision and constipation, which are usually more marked initially.

Many patients taking phenothiazines gain considerable amounts of weight and the precise reasons for this are not known, though increased appetitite, unsatisfactory diet and reduced motor activity may be involved. Various endocrine disturbances may occur, presumably through changes in prolactin metabolism; these can include menstrual irregularity, lactation and breast engorgement (sometimes also in males) and reduced male libido. The threshold for epileptic seizures may be reduced, though it is very rare for this to be a clinical problem in patients who were not previously epileptic. Another metabolic effect is the deposit of pigment, causing purplish discolouration of exposed skin areas and opacities in the cornea and lens; this may eventually cause visual acuity to be affected. As mentioned earlier, thioridazine in high doses may also cause pigmentary retinopathy.

Various hypersensitivity reactions can also occur, particularly with chlorpromazine. Skin rashes are not usually very troublesome, except for those resulting from exposure to strong sunlight; patients taking chlorpromazine must carefully avoid this. Jaundice was at one time estimated to occur in about 1% of patients on chlorpromazine, but now seems to be uncommon; it begins in the first few weeks of treatment and is of a cholestatic type. The drug must be stopped and jaundice then usually disappears fairly quickly. Leukopenia has been reported, but is very rare.

Management of the side-effects of neuroleptics may take several forms. If any serious problem has emerged, that particular drug should be withdrawn immediately and probably never used again. A prominent note should be made in the case-record. Other doctors treating the patient should be specifically informed. In other cases, a reduction of dosage, and the addition of extra therapy (such as anti-parkinsonian) may be sufficient. Coleman and Hayes (1975) warn against the routine use of anti-parkinsonian agents, which may not prevent emergence of extrapyramidal symptoms, may increase the incidence of anti-cholinergic side-effects, such as dryness of the mouth and constipation and may possibly interfere with the therapeutic action of the neuroleptic.

If parkinsonism has become troublesome, one of the usual treatments, such as benzhexol, 2–4 mg t.d.s. or orphenadrine, 50–100 mg t.d.s. may be given; amantadine, 100–200 mg per day is a possible alternative, but laevo-dopa should be avoided, as it may itself cause adverse mental changes. Amantadine is said to be particularly effective for akathisia and dystonia, and not to cause anticholinergic side-effects (Kelly and Aluzzahab, (1971). Unfortunately, no treatment has yet been shown consistently to help tardive dyskinesia and even reducing the dose of neuroleptic may initially cause a paradoxical worsening. Good results have been claimed with the use of other neuroleptics, such as thiopropazate, but it seems that these effects are only temporary. It is still a biochemical mystery why drugs which block dopamine receptors eventually cause them to be overactive in this way (Marsden, 1976).

Finally, the possibility of depression as a side-effect must be considered. Though it is quite widely believed among clinicians that depression may be a consequence of phenothiazine therapy, there is no convincing evidence for this. Indeed, neuroleptics in moderate doses are often used to relieve the agitation and anxiety associated with depressive illness. Mood swings may certainly occur in schizophrenia and suicide is far more common than in the general population (Markowe *et al.*, 1967), but there is no reason to link these directly with the use of tranquillizers. Patients do, however, quite commonly complain that they feel "damped down" when taking medication and this may be one of their main reasons for discontinuing it. The question will be discussed further in connection with depot neuroleptics.

Acute Treatment

Acute episodes of schizophrenia, whether first onset or relapse, are always a disturbing and emotionally traumatic experience—both for the patient and for those around him. Though it has been shown possible, using appropriate medication, to manage most such conditions in the home or at a day hospital, this does not mean that it is right to do so. In fact, there are strong reasons in favour of the initial period being usually spent within a hospital, where day-to-day interactions with properly trained professional staff would be much less emotionally tense than those in certain families (see Chapter 6). Such a period of "retreat" will itself help in recovery, whereas family relationships which have been damaged by the psychosis could well set up a vicious circle of further disturbance. This assumes that there is a hospital which provides a socially acceptable milieu, has well trained and competent medical and nursing staff, and is reasonably near the patient's home, so that links with the family are not disrupted. It also presupposes an effective and sympathetic referral service. Unfortunately these conditions frequently do not obtain (see Chapter 10) and the best choice possible has then to be made among options that are available. But the pharmacological treatment of acute schizophrenia is likely to be most successful in the setting of a good in-patient unit, with good community relations, whether it is in a general hospital or part of a larger psychiatric institution.

It will be recalled that phenothiazines are quite rapidly absorbed by mouth, although there is much variation between individuals, and even in the same person at different times. It is a matter of clinical judgement in any particular case to decide whether oral treatment will be sufficient at the beginning, or whether the degree of disturbance requires injections, which give much quicker and more reliable absorption. But there is also the problem that psychotic patients may not actually swallow tablets (even under nursing observation), so that oral medication may better be given as an elixir initially. When there is a marked degree of disturbed behaviour or subjective distress, an initial injection will probably be advisable; chlorpromazine, 50–100 mg intramuscularly is suitable for this in most cases. However, if there should be uncontrolled disturbance or aggression, and particularly if suitable accommodation or staff are not available, then an intravenous injection of haloperidol, 5 mg can be of great value. Injections can be repeated, e.g. on an eight-hourly basis, but it should rarely be necessary to continue them beyond the first two days. except during periods of special difficulty.

Initially, it will often be helpful to use a drug which has some sedative effect, as well as its specific neuroleptic action. For this purpose, chloi-promazine has remained the standard preparation and can be given in a starting dose of 200–300 mg, unless there are any physical complications or the patient is over 60, when smaller amounts should be used. From then on, medication is usually in the range of 100–300 mg, three times daily, and it is unusual to go beyond a total of 1,000 mg in 24 hours. The first objective of treatment is to control both disturbed behaviour and subjective abnormalities, such as delusions or hallucinations, which are likely to distress the patient and result in further symptoms. At the same time, regular clinical assessment is needed to see that excessive side-effects are avoided. As soon as the patient has begun to improve, some reduction of the initial dosage will usually be possible and this will be particularly welcome if, for instance, excessive drowsiness or extra-pyramidal symptoms have appeared.

Following this first period, medication should be continued at a fairly uniform level for several weeks, though some upward or downward adjustments may be needed in response to clinical changes in the patient. As mentioned earlier, there is little to choose between any of the major tranquillizers in respect of their antipsychotic effectiveness. Therefore, the particular drug used at this stage will depend largely on the response of each individual patient, and particularly on the sensitivity to side-effects. If, for example, chlorpromazine continues to produce marked drowsiness, changing to an equivalent dose of trifluoperazine may be useful. The dangers resulting from frequent changes of drugs, without giving any one of them a reasonable chance, have already been sufficiently emphasized. One would expect to see a significant degree of improvement within two to three weeks of beginning neuroleptic therapy for an acute schizophrenic episode. However, this raises the somewhat controversial question of whether or not progress is likely to be accelerated or heightened in quality by also administering ECT. The general tendency now is to use ECT rather infrequently in the treatment of schizophrenic illnesses, but many clinicians believe it still has a useful place, particularly for some paranoid conditions where medication achieves only a partial remission initially. It often seems to speed improvement if catatonic or marked depressive features are present and the same may sometimes be true for hebephrenic states in younger patients. However, Clare (1976) rightly points out that, "In the absence of conclusive evidence, one way or the other, it would seem prudent to maintain a cautious attitude towards a treatment that is empirical". It is also possible, of course, to use antidepressive medication when mood disorder is troublesome, but this is usually much slower in achieving relief than ECT.

Longer-term Treatment

Treatment of the acute phase may be concluded more or less successfully, but unfortunately this is not the end of the story, as it would be for many medical or surgical conditions. It has been suggested in earlier chapters that schizophrenia indicates a biological vulnerability in the organism. Once the illness has appeared, there is a definite risk that it will recur. The extent of this risk in individual patients has to be assessed clinically, making use of whatever guidance is available from scientific research. It is important to make such a judgement because the continued prescription of medication must be based on it.

It has been pointed out that the rate of relapse in untreated patients is one of the most important indices for determining the effectiveness of neuroleptics. This is by no means as easy as it might seem. Many of the methodological problems involved have been analysed by Wing *et al.* (1973). In the first place, American studies include many patients who would not receive a diagnosis of schizophrenia in Britain; secondly, most withdrawal investigations have occurred in hospital, where patients are largely protected from the stresses which often precipitate relapse in outside life; thirdly, some reports must be discounted because they have mixed acutely ill with chronic patients and the two will clearly respond quite differently to the same medication; fourthly, there was often much doubt as to whether or not patients had actually taken prescribed tablets.

In a study of the preventive value of oral medication, Leff and Wing (1971) avoided these pitfalls. First, the diagnosis was checked by computer analysis of clinical data obtained with a standardized schedule (PSE); secondly, the subjects involved were all out-patients; thirdly, the patients had all recovered from an acute schizophrenic illness;

fourthly, multiple checks were made as to whether or not the patients had taken their medication, particularly the use of riboflavine as a tracer, which could be identified in urine tests. Out of an initial total of 116 patients, only 35 actually entered the placebo-controlled trial, but the progress of the whole group was followed-up for a year. Reasons for patients not entering the medication trial were: (a) they had stopped medication of their own accord before the trial began, (b) their adjustment was considered by their clinicians to be too precarious to risk the possibility of placebo being substituted for active drug; or (c) their prognosis was considered by their clinicians to be good enough for them not to need maintenance therapy.

Amongst those patients who took part in the trial striking differences were found between the ones on an active drug (33% relapse) and those receiving a placebo (83% relapse). However, since only about one-third of the original total were in the trial, the results cannot be generalized to schizophrenic patients as a whole. "Unless trial patients are viewed in the setting of the population from which they are selected, the conclusions drawn about therapeutic efficacy may be over-optimistic." In fact, the prognoses made by the clinicians concerned about patients excluded from the trial for either reason proved remarkably accurate (at least in terms of the available treatment regime). The group with a good prognosis were characterized by having had a first episode of illness with an acute onset, symptoms of "endogenous" depression in the clinical picture and a good premorbid personality. Leff and Wing propose that in-patients of this kind, it might be justifiable to withhold maintenance treatment after the acute illness has settled. (See also the discussion of favourable social environments in Chapter 6.) Those patients who were excluded on account of poor prognosis did badly, even though kept on their original treatment.

There are several indications as to how treatment prospects could be improved. In the first place, those patients who stopped medication themselves soon after discharge from hospital had a high relapse rate (66·7%), and it is reasonable to suppose that a different type of treatment regime, in which most remained on regular medication, would have prevented many relapses. Secondly, even in the group with a poor prognosis, it is possible that a regular injection regime (for reasons such as higher absorption and more regular supervision) would have resulted in a better outcome for at least some of them. In fact, Leff and Wing advise that it would be wrong to exclude such patients from maintenance treatment, since a proportion would almost certainly benefit. The trial also identified characteristics of patients who were particularly likely to default from the follow-up regime; these tended to be younger, unmarried males of poor heterosexual adjustment and subject to situational anxiety. Such patients should preferably have extra supervision. Finally, it may be asked why one-third of the controlled trial patients known to be taking the active drug still relapsed. The reasons are probably both pharmacological (inadequate absorption) and social (life events and family stress).

How long, then, should maintenance neuroleptic treatment be continued in schizophrenia? Unfortunately, no clear answer can yet be given to this very important question, though the study described above showed that experienced psychiatrists usually have a fairly shrewd idea of patients' need for medication, on regular clinical indications. However, the evidence summarized in Chapter 6 about the protective effect of neuroleptics against social and family stresses suggests that this protection may be needed for a very long time, since the patient's susceptibility to these factors is unlikely to change much. Leff (1972) suggests that schizophrenic patients control their degree of social activity according to what they can tolerate and that maintenance medication increases their level of tolerance for social stimulation. If that is so, there is a strong argument for continuing the drugs indefinitely. In his view, reported trials of prophylactic medication provide no evidence that the effectiveness of this treatment can be related to duration of previous illness. Therefore, the view that schizophrenia generally "burns itself out", removing the need for further medication, cannot be accepted. Certainly, the consequences of further relapse are usually such that it is wise to be very cautious indeed before stopping maintenance drugs for most schizophrenics.

This approach, is not universally accepted. Concern about the long-term unwanted effects of continued neuroleptic treatment is genuine and the frequency of tardive dyskinesia in particular makes some psychiatrists suggest that "the cure is worse than the disease" (Gordon and Cole, 1976). As with any form of medical treatment, it is basically a matter of balancing costs and benefits, not forgetting that the costs must include great professional and administrative effort, and health education, if treatment compliance is to be maintained over long periods. But review of all the relevant circumstances should lead to a conclusion that is in favour of prophylactic treatment in most cases. However, dosages should regularly be reviewed to ensure they are no more than the minimum which will avoid relapse in any particular patient—a process of titration which needs both professional skill and knowledge of the individual concerned.

Assessing possible long-term disadvantages of medication is a difficult matter. Ideally, there should be reliable base-line measures of clinical state and of somatic function, as well as a control group not receiving the same form of treatment. However, clinicians rarely have both the foresight and the resources to look ten or 15 years ahead, maintaining contact with a group of patients throughout. As far as controls are concerned, it is ethically impossible to withhold what seems to be the best available treatment for more than a limited time. But systematic investigation is important if we are to have any clear idea as to whether the prevalence of abnormalities in a treated group is genuinely different from that in groups having other treatments or no treatment at all. Imlah (1978) has reported a detailed study of all 69 patients who commenced treatment with fluphenazine deconoate at a special maintenance clinic in 1969 and remained continuously on this medication for five years. At the end of this period, there was no evidence of haemotological or biochemical abnormality that could be related to the treatment; ten patients showed some electrocardiographical abnormalities, but none were significant; 20 patients showed extrapyramidal features, possibly associated with the medication, but all were mild, except in one case (four with oral dyskinesia had this before starting treatment); 11 patients had lens or corneal opacitics, not significantly affecting vision, but all had been on high dosage phenothiazines for a long time before starting injections. Imlah's conclusion is that the group showed a highly satisfactory result on the whole, in the absence of serious physical complications from treatment.

At the same time, the interrelationship of pharmacological and social factors (discussed in Chapter 6) must always be borne in mind and there are a number of research studies relevant to this theme. Hogarty et al. (1973, 1974) followed-up for two years a sample of 374 schizophrenic patients who had been discharged from mental hospitals. These were divided into four subgroups, who received respectively: placebo only; placebo with sociotherapy (social casework and vocational counselling); chlorpromazine; and chlorpromazine and sociotherapy. Whilst the drug versus placebo comparison was blind, it was clearly not possible to conceal the difference between receiving sociotherapy and not doing so. By the end of two years, 80% of patients on placebo had relapsed, compared with 48% of those on active drugs; however, half of all those who relapsed had already stopped taking medication. Patients who received active drugs with sociotherapy did better than those taking the drug alone; sociotherapy reduced the rate of relapse amongst those who had survived in the community for six months, but after a year, only had an effect in those on active drugs. It was concluded that maximum benefit came from a combination of medication and sociotherapy, continued for at least a year after discharge from hospital.

In a long-term follow-up of patients treated with neuroleptics in the home, Davis *et al.* (1972) concluded that not only the medication was needed, but also continuous family supervision by professional workers —in this case, community nurses. The patients were often found to be a serious disorganizing factor in multi-problem families, who received much emotional support and practical guidance in the course of the nurses' visits. When these visits ended, after two and a half years, a large proportion of those patients on placebo who had so far remained out of hospital relapsed sufficiently to require readmission. At this point, 34% of the placebo patients had remained in the community throughout, compared with 77% of the drug patients. "Aggressive home care", in addition to medication, was felt to be significant in preventing or retarding deterioration in several respects for these schizophrenic patients at home.

It was noted above, in connection with assessing the efficacy of drugs in schizophrenia, that a patient's hospitalization experience will depend not only on the medication he receives, but also on the hospital's policy or organizational structure. Relevant to this can be even such mundane matters as the financial arrangements under which patients remain in hospital, which may explain the high rate of chronicity in Japan (Kuwabara, 1976) markedly out of line with trends in most other countries. It is now generally accepted that schizophrenics respond best to an atmosphere which avoids undue arousal, but provides a reasonable level of stimulation; it should therefore be the clinician's aim to combine this with appropriate medication.

Chronic Patients in Hospital

In spite of determined efforts to avoid long stay in hospital, large numbers of schizophrenic patients remain, because of a combination of clinical and social handicaps. Many of them have been receiving neuroleptics continuously for years and it is a matter of some importance to know whether or not this is really necessary. The method of relapse measurement after withdrawal of treatment has been used to evaluate the results. Such studies suffer from methodological drawbacks, which have been summarized by Andrews *et al.* (1976); however, two American exceptions to these criticisms are the trials of Caffey *et al.* (1964) and by Prien *et al.* (1968). A review of the literature by Prien and Klett (1970) suggested that at least 40% of chronic in-patients could be

G

expected to relapse after medication was withdrawn. In their own study of 36 patients, Andrews *et al.* found that 35% of those on placebo relapsed (up to 29 weeks after active medication was stopped) compared with 7% of patients remaining on drugs. Most of those who relapsed showed a noticeable increase in social withdrawal for several weeks beforehand, but this improved rapidly when active medication was reintroduced. It was concluded that most long-stay patients should have a periodic withdrawal of medication, on a trial basis, but only as a cooperative undertaking between the doctors and nurses concerned. Otherwise, staff anxieties could well communicate themselves to some patients and result in them becoming clinically worse.

An uncontrolled but scrupulous study by Morgan and Cheadle (1974) came to rather different conclusions. This surveyed all 475 chronic schizophrenic patients who had been admitted to a specialized regional hospital for rehabilitation over a seven and a half year period. Only 18 had not been receiving neuroleptics at the time of transfer and these patients were put on drugs after arrival; the sample was under the care of the senior author for between one to seven years. After careful assessment, it was thought possible to stop medication for 74 patients (more than once in some cases) but only five were considered no worse as a result and in all the others treatment was resumed. Relapse occurred after an average of four and a half months from drug withdrawal, but the interval was much longer in some patients. The difference between these results and others, which have shown only a low relapse rate after drugs were withdrawn in chronic patients, was probably related largely to the active rehabilitation regime. This involved much more arousal and social stress than is usual for long-stay mental hospital patients, so that the protective effect of medication—described earlier—would be needed to a greater extent.

The studies of Wing *et al.* (1964) and Wing and Brown (1970) suggest that high doses of phenothiazines are less necessary in protected hospital environments, and the work on family relationships summarized in Chapter 6 shows that some patients in supportive family environments may not need medication at all. The interactions between social and pharmacological treatment are discussed by Wing *et al.* (1972).

Long-acting Injections and Continuity of Care

Studies which have shown the prophylactic value of neuroleptics, when taken over long periods, have also indicated the difficulties of maintaining cooperation from patients; a subject comprehensively reviewed by

Blackwell (1977). The familiar problems of getting people to take medication daily for any length of time in medical conditions (such as diabetes or tuberculosis) are compounded, in the case of schizophrenia, by the fact that many of the patients concerned do not show insight, have serious personality defects or lack responsible relatives. These extra problems are the more likely to arise because of the long period of risk, exceeding that for almost any comparable disease, with the possible exception of diabetes. The number of affected individuals, multiplied by the number of years during which they need prophylactic medication, results in an enormous demand on mental health services. However, the potential gains, in terms of reduced morbidity and hospitalization, are just as great.

A poor level of patient cooperation has been illustrated in studies such as those of Renton *et al.* (1963), showing that 46% of a sample of schizophrenic out-patients were not taking their prescribed tablets, and of Willcox *et al.* (1965), giving a failure rate of 48% in a mixed group of psychiatric out-patients. At the same time, psychiatrists who were trying to supervise clinically the increasingly large number of schizophrenic patients living outside hospital found that patients whom they knew would stay well on regular medication were repeatedly breaking down because of failure to continue taking drugs. Both the demonstrated success of neuroleptics in preventing relapse and the trend towards community care made this an important issue in psychopharmacology. It was largely a technical problem to find a way of maintaining a fairly constant level of neuroleptic, which did not depend on the regular swallowing of tablets. In other words, a completely new form of "delivery system" had to be found.

It was mentioned earlier that phenothiazines of the piperazine subgroup are relatively much more potent than the others; in fact, weight for weight, fluphenazine is 25 times more powerful than chlorpromazine. This meant that a relatively small dose could have a significant neuroleptic action for a fairly long time, if only it could be absorbed slowly. This objective was achieved, firstly by converting fluphenazine to an acid ester (enanthate) and then by dissolving the drug in sesame oil. When this preparation was injected intramuscularly, it was found to be effective for 12–14 days. Thus, the technological problem was solved and fluphenazine enanthate was first used clinically in the USA in 1963; it became available in the UK in 1966. Conversion to another ester (decanoate) increased the effective length of action to about four weeks, and this preparation came into use a couple of years later. Thus, the long-acting or depot tranquillizers entered clinical psychiatry.

Like all claims for advance in medicine, this one was properly received critically. But, in fact, it was simply a case of old wine in new bottles. The new preparations had no actions that were not already well known, but these actions were more consistent, and often more potent, depending on dosage. It has been emphasized that even when chlorpromazine is actually taken by mouth its absorption tends to vary unpredictably. Though the difficulties of measuring phenothiazine in human plasma have been formidable, available evidence indicated that depot injections produced an effective level of drug in the body, and that this could be maintained indefinitely by an appropriate regime of injections, e.g. once a month or so. This meant, though, that unwanted side-effects would occur, as well as therapeutic ones and since the total action of the drug was generally more effective than with oral medication, side-effects might also be more troublesome. But, making allowance for variations in absorption, both the good and the bad effects of long-acting tranquillizers must be more or less the same as those from equivalent dosages of the same substance by mouth.

Hence a whole shoal of red herrings. Some have been related to alleged ill-effects, such as depression from depot fluphenazine (de Alarcon and Carney, 1969). Others have questioned whether the injection regime has any prophylactic value (Watt and Shepherd, 1975). In each case, the question must be turned back to ask—does this also apply to the same phenothiazines taken by mouth (remembering that they tend to be rather less effective and consistent)? Attention to such basic clinical pharmacology shows that most of the "special" problems of depot neuroleptics are not special at all.

One technique of evaluation is to compare the length of hospital care during equal periods of time before and after beginning the depot regime, i.e. the "mirror-image method". (To avoid bias, the episode in which injections were started was excluded altogether.) If it is assumed that the natural history of schizophrenia shows no general tendency towards improvement, any improvement following institution of the new regime can be attributed to the regime itself. This is not, however, a trial of medication versus placebo or no intervention; in the reported studies, all patients had been treated with other methods, usually oral neuroleptics, before depot injections were started. The comparison is between *regimes* and not between substances. In some cases, hospitalizations will not be related to adverse clinical change, but in a large series such contaminating effects are insignificant. In one such study (Johnson and Freeman, 1972), 73 schizophrenic patients, followed-up for at least two years, had a total experience of hospitalization, after starting injections, only 48% of that experienced beforehand. Because the assumption of a deteriorating "natural" course of schizophrenia is questionable (see Chapter 1) and because the enthusiasm of the proponents of a new form of treatment can itself change the service outcome it was also necessary to undertake a controlled trial. In a study by Hirsch *et al.* (1972), a group of 74 severely chronic schizophrenic outpatients were assigned to active or placebo injections and reassessed either at relapse or after nine months. Only 8% of those on active injections relapsed, compared with 66% of those on placebo. The same advantage of active drug over placebo was seen when the patients were compared on social measures, such as the degree of burden on their relatives (Stevens, 1973a).

It has been suggested that series of this kind may exaggerate the benefit of the regime because they consist only of patients who have remained within it. Those patients who do not need, or who refuse, treatment will have different prognoses. Many will discontinue medication because they have not responded to it. Thus, the value of any regime can only be assessed in comparison with the progress of all patients from a defined area who might benefit from treatment. No such study has so far been published. The only epidemiologically based series so far is that of the present author in Salford, where every schizophrenic patient receiving depot tranquillizers since 1966 has been followed-up. The area concerned is the pre-1974 city, with an average population over the survey period of 127,000; all psychiatric contacts of the population have been recorded since 1968 by a Case Register (Fryers, *et al.*, 1970). Using the mirror-image method, annual cohorts have been examined for their pre- and post-treatment hospitalization experience. The sample has the following criteria: (a) diagnosis of schizophrenia personally confirmed, (b) still in receipt of depot tranquillizers at follow-up, (c) at least one hospitalization before injections were begun, (d) follow-up of at least 12 months. When the figures for all cohorts were totalled together, results for 141 patients on 30 June 1977, showed that their pre-injection hospitalization was 17,563 days and the post-injection total was 3,291 days. Comparison of annual cohorts has not confirmed the view that the prophylactic benefit tends to diminish over time. Further data, which will relate this treated group to all diagnosed schizophrenic patients in the local population, and record the numbers who have discontinued treatment for various reasons, are still incomplete. It is not, of course, suggested that administrative trends of this kind, which are common throughout the National Health Service, are attributable solely to the use of injected forms of medication. Other influences are discussed in Chapters 9 and 11.

Fluphenazine is not the only neuroleptic now available as a depot preparation but the only other one of significance is flupenthixol, which is also used in the decanoate form. In low oral dosage, this drug has proved to be a useful antidepressive. At the levels used for antipsychotic action, it has caused occasional reported cases of mania or severe insomnia. However, earlier suggestions that it would, concurrently with its tranquillizing effect, relieve depressed mood, apathy and social withdrawal have not been confirmed (Floru and Wittek, 1975; Kelly *et al.*, 1977). It also causes extrapyramidal side-effects, though possibly to a slightly less extent than fluphenazine; it is not yet clear whether this may be due to the use of non-equivalent doses.

The dose of fluphenazine decanoate is usually 12·5 mg initially, though in elderly patients it may be advisable to begin with 6·25 mg or even less (Ayd, 1975). If this test dose is well tolerated, a second injection may be given in 7–14 days, depending on the patient's condition; the strength of this dose can also be varied, though it is not usual to go beyond 25 mg at this point. From then on, it is a matter of clinical skill as to how the dosage and frequency of injections should be determined. Flexibility is important and it should not be assumed that 25 mg monthly is the norm. Once the patient is well stabilized, a very slow reduction of medication may be attempted, but it is always wise to err on the side of caution. Anti-parkinson drugs may also be needed, but only if there are definite indications and they should be withdrawn as soon as possible. The dosage of flupenthixol is usually 20–40 mg, at similar intervals.

Starting a patient on a regime of depot injections is one thing, but maintaining it for the length of time needed for adequate prophylaxis is another. In one study (Johnson and Freeman, 1973) it was found that 18% of a group of patients defaulted from the regime within a year. This proportion will obviously become cumulative over time, unless energetic steps are taken to correct it. If so, it is very likely that those patients who are most in need of continuous medication will be the ones to default most quickly. It is therefore advisable for every psychiatric service to have a register of psychotic patients requiring regular treatment and this may be based on a unit of population such as the NHS Health District. (Manic patients on lithium treatment need a similar register.) The register will need to maintain constant linkage with clinical and social services, so that patients most at risk will receive some form of continuous monitoring.

Depot injections are usually given at hospital clinics and it is important for the hours of these to be flexible so that patients can attend them without loss of working time. However, it may often be helpful for some of this work to be decentralized to group practice health centres, which will be nearer to the homes of many patients. If so, it is advisable for the injection to be given there by psychiatric community nurses. Scrupulous record-keeping is essential. In every area, there is bound to be a central group of patients who will not attend regularly for injections, in spite of encouraging letters and even visits. These patients may be among the most vulnerable of all to relapse, but this risk can be minimized by regular visits from psychiatric community nurses. The nurse can often give valuable help to the patient, and to the relatives or other supporters.

Community nursing has made great progress, during the past ten years, not only because of supervising medication. The latter does, however, provide a basis for effective prophylaxis of recurrent schizophrenia, if suitable management and information systems can be created which are capable of dealing continuously with large numbers of patients over prolonged periods. It illustrates once again that the use of medication in schizophrenia is intimately bound up with social and administrative factors; none of these aspects can be neglected if treatment is to be successful.

8 | Psychological Aspects of Treatment of In-patients

H. Gwynne Jones

It has been accepted, throughout this book, that "schizophrenia" is not a unitary condition.* Even when a restricted definition is used, there are marked differences between the acute and the chronic condition, which must be reflected in differences in methods of treatment and care. This chapter will be concerned chiefly with psychological methods of treatment that have been used with long-stay in-patients: mainly those referred to in Chapter 1 as the "old" long-stay. The swing of the pendulum from the appalling conditions of "community" care in the early nineteenth century to the moral treatment of the first county mental hospitals, and then back to custodial care for a prolonged period, with a yet further swing to come after the Second World War, when the concepts of the therapeutic community, rehabilitation, and early discharge were re-introduced, has already been described.

This chapter is concerned with some of the psychological principles that underlie these environmental approaches; in particular, the concepts of behaviour therapy and behaviour modification. By way of completing the picture, however, a number of other approaches will be considered first.

Psychotherapy

Simple supportive psychotherapy in the sense of examining a patient's social and other difficulties with him in an encouraging way and helping him to adjust to them without attempting any radical alteration of his

* See p. viii.

G*

personality is as essential an aspect of the treatment of schizophrenia as of any other psychiatric condition. The approach is dealt with in more detail in Chapter 9. "Counselling" is also an important concept, particularly when based on a detailed knowledge of the practical problems that schizophrenia poses to an affected individual and family, so that really skilled advice on management can be given when a chronically handicapped patient, or one at risk of relapse, is living in an unprotected environment. All professional people, whatever their discipline, should be familiar with its elements. Further consideration is given in Chapter 11.

"Dynamic" individual psychotherapy of a psychoanalytic or related orientation is not generally considered a treatment of much value in schizophrenia. Some psychoanalysts do treat schizophrenic patients but there is little evidence to suggest that they are successful (Feinsilver and Gunderson, 1972). Rogers *et al.* (1967) treated chronic and acute schizophrenic patients by client-centred techniques which emphasize genuineness, unconditional positive regard and accurate empathy, and compared their findings with those from matched control subjects receiving a milieu type of therapy. They claim an advantage for the client-centred approach in respect of improvement in emotional expression, less "denial" and an improved discharge rate.

May (1976b) in his comparative study of treatment methods in schizophrenia found group psychotherapy to be more effective than individual psychotherapy and group therapy centred on social and occupational problems superior to group therapy attempting to promote deep psychological insight. Freeman *et al.* (1958), while emphasizing the importance of relationship factors in therapy, considered the nurse–patient relationship to be of prime importance and described a training scheme to help nurses to establish appropriate therapeutic relationships. The quality of the relationships involved is an important non-specific factor in any form of therapy.

Family Therapy

Family therapy aims at the improvement of the functioning of a family based on its assessment and analysis as a unitary integrated structure of interacting parts. In a sense it is group therapy applied to the family group but all members may not be present on any single occasion. As might be expected from the various theories discussed in Chapter 6, one form of family therapy has been particularly associated with and developed from the treatment of young people with acute schizophrenia. Equally to be expected from the diversity of the various theoreticians there is no agreed orthodox manner of procedure. A good favourable review of this approach is provided by Fox (1976). He admits that there is little evidence for the efficacy of family therapy but points to the inadequacies of the trials reported and to the difficulties of outcome research for any form of psychotherapy. Family counselling, based on a knowledge of all the somatic, psychological and social factors influencing the course, is discussed in Chapter 11.

The Individual Case Approach

The treatment approaches considered so far derive either from general psychosocial principles or some variant of psychoanalysis. The processes involved could also be described in terms of the concepts and principles of academic experimental psychology and other approaches derive directly from those principles. Shapiro (1966), who has had an important influence on British clinical psychology, has long advocated an individual case approach, in which the clinical assessment and treatment of a psychiatric patient is treated as a form of scientific research. Hypotheses derived from the initial observations and case-data are experimentally tested. This has the advantage of self-correction. Failure of validation forces modification of the initial hypothesis and leads to further experimental testing. The formal discipline of this approach and its sceptical foundations foster the exploration of alternative explanations. More important still, it leads naturally to the design of treatment procedures. The most convincing validation of a hypothesis is the achievement of experimental control of an abnormality by the manipulation of some independent variable. Treatment is essentially the extension of such control on a more enduring basis into the patient's normal environment. Thus the goal of assessment is the design of procedures capable of modifying the patient's reactions to events or of ways of modifying the environment so as to alter the essential nature of the experienced events. This treatment is also embarked on in a sceptical experimental manner. The initial treatment model is likely to need modification or even to be abandoned in the light of the observed effects. It was partly the application of this approach that led to the early application of behaviour therapy in Britain. Shapiro himself has concentrated more on assessment than treatment. He has described several examples (1966) and Jones (1960) described a number of assessment and treatment cases. Very few of these were concerned with schizophrenia but more recent studies have been undertaken, using the techniques of operant behaviour modification to be described later. Shapiro tends to neglect the operant analogues of his approach and the impressive contribution of behaviour modifiers to single case methodology (for example, Liberman *et al.*, 1973a).

Bannister's "Construct Theory" Approach

Bannister (1962a,b, 1963, 1965; Bannister and Fransella, 1966; Bannister *et al.*, 1975), within the framework of Kelly's (1955) Personal Construct Theory, has elaborated a theory of the nature of schizophrenic thought disorder, its aetiology and, by implication, the aetiology of the type of schizophrenia of which thought disorder is a manifestation. Construct theory postulates that an individual's view of his world, particularly his social world, is structured by his attempt to make sense of it in terms of a set of bipolar dimensions or constructs which are an idiosyncratic product of his experience. In this way he generates expectations, and his construct system is modified according to the fate, validation or invalidation, of these expectations.

A person's construct system may be explored fairly objectively by means of a flexible assessment technique, the Repertory Grid, which Bannister employed to provide an operational definition of thought disorder, and which would discriminate between thought disordered schizophrenic patients and all other groups. Essentially, what is measured by this psychometric test is the degree or tightness of relationships between constructs and the consistency with which these relationships are maintained from occasion to occasion. Thought disorder is indicated by weak and inconsistent relationships, i.e. "loose construing". For example, a normal person might be expected to describe people he has already selected as "honest" as also being "good", and those he selected as "dishonest" as "bad"; i.e. he shows a high correlation between his use of the two constructs "honest-dishonest" and "good-bad". Thought disordered schizophrenic patients display lower correlations between such construct pairs. (There are analogies with other theories of schizophrenic thought disorder described in Chapter 5, although Bannister's experimental technique is not as rigorous.)

To explain the aetiology of this condition, it is argued that if someone construes a situation in such a way as to derive an expectation which is not confirmed, his initial reaction might be to relocate the relevant "element" at the opposite pole of the construct; e.g. a person initially seen as kind may be reconstrued as unkind. However, if the new construct is subsequently itself invalidated, and such shuttling to and fro between the poles continues, the predictions via that particular construct become vague and untrustworthy and its relationships with other normally related constructs become loosened: a person seen as kind may no longer be expected with any confidence to be sincere or dependable. The consequent vague and imprecise predictions are therefore protected from further invalidation.

The similarity between this invalidation hypothesis and Bateson's "double-bind" and related concepts is close, but Bannister's operational measures allowed him to test his theory experimentally by attempting to produce a specific area of "thought disorder" in normal subjects by controlled "validation" and "invalidation" of their judgements from photographs of people in terms of provided constructs. As predicted the relationships between serially invalidated constructs became progressively closer to random.

Thus encouraged, Bannister proceeded to the third and vital stage of his research, an experimental treatment designed to decrease the thought disorder displayed by actual schizophrenic patients. The treatment consisted, as the theory demands, of long-term serial validation to tighten the weak construing. The construct systems of individual long-stay patients were closely examined for relative islands of meaning within the general loose structures. Each patient was then seen in fortnightly individual sessions over some two years to provide the validation necessary to further tighten these areas, enhance their relationship with neighbouring areas, and stabilize the network of constructs generally. Nurse–patient interactions on the ward were also structured to the same end. Control patients received "total push" treatment over the same period and both groups were compared on a variety of measures. There was a tendency for some differences between the two groups to be in the predicted direction, but overall the results were inconclusive or negative. Bannister suggests that an adequate test of his hypothesis requires a far greater degree of environmental control.

Behavioural Approaches

Behaviour therapy represents an attempt to apply the techniques and principles of experimental psychology, especially those relevant to learning, to the modification or elimination of maladaptive behaviours, and

their replacement by adaptive alternatives. It is essentially re-educational
in its approach. Its advocates often claim that the abnormal or maladaptive behaviour requiring modification is itself learned. Even when
it is recognized that the abnormalities may have a different pathological
basis, the manifestations are regarded as mainly requiring active here-
and-now applications of techniques of behavioural learning, unlearning,
and relearning.

There are, in a sense, two main types of behavioural treatment. One,
to which the term "behaviour therapy" is sometimes restricted, has a
relatively broad theoretical basis in psychological learning and personality theory. It now embraces too wide a range of techniques to be
described here in detail, especially as few of these have in fact been
applied to schizophrenia, and several excellent accounts are now available elsewhere (for example, Yates, 1970). Its theoretical basis and
range of application has in fact widened a great deal in recent years
(Jones, 1971, 1974) to recognize, allow for and exploit mediating cognitive processes (Mahoney, 1977; Boneau, 1974), and the importance
of modelling, vicarious experience and other social forms of learning
(Bandura, 1971; Mischel, 1973). Behaviour therapy has been mainly
applied to neurotic conditions but many of the processes which it
exploits must play important roles in the treatment of any disorder.

"Behaviour modification", the preferred term for the other main type
of behavioural treatment, has a narrower theoretical basis, but one
considered by its exponents to be sufficient for almost all practical
applications of psychology. This is the operant conditioning paradigm
of B. F. Skinner (1938) and its later elaborations. Operant behaviour is
defined as behaviour whose form or rate is governed by its consequences,
but its control and modification requires more than common-sense
administration of rewards and punishments. The first task is a careful
analysis of the relevant initial behaviour patterns and the objective
definition of the desired terminal repertoire. The second and crucial
task, which may involve trial and error testing, is the devising of a
learning programme to progressively modify or "shape" the initial
repertoire in the direction of the target by reinforcing successively
closer approximations. The reinforcement must be effective for the
particular individual. Cigarettes, sweets or similar "primary" rewards
may be used or may be replaced by generalized reinforcers, such as
tokens exchangeable for more direct rewards. Attention, praise and
approval can also be very powerful social reinforcers. Aversive reinforcement (or punishment) can have dramatic effects on behaviour but,
apart from ethical considerations, is in the long term an inefficient aid to

programming. It tends only to block undesired behaviour temporarily and has unpredictable and disruptive side-effects. Apart from the planning of reinforcement schedules, programming requires environmental manipulation. Novelty is likely to evoke novel behaviour which then becomes available for shaping. Also, behaviour which is appropriate in one situation may not be in another. Thus the training has to embrace the discrimination of environmental cues. Arbitrary additional cues may be introduced to facilitate this learning and then gradually "faded" out. Models may also be provided and imitation encouraged and reinforced. A major problem, even when appropriate target behaviour is achieved in a laboratory or clinic, is its transfer into the patient's normal environment. The best solution to this problem is to carry out the training in that environment. Thus, one strong recent trend in behaviour modification has been for the psychologist who designs the programme to withdraw into a consultant/teacher role and to train parents, teachers or other appropriate agents in the techniques.

Inadequate social skills are often evident in psychiatric patients of various types and some behaviour therapists have attempted to develop formal methods of social skills training. In Britain, Argyle has studied social skills with an emphasis on modes of non-verbal communication, and has developed a form of training involving a range of techniques, including, for example, modelling, role-playing and televisual playbacks. This has been formally evaluated in a clinical setting for the treatment of milder personality disorders (Argyle et al., 1974). Goldstein's similar "Structured Learning Therapy" (1973; 1974) is described in a training manual and has been applied to schizophrenic and similar patients. This focuses on coping and mastery of skills such as beginning, participating in and ending a conversation; making a complaint; asking for help; rehearsing stressful encounters; dealing with aggression; life-planning and self-control. The actual training has four components applied during group training sessions. Tapes are played depicting successful behaviour to allow modelling. The patients are then trained in, and practise and rehearse, similar behaviour in role playing. Each role-play is then followed by a corrective feedback period and social reinforcement (praise) given as the role-playing approximates more closely to the taped model. Throughout, the training is directed to concrete behaviour of a flexible type, and broad and general evaluative comments from trainer or group members are avoided. Finally, in order to facilitate transfer of the learning to real-life settings, appropriate homework is prescribed.

It is clear that enduring social learning of this and other types requires that the relevant behaviour ultimately comes under the control of the learner himself. Therefore, contrary to popular belief, behaviour therapists specifically aim to train their patients in self-control, self-regulation or self-management. Various behavioural methods have been developed during recent years (for example Bandura, 1971; Kanfer and Karoly, 1972; Mahoney, 1974, 1977). Most of these involve self-generated stimulation. The patient consciously self-monitors his behaviour and reinforces it positively or negatively by feedback stimulation, the anticipation of outcomes, or by symbolic self-evaluation. Of course, this requires a high degree of cooperation from the patient which itself may need to be gradually shaped by external reinforcement. However, this can be a self-accelerating process, in that experimental evidence from both humans and animals tends to show that freedom to choose and to self-regulate reinforcements are themselves reinforcing. Whether this evidence is relevant to a condition like schizophrenia, in which cognitive deficits (see Chapter 5) are marked, is a moot point.

Extreme behavioural theories of the aetiology of schizophrenia tend to parallel, but in overt behavioural and environmental terms, the covert cognitive and affective theories, such as those put forward by Bannister or Bateson. Thus Ullman and Krasner (1969) suggest that schizophrenic behaviour is the result of repeated failure of reinforcement for certain sequences of behaviour, from which the schizophrenic patient learns not to attend to the usual environmental cues related to reinforcement, especially the social stimuli to which normal people respond. They have more far-fetched explanations of delusions and hallucinations, which Bandura (1971) considers to be products of learning through the direct reinforcement and modelling provided by deviant parents.

Causes and effects may well be confused in these theories, for which there is little convincing empirical support. Nevertheless, many operant conditioners have accepted this point of view, and have taken the success of operant techniques in modifying the behaviour of (mainly chronic) schizophrenic patients as confirmation.

Impressed by Lindsley's (1956) original research demonstration that schizophrenic patients are subject to the normal laws of learning, Ayllon and Michael (1959) investigated the unconscious and often unfavourable influence of the psychiatric nurse and demonstrated how, by training nurses in simple behavioural techniques such as systematic transfer of attention from unwanted to desirable behaviour, "psychotic" behaviours could be reduced. Milby (1970) showed how this approach could increase interpersonal interactions by initially severely withdrawn patients.

Isaacs *et al.* (1960) reported an impressive reinstatement of speech by operant "shaping" in a severely withdrawn patient who had been mute for 19 years. Others (for example Sherman, 1965; Wilson and Walters, 1966) added imitation procedures to similar treatments of mutism, and Baker (1971) in this country carried out a controlled study with 18 mute chronic schizophrenic patients which confirmed the value of these approaches.

Treatment of this nature inevitably includes elements of social skills training. Gutride *et al.* (1973) showed in a controlled study that very brief periods of Goldstein's "Structured Learning Therapy" were effective, and superior to a form of psychotherapy in improving the social behaviour of groups of acute and chronic schizophrenic patients, and that this improvement was maintained outside the treatment setting. Liberman and his colleagues (1972, 1973b) used similar brief techniques in their successful and innovative community clinic run on largely behavioural lines in California. Bloomfield (1973) trained a group of chronic schizophrenic out-patients to become more "assertive" in social interactions, not only by expressing displeasure when required but also in positive ways. It should, of course, be recalled that the term "schizophrenia" may not be applied in the same way, in these studies, as it is in Britain.

These behavioural group therapies for schizophrenic patients who have returned to or not left the community are perhaps the most promising development in this field but the major applications of behaviour modification remain ward-based especially in the form of the "token economy" introduced by Ayllon and Azrin (1968). In a token economy, tokens, usually plastic discs, are used as generalized conditioned reinforcers by ward staff to reward patients for appropriate behaviour in areas such as self-care, recreational and work skills. The tokens are then used by the patients to "purchase" goods, amenities or privileges. Social reinforcement in the form of verbal praise and informational "feedback" is usually provided at the same time as tokens are presented. Thus a nurse might say, "Good. Well done. Here are three tokens. Your work is improving." Large groups of patients can be treated in this way without losing the possibility of flexible application as required by individuals. Numerous reviews of this approach are now available (for example, Davison, 1969; Liberman, 1970; Carlson *et al.*, 1972; Kazdin and Bootzin, 1972; Gripp and Magaro, 1974). It is clear that token economies can reduce the psychotic behaviour of chronic regressed patients at least to the degree that other techniques of rehabilitation can achieve, and enable patients to undertake productive work or even be discharged from hospital. Following Ayllon and Azrin's original report, more sophisticated systems emerged (for example, Atthowe and Krasner, 1968) with variations of "mini-economy" to encourage independence and originality.

Work has also continued (and emerged from token economies) on the more individual treatment of specific aspects of schizophrenic pathology. For example, Liberman *et al.* (1973c) attempted to reduce the delusional talk of four chronic paranoid patients by providing as reinforcement "evening chats" and refreshments with a therapist of choice. The length of this "chat" varied with the amount of rational speech produced during an earlier day session, which terminated if the patients spoke irrationally. Delusional speech was much reduced during the daily interviews and the evening chats but this did not generalize to normal ward interactions, where one of the four actually increased his delusional talk. However, Patterson and Teigen (1973) followed up one of the four, giving him specific ward training. This patient improved and was later discharged. Wincze *et al.* (1972) found that contingent tokens decreased delusional speech in seven of nine patients while feedback in a control group was effective for five out of ten patients. The reduction achieved varied from 20% to complete suppression.

Meichenbaum (1969) tackled schizophrenic thought disorder in an interesting and fruitful way. He reinforced relevant, logical and abstract interpretations of proverbs in a controlled study involving separate evaluation of token and social reinforcement. The reinforced groups improved more than control groups, not only on the specifically rein-forced type of behaviour but also on more general measures of thinking with the tokens apparently being more effective than social reinforce-ment. A side-observation was that some patients talked out loud to themselves, giving themselves instructions to "be coherent", etc. There-fore, following Cameron, he set out actually to train such patients to talk to themselves in this way (Meichenbaum and Cameron, 1973). Modelling and social approval were applied and, gradually, each patient was taught to internalize his thinking while maintaining his level of problem solving. Finally he was required to maintain both thinking and performance while a distracting tape was played. At a later stage this self-instruction was applied to more complex, sequential problems and self-reward was introduced. As with motor behaviour, complex sequences were taught by a "chaining" technique. The individual ele-ments are first dealt with separately, then the patient has to produce two elements in sequence for reinforcement, then three and so on. Finally, the patient was trained to become sensitive to cues of incomprehension in others. These patients reduced their disordered talk and improved their problem-solving performance more than control patients reinforced for correct performance but without training in self-instruction. This is a good example of behaviour modifiers turning their attention to covert, cognitive processes and to self-management (see also Chapter 11).

Hallucinations are essentially subjective phenomena, but patients' reports of their "voices" provide a basis for behavioural treatments and several single-case studies have been reported. Rutner and Bugle (1969) studied the hallucinatory voices of a long-term female patient, which were of a controlling nature and severely affected the patient's mood. She privately recorded their occurrence for three days. Her daily frequency chart was then put on public display and she received praise from staff and other patients when a reduction was evident. During the initial three days, hallucination frequencies were 181, 80, and 11; during the public display period they declined to zero after 13 days. No hallucinations were reported during a six month follow-up and the patient improved in other ways. The fact that the major decline occurred during the private recording period especially interested Reybee and Kinch (1973) who, in an unpublished study, investigated further the focusing of attention on hallucinatoiy voices. Two long-stay male patients with continuous "voices" were first required, in a "general focusing" stage, to self-rate the voices' frequency retrospectively at intervals during the day. This produced no change, but a "specific focusing" stage, during which for three sessions a week they sat silently in front of an event-recorder and pressed the button each time a voice was heard and continued pressing until it stopped, produced a steady decrease over seven weeks from a 50% to a 10% rate in one patient, and from 20% to 10% in the other. Both showed a plateau at 10% and there was no generalization from the laboratory to the ward setting. This lack of generalization from one setting to another was also discussed by Wing and Freudenberg (1961).

Haynes and Geddy (1973) used a "time-out" technique to suppress hallucinations in a 45-year-old woman who had been in hospital over 20 years. She made little or no contact with others and could not repeat her subjective experiences. Episodes during which she either mumbled to herself or yelled loudly without any apparent provocation were taken as representing "hallucinatory behaviour". "Time-out" refers to the removal of positive reinforcement for an interval after the display of undesirable behaviour; in this instance the removal of the patient from the ward to social isolation in a small unfurnished room for ten minutes.

Owing to the frequency of the hallucinatory behaviour, time-out could only be applied on some occasions—about four times a day. From a base-line frequency of occurrence, in about 80% of observation periods there was a decline to about 30% after 35 days when a plateau was reached.

Behaviour therapy as well as behaviour modification techniques have also been applied to auditory hallucinations. For example, Slade (1972) treated a 19-year-old acute schizophrenic man by systematic desensitization, first carrying out a situational analysis of environmental conditions, mood states, and hallucinations, based on the patient's self-ratings. It seemed that the mood state deteriorated during hallucinatory periods, tension mounting before the hallucination and declining subsequently. Therefore, situations were sought which were tension provoking and during these the patient was taught to relax by presenting a hierarchy of situations in imagination. Mood states improved and episodes of "voices" were significantly reduced in frequency, with further improvement during follow-up. However, there was an increase in guilt and the patient was later re-admitted with depression but free of hallucinations.

The examples of behavioural treatment approaches which have been described are only a selection of those available but they illustrate the range of techniques and the complexity of the processes involved. Apart from specific elements determined by the underlying behavioural rationale, many non-specific factors are shared with other methods of treatment. What is non-specific in behavioural treatment may well include specific aspects of other treatments, especially some of the environmental treatments described earlier. It may be useful to end this chapter with a fairly detailed account of an investigation with which the writer has been particularly concerned (Baker *et al.*, 1977), which was designed to unravel some of the crucial factors in the type of behaviour modification procedures, especially token economies, which have proved useful in the treatment of chronic schizophrenia.*

* This report describes a project carried out between 1970 and 1976 at Stanley Royd Hospital, Wakefield, and supported by grants from the Department of Health and Social Security, the Medical Research Council and the Mental Health Research Fund. Apart from the five named authors who were involved throughout, others served for varying periods on the research staff and contributed a great deal: Drs K. Hutchinson, G. W. K. Bridges and K. Vaddadi, psychiatrists; Mr R. J. Butler, psychologist; Messrs H. Ineson and R. Agbah, nurses; Mrs J. Needham, secretary. Various members of the hospital staff also provided close and valuable support.

A Study of a Token Economy

When this study was originally planned no adequate field study of a token economy had been completed in Britain, although great interest had been excited by the American results. (There are now more than 30 active programmes in Britain.) It was clear that behavioural defects of the type associated with institutionalism—poor appearance, work habits, speech, self-help and the like—could be vastly improved by changes in social environment (Wing and Brown, 1961, 1970). There was also evidence that environmental changes were of great importance in influencing more active symptoms such as delusions and hallucinations (Brown *et al.*, 1972; Wing *et al.*, 1964). It was not, however, clear whether token economies could be used to influence symptoms such as delusions and hallucinations. In particular, since control groups had seldom been used, the treatment effects of token economies might to a large degree be attributable to the increased amount and improved quality of attention received by patients, although within-treatment controls had indicated that not all the improvement could be accounted for in this way. It was also striking that very few of the programmes described in the literature had survived the period of active installation and investigation by researchers, to become the regular and established routine of the hospital. Breakdown appeared to be part of the natural history of token economies (see Hall and Baker, 1973).

Thus the initial objectives were:

(1) to test whether token economy procedures were feasible in a British psychiatric hospital and to assess their potential as standard hospital procedure;

(2) to assess their efficiency using carefully matched control groups and with reference to a wide range of target behaviours;

(3) to assess the degree of residual defect remaining if and when improvement ceased;

(4) to assess the specific contribution to this improvement of contingent token reinforcement;

(5) subsidiary objectives concerned the development of assessment methods, nurse selection and training, and patient selection.

Despite the intention to establish control groups, the first 31 weeks of the research were designed on the basis of within-subject controls. This phase was intended to provide a training period for staff, to develop a set of assessment procedures and to establish the optimum package of therapeutic procedures, i.e. to decide the form of token economy which was to be applied to the experimental group in the main study. However, this pilot study (see Baker *et al.*, 1974) also produced interesting independent findings complementing those which came from the later main study. Seven male schizophrenic patients were involved. They had been in hospital from eight to 28 years and presented a wide range of symptoms, including delusions, affective flattening and speech disturbance. All displayed varying degrees of social withdrawal and a more equal share of socially embarrassing behaviour as rated on the Wing Ward Behaviour Scales (Wing, 1961).

These patients were brought together in a specially allotted small ward where their treatment passed through six stages:

(1) *Base-line* (6 weeks). Continuation of previous ward management and drug regime. Mainly custodial care and maintenance dosage of phenothiazines.

(2) *Activity* (3 weeks). As token economies involve increased stimulation and patient activity, an attempt was made to apply this component alone by intensive occupational therapy, work schedules, visits and on-ward social activities (Rosenthall *et al.*, 1972). The activities were matched to patients so as to stretch their capacities.

(3) *Free token phase* (7 weeks). Forty-five free tokens, not contingent upon behaviour, were issued daily. Patients paid nine of these for bed and board and could spend the remainder in an attractive ward shop. Quite strong salesmanship was necessary to persuade some patients to spend.

(4) *Contingent token phase* (14 weeks). The system was explained to the patients and then introduced gradually, starting with payment for ward tasks and withdrawing the free tokens in stages. The target behaviours subsequently rewarded by tokens included self-care, good appearance, prescribed and additional voluntary tasks, speech and social interaction, and also self-initiated activities which were fostered by fading-out the prompting usually provided by nurses.

This programme made great demands on the nurses, who had to adopt elaborate checking and assessment procedures. Token values were adjusted as a patient improved in any one area, and token earnings and expenditure were recorded on charts designed to guide nurses through the daily programme and to monitor the patients' performance. At a later stage Ineson (1976) wrote a 58-page manual of practice on such a ward.

(5) *Post treatment phase* (1 week). Baseline conditions were resumed.

(6) *Follow-up* after 8 weeks.

Assessment was by continuous and before and after measures. These included rating scales for dressing and initiative and the Wing Ward Behaviour Scale completed by nurses, a modification by Hamilton of the Lorr Standardized Psychiatric Rating Scale (Hamilton, 1960), a structured clinical interview (Burdock and Hardesty, 1968), and individual psychometric tests.

The measures showed considerable improvement overall, especially in the target areas of dressing and initiative but with a very wide range of individual differences. However, the improvement typically occurred early, sometimes dramatically so, before the contingent token phase. Thus the effects of better care and increased stimulation appeared to overshadow the contingency effects. The non-target items, owing to the process of target selection, started at a good level. Nevertheless, those for dressing did improve but only initially. Those for initiative actually showed a tendency to deteriorate during the contingency period which may reflect focusing of attention on to the target items.

Social withdrawal improved significantly over the first three periods, reaching a plateau which was maintained throughout the contingency phase. However, socially embarrassing behaviour showed a strikingly reciprocal pattern with significant deterioration during the contingent token phase. A withdrawn patient is inactive in all ways, socially embarrassing or otherwise: it seemed that less withdrawal allowed psychopathological behaviour to manifest itself afresh in an overt manner. This interpretation was supported by the Hamilton-Lorr ratings which followed a generally similar path to the social withdrawal ratings but with deterioration during the contingent token phase in the areas of thought disorder, emotional disturbance and catatonic symptoms. Thus there was some indication that positive symptoms reacted differently to the clinical poverty syndrome.

In summary, the patients undoubtedly improved as a consequence of the programme but there was little evidence that specific token contingency was the main factor in this improvement. As many other studies have shown, there is room for improvement following a long period of neglect (Wing and Brown, 1970). The major challenge is posed by patients who have not improved, even following many years of a positive regime (Catterson et al., 1963). It was also shown that it is necessary to follow-up patients for some time and that the nature of the post-treatment environment is an important factor in determining the outcome. Apart from the general regime, individual patients received individualized, intensive operant programmes, along the lines of case studies in the literature already reviewed, for specific behavioural abnormalities such as auditory hallucinations, irrelevant speech, These were sometimes very effective.

For the second, 15-month, main study (Hall *et al.*, 1977) three groups of six patients each were assembled from a pool of patients similar to those recruited for the pilot study. These were matched as closely as possible in threes for age, length of stay, ward behaviour and psychiatric symptoms. The triplet members were then randomly assigned to the three groups. Members of the control group remained on their own wards and received no special treatment except that they were assessed at the same times as the other two groups. The latter transferred to the experimental ward for their base-line assessment and a structured activity programme as piloted. This also continued into the next or token stage which differed for the two groups. The "contingent token groups" (CT) were treated as in the contingent phase of the first study. Thus for these patients, the performance of a target behaviour was reinforced with praise and attention (i.e. *social reinforcement*), an appropriate number of tokens (i.e. *token reinforcement*), and the patients received an explanation of why the tokens were awarded (i.e. *informational feedback*). The other "non-contingent token group" (NCT) received similar contingent social reinforcement and informational feedback and tokens matched in number to their CT partner's previous day's earnings at ten arbitrary and varied times of the day. Time-sampling observational methods were employed to ensure that equal amounts of attention were directed to each group. Thus, the token contingency was the essential difference between the two experimental groups. The NCT group were in fact exposed to a regime very similar to that advocated by Russell Barton (1976). By the overall design it was hoped to control change of physical environment, specification of goals, amount of stimulation and ward atmosphere.

The ward activity programme was essentially as in the pilot study, but with a wider and more complex range of activities and jobs. The range of target behaviours was similar to the pilot study, but tokens were allocated in different amounts. Each patient's token income sheet was marked up individually for each day, noting differences of token values, etc. For certain behavioural areas systematic variable-ratio schedules of reinforcement were used. These were progressively "thinned out" until no reinforcement was necessary. Care was taken to balance social reinforcement schedules for both groups of patients.

Care was also taken not to reinforce NCT patients accidentally. For example, if patients were absent without leave from the ward, they did not receive any tokens due to them on return, as this might have constituted token reinforcement for absconding. Control patients were also cushioned from very wide fluctuations in token earnings, although the total amount received was exactly the same as their token mates.

Two changes were made to the assessment procedures. The frequency of some measures was reduced, because of the increased work-load produced by more patients and a more varied regime, and also because the longer experimental phases required less frequent measurement. However, the range was broadened by the use of three separate verbal ability tests, additional rating scales and two separate time-sampling procedures to record spontaneous speech produced by patients and attention paid by nurses. Assessments were related to standard four-week periods, so that any individual changes in required levels of target behaviour were also re-set every four weeks. Regular reliability checks were carried out throughout the study.

The base-line and assessment period lasted for 12 weeks. The next 48 weeks were then devoted to the treatments as described and then the token system was maintained for a further 12 weeks during which post-treatment assessments were made. These periods are longer than in most other related studies but one of the findings was that, at each stage, the effects took a surprisingly long time to stabilize.

Over the entire period both CT and NCT groups improve in similar ways to a similar extent. The on-ward control group, on the contrary, actually showed some deterioration illustrating the need for prophylactic as well as therapeutic measures. The improvement shown by the experimental groups cannot be due to contingent tokens but to some factor common to both groups. This does not exclude social and informational forms of reinforcement. Again, contingent tokens were found to be the most useful when applied in individual sessions for specific purposes. The tokens also served a useful purpose in the general programme by directing staff attention to particular problem areas. The CT patients also showed greater improvement than NCT patients during the early stages of the token stage, which could explain the apparent overall superiority of contingent tokens in some studies with brief experimental treatment periods. Other more thorough recent studies support the present finding.

Improvement was most marked in both groups in the areas of social withdrawal (especially in the areas of social interest and mixing), appearance and routine behaviour. Again there was evidence that the initial improvement of CT patients was accompanied by some deterioration in relation to symptoms such as hallucinations, emotional and motor abnormalities and agitation, but not to withdrawal and thought disorder. However, this deterioration was only temporary, with a subsequent return to initial levels and ultimate (post-experimental period) improvement (Baker *et al.*, 1977). Again this points to the importance of allowing sufficient time for effects to stabilize. The pilot study (and others in the literature) did not allow sufficient time for this.

Non-target items showed some tendency to deteriorate over the length of the study and, within particular target areas, improvement was most marked for items on which patients were initially worse. However, the regime overall appeared to be most beneficial for patients in the middle range of severity of condition. The gains of the very deteriorated, although significant, really produced slight clinical pay-off, a factor to be noted in considering the cost efficiency of this type of programme. Some of the higher level patients also appeared not to be helped by the inevitable degree of control necessary to operate the programme. For them, a more flexible regime allowing greater independence would be advantageous.

Compared with the pilot study, there were some unexpected and anomalous changes in individual's behaviour during the relatively lengthy base-line phase. These tend to indicate that suggestive and attitudinal factors related to staff training and expectations concerning novel treatments were operating.

Paradoxical effects of treatment were also shown by several individuals. For example, one patient was noted early on to be eating less than one-third of the meals provided. As his weight remained stable it seemed that this must have been his unnoticed regular intake on his previous ward. However, when the programme required token payment for meals he ate more. Later his intake was fully normalized on an individual contingency programme.

A female patient on a later established, parallel token ward spent most of her day off the ward. She was given tokens every time she was observed on the ward and reacted (quite sensibly) by waiting for payment and then immediately departing. Then she was required to pay three tokens to leave and received a handful if she returned after a specified time, say half an hour. This worked at first but she gradually deteriorated until the programme was discontinued and she was allowed to leave as she pleased. This resulted in a dramatic reduction in her off-ward time.

For the writer, who does not subscribe to a strict operant view of man, but in the context of a more cognitive learning theory, sees him as a complex but integrated, information-processing and self-regulating organism, several of these apparent anomalies make sense. The highly organized structure of a token economy and its intrinsic informational feedback provide the basis for improved self-control by those patients who improve. Others cannot cope, while others again (those initially at a high level) may find the new structure a frustrative interference with other forms of information flow which impairs their freedom of action.

Thus, in setting up regimes of this nature, it would seem advisable to select relatively homogeneous groups of patients and to match and adjust the complexity of the programme to their initial and changing level of functioning allowing for the incorporation of specially tailored individual programmes to deal with specific problems. For this to be achieved successfully, thorough training and the full cooperation of the ward staff is essential. The general programme is in the hands of the nurses and, although the design of individual programmes may be the particular province of clinical psychologists, these too may be passed over when established. The operant paradigm provides a valuable technological framework not only for programme design but also for training staff and, in treatment, the evidence indicates that it does not embrace all the therapeutic factors.

One of the main objectives of the investigation was to test the viability of such systems within the routine of a typical mental hospital. This means that the programme cannot operate in isolation but must form part of an overall rehabilitation system, preferably involving several wards, planned occupational therapy, half-way houses, and other aids to rehabilitation. When the main experiment ended, attention was therefore paid to these contextual elements, and the experimental ward routine was changed so as to take account of the experimental findings and to prepare for the withdrawal of the researchers and the hand over to the hospital clinical team.

All patients (CT and NCT) moved to a contingent token programme and the assessment procedures were reduced and simplified. Few changes were noticed in the NCT patients' behaviour except that there were more frequent requests for "floating" tasks. The continuing assessment did show the slow but significant improvement over the following three years in socially embarrassing and symptomatic behaviour which had initially deteriorated during the experimental period. As the hospital rehabilitation system developed, patients were transferred elsewhere to be replaced by means of a standardized selection procedure. Ineson's (1976) manual describes the final form of the programme.

Meanwhile, senior nurses had become interested in developing a similar programme in an adjacent female ward. With psychiatric cooperation a homogeneous group of 12 patients was selected and two qualified and other student nurses were allocated. No formal research was attempted but it was intended to explore how much such patients could improve on a small ward with a favourable staffing ratio by applying an activity and social interaction regime without tokens. The permanent staff members first spent two weeks on the male token ward with the interesting consequence that they became wedded, despite the reverse encouragement of the research team, to the introduction of tokens on the female ward. A token programme was therefore established and, largely under the guidance of Mr R. J. Butler, then a graduate psychologist working as a nursing assistant, took an initially rather different form from the previous one and developed in very different ways, with a strong emphasis on community facilities and individual programmes (Butler, 1977). When a patient's target behaviour reached appropriate levels, weaning from tokens was begun by reducing their number and by making them contingent upon longer chains of behaviour. Delayed reinforcement was only really successful with the least withdrawn patients and when token earnings were high and stable.

Seventeen patients had passed through this ward by the end of the study. Of these, four failed to respond and moved to other wards. Seven of initial low level improved but not to discharge level, two moved to a pre-discharge ward, one worked outside the hospital but still lived in, and one was discharged home.

Meanwhile, a multi-ward rehabilitation programme had been established as the final phase of the project. This had a service rather than a research orientation. One reason for its development was that patients who had improved on the token economy still lacked skills related to budgetting, shopping, cooking and other essential activities of community life. Therefore, a series of services was established to enable these and other patients to progress by stages from hospital to community. Rehabilitation is a major topic of the next chapter but, for the sake of completion, this chapter ends with a brief outline of the current rehabilitation system at Stanley Royd Hospital:

(1) *Selection Committee*. Patients may be referred from any ward to a small multidisciplinary selection committee which meets weekly. This committee decides whether a patient is to be accepted into the system and, if so, whether into the pre-discharge ward or into the male or female token economy. Motivation towards discharge is an important criterion.

(2) *Token Economies*. Only a minority of patients enter these wards. These patients are not at a sufficiently high level to move directly to the pre-discharge ward but are thought capable of being raised to that level. If and when improvement is sufficient they are transferred to the pre-

discharge ward. If that level cannot be reached they return to an ordinary ward.

(3) *Pre-discharge Ward*. This is a 40-bed ward of average staff–patient ratio. Training in community skills is provided by occupational therapists and practical preparations are made for discharge. From here patients may be discharged directly into the community, to relatives, flats, hostels, etc. or enter an alternative, smaller stream by transferring to the Preparatory House.

(4) *Preparatory House*. This is a small, pleasant house within the hospital grounds with a fair degree of privacy and good domestic facilities. Groups of four patients, selected for compatability, live here, buy their own food, cook, work, etc. but are given support as required. "Housekeeper" patients receive practical training in relevant skills from the occupational therapist and group discussions are run by a social worker. Usually two patients are "housekeepers" and two have full-time occupations. This house has proved an essential part of the system. Incompatible patients, or those whose clinical condition deteriorates, are returned to the pre-discharge ward. Those who complete the training move into the community either in one of the ways mentioned or into a group home.

(5) *Group Homes*. Four of these have been established in surrounding districts with charity support. They are usually semi-detached houses in well populated areas: two are all-male, one all-female, and one mixed. Support is provided by community nurses or social workers.

Of 87 patients followed through, 23 were not selected and 24 were discharged. Of the latter, 12 went to group homes, two to relatives, two to hostels, two to flats and six to no fixed abode. Their mean stay in the rehabilitation system had been eight and a half months. Fifteen patients were "stuck" on the pre-discharge ward (mean stay 22·7 months), 16 had been transferred from the pre-discharge ward and nine had been selected for the token economies. Six of these nine had been adequately prepared for the pre-discharge ward and one was unsuccessful. The mean length of token treatment was 15·3 months.

During the last year of the research project, responsibility for those parts of the system controlled by research staff was transferred to hospital staff. A gratifying aspect of this project is that what started as a small scale, single ward research project affecting a handful of patients has become a well-established hospital-wide rehabilitation scheme. The place of token economies is small but apparently important, so long as the overall rehabilitation context is kept at a high standard. The principles of rehabilitation, both in the in-patient and in the wider community setting, will be considered in the next chapter.

9 | Social Forms of Psychiatric Treatment

Douglas Bennett

We have seen that the course and outcome of "schizophrenia"* is not uniform. Some patients suffer an acute attack, characterized by typical first-rank symptoms and diagnosed according to strict clinical criteria, but subsequently never experience another. On the other hand, up to one quarter of all those who have a first attack are found to be substantially socially disabled five years later. The factors that influence the course —genetic, pharmacological, and social—have been discussed in some detail. In this chapter, we shall discuss the application of this knowledge, and of more empirical clinical experience, to problems of rehabilitation and resettlement.

Rehabilitation is the process of helping a physically or psychiatrically disabled person to make the best use of his residual abilities in order to function at an optimum level in as normal a social context as possible (Wing, 1963). In rehabilitation, we try to help a disabled person to adapt or readapt. In pursuing this aim, we seek to reduce or limit the extent of the individual's disabilities and to develop compensatory adaptive skills. Even if some disabilities are permanent, the disabled may still be helped to adapt if alterations or adjustments can be made in the environment. The aim of rehabilitation is resettlement, the success of which is judged by the extent to which the disabled individual is able to work independently, to sustain ordinary domestic and family responsibilities, and to make enjoyable and creative use of his leisure time. Such a standard is very high, even for non-handicapped individuals, and it is not applicable to many people with schizophrenic disabilities. For chronically disabled people, resettlement always means something less

* See p. viii.

than the ideal, but this does not imply any relaxation of standards for rehabilitation. On the contrary, the more disabled the individual the more important it is to design an effective programme of rehabilitation in order to attain an optimum resettlement.

This distinction between rehabilitation and resettlement is often overlooked. For example, it may be assumed that simply discharging a patient from hospital is a criterion of successful resettlement. Discharge rates, or figures about length of stay, are used as indices of outcome, without further data about level of social functioning or quality of life. Similarly, it may be assumed that someone who is living at home, or who is employed, need not be considered for rehabilitation, because he or she is already "resettled". Rehabilitation means decreasing disabilities as far as possible, maintaining them at a low level, and increasing assets in order to compensate for any disabilities that are irreducible. Only after a lengthy period of rehabilitation is it possible to make a guess as to the optimal level of settlement that an individual can achieve.

Employment Rehabilitation Centres (ERCs) provide an example of how confusing terminology can be. Although they do have certain rehabilitation functions they are, on the whole, more directed towards resettlement, i.e. placement in jobs. They try not to accept schizophrenic patients who are unlikely to find work after a six- to eight-week course. Such people do, of course, exist but the main value of an ERC in chronic schizophrenia is as the end-point in a long process of preparation (Beach, 1975). Yet many psychiatrists refer unprepared patients to ERCs, on the assumption that they will be "rehabilitated". It is not surprising if psychiatrists and ERC staff become pessimistic about the possibility of the centres helping schizophrenic patients.

The process of rehabilitation often has to be prolonged and it must be based on an accurate assessment of the disabilities that are likely to occur in chronic schizophrenia and of the ways in which these are maintained or altered by environmental influences. The intrinsic impairments, extrinsic disadvantages, and adverse secondary reactions that commonly occur in schizophrenia have been described in Chapter 1 and their social reactivity has been considered in Chapters 6 and 8. Before discussing methods of assessment it is important to mention some of the sociological concepts that underlie rehabilitation procedures.

Theoretical Views of Rehabilitation

Phillips (1968) suggests that a person's adaptation is his response to the complexities of living in society. Pathological reactions and disabilities which undermine a person's adaptation have to be considered in the context of his more positive adaptive capacities. Phillips views adaptation as a developmental process in which the individual must, at each age, meet increasing expectations not only that he should be more independent, but should undertake responsibility for others. Phillips suggests that a person's adaptation requires a degree of social competence which is a composite measure of his intellectual capacity for mastery of the objective world, his social capacity for relationships with others and his acceptance of principles which guide interpersonal behaviour and enable him to choose between alternative paths of action. A person's capacity for adaptation will, therefore, be determined in part by his premorbid social competence. This will be undermined by the schizophrenic disorder. At the same time, failure through a lack of competence to meet the expectations of society in family life or employment may cause stress which activates schizophrenic symptoms.

Social competence depends in part on a person's natural endowment but also on the socialization process by which he acquires the knowledge, skills and disposition which make him a more or less able member of society. While there is a tendency to concentrate on socialization in childhood, this process cannot prepare a person for all the roles which he will be expected to fill in later years (Brim and Wheeler, 1966). Socialization plays an important part in the rehabilitation process, as it seeks to help a disabled person to acquire or regain the habits, beliefs, attitudes and motivation which will enable him to perform satisfactorily in the roles expected of him in society. Brim and Wheeler (1966) suggest that before a person is able to perform satisfactorily in a role he must know the behaviour and values expected of him, must be able to meet role requirements and must desire to practise the behaviour and pursue the appropriate ends. Most institutions for adult socialization, such as universities, or the army, screen out those who do not have appropriate abilities, motives and values for the anticipated roles; they get rid of potential failures. A system such as a hospital which attempts to re-socialize the mentally ill has to get rid of its successes and keep its failures. One cannot screen out patients from rehabilitation, but one can try to recognize the specific needs and limitations of individual patients, define one's aims and avoid a wasteful approach to rehabilitation based "on faith, hope and rule of thumb" (Lewis, 1955).

A person with chronic schizophrenia not only has limited competence; he also has a clinical condition which is highly responsive to social stress. Mechanic (1970) does not see stress as the stimulus acting on a person nor that person's response to the stimulus, but as the discrepancy

H

between the demands presented to the individual and his capacity to deal with them. If the patient with schizophrenia can deal with problems in the family, employment or elsewhere, using the skills, knowledge and social techniques he has acquired, relapse will not occur. The gap between social expectations and the patient's capacity to meet them is bridged by two factors: one, the skill in social performance which Mechanic calls "coping"; and the other, the intrapsychic mechanisms manifested in emotional responses of confidence or anxiety, which he calls "defence". The ability to deal with stress depends on the patient's skills and emotional stability, as well as on his motivation. Thus it is necessary to ask whether the patient *wishes* to cope with the stresses of life (or rehabilitation), whether he is actually able to do so, and whether he is confident that he can do so without breaking down. The answers will bear some relationship to each other, for the patient's wish to deal with his situation depends to some extent on whether he thinks he is able to do so, and his assessment of that ability depends in part on his self-confidence.

These theoretical formulations find support not only from clinical experience but from research on the rehabilitation of disabled people. Thus in a study of a rehabilitation unit, mainly for the physically disabled, Wing (1966) demonstrated how the acquisition of skill influenced self-confidence as well as diminishing anxiety and depression. Strauss and Carpenter (1972, 1973) examining the outcome of schizophrenic patients concluded that poor work and poor social functioning might be quite independent of the schizophrenic condition. Cumming (1963) too, has shown that many patients with schizophrenia before they were first admitted to hospital had a very limited social adaptation and were living on welfare payments. These findings underline the need in rehabilitation to examine the patient's previous social adaptation as well as his present social competence and to consider the process of socialization for social roles as well as identifying symptoms and disabilities. For it is on this basis that one must make assessments of a patient's function, plan interventions in the individual case and develop rehabilitation settings.

Rehabilitation for all psychiatric patients, as well as those suffering from schizophrenia, is principally directed to the recovery or initiation of appropriate social roles, as compared with the over-riding aim of restoring task performance in physical illness. But patients with schizophrenia do have difficulties in task performance which need consideration. When a selected group of schizophrenic patients were sent to an ERC and were compared with a group of non-schizophrenic entrants they did not show any significant difference in terms of good manual dexterity, taking trouble or in the completion and finish of work. They were, however, more socially withdrawn, lacking in skill, less industrious and less popular than non-schizophrenic controls. They lacked initiative and could only cope with the simplest work (Wing *et al.*, 1964). They are often slow workers and have difficulty in dealing efficiently with semi-complex psychomotor tasks (Wadsworth *et al.*, 1962).

Assessment

The first step in assessment is to discover the nature, severity and extent of the schizophrenic disabilities from the clinical history and an examination of the patient's mental state. An impression of a person's previous social adaptation is also obtained from the history. His intellectual development is not necessarily revealed by measures of intelligence. What one must discover from the history is how he has fulfilled this intellectual potential in his educational and occupational life. An individual's social development is estimated by a consideration of the stability of his interpersonal relationships, the degree of emotional involvement he has been able to initiate and sustain, and the diversity of these relationships in so far as they denote the presence of skills in interpersonal interaction. Finally one tries to assess his acceptance of the principles which guide interpersonal behaviour. This can be inferred from the extent to which he seems to be accountable for his acts and their consequences, in terms of adult independence from parents and the level of responsibility he has achieved in employment. One must form some impression too of his sense of obligation to others. This is often reflected in his marital history, which may also suggest his sense of reciprocity in his relations with others. Efforts to achieve a more accurate appraisal of previous social adaptation in employment have been reported (Watts and Bennett, 1977) and other measures of social adaptation will doubtless follow. An assessment should also be made of the patient's present competence and skill, and how these relate to the stresses, expectations of social and family life and employment which he will have to meet when he leaves hospital, and how far he is motivated to meet these. This requires some assessment not only of the expectations of family members but also of the "coping supports" which they afford the patient. Few people have to cope entirely alone; most find support in this task from family, friends and colleagues who advise, help and reassure them.

In physical rehabilitation it is relatively simple to introduce or reproduce, in the hospital, those aspects of the physical environment, such
as special kitchens or bedrooms, to which the patient has to adapt.
Human behaviour, too, can be observed easily enough, although it can
be distorted by hospital influences. But there are special difficulties in
judging the ability of a psychiatrically disabled patient to perform the
roles of daily life in a hospital setting; for hospitals reduce the demands
and stresses of daily life and assign disabled persons the role of patient
(Parsons and Fox, 1952). It is not usually possible to provide the cus-
tomary adult roles for the sick or disabled in hospital, therefore one is
forced to make one's assessment of behaviour, competence and role
performance in stages as the patient moves from low expectation wards
to those requiring more personal independence such as a day hospital
(where he is only a partial patient) and eventually community life.
With each subsequent move towards the daily life of the community a
more complete assessment is possible and will confirm, amplify or refute
views formed at an earlier stage.

Day hospitals are good settings for assessment, since the patient is
playing some roles in the family or elsewhere outside the hospital, and
his family are more easily contacted. Paid subcontract work is useful in
assessment because it provides the disabled person with a role where the
balance between expectations and reward represent the norms of employment outside hospital (Bennett, 1970). Many mental hospitals have
provided houses or flats where patients live independently and where
assessment of self-care skills and competence in a domestic role can be
made in a more "normal" social context. Otherwise such assessments
have to be made in the patient's home or lodgings and this presents
difficulties. Assessments of employability can only be made in hospital
if a realistic work setting is available, managed by staff with experience
of industry who are familiar with the outlook of employers, supervisors
and workers more than with the requirements of hospital life. In such a
realistic setting, using recently developed measures it is possible to make
valid and reliable predictions of the post-hospital employability of a
patient (Cheadle et al., 1967; Cheadle and Morgan, 1972; Griffiths,
1973; Watts, 1974). Most judgements of a patient's role performance,
attitudes and motivation are very subjective. It is obvious that a female
member of staff will see and assess a male patient's role in a different
manner from that of a male staff member. Further, a nurse or occupational therapist in contact with the patient all day will see aspects of his
behaviour which he would not reveal to a doctor or social worker who
interview him in an office. Differences in their outlook and in their

experience of the patient lead to staff disagreements about such matters as whether the patient can, or will, do this or that, or whether he is trying or not trying. At other times they question whether his behaviour is reasonable or appropriate to a person of his age and sex, and so on. It is important therefore in making such judgements to involve all the staff who work with the patient in such discussions; not only staff from different disciplines, but of differing age and sex and especially the junior staff who spend most time with the patient. While there is no alternative to such subjective and controversial assessments, it cannot be too strongly emphasized that no assessment should be made on the supposition that the individual cannot and would never be able to do this or that. In every case assessments should be based on the patient's actual performance. It is equally important to realize that assessements only hold good for the time and the situation where they were made. Rehabilitation does change disabilities, attitudes and competence, however slowly. If there is any doubt a further trial of an activity or role performance in an appropriate situation must always be preferred to stubborn reliance on an outdated assessment.

Finally it is important to assess the patient's family and social network in terms of their attitude and behaviour to the patient, and the amount of stress they, or the patient, experience. In most instances this is best done by discussion with the family and the patient rather than by asking a social worker to visit the family alone, although this may be advisable in some instances.

Rehabilitation Practice

The theoretical views outlined earlier have now to be translated into the principles and practice of rehabilitation. In the rehabilitation of patients with schizophrenia the clinician must help the patient to avoid situations which might be overstimulating or understimulating (see Chapter 6). The patient with schizophrenia has a marked tendency to withdraw socially. If there is no social stimulation this withdrawal is fostered, together with passivity, inertia and lack of initiative. On the the other hand, if the patient is overstimulated socially, he may well break down and once again develop florid psychotic symptoms (Stone and Eldred, 1959; Wing et al., 1964). For this reason, rehabilitation has to be arranged in a series of steps in which social expectations are slowly increased without stressing the patient so much that he breaks down and becomes floridly psychotic. When he has mastered one rehabilitation step he moves on to the next. Thus, in terms of Mechanic's model, he gains skill in coping without his illness being made worse and his confidence undermined. The patient should thus gain a sense of mastery which will in turn increase his motivation. This policy demands a graded series of living and work environments in the hospital and elsewhere, each with a progressively higher level of expectation in terms of work or social independence. A patient may not necessarily show the same level of emotional stability or skill in work as he does in the residential environment or vice versa, so advance may be quicker in one area than the other. Wards can be arranged in a progressive series where increasing social expectations correspond to a reduction in the ratio of nursing staff to patients as the patient moves through the rehabilitation process to resettlement. Similarly progress in employment can be arranged in stages; the hours of work and the complexity of the job to be done very steadily increased. The transfer of a patient to a situation with higher expectations should only be made after careful consideration of his capacity for such a move. In implementing this policy, rehabilitation becomes an essential part of a patient's total care; it is not located in a special department or a workshop. So while there may be a place for a consultant with a special interest in rehabilitation to be responsible for organizing the service, clinical responsibility for the rehabilitation of the individual patient must be a part of every psychiatric consultant's work (Tunbridge Report: DHSS, 1972).

In rehabilitation one should always aim to prepare the patient for community adjustment. Some patients may not achieve this, but the optimal outcome of rehabilitation is likely to result from setting expectations that are always a little above those of patient and relatives. When community readjustment is the aim, one has to help patients to play normal social roles. Task performance is important but not enough. As has been said, it is not easy to introduce normal roles into the mental hospital but something can be done to encourage patient's role performance even in long-stay wards. Wing and Brown (1970) in their study of three mental hospitals describe "Longfield Villa" in one of the hospitals. That villa housed the most severely handicapped female patients in the whole hospital. Yet these patients, mostly suffering from schizophrenia, got up, got their meals, did the chores, went to work, spent their leisure time, and organized their way of life as they would if they were not in hospital and not handicapped.

Ideally the last stage of rehabilitation should take place in a day setting where the patient gradually assumes his roles in the family and everyday life.

A controlled study of day hospital rehabilitation was undertaken in the Maudsley Day Hospital, and Vocational Resettlement Unit (Bennett, 1972) and the outcome was measured in terms of patients' attitudes, disabilities and social performance (Griffith, 1974; Stevens, 1973; Wing *et al.*, 1972). The experiment was unique in that the sample of patients was drawn from the Camberwell Register and so represented a district rather than a hospital population. Seventy-five patients were eligible for the study but only 28 patients were judged to be both suitable and willing to take part. They were divided into experimental and control groups with 14 patients in each. The control group patients were not admitted to the day hospital and their consultants were free to arrange treatment or rehabilitation as they wished. All the patients were severely handicapped; most were suffering from schizophrenia. A number of patients could not cope with the sudden transition from a home or institutional environment to the more complicated and demanding life in the day hospital and either had adverse reactions or stayed away. There was no significant difference in outcome between the experimental and control group. So while there are obvious advantages in rehabilitating patients in a more natural environment, this stage has to be approached by easy steps if patients with schizophrenia are not to be overstimulated. With hindsight, much more attention should have been paid to the patient's domestic environment (most were not living with families) for it is there that he spends 128 hours of the week compared with 40 hours in the day hospital.

The Setting for Rehabilitation

It is necessary now to say something of what is required in a rehabilitation setting. Rehabilitation takes place in a variety of settings, such as the ward, the hospital workshop, the day hospital or the family. No single setting is ideal for rehabilitation. Each has its advantages and disadvantages for any particular patient; it may be too stressful or offer too little stimulation, it may offer too much or too little staff supervision, it can be desocializing for the patient or present expectations he cannot meet. The setting alone cannot rehabilitate a patient. Rehabilitation has to be tailored to the individual's specific disabilities, his interests, motivations and his native or learned skills. But the setting can and should be organized to provide a certain general level of expectation. For example, the workshop presents general expectations about timekeeping and working and it provides adequate quantities of work suitable for patients with different interests and different abilities. Some work should require mental judgement and skill, such as concentration and accuracy, initiative and independent judgement. Other tasks exploit ability in interpersonal relationships and complex or simple repetitive manual skills. In the early stages of rehabilitation, disability rather than skill will determine what a patient can do. Later one has to concentrate on teaching and development of the skills which the patient lacks and on the improvement of those aspects of role performance which have been impaired.

All rehabilitation settings must be organized to foster everyday role performance, maintain independence and activity, provide a normally patterned day of work and leisure, and so on. Certain of these requirements were recognized by the pioneers of the "therapeutic community" approach. They set out to provide a setting in which the patient and staff communicated freely, examined each other's behaviour in small groups and dealt with each other in a "democratic" manner. This certainly did something to clarify the *emotional* obstacles to the patient's coping, in terms of his interpersonal relations. It emphasized responsibility and changed some aspects of the patient role. But its ideology confused rehabilitation and treatment (Cumming, 1969; Rapoport, 1960). While social adaptation was set as the aim, the practice was to try to change the patient's personality. The whole package of activities was assumed to be "therapeutic" but it was not clear which activities were effective or for which patient. Wing and Brown (1970) approached the problem of the effect of the social milieu on patients in a different way. They began with the established ward environments in three mental hospitals. Over a period of eight years they measured the social changes, for better or worse, which took place and then saw how these alterations paralleled changes in the measured disabilities of chronic patients with schizophrenia. They found that the most important single factor associated with improvement in patients' intrinsic handicaps was a reduction in the amount of time which patients spent doing nothing. A more restrictive ward seemed to play an independent part in maintaining "negative" symptoms. Increased contact with the outside world, a more optimistic mood among the nursing staff and an increased supply of personal belongings were less important as far as intrinsic disabilities were concerned. They were, nevertheless, of major importance in reducing secondary or extrinsic handicaps.

Rehabilitation in that context was "late" rehabilitation (Gastager, 1969): largely a matter of making the best of a bad job and reversing where possible the effects of past neglect, by alterations in the ward environment. It is important to note that while communication and staff attitudes can only be changed in staff and staff/patient groups, alterations in the other important variables require administrative action. In the "early" rehabilitation of patients who do not have a long hospital stay, restrictiveness, the deprivation of personal belongings and lack of contact with the outside world are of less importance. One finds that disabilities, while still present, and sometimes incapacitating, are, in general less severe. But social adaptation is not automatically restored by treatment alone; at least not at the highest possible level. Faced with this situation, the clinician is forced to pay more attention to the socialization of the patient for role performance.

Reference has already been made to Brim's theoretical view of what a person must be able to do if he is to perform satisfactorily in the roles of everyday life, Wheeler has attempted to link Brim's views to the requirements of a socialization setting (Brim and Wheeler, 1966). He suggests that such a setting must provide clear and unambiguous norms for the patient, must provide opportunities for learning and practising the required role performance, and must selectively reward the behaviour of the patient. Mechanic (1970) has also linked his analysis of the ways in which a person deals with stress to aspects of the social environment. The clinician establishing a rehabilitation setting should ensure that there are opportunities for patients to develop skills and competence with other persons which will enable them to deal with the needs, demands and challenges of society. There must also be an incentive system of rewards and punishment, and an evaluative system which supports the patient when he experiences emotional discomfort in trying to cope but at the same time corrects inappropriate responses. It will be seen that these formulations have much in common and taken together indicate essential elements for the organization of a rehabilitation setting. The setting should offer opportunities for the individual to learn and practise role performance, to develop skills and competence in instrumental tasks and in living and working with others. It should also motivate the patient. This learning must be realistically related to the demands of life in society.

One of the first attempts to provide these rehabilitation opportunities was the introduction of paid industrial work in mental hospitals (Wadsworth et al., 1958; Early, 1960; Wansbrough and Miles, 1968). This not only offered training in instrumental skill but, because it came into the hospital from the outside world, was realistically related to the expectations of society. More importantly the rates of pay had been negotiated between workers and industry and so represented that balance between

H*

society's expectations and rewards which is an essential part of a social role. The rate of pay provided clear and unambiguous norms and selectively rewarded the patients' efforts. Disabled patients must also be given opportunities to learn the skills of social interaction, of self-care, the care of children and domestic life. Such skills are not easily generalized to the community setting and present techniques will have to be modified (Shepherd, 1977). Attempts to modify the behaviour of the more chronic hospital patients with schizophrenia using a token economy approach have received wide attention. Hall *et al.* (1977) recently summarized their own studies and concluded that most improvement occurred in the areas of the patient's dressing and appearance, routine ward tasks, social mixing and interests. There was no improvement in socially embarrassing or symptomatic behaviour. They too found no evidence of response generalization and did not believe that the improvement which took place could be attributed to contingent token reinforcement, but felt that there might be reinforcement from contingent social reinforcement and feedback. Wheeler and Mechanic both argued the need for an incentive system which selectively rewards the patients' behaviour. Token economy methods have already been discussed in Chapter 8. The effect of money incentives in work are well reviewed by Goldberg (1967) who shows that the results are confusing. With money incentive, work output increased in most studies, although there seemed to be some differences between the responses of "paranoid" and "non-paranoid" patients. While patients certainly appreciated money, its incentive effect was not demonstrated (Wansbrough, 1971). Williams and Blackler (1971) in a review of motivation research concluded that if an individual is to change his mode of behaviour he should feel that such a change will increase his ability to predict events and exercise control over certain aspects of his life. So it is not surprising that not all patients were motivated by being paid small amounts of money which would not do much to change their lot in an institutional environment. Perhaps the most important motivation for patients is to recognize in the course of rehabilitation that they are achieving an increasing mastery over their lives. It is therefore necessary that the patient should know how he is doing, not only by giving him feedback about his work performances but also in terms of his performance in roles and in social interaction. This was one of the major conclusions drawn from the experiment by Wing and Freudenberg (1961).

It may be difficult to provide clear and unambiguous norms for role performance in a hospital rehabilitation setting. The setting of norms will depend largely on the development of a staff system of beliefs about a code of conduct towards the common interests of patients and their families, and the wider community, as well as to staff members (Bennett, 1969). The code of conduct in the old fashioned mental hospital was largely determined by hospital staff and management. It served their interests and their need to manage large numbers of mentally ill people. In rehabilitation the norms have to be those which secure adaptation not only in the hospital but in everyday life. There is also a need for an evaluative system in a rehabilitation setting for the patient with schizophrenia. If competence is to grow, time is needed for learning and too much or too little support, or too little disapproval may affect the patient's confidence or motivation to acquire the necessary skills. Too often support can be patronizing, if staff equate it with unlimited tolerance and acceptance, rather than with the instillation of spirit or hope. In these matters, staff often divide along sex lines; female staff representing the stereotypes of the caring mother and male staff that of the firm, demanding father. It takes time to establish and maintain an effective marriage of these attitudes (Bennett *et al.*, 1976; Skynner, 1975).

Little can be said here about teamwork. It is essential for successful rehabilitation, which demands detailed intervention in so many aspects of the patient's life and functioning. Many teams are set up; few function really well. If team members aie to produce the best results, they need much the same assistance as the rehabilitee they have to help. They too have to develop competence, they need motivation, feedback, clear norms and must develop roles appropriate to rehabilitation work. Even if they receive this direction and are well led, they still have to deal with the emotional conflicts generated in the care of handicapped people who do not recover completely. These emotional conflicts are inevitable, but they must be continually defused. A useful approach is for the whole staff team, without exception, to meet weekly with a "neutral" therapist, or "facilitator" who is skilled in understanding interpersonal relationships and is not otherwise involved in the work of the ward or unit. A detailed account of such a group has been given by Skynner (1975).

The Family and Rehabilitation

The relationships between the patient with schizophrenia and his family are dealt with in Chapters 6 and 10. But it is important here to note that while the patient can be seen as a "burden" on his family, the reverse is sometimes true. Families, faced with a sick member who seems unresponsive and uninterested in doing anything or getting back to work will experience feelings of frustration, despair, anger or guilt, very similar to those experienced by the rehabilitation staff. These feelings and the resulting attitudes of criticism or overconcern can, in turn, be a "burden" on the patient and even stimulate relapse (Brown *et al.*, 1962, 1972). Sometimes in the interests of family peace, former patients with schizophrenia are "institutionalized" in their own homes, and rehabilitation resisted by their families (Freeman and Simmons, 1963). Some families can be helped by practical advice on the management of their disabled member. In others, feelings can be relieved and attitudes changed. But if such means are ineffective, partial separation of the patient from his family by day centre attendance, or complete separation by providing an alternative residence with a degree of supervision appropriate to the patient's disabilities, may be a constructive step in rehabilitation.

Work and Rehabilitation

The importance of occupation and work has been stressed many times already, for it has many beneficial effects. Inactivity has a marked influence on the intrinsic impairments of schizophrenia as well as on the development of adverse secondary reactions. Work is important in minimizing extrinsic disabilities; it is part of the structure of daily life and, if paid, it socializes the patient by giving him a significant role. Work teaches the patient to cope with stress and it also prepares him for resettlement in employment (Bennett, 1975; Morgan, 1974). Assessment of a patient's capabilities, not just in task performance but in the work situation, gives a good idea of his capacity to sustain an important social role and to interact successfully with his peers and those in authority. Unfortunately, work is often seen as the whole, or a major part, of "rehabilitation", and the presence of paid industrial work in a hospital is taken to signify that the patient's readaption is being undertaken. This is not so. Work is simply an essential and flexible tool, which can be used at different stages in a person's rehabilitation, in conjunction with other approaches. In mental hospital rehabilitation it may be used to prevent the development of extra disability, while in a resettlement unit its purpose is to prepare the patient for the stresses of open employment or to assess his capacity for this. Thus, as the patient progresses, the hours of work will increase, so will the complexity of the task, the variety of the types of job available and the level of expectation of performance. Occupational therapy using traditional craftwork can be useful in preventing intrinsic disabilities, providing it occupies the patient for most of the working day. However, in craftwork or art, a person may be doing or making something purely for his own satisfaction. He then meets his own expectations and provides his own reward. In such a case it is an activity without a social role, and it has much less value in the later stages of rehabilitation (Miles, 1971).

Doctors and occupational therapists are often appalled by dull repetitive industrial jobs and wonder how anyone could do them. But the repetitiveness, the lowliness, or the nastiness of the job are subjective estimates. Nurses, for example, have to do some things which would disgust the most unskilled labourer if he did not see these activities in their social context. On the other hand, work does not have to be dull and uninteresting. There is no doubt that the nature of many of the tasks provided for patients with schizophrenia has been determined by a tendency to underestimate their capacities and by difficulties in securing more complex work and adequately supervising it by nurses and occupational therapists. It is quite possible, given skilled staff, to provide paid secretarial, clerical, research and data processing tasks, which are both acceptable and useful in the rehabilitation of university graduates (Bennett, 1972). At present there is little provision in this country for the rehabilitation of the more intelligent person disabled by schizophrenia; the need for this has been underestimated. While such patients are rarely able to adjust at their previous occupational level, they can be resettled in work which they find satisfying.

It is often suggested that the aims of rehabilitation should differ for men and women since women tend to perform socio-integrative, rather than instrumental, roles in society. While this is broadly true, the domestic division of labour in some families is, today, less clearly defined than formerly, as in Britain half the women of working age are employed outside the home. The general goals of rehabilitation such as responsibility improved interpersonal relationships and increased motivation are as important in the domestic role as in employment, while skill in domestic tasks can be refurbished by occupational therapists. However, there is much more to a married woman's role than being able to cook and shop. It makes heavy emotional demands and requires a nice judgement of priorities in balancing the needs of husband, children, other relations, neighbours and friends. Attempts have been made to help mothers with the task of child rearing and the maternal role. This is especially important for those who have spent significant periods of their own childhood in children's homes or have had disturbed relationships with their own parents (Lindsey et al., 1977). However, it must be admitted that while such problems are being tackled, they have not yet been satisfactorily mastered.

Resettlement

The ultimate aim of rehabilitation for people disabled with schizophrenia is to resettle them in work or domestic life. By resettlement, the Department of Employment means the attempt to secure for all disabled people "their full share within their capacity, of such employment as is ordinarily available". By the Disabled Persons Act (1944) employment for the physically or psychiatrically disabled is both protected and provided in various ways. Every employer of more than 20 workers is obliged to employ 3% of registered disabled persons. In every employment exchange there is a Disablement Resettlement Officer (DRO) who is responsible not only for placing disabled people in employment but for following up the individual and his employer, to see that the placing has been satisfactory to both. The disabled can also attend an ERC or obtain sheltered employment in a Remploy factory if they can work but are incapable of open economic employment. Someone disabled by schizophrenia is entitled to all these services. But if a disabled person is to be employed he must be able to perform the tasks required adequately and he must get some satisfaction from his work. From the employer's point of view he must not only be able to perform assigned tasks acceptably, his role behaviour in employment must also be acceptable. Fraser Watts finds that poor personal relationships with other workers or supervisors and low levels of drive and initiative are more often responsible for former psychiatric patients' failure to secure or hold a job than their poor task performance (Watts, 1977).

Psychological tests of intelligence or the use of special aptitude tests (such as the GATB) do not predict employability (Taylor, 1963; Allen and Loebel, 1972). Keenness for work and good relationships with employers, supervisors and workmates are what matters. The only way to decide whether or not a disabled patient shows these qualities is to observe his behaviour in a real work situation. Commonly this opportunity is provided in an ERC. Thus when the "medical" stage of rehabilitation is completed it may be useful to refer a disabled patient with schizophrenia to an ERC. But experience shows that there is often a wide gap between the patient's readiness for work as judged by hospital staff and the patient's employability as assessed by the staff of the ERC. They assume that patients referred will be employable in eight-to-ten weeks, but it is not uncommon that patients, while potentially employable, need a much longer period of industrial type preparation before they could be placed in work. There are two possibilities: one is to extend their time in the ERC; the other is to provide more realistic work preparation in hospital (Wing *et al.*, 1964). An example of the latter approach is a resettlement unit which was established at Netherne Hospital in 1957 (Bennett *et al.*, 1961). It sought to assess and prepare patients for resettlement by gradual exposure to working and living conditions similar to those in the community. Freudenberg (1967) showed that patients from this unit had a more stable work record after discharge than that of patients discharged from other wards in the same hospital. The patients admitted to this unit from 1959 to 1969 had unusually low readmission and unemployment rates after resettlement. Seventy-seven per cent of the admissions had moderate schizophrenic disabilities. Ekdawi (1972) believed that if more opportunities for sheltered employment had been available the results would have been even better.

There are still far too few opportunities for sheltered employment outside Remploy factories although studies have shown that many patients with schizophrenia could be employed at that level (Bennett and Wing, 1963; Wing *et al.*, 1964; Brown *et al.*, 1966). In spite of adequate preparation and more sheltered employment, only a proportion of disabled persons with schizophrenia will be employable. This does not depend only on their disability or attitudes, but also on where they live, the prevailing economic conditions, their personal circumstances and not least on their good fortune in finding suitable employment.

Failure in a placement should not be attributed automatically to the patient's unfitness for employment. The job might have been unsuitable. Some patients with schizophrenia will be employed most of the time, some will be marginally employed, and about 40% will be unemployed. Of the unemployed and marginally employed, some will be in hospital and some in the community. It is still uncertain how far resettlement in work is influenced by rehabilitation and how much by the patient's previous adaptive capacity. It is certainly influenced by the severity of the disabilities; even so adequate preparation does have an effect. We set our sights too high if we think of resettlement only in terms of the disabled patient's permanent return to a fully independent domestic and vocational role (Criswell, 1968). Some patients will achieve this, but many will have to be settled at different levels on the twin ladders of employment, or domestic and residential life (Early, 1965). For example, a patient may have to live in hospital and yet be able to go daily to independent employment in the outside world. Some will live at home and have to attend an occupational day centre. Others will live an independent life in a boarding house and yet be unemployed. Many such combinations are possible.

As has been suggested earlier, a patient who has been resettled is not settled once and for all. Many patients will relapse under stress although this risk may be lessened by adequately monitored after-care. For such patients, rehabilitation should not be viewed as a "progressive"process moving steadily towards permanent community readjustment. For them, for their families, and for the medical and social services, rehabilitation is best regarded as a continuous process of accommodation (Criswell, 1968).It is on that basis that clinical psychiatry, rehabilitation, resettlement and community care, should be conceived and organized. Every step in resettlement should be discussed with the patient's family, if the patient is still in contact with them, and it is intended that he should live at home. They too must be prepared, supported and motivated for the part they are going to play. Brown et al. (1966) found that 40% of patients were still living with parents and 37% with a spouse, at the time of admission. They were surprised to find that most patients gave rise to remarkably little complaint even when unemployed, although there were difficulties when the patient relapsed. They also showed that the divorce and separation rate of married patients was probably three times that of the general population; the figure for men being twice that for women.

Families do complain that they often have to put up with disturbing and distressing behaviour because of difficulties in securing the admission to hospital of the family member with schizophrenia. Brown et al. (1966) found that 43% of patients with schizophrenia were admitted under some compulsory order in 1956. Much depends both on legal requirements for admission and on the attitudes of the family, the doctor and social workers. Since the Mental Health Act 1959, compulsory admissions have decreased. In Camberwell, in 1964, 24% of patients were admitted under legal compulsion. This figure fell to 17% in 1969 and to 5% in 1974. During this period the provision of services was moving steadily from a distant mental hospital to the local area where it was possible to maintain effective aftercare in cooperation with social services. Since the local services were often more acceptable to patients and their families, more responsive to their needs, many of the social and clinical crises which led to compulsory admission could be prevented (Wing and Hailey, 1972).

Residential Services

Many patients do not have families, or their family is unable to accommodate them. In some instances, because the family has painful and unhappy memories of the patient's bizarre or disturbing behaviour, they are not willing to receive him. Some patients do not want to return to their families. For others the family provides an understimulating or overstimulating environment leading either to apathy and desocialization or to psychotic relapse.

These are some of the many reasons why disabled patients with schizophrenia may need somewhere to live other than their own homes. There are relatively few who are able to use, or afford such "normal" forms of residential provision as a council house or flat, an unfurnished flat, private hotel, boarding house or paying guest arrangement. In recent years more specialized forms of residential care for the mentally ill have been provided by local authorities and voluntary bodies (Wright, 1966; Fairweather et al., 1969; National Association for Mental Health, 1977). Finally there are in big cities those provisions which have been society's response to the needs of the homeless and destitute; Salvation Army hostels, common lodging houses and reception centres. Which facilities partially disabled patients with schizophrenia use depends largely on their social competence, initiative, behaviour and attitudes. Thus, although three-quarters of those using a number of local authority hostels for the mentally ill were suffering from schizophrenia, they were found to have fewer behavioural impairments than their contemporaries in mental hospitals (Hewett and Ryan, 1975; Hewett et al., 1975). However, they probably required more supervision than those who lived in bedsitting rooms provided by a housing association for ex-psychiatric patients (Birley, 1974). Some disabled patients are too paranoid in their attitudes to accept such placements, even if they are available (which they may not be) and prefer a more solitary life moving from place to place. Others, too disabled to care properly for themselves, slide into destitution. Others are not sane enough or socially competent enough to control their bizarre behaviour in public, and may commit some trivial offence which brings them into conflict with the law. As a result they are deemed to need a more supportive environment and are either sent to prison or go back to the mental hospital. In prison they serve a short sentence and are discharged. They are often unwilling to remain long in hospital and are not dangerous enough to themselves and others to be retained against their

will. Rollin (1963) studied the population of mentally abnormal offenders admitted to Horton Hospital in 1961 and 1962 and found 83%
suffered from schizophrenia, while 44% had previously served prison
sentences. Tidmarsh and Wood (1972) surveyed the population of destitute and homeless men admitted to the Camberwell Reception Centre in
1970. They found that most of those without prison sentences had not
been in hospital and most of those who had not been in hospital had
not been in prison either, while conversely those who had been in
either type of institution had usually been in both. Yet wherever they
go, these individuals, severely disabled by schizophrenia, are unable
to manage in society. They can only cope in an institution but this
does not seem to be acceptable to them and so they wander from prison
to doss house, on to the mental hospital, then to a hostel and back
again. Gunn (1977) compares them to "a stage army tramping round
and round, making a much greater impression than their numbers
warrant", simply because there are no facilities which will accept them
or which they will accept. Their difficulties are made greater by
the recent reduction in accommodation for the single homeless and
in furnished accommodation for rent. Aware of this problem, psychiatrists have mistakenly believed that many mentally abnormal offenders must suffer from schizophrenia. This is not so. Psychopathy,
alcoholism and mental retardation are the psychiatric conditions
having a special association with criminal behaviour. An American
study of 223 male and 66 female serious offenders leaving prison
showed that while 90% of the males were diagnosed as having a
psychiatric disorder, schizophrenia was only detected in 1% of the men.
While a majority of all patients admitted to Broadmoor have a diagnosis
of schizophrenia (Gunn, 1977) this must be set against the fact that
only 7% of all admissions to psychiatric hospitals are detained under
Sections 60, 65, 71 or 72, and of these over 18·6% go to the Special
Hospitals.

Our concern with the community readaptation of patients with
schizophrenia should not blind us to the needs of those patients who will
still require a prolonged hospital stay. They cannot cope with a community existence. In their care, too, we should not neglect the principles
of rehabilitation. They must be helped to adapt even if they cannot be
discharged. Too often they have been consigned to neglect in the socially
sterile back wards. It seems possible and not too difficult to offer them a
less "institutionally oriented" form of care where rehabilitation would
be directed to "sustaining their personalities" (Mathers, 1972; Miller
and Gwynne, 1972).

Conclusion

Rehabilitation has many facets and these include the planned step-by-step progress of the patients' social adaptation to eventual resettlement, community accommodation and adjustment for others sustaining the personality of the most disabled in hospital. The principles of effective rehabilitation can be more clearly defined. In practice they have been developed in a number of well known centres but these "tend to be isolated and largely dependent upon the drive and leadership of an individual doctor" (DHSS, 1972). There is still a lack of professional and public awareness of what can be done to rehabilitate patients with schizophrenia and this needs to be remedied.

10 | Social Work with Patients and their Families

Clare Creer

Previous chapters have looked at family influences upon the development and course of schizophrenia. This chapter will put forward some suggestions about how social work* intervention might be directed towards helping the relatives of the patient suffering from chronic schizophrenia who are supporting the patient (to whatever extent) in living outside hospital. Many patients suffering from chronic schizophrenia who would at one time have been kept in hospital indefinitely are now living outside. Yet at present the community medical and social facilities to cater for the needs of such chronically disabled patients are far from being provided on the scale required. Frequently it is the relative or relatives of a patient who in effect take on the role of the primary agent of community care, with all the responsibilities that entails.

In such cases the social worker's task could be interpreted as one of offering support to the relatives to help them in supporting the patient. Many patients suffering from chronic schizophrenia become totally cut off from their families, and this can seriously reduce the patient's chances of making any kind of life for himself outside a hospital setting. The social worker would therefore be concerned to find ways of reducing tensions between the patient and his family so as to avoid any total severing of relations between them. Some of the ways this might be achieved will be considered below.

---

* The author discusses the help that might be given by social workers. Everything she says is relevant to the practice of other professional helpers such as community nurses, general practitioners and psychiatrists(Ed.).

Apart from the family setting, the other major environmental influence upon the patient is the extent and quality of support offered to him by agencies outside the home. Whatever these agencies may offer in the way of sheltered employment, financial help, medical advice, or social activities may make an important contribution to shaping the framework of the patient's daily life outside hospital. This chapter will therefore also examine the ways in which the various services can be used to support the patient living in the community.

Most of the material which will be used to illustrate the arguments put forward comes from the survey published in 1974 in the report "Schizophrenia at Home" (Creer, 1975; Creer and Wing, 1974). This survey was carried out between March and December 1973. Eighty interviews were conducted with relatives of patients suffering from schizophrenia. Fifty of these interviews were undertaken with relatives who were members of the Schizophrenia Fellowship—a charitable fellowship aiming to promote the welfare of patients and their relatives. The value of talking to these relatives lay in the fact that they tended to be an articulate and thoughtful group. One potential disadvantage is that being a highly self-selected group they were unrepresentative. To attempt to counteract any bias in the results a parallel survey was undertaken of a randomly selected group of relatives (all residing in one defined area of inner-suburban London). If anything, this group was unrepresentative in the other direction, i.e. the relatives presented fewer problems than average because the patients were all in touch with services in an area where medical and social work standards were high. The national picture seems likely to fall somewhere between these two levels. The aim of the interview was to find out more about how the patients functioned at home, how they usually behaved, and what their daily lives were like. Relatives were encouraged to talk about the problems they were currently encountering which were connected with the illness, and also to describe their experiences with the various services available to the patient and to them. It was hoped to build up a picture of where services were inadequate and of how they could be improved.

While many accounts have been written of the problems and symptoms of sufferers from chronic schizophrenia, this study looked specifically at the problems as seen through the eyes of the relatives. As such it is perhaps of special interest to social workers who are concerned with helping relatives with their difficulties in coping with patients at home. Since much current concern in the social work profession centres around the need to evaluate the service we provide, the relatives' accounts of their experiences with services and their ideas about possible improvements are also particularly pertinent.

This chapter will consider whether social work intervention can be used to modify the effects of both family and outside agencies upon the patient's daily life and the course of his illness. An attempt will be made to suggest how supportive influences in the environment could be maximized and damaging ones reduced. The family life of the patient will be looked at first, and the effects of outside help examined in a subsequent section. The problems described by relatives interviewed in the 1974 survey fell into three main groups. The first of these concerned the patient's actual behaviour when it caused distress or disturbance to his family. The second group of difficulties arose around the relative's own reactions to the patient's illness. The third area where problems arose was in damage done in relatives' relationships with neighbours, friends, and the wider community brought about by the patient's illness. Each of these three areas of potential problems will be looked at, and then some suggestions offered as to how social workers may be able to intervene constructively.

Problems which Patients' Behaviour Could Cause in the Home and how Relatives Coped

Relatives describe two major problems: one is that patients can be withdrawn and lead almost completely solitary lives even though living under the same roof as their family, the other is that some patients are excessively active or behave in a socially embarrassing way.

Patients who behave violently, aggressively, or in an embarrassing way which draws public attention to the fact that they are ill present obvious difficulties for their families, but social withdrawal is far more widespread. It is a sadly accepted fact of everyday life for many of those who live with a schizophrenic patient. A patient's withdrawal from outside contact can lead to a considerable amount of suffering for his family. Most people expect social relationships to be rewarding. Many relatives who care for a patient and have perhaps stood by him loyally over years of illness feel hurt at how little the patient seems to return their caring. The commonest way in which a patient's withdrawal seems to manifest itself, is in difficulties in mixing with other people. One mother said of her son, "He just can't bear *people*—even to be in the same room as another person." This comment sums up the way many patients feel. Some patients cannot tolerate the physical presence of others for long even if no demands are being made upon them to talk or be sociable. As one mother said, "You just can't understand it. Here's someone you've known all these years and you've always got on well with, and suddenly he can't even stand being in the same room with you." Another mother described how her son would grab his cigarettes and make a dash for his room whenever the doorbell rang, so afraid was he of having to see or speak to a visitor.

Other patients like to be with other people as long as they do not have to interact with them directly. One such patient, for instance, enjoyed going to family parties as long as he could sit slightly apart and was not expected to speak to anyone. Another had said he liked to go and visit his aunt. His aunt was surprised to hear this as during these visits he would just sit in a chair and say nothing.

Many relatives refer to the patient's lack of conversation as a problem. If the patient is married and lives with husband or wife, the spouse will usually expect quite a lot of conversation and companionship from the patient. If a relative lives alone with the patient, the relative might want to spend some time chatting and generally enjoying the patient's company. One elderly lady who lived alone in a damp basement flat with her niece (the patient), said wistfully that she would have been glad of a chat in the evenings when her niece came back from the Day Centre. This lady could not get out much because of her arthritis. She was obviously rather lonely, but she said that each evening on her return from the psychiatric day centre, her niece would eat the meal she had ready for her in silence, and then go at once to her room.

Apart from a natural desire for some social contact, relatives also feel distress on another level. It is very hard to live with somebody who appears to be unhappy and yet to feel that all one's attempts to share the burden of the unhappiness are rejected. Often relatives want to be of some use by listening to the patient, learning what is troubling him, talking things over, or somehow conveying their concern and affection. The patient, however, may prefer to remain silent. The elderly aunt mentioned above was baffled by her niece's silence. "If only she'd unburden herself and tell me what's on her mind, I'm sure she'd be better. I can't make out if she's unhappy or what."

Another way in which a patient's withdrawal from the outside world can manifest itself is in a lack of desire to occupy himself in any way during the day. Many patients spend periods (and sometimes quite long periods) of the day doing nothing at all, simply sitting in a chair or lying on the bed staring vacantly into space. One mother described how, "in the evenings you go into the sitting-room and it's in darkness. You turn

on the light, and there he is, just sitting there staring in front of him.''
Other patients, whilst not doing absolutely nothing in this way, spend a
lot of time in rather pointless repetitive activities, such as brewing endless
cups of tea, or chain smoking for hours at a time.

Relatives are often unsure what to do about helping a patient to fill
the long series of empty hours stretching between breakfast and bed-
time. Some feel the patient's inactivity might be self-protective and that
he needs his periods of doing nothing in order to keep from relapsing.
One patient, a young man, had told his mother he had to lie on his bed
for several hours in the evening because he was "all fizzing up inside".
This young man was less handicapped than many in that he was able
to communicate so well why he behaved as he did. This enabled his
mother to understand and not feel unduly anxious about the hours he
spent on his bed. Also in this case the young man worked during the day
and his mother appreciated that this imposed a strain on him and felt
he needed his times of inactivity in order to compose himself and
"recharge his batteries".

Sometimes relatives fear that allowing the patient to spend too many
hours in complete inactivity might lead to increasing withdrawal.
Some encourage the patient to take up some hobby or interest. Often
however, it is an aspect of a patient's general withdrawal from life that
he has little interest in any outside activity. When a patient does attempt
some task, he may be clumsy and slow in movement. One mother
said she sometimes asked her daughter to vacuum the floor. The
daughter would take ages over it, vacuuming a tiny square of floor at a
time, and stopping every now and again in a "fixed" sort of posture.
Some patients neglect their appearance and personal hygiene, and this
can create problems in the home. Some relatives find ways of dealing
with this. One mother said she had found that if she asked her son directly
to change into clean clothes he got angry and refused. However if she
simply left a clean set of clothes hanging over a chair in his room, he
would sometimes put them on.

It may be because meal-times are such social occasions that many
patients behave oddly over meals. Some will not eat with other people
but will take their meals off to the bedroom and eat alone. Others are
suspicious about food, sniffing it dubiously, or sometimes hurting relatives' feelings by refusing to touch a carefully prepared dinner. Many
patients exist for long periods on extremely odd diets and relatives
worry about the effects on the patient's health.

Although problems of these kinds constitute the majority recounted
by relatives, there are also numerous instances when patients' behaviour

draws unwelcome and embarrassing attention to the patient and his family. Some patients suffer from bouts of restlessness when they rush around the house in a frenzy of pointless activity or pace up and down a room for an hour or more at a time. Sometimes a patient will do this at night and keep his relatives awake. Things are even worse if a patient's periods of restlessness take some noisier form, such as playing the same pop record over and over again very loudly at midnight. When neighbours are disturbed by such activity a whole new set of difficulties is created. Some relatives manage to persuade the patient to conceal such behaviour to some extent. The elderly aunt mentioned earlier, who was so puzzled and disappointed at her niece's lack of conversation, described how she had dealt with one problem of this kind. Her niece had a habit of pacing up and down in front of the house for an hour or so at a time. As the niece's appearance was rather odd anyway and she tended to mutter to herself, she was attracting a lot of attention from neighbours and people passing in the street. Fortunately the aunt had been able to persuade her niece to do her pacing "round the back where people can't see". This simple expedient had helped to ease tensions which were beginning to arise with neighbours and relieved the aunt of much embarrassment and anxiety.

Probably through their general lack of interest in and comprehension of the outside world many patients do not realize that their behaviour is off-putting and disturbing to other people. Odd behaviour is very handicapping socially, and although some patients have no desire for social contact anyway, there are others who actively seek it. These patients frequently suffer because they still wish to interact with others but do not have the social skills to do so. One young patient's parents described how he would "collar" any friend of his brother's who happened to call at the house, and would talk at the unfortunate friend non-stop until somebody in the family saw what was happening and came to the rescue. Other relatives described how patients would try to join in a conversation, but would somehow manage to make a remark so odd and out-of-tune with the general discussion that a dreadful silence would fall. The wife of a patient said regretfully and with some bitterness that, "we never get invited anywhere more than once".

Relatives describe numerous other ways that a patient's behaviour causes embarrassment in front of other people. A patient might sit in strange postures, make bizarre gestures or wierd grimaces. Some would talk or laugh to themselves from time to time, perhaps in response to voices which only they can hear. In some instances, relatives succeed in getting patients to control such behaviour in public. One mother said that if her son started to mutter to himself when outsiders were present, a quick if and quiet reminder from her was almost always sufficient to make him stop, or else he would leave the room and go somewhere on his own until he had finished. Perhaps this mother's success came partly from her calm but firm attitude to his problem. She did not make a fuss or show undue concern about her son's muttering, but she did make it quite clear to him that it was something he should do in private and not in front of other people. Of course relatives are not always so successful, particularly if a patient is highly disturbed or strongly preoccupied with delusional ideas.

Some patients express ideas of a delusional nature from time to time, perhaps saying that people are plotting against them or following them, or that their food is being poisoned. Relatives often feel in a quandary about how to respond to these remarks. If they express disbelief they fear the patient might feel more isolated than ever and might even decide they are in league with his persecutors. But they feel it would be wrong to agree with the patient and perhaps reinforce his belief in his unreal world. One patient, a middle-aged married lady, was relating how she had poured away several pints of milk recently, believing them to be poisoned. Her husband, who seemed very warm and tolerant towards her, but also deeply puzzled by her illness, became anxious when she spoke about this incident. He tried, rather nervously, to make a joke about it, saying, "Wasn't that a silly thing to do Annie? Fancy wasting all that milk. I don't know." But his wife became somewhat irritated at this, saying, "Well what would you do if a voice told you the milk was poisoned? I mean if you heard an actual voice?" Her husband, trying to appease her now, said, "Yes, I know it didn't seem silly at the time, but you know now it was the illness, don't you?" His wife however remained doubtful, replying, "I don't know. I still don't see how a voice can be an illness."

Sometimes a patient's delusional ideas involve his relatives. One young husband described how during her last relapse his wife had struggled with him on the very public walkway of the block of council flats where they lived, shouting out that he was trying to kill her. He now felt extremely embarrassed with the neighbours as he was sure they believed he ill-treated his wife. When a patient holds the belief that a relative is hostile towards him, he can become threatening or even violent. One mother said that she frequently reminded herself that however frightened she might feel of her son, "He is really much more frightened than I am." Several relatives feel as she did, that it is the patient's inner terror that makes him strike out at those he sees as his persecutors. In

other instances relatives think they can trace the reason for an outbreak
of violence back to some recent frustration the patient has suffered, such
as an unsuccessful attempt to join in some social activity. Nevertheless,
however understanding relatives might be, violence or threats of it can
make life impossible in the household. An atmosphere of tension in the
family tends to remain if an incident of violence has ever occurred, even
if this was a long time ago. Relatives do not forget such incidents, but
are particularly nervous of a recurrence if the previous violence has
come "out of the blue" and without any warning. One father recounted
how he had been taking his son somewhere in the car. There had been
no sign of anything amiss, and nothing had happened to upset his son
that day. But when the father turned round to reverse, his son suddenly
punched him hard, breaking his nose. Because there had been no
apparent reason for this sudden outbreak of violence the patient's
parents felt it could happen again at any time and that they were
powerless to prevent it.

Few relatives report problems arising out of the patient's sexual
behaviour. Most patients showed a complete lack of interest in sex (a
fact which causes problems when the patient is married). Most relatives
say they would welcome any indication of normal sexuality from the
patient.

To complete this discussion of problems associated with patients'
behaviour, a word should be said about patients who suffer from depression or suicidal ideas. Some patients have periods when they become
morose, sometimes weepy, and feel that life is not worth living. Depression sometimes seems to be associated with the patient's realizing that a
brother or sister, perhaps younger than himself, is being more successful
at work or in social life than he. Talk of suicide and attempts at suicide
are sometimes associated with depression. This is not always so however,
and suicide attempts can occur without prior warning, even when the
patient appears to be quite cheerful. Once again the unpredictability of
the patient's actions makes it difficult for his relatives to know what to
expect and how to prevent him from harming himself.

Problems for Relatives Connected with their own
Reactions to the Patient's Illness

Some relatives feel drained and exhausted by caring for the patient.
This anxiety arises most often when patients are unpredictable in their
moods and actions. Relatives speak of being "constantly on a knife-

edge", "living on your nerves", or "living on the edge of a volcano". The elderly mother of a patient described how she lay in bed in the morning listening for her son—if she heard him stamping and swearing about his room her heart would sink as she knew it would be "one of his bad days". Very often relatives keep some terrible past incident in their minds, the recurrence of which is a constant dread. One young man's sister told how her brother was once eating a meal with the family. Nothing was amiss, nothing out-of-the-ordinary had happened, and he appeared to be in quite a cheerful frame of mind. At some point he left the room, and after a while somebody realized he had been gone a long time and went to look for him. He was found to have taken an overdose and had to be rushed into hospital. Several relatives said that the strain and tension of living with someone who is so unpredictable, and whose moods can change so suddenly, is hard to imagine for anyone who has not experienced it.

As well as the anxiety they suffer, many relatives feel guilty about the patient's illness. Parents, in particular tend to feel they are to blame in some way. Such feelings are exacerbated when doctors or social workers imply that they are at fault and have caused the illness.

Guilt can give rise to depression, which is a reaction relatives mention frequently. Depression also results from exhaustion and a feeling of pointlessness. Elderly relatives are particularly susceptible to this. They find that they have all the strains and demands on their time which might be associated with bringing up a small child. It is worse if they can see no end in view; the patient will never be independent or able to look after himself. None of the rewards from watching young children grow and develop are available. There is also the worry of knowing they are getting on in years and that the patient may not be able to cope if they fall ill or die.

In some cases, the depression relatives feel is closely akin to mourning. Many feel a permanent sense of grief because the person they had known no longer seems to exist. If the patient occasionally still shows glimmerings of his former personality, this often keeps hope alive in the relatives that he might somehow eventually be cured. Such hope can raise expectations too high. Some relatives say, paradoxically, that it is only once they have given up hope and decided the patient will never improve, that life seems to become more bearable.

Another reaction some relatives mention is anger. They say they have to "blow up" from time to time to relieve their feelings. On the other hand, many patients are terrified of any show of anger (even though they themselves might shout and be aggressive at times) so that relatives feel forced to contain their irritation as best they can. On a deeper level, many relatives feel an intolerable sense of frustration because nothing they do seems to help.

Some relatives do come to terms with their feelings about the illness, and the effect it has had on their lives, particularly when they have worked out ways to manage their problems, as the result of years of trial-and-error and a great deal of patience.

The Effects of Schizophrenia on Families' Relations with the Wider Community

In some cases families are divided because of their experience of schizophrenia. For example, one or two members might be prepared to stick by the patient but get no support from other relatives. Similarly, neighbours and friends vary in their reactions. In fact a common difficulty for relatives lies in the attitudes towards mental illness which are currently prevalent in our society. One husband in his forties, whose wife had only recently become ill, said, "When our friends heard about my wife's breakdown they seemed to look on it as some kind of catastrophe—they seemed to take the attitude that she'd never be right again—never be able to go out again or anything."

The effect on relatives' social life can be devastating. Relatives might feel unable to invite people to their homes because they fear they might be shocked or embarrassed by the patient's behaviour. Equally the relatives can be prevented from going out because the patient does not like being left alone for long. One mother spoke of the problems which arose with new social contacts. Sooner or later the conversation always turned to, "And do you have any children . . . Oh yes, and what does your son do?" "Mention mental illness," she said, "and an awful hush descends on the whole room." One mother had found least upset was caused in these circumstances by saying, "My son suffers from depression", as people seemed to find this a more socially acceptable condition than schizophrenia.

In What Ways can Social Work with the Families be of Help?

Quite a number of relatives, when asked, can remember with gratitude a particular doctor, nurse, or social worker who has been of great help at some stage, or some occasion when a specific service agency has given prompt and appropriate aid. This indicates that the potential exists for much useful help to be given. The uniform application of such knowledge as we have at present, could make a substantial difference to many families' problems.

How can the professional helper best apply what knowledge we currently have, in order to mobilize the supportive potential within a family? The first step is to assess what the relatives see as the main problems in living with the patient. In order to do this, it will be necessary to get as full a picture as possible of what the patient is like at home, how he usually behaves, how his daily routine goes, how handicapped he is, and in what areas. As the relatives bring up specific problems, the social worker can find out how they have been dealing with them, and whether their methods have met with any success. If the patient is behaving in ways which the relatives find unmanageable, the social worker can try to devise with them some more effective methods of handling this difficult behaviour. Such discussion must of necessity be very much a two-way process since the extent of our knowledge of the management of schizophrenia is as yet limited. Very often relatives who have coped with a patient for many years, have learned a great deal by trial-and-error about how to cope with a variety of problems. The knowledge they have built up can offer many ideas and guidelines about ways of coping with difficult behaviour which the social worker may usefully be able to pass on to other families facing similar problems.

When considering general principles about how to deal most constructively with a patient's behaviour, two basic guidelines need to be borne in mind. The first is that if a patient is not stimulated enough, he may become excessively withdrawn. The classic example of the effect of totally inadequate stimulation is the very withdrawn and institutionalized patient seen in the worst of the back wards of the old style mental hospitals. The second principle to remember is that if a patient is over-stimulated he may relapse with a predominance of florid symptoms, showing evidence for example, of hallucinations, delusions, over activity or even violence. Applying these two basic principles to the patient living with his family the aim would be to encourage the development of an environment within which the level of stimulation is optimum for that particular patient.

The relatives of a patient who tends to withdraw from the outside world can learn through experience that they should encourage him not to withdraw to excess. They might insist on the patient doing some small household task each day, even though supervising him in this might cost a lot in time and effort. Relatives who have coped with the illness for many years have often reached an agreement with the patient on how much he is expected to do, in other words they reach an understanding of how much stimulation is beneficial to him. The brother of a patient said that at one time he had frequently lost his temper with his sister because she did nothing around the house, and he would return from work each evening to find the place untidy and dirty. Now he no longer got angry about this because he had reached the conclusion that it was no use expecting her to do very much. However, instead, he insisted that she should always have the potatoes peeled ready for him to cook for their supper when he got home from work. He knew she would not remember this unless he left the potatoes out on the table each morning where she would notice them. He always left out the correct number as he knew it would be beyond her to work this out. He also told her not to worry about putting in the salt as he had found she was unable to judge this, and "would put in half the packet if I asked her to do it". Like many relatives, this brother had adjusted the demands he made of the patient to a realistic level. Whilst he put some pressure on her to do more than she would choose if left to herself, he had come to appreciate her limitations, as was shown in his understanding of the need to remind her daily in an indirect way of what he expected her to do.

On the other hand, too much emotional pressure upon the patient by his family can produce overstimulation. The same is true if relatives do not make it clear to the patient what is expected, or if they make confusing or complicated demands of him. The socially embarrassing type of behaviour is probably best controlled by a firm, but emotionally neutral, approach. One mother had had problems in the past when her son had broken windows and furniture. She now made it quite clear to him that he would have to go straight to hospital if such behaviour occurred again. She said her son knew she meant it and had therefore made the effort to control himself. This mother was tolerant of many of her son's odd habits but firm about anything which was actively antisocial. She had come to feel quite confident of her ability to cope. Her son, perhaps because of her confidence, seemed to have found a certain security within the framework of the expectations she laid down so unambiguously.

It is perhaps because changes in his environment can overstimulate the patient that too many changes occurring all at once have been shown to be a factor contributing to relapse. Such changes do not necessarily have to be distressing. A birth in the family, a marriage, or moving house, are as much possible precipitators of relapse as are death or illness in the family or the loss of a job. Social workers can assist families by advising them to try and plan such events so that too many do not occur all at once. When this is unavoidable, the family can at least be warned of the likely effects on the patient, and it may be possible to devise ways of offering the patient extra support during a temporarily stressful period.

Besides discussing ideas with relatives about how to manage difficult behaviour and what action to take to reduce the likelihood of relapse, social workers could also help by talking to relatives about the way they are feeling and how they are reacting to the patient's illness. Often relatives may not have had the opportunity to talk in this way, and it can be a relief to them. If they are, for example, becoming overwhelmed by feelings of grief or guilt, then talking about this can help them to work through and eventually cope with such feelings. However social workers need to remember that relatives are not always ready and willing to discuss such matters. Many will have mixed feelings about talking to a social worker, and these may have to be talked through first before the relatives are ready to trust the worker enough to discuss fully their feelings and anxieties concerning the patient. Some relatives for instance, may feel they are betraying the patient or talking behind his back if they tell the worker about problems they are having with him. Some may have a vague fear that the worker represents authority, and may admit the patient to hospital if they complain too much about him. One patient's sister said during interview, "I don't like saying anything about him, I feel like I'm betraying him. After all, blood is thicker than water. I wouldn't like them to say he had to go back into hospital." Alternatively, relatives may have grown so used to feeling depressed or anxious, that they are now scarcely aware of it; they may have ceased to expect life to be any different, and it may not occur to them to bring up as problems matters which other people would certainly regard as such. For reasons like this, relatives will often tend to be reticent and uncomplaining, so it is useful if the social worker has some idea in mind of what the relatives feelings and problems are likely to be. The worker is then much more likely to pick up allusions to problems which may actually be having a serious effect, but which the relative may only mention vaguely as a matter of small importance.

The skills required to help relatives to talk about and cope with their feelings, are the same ones used by social workers in dealing with people in distress in all kinds of contexts, not just in the field of mental illness. It is therefore disturbing to hear so many relatives say they have had experience of social workers who lacked understanding of their feelings.

I

Many felt social workers had dismissed them as over-anxious, or "just a fussing mother". It is important for those who have contact with the relatives to remember that they have much about which to be anxious. It is questionable whether anybody can reasonably be expected to retain an appearance of balanced calm whilst living under the kinds of stresses some relatives face, often over very long periods. Bearing this in mind, it should be possible for social workers to use their traditional skills to some effect in helping relatives to become aware of, and thus to begin to cope with, any disabling reactions they may experience in response to the patient's problems.

The third way in which attempts can be made to modify the patient's family environment, is by helping to reduce the effects of the isolation or even ostracism which some relatives suffer within the wider community because of the patient's socially unacceptable handicaps. This is an area where it can be difficult to effect any change, since it has to do with the widespread and deeply seated unfavourable attitudes towards mental illness held by many people in the community. The most feasible way to approach the problem seems to be by introducing relatives to such self-help groups as the National Schizophrenia Fellowship, 29 Victoria Road, Surbiton, Surrey, where they can gain support and companionship from other relatives who can understand their problems from their own first-hand experience. Such a group can also do much towards educating the public towards a more understanding attitude to mental illness.

The Co-ordination of Services as a Means of Improving the Patient's Day-to-day Environment

If efforts can be made to obtain the maximum possible help from all the various services, this can make a marked difference to the pattern of a patient's daily life. Some relatives who have had years of experience of the illness have built up a substantial knowledge of the services available in their locality, and of how to make use of them. It is unfortunate that it seems to take a long time to reach this stage and that chance often seems to play a large part in the extent of relatives' awareness of the use of services. Many relatives make their initial approach for help to the general practitioner or to the local Social Services office. Some relatives have had the experience of being told by their family doctor to go and see a social worker, and by the social worker that the doctor was the only person that could help them. Some relatives feel that Social Services seem to operate a purely crisis-oriented service, observing that in a crisis, when the patient becomes highly disturbed, and a compulsory admission to hospital needs to be arranged at once, Social Services often give prompt and efficient service. But this frequently proves to be the end of the matter, and no further contact is offered. Similarly relatives complain that in the initial stages of the illness, before the patient has become so ill as to constitute a danger to himself or others, little interest is shown in the problem. In fact, many relatives who have approached the Social Services office with worries at this stage of the illness, have the impression that they are regarded as "over-anxious" and their accounts of their difficulties seem to be briskly dismissed.

Given the harsh reality of the present scarcity of resources in the Social Services field, it seems important to look at what social workers could theoretically do if they had the time, the knowledge, and the resources. Some will have both the desire and the opportunity to devote time to supportive and preventive work with psychiatric patients living in the community. (Those who occupy posts attached to psychiatric hospitals may have more opportunity for this than others.) This chapter has already looked at ways in which social workers can offer advice and guidance to families in the day-to-day management of the illness. The other kind of help the social worker can give is to ensure that the patient and his family are in touch with all the requisite services. When dealing with numerous other types of problem, social workers generally regard it as part of their role to co-ordinate whatever services are appropriate to a client's need. This aspect of the social worker's task is particularly vital in dealing with the patient suffering from schizophrenia and living in the community. In many areas of the country the services which do exist are thin on the ground. Nevertheless relatives are sometimes not in touch even with those which are available in their locality.

To begin with medical services, one of the most valuable assets to any patient and his family is a sympathetic general practitioner. Such a GP can be helpful in giving the initial diagnosis and in explaining the meaning of it to the relatives. He can also convey this information to the patient if he feels the patient is sufficiently rational to be able to make sense of it and if he thinks the information will have a positive rather than a negative effect upon the patient's state of mind. Many relatives wait for long periods before receiving any clear statement about diagnosis. Some eventually learn the diagnosis by indirect means, such as by seeing it written by the family doctor on the patient's Sickness Certificate. A sympathetic doctor can also be of help in sorting out problems which arise with a patient's medication. One patient's sister described how worried she had been because her brother had refused to go to the surgery for his three-weekly injection. She had phoned the doctor, who had been most cooperative. He called to the house and told the patient he had wondered why he had not come in for his injection. He had not mentioned that the sister had rung him, as the sister had felt the patient would have been angry with her. The doctor talked with the patient about the way he was feeling, and discussed with him various odd ideas which were preoccupying and disturbing him at the time. He then persuaded the patient to have his injection.

Not all doctors are as understanding or as approachable as this. Many relatives have doubts and fears about a patient's medication, but feel their doctor is too busy to be approached. Relatives often receive no explanation about the medication the patient is receiving, nor any indication of how important it is that he takes it regularly. One husband who clearly did not realize the importance of his wife taking her medication regularly said, "I leave all that to her. I would not know if she remembers to take it or not. I have enough to do without thinking about her tablets as well." This husband certainly did have "enough to do" as his wife had "spells" lasting for a few days every four weeks or so, when she seemed incapable of doing anything, and would just sit in a chair, and would not wash or eat. Then the husband had to take time from work to care for her and their four small children. Yet nobody had looked into the possibility that these "spells" were linked to the patient's not taking her medication. Nobody had suggested to the husband that this could be the case.

Some relatives worry whether a patient will "get addicted" to his tablets, and have anxieties about the effects of long-term medication. Here an opportunity for discussion with a sympathetic GP is helpful. Relatives also need to have some information about possible side-effects. Some have not been told about such unexpected side-effects as the patient's eyes rolling involuntarily upwards. In such cases they do not know whether the phenomenon is a side-effect, another symptom associated with schizophrenia, or an indication of something physically wrong with the patient. If relatives are nervous about approaching the family doctor but have some medical problem they wish to discuss, the social worker can intervene by approaching the doctor on their behalf. Often social workers are themselves unsure of the value and effects of medication and in any case they are not qualified as the doctor is to give relatives information of this kind. When a patient is in hospital more could be done to ensure that relatives have the opportunity to discuss their anxieties with a doctor there. Again many find hospital doctors unapproachable or unwilling to include them in plans made for the patient's treatment.

Very often it makes a great contribution towards easing family tensions if arrangements can be made for the patient to spend part of the day out of the home. If there is a Psychiatric Day Centre, Rehabilitation Centre or any form of sheltered employment available in the vicinity this can be of considerable help. Such services increase the amount of stimulation present in the patient's daily routine by providing several hours of occupation each day. At the same time these services can reduce undesirable overstimulation by reducing the amount of time spent each day by the patient in contact with his family. This is particularly valuable if the relatives are inclined to place emotional pressure upon him or have rather high expectations of his behaviour. Also, by providing a break for relatives, day-care services can make it more possible for them to offer the right kind of support to the patient during the part of the day that they do have the care of him.

In some cases it is the fact that relatives are unable to have a break that makes life intolerable. It would help relatives in this position if any ways could be found of giving them temporary relief, either by arranging a short period of care for the patient while they could have a holiday, or perhaps by encouraging the patient to attend a social club (if there is one locally catering to the needs of psychiatric patients) so that the relatives could have the occasional "evening off". In some cases however, more radical measures are necessary. Many patients would do better, and their families would be enabled to offer much greater support, if the patient could be accommodated somewhere other than in the household with the relatives. Again we are faced with the problem of scarcity of resources. The provision of long-term forms of sheltered accommodation is extremely inadequate to the need. Even if a hostel place is found for a patient, many patients prefer to remain with relatives, or may exhibit behaviour too difficult to be acceptable within a hostel. The patient often ends up by returning to the relatives, and while the relatives may accept this as inevitable, they often wish things could be otherwise.

One area where relatives often mention problems is that of finance. Here help is theoretically available uniformly throughout the country in the form of various types of benefit but obtaining the financial assistance to which the patient is entitled often seems to be a formidable task, and problems are common. A major problem is that the scheme of sickness and unemployment benefits is designed to cater for people who live at a permanent address and are either temporarily out of work or are sick, but still capable of obtaining a certificate to prove sickness from their

GP and of sending this in to the approrpriate office. Patients suffering from schizophrenia often move about a good deal, take jobs they are too ill to manage, and then give them up after a few days or weeks. The patient is then not eligible for unemployment pay because he has left the job of his own accord. However, he is no longer eligible for sick pay either, without going through the whole process of application again, since he has been in employment. He could claim Supplementary Benefit, but arranging this quickly is notoriously difficult. If he has no permanent address it is even harder. Patients often take one look at the queue in their local Supplementary Benefits office, or at all the questioning and form-filling which is required, and give up. Many relatives take over this side of things completely. Some patients go every week to the employment exchange and sign on to obtain unemployment pay, but many find this weekly encounter with officialdom too much. Many relatives struggle through the system so many times on the patient's behalf that they know how to work it. Even so, there can be sudden unexpected disruption just when relatives think that the finances, at least, have been sorted out. One mother whose son had been on sick benefit for some time suddenly received a notice for him to attend for DHSS medical examination. He did so, was pronounced fit for work, and his benefit instantly stopped. Fortunately, in this case a sympathetic GP stepped in and sorted matters out. This patient was fortunate in having relatives to fight for him and a GP to support them.

Many relatives say how difficult it is to get some form of benefit started for the patient; if initial arrangements are made, however, then the benefit comes through automatically without any further effort on the patient's part. This applies as long as the patient's circumstances do not change, for example as long as he does not move, or suddenly take a job and then drop it again. Where patients have relatives who lack the ability to cope with officialdom, or where patients are no longer in touch with their families, it seems highly possible that they will not get the benefits to which they are entitled. Patients who become destitute are of course at risk of becoming dragged down by a whole host of secondary problems.

This section has examined some of the ways in which existing services are functioning from the relatives' point of view. Relatives' descriptions of their experiences with services produce a picture of an extremely patchy system of services over the country. Most relatives can recall one or two occasions when they have received excellent service from one particular source. But they recount far more instances when services had been unhelpful. The hopeful part of the picture is that on the occasions when the right kind of help is offered to families at the right time, it makes an invaluable contribution to their ability to cope with the patient at that point. Looking towards the future with this in mind, it is possible to see how services which at present scarcely exist could be of enormous help to families. Even taking the present situation and assuming no new services can be provided and no expansion of present ones is likely, much could still be done to obtain a better and more consistent standard of care from those which exist already. It is here suggested that social workers, community nurses, and doctors should see it as part of their role to seek out and obtain the maximum benefit from all existing services. These services should be used in any feasible way to modify the routine of a patient's daily life so as to alleviate the pressures on the patient and his family, and to support their strengths in any way possible.

The Management of Schizophrenia

11

J. K. Wing

The Concept of Management

The concept of management is well-recognized in physical medicine. It includes all the elements of secondary and tertiary prevention: early detection and treatment in order to limit the development of impairments as far as possible, prevention of unnecessary secondary reactions, and encouragement of compensatory abilities. Thus it also includes rehabilitation and the containment of disability. In spite of the bureaucratic sound of the word, connotations of officialdom and authoritarianism should not be read into it, although effort, imagination, sympathy and specific knowledge on the part of professional workers are required to keep them at bay. Above all, the concept of management demands a full understanding of the various ways in which handicaps can develop. These have been outlined in Chapter 1, in terms of acute syndromes, intrinsic impairments, extrinsic disadvantages, and secondary personal reactions. In the case of chronic conditions, management is basically a matter of helping affected individuals, their relatives, and the community at large, to live with schizophrenia.

In this chapter, we shall draw upon material presented throughout the book in order to illustrate the problems that constantly arise during the management of schizophrenia (particularly its chronic forms), and in order to redress the balance somewhat, we shall begin by trying to look through the eyes of the affected individual (Sommer and Osmond, 1960).

1*

Self-help

Everyone has to learn to live with himself or herself and everyone has handicaps of some sort. People who are severely affected by schizophrenia have more adjustments to make than most and fewer abilities with which to try to cope. The acute symptoms of schizophrenia carry a strong sense of conviction which cancels out the good advice of relatives and professional helpers. Since many patients have always been rather detached from social opinion, and the first onset often occurs during the rebellious teens, it is not surprising that patients find themselves at odds with the world in general and their family in particular. The surprising thing is that some, after prolonged experience and suffering, do begin to recognize what circumstances make things better or worse, and therefore learn what to avoid and what to foster (Wing, 1975). These gifted ones have to speak for the rest and it is important that professional people and relatives try to learn from them. The following discussion of factors potentially under the control of patients is based on patients' own experiences.

The most obvious is whether to accept medication. Some discover by trial and error that symptoms tend to occur after discontinuing it. They have to balance the side-effects, particularly the "dampening" effect that some complain of, against the relief from acute distress and disablement. Many studies of patients advised to continue medication over long periods for conditions such as tuberculosis, parkinsonism, epilepsy and diabetes, have demonstrated similar problems and roughly equivalent proportions (up to one third) who discontinue medication. Explanations about the types of drugs available, the corrective effects of others, the reasons for varying the dose (e.g. increasing in anticipation of stress, decreasing in sheltered surroundings), particularly if they match the patient's experience, may prove very helpful.

Some patients eventually learn to recognize situations that act as triggers to release unpleasant subjective experiences. One said: "There is a sensitivity in myself and I have to harden my emotions and cut myself off from potentially dangerous situations. . . . When I get worked up I often experience a slight recurrence of delusional thoughts." He learned to avoid arguments on religious or political subjects that made him emotionally upset. Another found that there were situations, such as sitting in a train when it was not moving, when he would tend to have abnormal perceptual experiences. For example, the eyes of other passengers seemed to "radiate". He found that he could deliberately turn his attention to something else, or practise a relaxation technique, and that the process of delusion formation could thus be interrupted. Another man knew that he only experienced hallucinations when he had nothing to occupy his mind and used this lesson constructively. He still heard voices last thing at night before going to sleep but quite enjoyed the experience and did not worry about it. A very intelligent woman learned, after bitter experience, to choose her man friends from people who were not her intellectual equals, because she did not become so involved with them and could control the situation better.

A less precise version of these techniques is social withdrawal, which is often used quite unconsciously by patients to avoid situations they find painful. The process can of course go too far and then entails risks of its own, since understimulation can lead eventually to unnecessary slowness, underactivity and apathy. However, withdrawing from excessive social intrusion, to which schizophrenic patients are very sensitive, is often found preferable to being forced into unwanted social interaction. This mechanism may appear unhealthy to family members and professional advisers, but it can be a sensible reaction. It takes a good deal of insight for the patient to use it rationally.

Finding work within the patient's competence is another important means of coping. Many are unable to work under pressure, or to take responsibility for other workers, or to cope with complex decision-making. A steady undemanding job, at not too great a pace, can be a great help, though difficult to find outside sheltered environment. Even such work may require a great deal of attention from patients who find concentration exhausting; a fact that many relatives and hostel supervisors find difficult to understand (Hewett et al., 1975).

Knowing how others will react to a recital of delusions or to odd behaviour such as talking to oneself, is a further useful acquisition if the patient can use the knowledge to behave accordingly when in company. Many patients do come to realize that only certain people can be trusted to hear such private matters.

Even more insight and control is needed to go further, and to work out ways of helping other people understand and accept one's own handicaps without antagonizing or boring them. Many patients never attain any degree of conscious insight at all, although various techniques of coping, particularly social withdrawal, are used unconsciously. More could attain some insight if relatives and professional people could acquire the skill to help.

The Problems of Relatives

It is generally accepted nowadays that handicapped people are better off living with their relatives than in segregated communities and this assumption is at the root of recent plans for services (DHSS, 1975). Ordinarily, children grow up, marry and set up their own independent households. The situation of elderly parents with an adult handicapped son or daughter at home is an unusual and difficult one. The social expectations involved are not as hard to live up to as in the case of a husband or wife with a handicapped spouse, since here the problems of raising children, looking after a household, or earning a living wage, give rise to far greater pressure on the patient (Brown *et al.*, 1972). Women patients are more likely to be married than men, and there is a high rate of divorce, particularly among men (Brown *et al.*, 1966).

Experience with a large number of families suggests that, although there is great variation in ways of reacting, certain patterns can be observed. There is the initial period of coming to terms with the onset and early course of schizophrenia. Often, patient and relatives find it difficult to recognize that a serious and possibly chronic disorder is present and there is an attempt to normalize abnormal behaviour. There follows a period of turbulance in which great strains are placed on relatives and which may result in the patient leaving or even in complete break-up of the family. Subsequently, if contact is not lost, patient and relative often come to acquire a tolerance which neither had earlier. The relative, however, does so at the expense of restricting his or her life. Often the parents of unmarried or separated patients are elderly widows who are glad to have some companionship and someone to do a bit of shopping for them if they are physically disabled, who are not too bothered by not being able to live a life of their own. The major worry then is—what will happen in the future, when the parent dies?

This contented, if restricted, outcome for family life is sometimes only reached after a lengthy and profoundly distressing time, during which the patient's condition is unstable and the relatives do not know what will happen next. It is not surprising that some patients become homeless drifters, moving from lodging house to reception centre to sleeping rough, while others find refuge in long-stay hostels, homes or hospitals but are still essentially "homeless single persons". There do not have to be many patients becoming destitute from each district each year in order to account for the large numbers found in Salvation Army hostels and reception centres (Leach and Wing, 1978; Tidmarsh and Wood, 1972; Wood, 1976).

The results of a recent survey of relatives' experiences are described in Chapter 10. Relatives acquire considerable experience of coping with schizophrenia and, as was made clear in Chapter 6, many are tolerant and supportive, but their methods are inevitably trial and error. Some learn not to argue with a deluded patient; others never learn. Some discover just how far they can go in trying to stimulate a rather slow and apathetic individual without arousing resentment. Others push too hard, find their efforts unrewarded or that they make matters worse, and then retreat into inactivity themselves. Some never give up intruding until the patient is driven from home.

One of the most important problems is the fluctuating insight of the patient. By contrast, the parents of a severely retarded person know where they stand; he will never be able to make independent judgements about important sectors of his life but will have to have them made for him. At the other extreme, a blind person, although necessarily dependent on others for certain kinds of help, can otherwise take full responsibility for his own decisions. The situation is quite different when an individual becomes acutely psychotic and unable to make rational judgements, without recognizing the fact, and later recovers without remembering why it was necessary for others to act for him. Failure by professional people to recognize the real difficulties inherent in this situation is the cause of much complaint from relatives.

In spite of all the work that has been carried out with families one of the commonest criticisms they make is that, when they ask for advice from professional people as to the best way to cope, they receive no useful answer or the question is simply turned back at them, their own amateur efforts being received with polite disdain or, worse, as evidence of their own abnormality. The discussion of possibilities of self-help for patients gives some clues as to how to advise relatives, as does the work described in Chapter 6, the experience of experts outlined in Chapters 8 and 9, and above all the cumulative experience of the relatives themselves, described in Chapter 10. It is encouraging to find how many relatives do manage to discover a way of living with schizophrenia that provides the patient with a supportive and non-threatening home.

The major factors are creating a non-critical accepting environment, providing an optimal degree of social stimulation, keeping expectations realistic, learning how to cope with fluctuating insight and how to respond to delusions or bizarre behaviour, making use of whatever medical and social help is available (including tactfully educating professionals who know less than relatives), and helping the patient to help himself. Voluntary organizations such as the National Schizophrenia

Fellowship can do much to raise morale, educate each other and the public, and to experiment with new ways of providing services.

Professional Advisers

The two sections on factors at least partially under the control of patients and relatives set the background for a discussion of the role of professional advisers. Their corporate task is to identify, assess, treat, advise and care for people with schizophrenia and to prescribe services. Sufficient has been said to cover all these duties except the last, which is mainly outside the scope of this book. A further word may be useful on the subjects of counselling and of rehabilitation.

Dr Brian Davies (1977), President of the Association of Directors of Social Services, said that the essence of counselling the relatives of disabled people was that the adviser had to know as much about the disability as they did. This not unreasonable requirement demands considerable experience, which many professional people thrown in at the deep end do not possess. Psychiatric nurses perhaps have as much experience as anyone of the various ways in which it is possible to cope with the behaviour of people with schizophrenia, since they themselves take the place of relatives when the patient is in hospital. When acting as community nurses they can enlarge this experience by entering the patients' homes (including homes or hostels) and learning from their relatives. They have the backing of hospital services and, if they were available in an emergency (particularly at night and at weekends), could provide the main body of counsellors. Psychiatrists often seem not to be able to give advice on crucial questions of how to cope, but fall back on evasions which seem to patient and relative to be implicit confessions of ignorance. The way to learn is to listen with an open but critical mind. The training of social workers for this form of counselling is woefully inadequate but suggestions for improvement have been made (CCETSW, 1974).

Counselling cannot be separated from other aspects of long-term management such as assessment, treatment, rehabilitation and resettlement. Once the assessment of impairments, disadvantages and personal reactions has been made, the aims of patient and relatives are realistically weighed against the possibilities. A series of limited objectives, defined in terms of social performance, is formulated, each of which should be attainable by specified forms of therapeutic action. The programme then proceeds by trial and error, with frequent modifications as each objective is or is not reached, and as the participants' aims change. Once an optimal level is reached the aims are to prevent relapse or increase in handicap and to continue to develop any assets available.

The particular techniques to be used to achieve each objective within a staged rehabilitation programme are drawn from the full range of those available: medication, group pressures, vocational training, reinforcement, counselling and support. Probably the most important element, however, is the process of working out a series of limited objectives, each of which is attainable because not impossibly distant from the present situation, so that progress can be seen to be achieved. This is highly rewarding for everyone concerned. If no such progress can be made, or a plateau of achievement has been reached, this is a positive, not a negative, reason for resettlement at that level. A cardinal principle of rehabilitation, however, is that functions that the individual is unable to carry out for himself should, whenever possible, be carried out for him, in the hope that active function will eventually return. In chronic schizophrenia, this means that the level of social stimulation should not be allowed to fall too low (so long as there are no adverse reactions) even though there is no apparent response. The fact that handicap is not increasing is a sign of success.

The survey of relatives' opinions described in Chapter 10 showed that each aspect of management mentioned here could be carried out effectively and sympathetically. If a service could be created that would deal with all aspects of care at a reasonable standard—including recognition, assessment, crisis intervention, treatment, counselling, rehabilitation, security, supervision, care and shelter—it is certain that much morbidity could be avoided. Experienced professional helpers can do much, even within the present framework of services, but the range available is far from adequate.

In turning from a system of services gathered together on one site, which is what the large hospitals provided, to a system in which these functions are geographically fragmented, there are many advantages but also two large risks, neither of which has so far been avoided. The first is that the many small-scale alternatives that are needed to substitute for the previous large-scale units will not be comprehensively provided. They have to be set up by local authorities assisted by the useful efforts of voluntary associations, and it takes time, motivation, and the expenditure of public money to create them. Virtually no district in the country yet has its full complement. Particularly lacking are facilities where severely disabled or disturbed schizophrenic patients can live a life that reaches the highest quality possible, with facilities for

sheltered work and sheltered leisure time as well as residential accommodation (Mann and Cree, 1976). Not many patients need all these
facilities at once but there are some, and many others need some part of
them. The District General Hospital Unit cannot provide the domestic
and vocational milieu required. The other major risk of fragmentation is
that a number of small unsatisfactory services will be created instead of
one large one, with the added danger that supervision is more difficult
and the problems of communication more complicated. It should be
said that many of the smaller units run by statutory authorities and
recognized voluntary associations are, in fact, very satisfactory (Hewett,
et al, 1975) but the same is not true of unsupervised accommodation.

Matters such as these are important because two-thirds of the population of residential units and day centres for the adult mentally ill are now
long-stay and by far the commonest diagnosis is schizophrenia. Psychiatrists and social workers have the opportunity to influence local services
through the local planning machinery, and to encourage and participate
with voluntary organizations in setting up housing associations, hostels,
sheltered workshops, social clubs, restaurants, leisure activities (particularly at weekends), and counselling services in which relatives and
patients play an active part. Clinical workers do not always see it as part
of their job to help construct services as well as to run them, still less to
recognize laymen as equal partners in the enterprise, but the rewards to
all parties, and above all to patients, are well worth the adjustment of
attitudes that is needed.

The authors of this book have attempted to present all the many facets
of our current knowledge about schizophrenia. It is not negligible. The
medical profession is nowadays frequently criticized for an undue pre-
occupation with the biological basis of disease and physical methods of
treatment, and for taking no interest in all the other problems (many
of much greater importance) that patients bring to their doctors. Social
workers are beginning to be criticized in a different, but equivalent, way,
as they apply this or that technique which is of limited relevance to the
problems of their clients. Psychiatrists are perhaps less deserving of such
criticism than some other branches of the medical profession but we
hope that this book makes plain that biological, psychological and social
factors must always be considered in the interests of helping handicapped people and their relatives. Curing or alleviating disease is one
important part of this aim.

We cannot do better than end by quoting a letter written to the
British Medical Journal, on the subject of "Management of childhood
epilepsy" (Balme, 1977). The writer criticized a leading article on the

subject because it dealt only with drugs. It left out the problems of going to school, climbing trees, swimming, camping, getting married, having children, drowning in bathwater three inches deep. It did not mention fire guards, protection of staircases or removal of bathroom locks. "It is as if your expert on epilepsy saw patients only in a hospital clinic, left the clinic only to go to the laboratory, and never saw the results in the home, in plastic surgery wards, and in the cemeteries, of such neglect of management."

References

Ackner, B., Harris, A. and Oldham, A. J. (1957). *Lancet* **1**, 607.

Adelstein, A. M., Downham, D. Y., Stein, Z. and Susser, M. W. (1968). *Soc. Psychiat.* **3**, 47.

Alexander, F., Curtis, G. C., Sprince, G. and Crosley, A. P. (1963). *J. nerv. ment. Dis.* **137**, 135–142.

Allen, G., Harvald, B. and Shields, J. (1967). Measures of twin concordance. *Acta genet.* (Basel) **17**, 475–481.

Allen, M. G., Cohen, S. and Pollin, W. (1972). *Am. J. Psychiat.* **128**, 939–945.

Allen, R. V. and Loebel, R. (1972). *Can. J. behav. Sci.* **4**, 101–117.

Ananth, J., Ban, T. A., Lehmann, H. E. and Bennett, J. (1970). *Can. psychiat. Ass. J.* **15**, 15–20.

Andrews, P., Hall, J. N. and Snaith, R. P. (1976). *Br. J. Psychiat.* **128**, 451–455.

Angrist, B., Sathananthan, G. and Gershon, S. (1973). *J. psychiat. Res.* **11**, 13–23.

Angrist, B., Sathananthan, G., Wilk, S. and Gershon, S. (1974). *Psychopharmac.* **31**, 1–12.

Angst, J. (1966). *Monogr. Gesamtgeb. Neurol. Psychiatr.* **112**. Springer-Verlag, Berlin.

Angyal, A. and Blackman, N. (1940). *Archs Neurol. Psychiat.* **44**, 611–620.

Angyal, A. and Sherman, M. A. (1942). *Am. J. Psychiat.* **98**, 857–862.

Antun, F., Burnett, G. B., Cooper, A. J., Daly, R. J., Smythies, J. R. and Zealley, A. R. (1971). *J. psychiat. Res.* **18**, 63–67.

Argyle, M., Bryant, B. and Trower, P. (1974). *Psychol. Med.* **4**. 435–443.

Asperger, H. (1944). *Arch. Psychiat. Nervenkr.* **117**, 76–136.

Asperger, H. (1960). *In* "Jahrbuch für Jugendpsychiatrie und ihre Grundgebiete" (Ed. Villinger, W.). Stuttgart.

Astrup, C. and Ødegaard, Ø. (1960). *Acta psychiat. scand.* **35**, 289.

Atthowe, J. M. and Krasner, L. (1968). *J. abnorm. Psychol.* **73**, 37–43.

Ayd, F. J. (1961). *J. Am. med. Ass.* **175**, 491–500.

Ayd, F. J. (1975). *Am. J. Psychiat.* **132**, 491–500.

Ayllon, T. and Azrin, N. H. (1968). "The Token Economy: a motivational system for therapy and rehabilitation". Appleton-Century-Crofts, New York.

Ayllon, T. and Michael, J. (1959). *J. exp. Analysis Behav.* **2**, 323–334.

Axelrod, J. (1961). *Science* **134**, 343–344.

Axelrod, J. (1962). *J. Pharmac. exp. Ther.* **138**, 28–35.

Babcock, H. (1933). "Dementia Praecox: A Psychological Study". Science Press, Lancaster, Pa.

Babigian, H. M. (1975). *In* "Comprehensive Textbook of Psychiatry II" (Eds Freedman, A. M., Kaplan, H. and Sadock, B. J.) Vol. 1. Williams and Wilkins, Baltimore.

Bagshaw, M. H., Kimble, D. P. and Pribram, K. H. (1965). *Neuropsychologia* **3**, 111–119.

Baker, R. (1971). *Behav. Res. Ther.* **9**, 329–336.

Baker, R. D., Hall, J. N. and Hutchinson, K. (1974). *Br. J. Psychiat.* **124**, 367–384.

Baker, R. D., Hall, J. N., Hamilton, M., Jones, H. G. and Rosenthall, G. (1977a). Clinical applications of behaviour modification techniques with long-stay psychiatric patients. DHSS Research Report.

Baker, R. D., Hall, J. N., Hutchinson, K. and Bridge, G. W. K. (1977b). *Br. J. Psychiat.* (in press).

Baldessarini, R. J. (1975). *Int. Rev. Neurobiol.* **18**, 41–67.

Baldessarini, R. J. (1977). *New Engl. J. Med.* **297**, 988–995.

Balme, H. W. (1977). *Br. med. J.* **2**, 1284.

Ban, T. A. and Lehmann, H. E. (1975). *Can. Psychiat. Ass. J.* **20**, 103–112.

Bandura, A. (1971). "Principles of Behaviour Modification". Holt, Rinehart and Winston, London.

Banerjee, S. and Snyder, S. H. (1973). *Science* **182**, 74–75.

Bannister, D. (1962a). *Acta psychol.* **20**, 104—120.

Bannister, D. (1962b). *J. Ment. Sci.* **108**, 825–842.

Bannister, D. (1963). *Br. J. Psychiat.* **109**, 680–686.

Bannister, D. (1965). *Br. J. Psychiat.* **111**, 377–382.

Bannister, D. and Fransella, Fay (1966). *Br. J. soc. clin. Psychol.* **5**, 95–102.

Bannister, D., Adams-Webber, J. R., Penn, W. I. and Radley, A. (1975). *Br. J. soc. clin. Psychol.* **14**, 169–180.

Barry, H. and Barry, H. (1961). *Archs gen. Psychiat.* **5**, 292.

Barry, H. and Barry, H. (1964). *Archs gen. Psychiat.* **11**, 385.

Barton, R. (1976). "Institutional Neurosis", 3rd edn. John Wright, Bristol.

Bateson, G., Jackson, D., Haley, J. and Weakland, J. (1956). *Behav. Sci.* **1**, 251–264.

Beach, W. C. (1975). *Heatlh Trends* **7**, 31–35.

Bedenić, B., Kesić, B., Korbar, M. *et al.* (1972). Differential rates of psychoses in Croatia, Yugoslavia: Final Report, Aagreb. Zndrija Stampar School of Public Health.

Belmaker, R. H., Ebbesen, K., Ebstein, R. and Rimon, R. (1976). *Br. J. Psychiat.* **129**, 227–232.

Bennett, D. H. (1969). *Soc. Psychiat.* **9**, 4–18.

Bennett, D. H. (1970). *Soc. Psychiat.* **5**, 224–230.

Bennett, D. H. (1972). *In* "Evaluating a Community Psychiatric service: The Camberwell Register 1964–71" (Eds Wing, J. K. and Hailey, A. M.) 275–282. Oxford University Press, London.

Bennett, D. H. (1975). *In* "Psychiatrie der Gegenwart: Forschung und Praxis" (Eds Kisker, K. P., Meyer, J.-E., Muller, C. and Strömgren, E.) Vol. 3, 743–778. Springer-Verlag, Berlin.

Bennett, D. H. and Wing, J. K. (1963). *In* "Trends in the Mental Health Service" (Eds Freeman, H. and Farndale, J.) Chapter 27. Pergamon, Oxford.

Bennett, D. H., Folkard, S. and Nicolson, A. (1961). *Lancet* **2**, 539–541.

Bennett, D. H., Fox, C., Jowell, T. and Skynner, A. C. R. (1976). *Br. J. Psychiat.* **129** 73–81.

Bidder, T. G., Mandel, L. R., Ahn, H. S., van den Heuval, W. J. A. and Walker, R. W. (1974). *Lancet* **1**, 165–166.

Birley, J. L. T. (1974). *Psychiat. Q.* **48**, 568–571.

Birley, J. L. T. and Brown, G. W. (1970). *Br. J. Psychiat.* **116**, 327.

Blackwell, B. (1977). *Br. J. Psychiat.* **129**, 513–531.

Bleuler, E. (1911). "Dementia Praecox or the Group of Schizophrenias" (Trans. J. Zinkin, 1950). International University Press, New York.

Bleuler, E. (1919). "Das Autistisch-Undisziplinierte Denken in der Medizin und seine Überwindung". Springer-Verlag, Berlin.

Bleuler, M. (1972). "Die schizophrenen Geistesstörungen im Lichte langjähriger Kranken- und Familiengeschichten". Thieme, Stuttgart.

Bloomfield, H. H. (1973). *Behaviour Therapy* **4**, 227–281.

Bockoven, J. S. (1956). *J. nerv. ment. Dis.* **124**, 167.

Bodmer, W. F. (1976). *Neurosci. Res. Prog. Bull.* **14**, 66–69.

Boneau, C. A. (1974). *Am. Psychol.* **29**, 297–309.

Böök, J. A. (1953). *Acta genet. Statist. med.* (Basel) **4**, 1.

Böök, J. A. (1961). *In* "Causes of Mental Disorders: a Review of Epidemiological Knowledge". (Eds Gruenberg, E. M. and Huxley, M.). Millbank Memorial Fund, New York.

Bosch, G. (1962). "Der frühkindliche Autismus". (Trans. D. and I. Jordan, 1970). Springer, Berlin.

Boulton, A. A. (1971). *Nature* **231**, 22–28.

Bourdillon, R. E., Clarke, C. A., Ridges, A. P., Sheppard, P. M., Harper, P. and Leslie, S. A. (1965). *Nature* **208**, 453–455.

Bourne, H. (1953). *Lancet* **ii**, 964.

Bowers, M. B. (1974). *Archs gen. Psychiat.* **31**, 50–54.

Bowers, M. B. and Freedman, D. X. (1966). *Archs gen. Psychiat.* **15**, 240–248.

Brill, H. and Patton, R. E. (1962). *Am. J. Psychiat.* **119**, 20.

Brim, O. G. and Wheeler, S. (1966). "Socialization after Childhood: two essays". John Wiley, New York.

British Medical Journal (1974). Editorial: Unity and diversy in schizophrenia. *Br. med. J.* **4**, 673–674.

Broadbent, D. E. (1958). "Perception and Communication". Pergamon Press, New York.

Broadbent, D. E. (1970). *In* "Attention: Contemporary Theories and Analysis" (Ed. Mostofsky, D.). Appleton-Century-Crofts, New York.

Broadbent, D. E. (1971). "Decision and Stress". Academic Press, London and New York.

Brockington, I., Crow, T. J., Johnstone, E. C. and Owen, F. (1976). *In* "Monoamine Oxidase and its Inhibition", CIBA Foundation Symposium No. 39 (new series), (Eds Wolstenholme, G. E. W. and Knight, J.). Elsevier, Amsterdam; Excerpta Medica, North-Holland.

Broekma, V. and Rosenbaum, G. (1975). *J. abnorm. Psychol.* **84**, I, 30–35.

Broen, W. E. (1966). *Psychol. Rev.* **73**, 579–585.

Broen, W. E. (1968). "Schizophrenia research and Theory". Academic Press, New York and London.

Broen, W. E. and Storms, L. H. (1961). *Psychol. Rev.* **68**, 405–415.

Brooke, E. M. (1957). *Int. Congr. Psychiat.* (Zurich) **3**, 52.

Brown, G. W. (1959a). *Br. med. J.* **ii**, 1300–1302

Brown, G. W. (1959b). *Millbank Memorial Fund Q.* **37**, 101–131.

Brown, G. W. (1960). *Acta psychiat. neurol. scand.* **35**, 414–430.

Brown, G. W. (1967). *In* "Recent Developments in Schizophrenia" (Eds Coppen, A. and Walk, A.) *Brit. J. Psychiat. Spec. Publn* No. 1. Headley, Ashford, Kent.

Brown, G. W. and Birley, J. L. T. (1968). *J. Hlth soc. Behav.* **9**, 203–214.

Brown, G. W. and Birley, J. L. T. (1970). *In* "Psychiatric Epidemiology" (Eds Hare, E. H. and Wing, J. K.). Oxford University Press, London.

Brown, G. W. and Rutter, M. (1966). *Human Relations* **19**, 241–263.

Brown, G. W., Carstairs, G. M. and Topping, G. G. (1958). *Lancet* **2**, 685–689.

Brown, G. W., Monck, E. M., Carstairs, G. M. and Wing, J. K. (1962). *Br. J. prev. soc. Med.* **16**, 55–68.

Brown, G. W., Bone, M., Dalison, B. and Wing, J. K., (1966). "Schizophrenia and Social Care", Maudsley Monograph No. 17. Oxford University Press, London.

Brown, G. W., Birley, J. L. T. and Wing, J. K. (1972). *Br. J. Psychiat.* **121**, 241–258.

Brown, G. W., Harris, T. O. and Peto, J. (1973). *Psychol. Med.* **3**, 159–176.

Brown, G. W., Bhrolchain, M. N. and Harris, T. (1975). *Sociology* **9**, 225–254.

Bruder, G. E., Sutton, S., Babkoff, H., Gurland, B. J., Yozawitz, A. and Fleiss, J. L. (1975). *Psychol. Med.* **5**, **3**, 260–272.

Bruderlein, F. T., Humber, L. G. and Voith, K. (1975). *J. Med. Chem.* **18**, 185–188.

Brune, G. G. and Himwich, H. E. (1962a). *Archs gen. Psychiat.* **6**, 324–328.

Brune, G. G. and Himwich, H. E. (1962b). *Archs gen. Psychiat.* **6**, 324–328.

Buchsbaum, M. S. (1975). *In* "Biology of the Major Psychoses" (Ed. Freedman, D. Y.). Raven Press, New York.

Buchsbaum, M. S. (1976). *In* "Consciousness and Self-Regulation I" (Eds Schwartz, G. E. and Shapiro, D.), Chapter 3. Plenum, New York.

Buchsbaum, M. S. and Silverman, J. (1968). *Psychosom. Med.* **30**, 12–22.

Buchsbaum, M. S., Coursey, R. D. and Murphy, D. L. (1976). *Science* **194**, 339–341.

Buck, C., Hobbs, G. E., Simpson, H. and Wanklin, J. M. (1975). *Br. J. Psychiat.* **127**, 235–239.

Bull, H. C. and Venables, P. H. (1974). *Br. J. Psychiat.* **125**, 350–354.

Bunney, B. S. and Aghajanian, G. K. (1976). *In* "Antipsychotic Drugs: Pharmaco-dynamics and Pharmacokinetics" (Eds Sedvall, G., Uvnas, B. and Zotterman, Y.) 305–318. Pergamon Press, Oxford.

Burdock, E. I. and Hardesty, A. S. (1968). *J. abnorm. Psychol.* **73**, 62–69.

Burt, D. R., Creese, I. and Snyder, S. H. (1976). *Mol. Pharmac.* **12**, 800–812.

Butler, R. J. (1977). *J. adv. Nursing* (in press).

Caffey, E. M., Diamond, L. S., Frank, T. V., Grasberger, J. C., Herman, L., Klett, C. J. and Rothstein, C. (1964). *J. Chron. Dis.* **17**, 347–358.

Cameron, N. (1938). *Psychol. Monogr.* **50**, 1–33.

Carlson, C. G., Hersen, M. and Eisler, R. M. (1972). *J. Nerv. ment. Dis.* **155**, 192–204.

Carlsson, A. (1959). *Pharmac. Rev.* **2**, 490–493.

Carpenter, W. T., Strauss, J. S. and Muleh, S. (1973). *Archs gen. Psychiat.* **28**, 847–852.

Carpenter, W. T., Fink, E. B. and Narasimhachari, N. (1975). *Am. J. Psychiat.* **132**, 1067–1071.

Carter, C. O. (1976). "An ABC of Medical Genetics", 3rd edn. The Lancet, London.

Carter, M. and Watts, C. A. H. (1971). *Br. J. Psychiat.* **118**, 453–460.

Catterson, A., Bennett, D. H. and Freudenberg, R. K. (1963). *Br. J. Psychiat.* **109**, 750.

Cawley, R. H. (1967). *In* "Recent Developments in Schizophrenia" (Eds Cooper, A. and Walk, A.). Headley Brothers, Ashford, Kent.

Central Council for Education and Training in Social Work (1974). "People with Handicaps need Better Trained Workers", Paper No. 5. CCETSW, Clifton House, Euston Road, London.

Chapman, J. (1966). *Br. J. Psychiat.* **112**, 225–251.

Chapman, J. A. and McGhie, A. (1962). *J. ment. Sci.* **108**, 455–462.

Chapman, L. J. (1958). *J. Abnorm. soc. Psychol.* **65**, 374–379.

Cheadle, A. J. and Morgan, R. (1972). *Br. J. Psychiat.* **120**, 437–441.

Chloden, L. W., Kurland, A. and Savage, C. (1955). *J. nerv. ment. Dis.* **122**, 211–221.

Clark, R. E. (1949). *Am. J. Sociol.* **54**, 433.

Clausen, J. A. and Kohn, M. L. (1959). *In* "Epidemiology of Mental Disorder" (Ed. Pasamanic, B.). Am. Ass. Advance Sci., Washington, D.C.

Clausen, J. A. and Kohn, M. L. (1960). *In* "The Etiology of Schizophrenia" (Ed. Jackson, D.). Basic Books, New York.

Clayton, P. J., Rodin, L. and Winokur, G. (1968). Family History Studies: III. *Comprenhens. Psychiat.* **9**, 31–49.

Clemens, J. A., Smalstig, E. G. and Sawyer, B. D. (1974). *Psychopharmac.* **40**, 132–135.

Cohen, S. M., Allen. M. G., Pollin, W. and Hrubec, Z. (1972). *Archs. gen. Psychiat.* **26**, 539–546

Coleman, J. H. and Hayes, P. E. (1975). *Dis. nerv. Syst.* **36**, 591–593.

Connell, P. (1958). "Amphetamine Psychosis". Chapman and Hall, London.

Cooper, B. (1961). *Br. J. prev. soc. Med.* **15**, 17.

Cooper, B. and Morgan, H. G. (1973). "Epidemiological Psychiatry". Thomas, Springfield.

Cooper, J. E., Kendell, R. E., Gurland, B. J., Sharp, L., Copeland, J. R. M. and Simon, R. (1972). "Psychiatric Diagnosis in New York and London", Maudsley Monograph No. 20. Oxford University Press, London.

Creer, C. (1975). *Social Work Today* **6**, 2–7.

Creer, C. and Wing, J. K. (1974). "Schizophrenia at Home". National Schizophrenia Fellowship, 78 Victoria Road, Surbiton, Surrey.

Creese, I. N. R. and Iversen, S. D. (1974). *Brain Res.* **55**, 369–382.

Creese, I. N. R. and Iversen, S. D. (1975). *Brain Res.* **83**, 419–432.

Creese, I. N. R., Burt, D. R. and Snyder, S. H. (1976). *Science* **129**, 481–483.

Criswell, J. H. (1968). *Rehab. Lit.* **29**, 162–165.

Crocetti, G. M., Kulcar, Z., Kesic, B. and Lemkau, P. V. (1964). *Am. J. publ. Hlth* **54**, 196.

Crow, T. J., Deakin, J. F. W., Johnston, E. C. and Longden, A. (1976). *Lancet* **2**, 563–566.

Cumming, E. (1969). *Int. J. Psychiat.* **7**, 204–208.

Cumming, J. H. (1963). *Psychiat. Q.* **37**, 723–733.

Curnow, R. N. and Smith, C. (1975). *Jl. R. statist. Soc.* A, **138**, 131–169.

Curry, S. H. (1976). *Br. J. clin. Pharmac.* **3**, 20–28.

Davies, B. M. (1977). *In* "The Younger Disabled: Proceedings of Social Services Conference, 1976". Association of Directors of Social Services.

Davis, A. E., Dinitz, S. and Pasamanick, B. (1972). *Am. J. Orthopsychiat.* **42**, 375–388.

Davis, J. M. (1965). *Archs gen. Psychiat.* **13**, 552–572.

Davis, J. M. (1974). *J. psychiat. Res.* **11**, 25–29.

Davis. J. M. (1975). *Am. J. Psychiat.* **132**, 1237–1245.

Davison, B. C. C. (1973). *Br. J. Psychiat. Spec. Publn.* No. 8. Headley, Ashford, Kent.

Davison, G. C. (1969). *In* "Behaviour Therapy: appraisal and status" (Ed. Franks, C. M.). McGraw Hill, New York.

Davison, K. (1976). *In* "Schizophrenia Today" (Eds Kemali, D., Bartolini, G. and Richter, D.) 105–133. Pergamon Press, Oxford.

Davison, K. and Bagley, C. R. (1969). In *Br. J. Psychiat. Spec. Publn.* No. 4, 113–184. Headley, Ashford, Kent.

De Alarcon, R. and Carney, M. W. P. (1969). *Br. med. J.* iii, 564–567.

Dellas, M. and Gaier, E. L. (1970). *Psychol. Bull.* **73**, 55–73.

Department of Health and Social Security (1972). "Rehabilitation", Report of the Tunbridge Committee. H.M.S.O., London.

Department of Health and Social Security (1975). "Better Services for the Mentally Ill", Cmnd. 6233. H.M.S.O., London.

Dohan, F. C. (1966). *Acta. psychiat. scand.* **42**, 1–23.

Dohrenwend, B. P. and Dohrenwend, B. S. (1969). "Social Status and Psychological Disorder: A Causal Inquiry". Wiley, New York.

Douglas, F. J. and Pribram, K. H. (1966). *Neuropsychologia* **4**, 197–220.

Douglas, R. J. (1967). *Psychol. Bull.* **67**, 416–442.

Dunaif, S. and Hoch, P. H. (1955). *In* "Psychiatry and the Law" (Eds Hoch, P. H. and Zubin, J.). Grune and Stratton, New York.

Dunham, H. W. (1965). "Community and Schizophrenia: An Epidemiological Analysis". Wayne State University Press, Detroit.

Dykes, M. and McGhie, A. (1976). *Br. J. Psychiat.* **128**, 50–56.

Early, D. F. (1960). *Lancet* **2**, 754–757.

Early, D. F. (1965). *In* "Psychiatric Hospital Care" (Ed. Freeman, H.) 165–172. Bailliere, Tindall and Cassell, London.

Easterbrook, J. A. (1959). *Psychol. Rev.* **66**, 183–200.

Eaton, J. W. and Weil, R. J. (1955). "Culture and Mental Disorders". Free Press, Glencoe, Illinois.

Edwards, J. H. (1972). *In* "Genetic Factors in 'Schizophrenia' " (Ed. Kaplan, A. R.) 310–314. Thomas, Springfield, Illinois.

Ehringer, H. and Hornykiewicz, O. (1960). *Klin. Wschr.* **38**, 1236–1239.

Ekdawi, M. Y. (1972). *Br. J. Psychiat.* **121**, 417–424.

Elston, R. C. and Campbell, M. A. (1970). *Behav. Genet.* **1**, 3–10.

Emmerich, D. S. and Levine, F. M. (1970). *Dis. nerv. Syst.* **31**, 552–557.

Erlenmeyer-Kimling, L. (1972). *Int. J. ment. Hlth* **1**, 1–2.

Erlenmeyer-Kimling, L. (1975). *In* "Life History Research in Psychopathology" (Eds Wirt, R. D., Winokur, G. and Roff, M.) Vol. 4, 23–46. University of Minnesota Press, Minneapolis.

Erlenmeyer-Kimling, L. and Paradowski, W. (1966). *Am. Nat.* **100**, 651–665.

Enna, S. J., Bennett, J. P., Burt, D. R., Creese, I. and Snyder, S. H. (1976). *Nature* **263**, 338–341.

Essen-Möller, E. (1941). *Acta psychiatr. neurol. scand. Suppl.* **23**.

Essen-Möller, E. (1955). *Acta genet. Statist. med.* **5**, 334–342.

Essen-Möller, E. (1977). *Acta psychiat. scand.* **55**, 202–207.

Etzioni, A. (1961). "A Comparative Analysis of Complex Organizations". Free Press, New York.

Eysenck, H. J. (1972). In "Genetic Factors in 'Schizophrenia' " (Ed. Kaplan, A. R). 504–515. Thomas, Springfield, Illinois.

Fairweather, G. W., Sanders, D. H., Cressler, D. L. and Maynard, H. (1969) "Community Life for the Mentally Ill". Aldine, Chicago.

Falconer, D. S. (1965). *Ann. hum. Genet.* **29**, 51–76.

Farina, A., Garmezy, N. and Barry, H. (1963a). *J. abnorm. soc. Psychol.* **67**, 624.

Farina, A., Barry, H. and Garmezy, N. (1963b). *Archs gen. Psychiat.* **9**, 224.

Faris, R. E. L. and Dunham, H. W. (1939). "Mental Disorders in Urban Areas". University of Chicago Press, Chicago.

Farley, J. D. (1976). *Acta psychiat. scand.* **53**, 173–192.

Feinsilver, D. B. and Gunderson, J. G. (1974). *Schiz. Bull.* **34**, 241–256.

Ferreira, A. J. (1963). *Archs gen. Psychiat.* **8**, 68–73.

Ferreira, A. J. and Winter W. D. (1965). *Archs gen. Psychiat.* **13**, 214–223.

Ferreira, A. J., Winter, W. D. and Poindexter, E. J. (1966). *Family Process* **5**, 60–75.

Fieve, R. R., Rosenthall, D. and Brill, H. (Eds) (1975). "Genetic Research in Psychiatry". John Hopkins University Press, Baltimore and London.

Fischer, M. (1973). *Acta psychiat. scand. Suppl.* **238**.

Floru, L., Heinrich, K. and Wittek, F. (1975). *Int. Pharmacopsychiat.* **10**, 230–239

Foulds, G. A. and Bedford, A. (1975). *Psychol. Med.* **5**, 181–192.

Foulds, G. A. and Dixon, P. (1962). *Br. J. clin. soc. Psychol.* **1**, 199.

Fowler, R. C. and Tsuang, M. T. (1975). *Comprehens. Psychiat.* **16**, 339–342.

Fox, R. E. (1976). In "Clinical Methods in Psychology" (Ed. Weiner, I. B.). Wiley, New York.

Frantz, A. G. and Sachar, E. J. (1976). In "Antipsychotic Drugs: Pharmacodynamics and Pharmacokinetics" (Eds Sedvall, G., Uvnas, B. and Zotterman, Y.) 421–436. Pergamon Press, Oxford.

Freedman, D. G. (1968). In "Genetic and Environmental Influences on Behaviour" (Eds Thoday, J. M. and Parkes, A. S.) 37–62. Oliver and Boyd, Edinburgh.

Freeman, H. and Rodnick, E. H. (1942). *Archs Neurol. Psychiat.* **48**, 47.

Freeman, H. E. and Simmons, O. G. (1963). "The Mental Patient Comes Home". Wiley, New York.

Freeman, J. M., Finkelstein, J. D. and Mudd, S. H. (1975). *New Engl. J. Med.* **292**, 491–496.

Freeman, T., Cameron, J. L. and McGhie, A. (1958). "Chronic Schizophrenia". International Universities Press, New York.

Fremming, K. H. (1951). "The Expectation of Mental Infirmity in a Sample of the Danish Population". Occasional papers on Eugenics, No. 7. London, Cassell.

Freudenberg, R. K. (1967). *Psychiat. Q.* **41**, 698–710.

Freyhan, F. A. (1959). *Am. J. Psychiat.* **115**, 577–585.

Friedhoff, A. J. and van Winkle, E. (1962a). *Nature* **194**, 897–898.

Friedhoff, A. J. and van Winkle, E. (1962b). *J. nerv. ment. Dis.* **135**, 550–555.

Friedman, E., Shopsin, B., Sathanathan, G. and Gershon, S. (1974). *Am. J. Psychiat.* **131**, 1392–1398.

Fromm-Reichmann, F. (1948). *Psychiatry* **11**, 263–273.

Fuller, R. W. (1976). *Life Sci.* **19**, 625–628.

Gardos, G. and Cole, J. O. (1976). *Am. J. Psychiat.* **133**, 32–36.

Gardos, G., Cole, J. O. and Orzack, M. H. (1973). *Psychopharmac. (Berlin)* **29**, 221–230.

Garmezy, N. (1974). *Schiz. Bull.* **8**, 14–90, **9**, 55–125.

Garratt, F. N. (1976). *Lancet* **ii**, 1303.

Gastager, H. (1969). *Psychother. Psychom.* **17**, 34–41.

Gerard, D. L. and Houston, L. G. (1953). *Psychiat. Q.* **27**, 90.

Gerard, D. L. and Siegel, J. (1950). *Psychiat. Q.* **24**, 47.

Goddard, G. V. (1964). *Psychol. Bull.* **62**, 89–109.

Goffman, E. (1961). "Asylums: Essays of the Social Situation of Mental Patients and Other Inmates". Doubleday, New York.

Goldberg, D. (1967). *Soc. Psychiat.* **2**, 1–13.

Goldberg, E. M. and Morrison, S. L. (1963). *Br. J. Psychiat.* **109**, 785.

Goldberg, S. C., Frosch, W. A., Drosman, A. K., Schooler, N. R. and Johnson, G. F. S. (1972). *Archs gen. Psychiat.* **26**, 367–373.

Goldberg, S. C., Schooler, N. R., Hogarty, G. E. and Roper, M. (1977). *Archs gen. Psychiat.* (in press).

Goldfarb, W., Spitzer, F. L. and Endicott, J. (1976). *J. Autism Childhood Schiz.* **2**, 327–338.

Goldhamer, H. Marshall, A. (1953). "Psychosis and Civilisation Glencoe". Free Press, Illinois.

Goldstein, A. P. (1973). "Structured Learning Therapy: towards a psychotherapy for the poor". Academic Press, New York and London.

Goldstein, A. P., Gershaw, N. J., Sprafkin, R. P. (1974). "Trainer's Manual for Structured Learning Theraphy", 3rd edn. Syracuse University.

Goodman, N. (1957). *Br. prev. soc. Med.* **11**, 203.

Gottesman, I. I. and Erlenmeyer-Kimling, L. (eds) (1971). *Soc. Biol. Suppl.* Vol. 18.

Gottesman, I. I. and Shields, J. (1966). *In* "Progress in Experimental Personality Research" (Ed. Maher, B. A.) Vol. 3, 1–84. Academic Press, New York and London.

Gottesman, I. I. and Shields, J. (1967). *Proc. nat. Acad. Sci.* **58**, 199–205.

Gottesman, I. I. and Shields, J. (1972). "Schizophrenia and Genetics: a Twin Study Vantage Point". Academic Press, New York and London.

Gottesman, I. I. and Shields, J. (1973). *Br. J. Psychiat.* **122**, 15–30.

Gottesman, I. I. and Shields, J. (1976). *Schiz. Bull.* **2**, 360–401.

Green, A. R. and Grahame-Smith, D. G. (1976a). *Nature* **262**, 594–596.

Green, A. R. and Grahame-Smith, D. G. (1976b). *Nature* **260**, 487–491.

Greengard, P. (1976). *In* "Antipsychotic Drugs: Pharmacodynamics and Pharmacokinetics" (Eds Sedvall, G., Uvnas, B. and Zotterman, Y.) 271–288. Pergamon Press, Oxford.

Griffith, J. D., Cavanaugh, J. H., Held, J. and Oates, J. A. (1972) *Archs gen. Psychiat.* **26**, 97–100.

Griffith, R. D. P. (1973). *Br. J. Psychiat.* **123**, 403–408.

Griffith, R. D. P. (1974). *Psychol. Med.* **4**, 316–325.

Gripp, R. F. and Magaro, P. A. (1974). *Behav. Res. Ther.* **12**, 205–228.

Gruenberg, E. M. (1957). *In* "Explorations in Social Psychiatry" (Eds Leighton, A. H., Clausen, J. A. and Wilson, R. N.). Basic Books, New York.

Gruzelier, J. and Hammond, N. V. (1976). *Res. Commun. Psychol. Psychiat. Behav.* **1**, 33–72 (a).

Gruzelier, J. H. and Venables, P. H. (1972). *J. Nerv. ment. Dis.* **155**, 277–287.

Gruzelier, J. H. and Venables, P. H. (1975). *Psychophysiol.* **12**, 66–73.

Gunn, J. (1977). *Br. J. Psychiat.* **130**, 317–329.

Gutride, M. E., Goldstein, A. P. and Hunter, G. F. (1973). *J. consult. clin. Psychol.* **3**, 408–415.

Haase, H. J. and Janssen, P. A. J. (1965). "The Action of Neuroleptic Drugs". Year Book Medical Publishers, Chicago.

Häfner, H. and Reimann, H. (1970). *In* "Psychiatric Epidemiology" (Eds Hare, E. H. and Wing, J. K.). Oxford University Press, London.

Hajdu-Gaines, L. (1940). *Psychoanal. Rev.* **27**, 421–438.

Haley, J. (1959a). *Psychiat.* **22**, 321–332.

Haley, J. (1959b). *J. nerv. ment. Dis.* **129**, 357–374.

Haley, J. (1960). *Am. J. Ortho-psychiat.* **30**, 460–467.

Haley, J. (1968). *J. Albnorm. Psychol.* **73**, 559–565.

Hall, J. N. and Baker, R. D. (1973). *Behav. Res. Ther.* **11**, 253–263.

Hall, J. N., Baker, R. D. and Hutchinson, K. (1977a). *Behav. Res. Ther.* (in press).

Hall, J., Baker, R. and Jones, G. (1977b). Dept. Psych. Psychiat., University of Leeds (mimeo).

Hamilton, M., Smith, A. L. G., Lapidus, H. E. and Cadogan, E. P. (1960). *J. ment. Sci.* **106**, 40–55.

Hanson, D. R., Gottesman, I. I. and Heston, L. L. (1976). *Br. J. Psychiat.* **129**, 142–154.

Hare, E. H. (1956). *J. ment. Sci.* **102**, 753.

Hare, E. H. (1975). *Am. J. Psychiat.* **132**, 1168.

Hare, E. H., Price, J. S. and Slater, E. (1972). *Br. J. Psychiat.* **121**, 515–524.

Harris, A., Linker, I., Norris, V. and Shepherd, M. (1956). *Br. J. prev. soc. Med.* **10**, 107–114.

Harrow, M. and Quinlan, D. (1977). *Archs gen. Psychiat.* **34**, 15–21.

Harrow, M., Tucker, G. J. and Shields, P. (1972). *Archs gen. Psychiat.* **27**, 40—45.

Hasenfus, N. and Magaro, P. (1976). *Br. J. Psychiat.* **129**, 346–349.

Haynes, S. N. and Geddy, P. (1973). *Behav. Ther.* **4**, 132–127.

Helgason, T. (1964). *Acta psychiat. scand.* **40** (Suppl. 173).

Helmsley, D. R. (1975). *Br. J. soc. clin. Psychol.* **14**, 81–89.

Hernandez-Peon, R., Scherrer, H. and Jouret, M. (1956). *Science* **123**, 331–332.

Heston, L. L. (1966). *Br. J. Psychiat.* **112**, 819–825.

Heston, L. L. (1970). *Science* **167**, 249–256.

Heston, L. L. and Denney, D. (1968). *In* "The Transmission of Schizophrenia" (Eds Rosenthal, D. and Kety, S. S.), 363–376. Pergamon Press, Oxford.

Hewett, S. and Ryan, P. (1975). *Br. J. hos. Med.* **14**, 65–70.

Hewett, S., Ryan, P. and Wing, J. K. (1975). *J. soc. Policy* **4**, 391–404.

Higgins, J. (1976). *J. Psychiat. Res.* **13**, 1–9.

Hilgard, J. R. and Newman, M. F. (1963). *Am. J. Ortho-psychiat.* **33**, 409.

Himwich, H. E. (1970). *In* "Biochemistry, Schizophrenia and Affective Illnesses" (Ed. Himwich, H. E.). Williams and Wilkins, Baltimore.

Hirsch, S. R. and Leff, J. P. (1971). *Psychol. Med.* **1**, 118–127.

Hirsch, S. R. and Leff, J. P. (1975). "Abnormalities in Parents of Schizophreics", Maudsley Monograph No. 22. Oxford University Press, London.

Hirsch, S. R., Gaind, R., Rohde, P. D., Stevens, B. C. and Wing, J. K. (1973). *Br. med. J.* **1**, 118–127.

Hoch, P. H. and Polatin, P. (1949). *Psychiat. Q.* **23**, 249.

Hockey, G. R. J. (1970). *Q. J. exp. Psychol.* **22**, 28–36 (a).

Hockey, G. R. J. (1970). *Q. J. exp. Psychol.* **22**, 37–42 (b).

Hoffer, A. (1973). *In* "Orthomolecular Psychiatry" (Eds Hawkins, D. and Pauling, L.) 202–262. W. H. Freeman and Co., San Francisco.

Hoffer, A., Osmond, H., Callbeck, M. J. and Kahan, I. (1957). *J. clin. exp. Psychopath.* **18**, 131–158.

Hogarty, G. E. and Goldberg, S. C. (1973). *Archs gen. Psychiat.* **28**, 54–64.

Hogarty, G. E., Goldberg, S. C. and Schooler, N. R. (1974a). *Archs gen. Psychiat.* **31**, 609–618.

Hogarty, G. E., Goldberg, S. C., Schooler, N. R. and Ulrich, R. F. (1974b). *Archs gen. Psychiat.* **31**, 603–608.

Hollinghead, A. B. and Redlich, F. C. (1958). "Social Class and Mental Illness". Wiley, New York.

Hollister, L. E. (1962). *Ann. N.Y. Acad. Sci.* **96**, 80–88.

Holzman, P. (1968). Perceptual aspects of psychopathology. Paper presented at the meeting of the American Psychopathological Association (February).

Holzman, P. S., Proctor, L. R. and Huges, D. W. (1973). *Science* **181**, 179–181.

Holzman, P. S., Proctor, L. R., Levy, D. L., Yasillo, N. J., Meltzer, H. Y. and Hurt, S. W. (1974). *Archs gen. Psychiat.* **31**, 143–151.

Holzman, P. S., Levy, D. L. and Proctor, L. R. (1976). *Archs gen. Psychiat.* **33**, 1415–1420.

Hordern, A. and Hamilton, M. (1963). *Br. J. Psychiat.* **109**, 500–509.

Hoskins, R. G. (1946). "The Biology of Schizophrenia". Norton, New York.

Hunt, J. McV. and Cohen, C. (1944). *In* "Personality and Behaviour Disorders" (Ed. Hunt, J. McV.). Ronald Press, New York.

Hunter, R., Earl, C. J. and Thornicroft, S. (1964). *Proc. R. Soc. Med.* **57**, 758.

Hsu, L. L. and Mandell, A. J. (1973). *Life Sci.* **13**, 847–858.

Huxley, J., Mayr, E., Osmond, H. and Offer, A. (1964). *Nature* **253**, 220–221.

Idanpaan-Heikkila, J., Alhava, E., Oikinuora, M. and Palva, I. (1975). *Lancet* ii, 611.

Ineson, H. (1976). A manual of practice on a token economy ward. Unpublished Report, Stanley Royd Hospital.

Inouye, E. (1963). *Proc. Third Int. Congr. Psychiat. 1961* **1**, 524–530. University of Toronto Press, Montreal.

Isaacs, W., Thomas, J. and Goldiamond, I. (1960). *J. Speech Hearing Disorders* **25**, 8–12.

Iversen, L. L. (1975a). *In* "Handbook of Psychopharmacology" (Eds Iversen, L. L., Iversen, S. D. and Snyder, S. H.), Vol. 3, 381–442. Plenum, New York.

Iversen, L. L. (1975b). *Science* **188**, 1084–1089.

Iversen, S. D. (1977). *In* "Handbook of Psychopharmacology" (Eds Iversen, L. L., Iversen, S. D. and Snyder, S. H.), Vol. 8, 333–384. Plenum Press, New York (in press).

Jablensky, A. and Sartorius, N. (1975). *Psychol. Med.* **5**, 113.

Jacobs, S. and Myers, J. (1976). *J. nerv. ment. Dis.* **162**, 75.

Jacobs, S., Prusoff, B. A. and Paykel, E. S. (1974). *Psychol. Med.* **4**, 444.

Jacquet, Y. F. and Marks, N. (1976). *Science* **194**, 623–634.

Janowsky, D. S., Huey, L., Storms, L. and Judd, L. L. (1977). *Archs gen. Psychiat.* **34**, 189–194.

Janssen, P. A. J. (1976). *In* "Antipsychotic Drugs: Pharmacodynamics and Pharmaco-kinetics" (Eds Sedvall, G., Uvnas, B. and Zotterman, Y.). Pergamon Press, Oxford.

Janssen, P. A. J., Niemegeers, C. J. E. and Schellekens, K. H. L. (1967). *Arzneimittel-Forsch.* **17**, 841–854.

Jaspers, K. (1963). "General Psychopathology" (Trans. J. Hoenig and M. W. Hamilton). Manchester University Press, Manchester.

Johnson, D. A. W. and Freeman, H. L. (1972). *Practitioner* **208**, 395–400.

Johnson, D. A. W. and Freeman, H. L. (1973). *Psychol. Med.* **3**, 115–119.

Johnstone, E., Crow, T. J., Frith, C. D., Carney, M. W. P. and Price, J. S. (1978). *Lancet* **1**, 8–48.

Jones, H. G. (1960). *In* "Handbook of Abnormal Psychology" (Ed. H. J. Eysenck). Pitman, London.

Jones, H. G. (1971). New horizons in behaviour therapy. *In* "Behaviour Therapy in the 1970s" (Eds Burns, L. E. and Worsley, J. L.). John Wright, Bristol.

Jones, H. G. (1974). *Bull. Br. Psychol. Soc.* **24**, 279–290.

Jones, K. (1972). "A History of the Mental Health Services". Routledge, London.

Jones, M. (1953). "The Therapeutic Community". Basic Books, New York.

Juda, A. (1953). "Höchstbegabung: ihre Erbverhältnisse sowie ihre Beziehungen zu psychischen Anomalien". Urban u. Schwarzenberg, Munich and Berlin.

Jung, C. G. (1906). "The Psychology of Dementia Pracox" (Trans. A. A. Brill). Nervous and Mental Diseases Monographs, 1936.

Kakimoto, Y., Sano, I. and Kanazawa, A. (1967). *Nature* **216**, 1110–1111.

Kallman, F. J. (1946). *Am. J. Psychiat.* **103**, 309–322.

Kallman, F. J. (1950). *Int. Congr. Psychiat. Rapp.* **6**, 1–27. Hermann, Paris.

Kanabus, P., Kryas, G. and Matsumoto, H. (1973). *Nerv. Super.* **15**, 124.

Kanfer, F. H. and Karoly, P. (1972). *Behav. Ther.* **3**, 398–416.

Kanner, L. (1942–3). *Nerv. Child* **2**, 217.

Karlsson, J. L. (1968). *In* "The Transmission of Schizophrenia" (Eds Rosenthal, D. and Kety, S. S.) 85–94. Pergamon Press, Oxford.

Karlsson, J. L. (1973). *Br. J. Psychiat.* **123**, 549–554.

Kasanin, J. (1933). *Am. J. Psychiat.* **13**, 97.

Kay, D. W. K., Roth, M., Atkinson, M. W., Stephens, D. A. and Garside, R. F. (1975). *Br. J. Psychiat.* **127**, 109–118.

Kazdin, A. E. and Bootzin, R. R. (9172). *J. Appl. Behav. Anal.* **5**, 343.

Kebanian, J. W., Petzold, G. L. and Greengard, P. (1972). *Proc. natn. Acad. Sci. U.S.A.* **69**, 2145–2149.

Kelly, G. A. (1955). "The Psychology of Personal Constructs" 2 Vols. Norton, New York.

Kelly, H. B., Freeman, H. L. and Schiff, A. A. (1977). *Int. Pharmacopsychiat.* **12** (in press).

Kelly, J. T. and Alluzzahab, F. S. Snr. (1971). *J. clin. Pharmacol.* (U.S.A.) **11**, 211–214.

Kelly, P. H., Seviour P. W. and Iversen, S. D. (1975). *Brains Res.* **94**, 507–522.

Kendig, I. and Richmond, W. V. (1940). "Psychological Studies, in Dementia Praecox". Edwards, Ann Arbour, Michigan.

Kennedy, P. F. (1975). *In* "New Perspectives in Schizophrenia" (Eds Forrest, A. and Affleck, J.). Churchill Livingstone, Edinburgh.

Kety, S. S. (1959a). *Science* **129**, 1528–1532.

Kety, S. S. (1959b). *Science* **129**, 1590–1596.

Kety, S. S. (1967). *New Engl. J. Med.*, **276** 325–331.

Kety, S. S., Rosenthal, D., Wender, P. H., Schulsinger, F. and Jacobsen, B. (1975). *In* "Genetic Research in Psychiatry" (Eds Fieve, R. R., Rosenthal, D. and Brill, H.) 147–165. John Hopkins University Press, Baltimore and London.

Khosla, T., Newcombe, R. G. and Campbell, H. (1977). *Br. med. J.* **1**, 341–344.

Kidd, K. K. (1975). *In* "Genetic Research in Psychiatry" (Eds Fieve, R. R., Rosenthal, D. and Brill, H.) 135–145. Johns Hopkins University Press, Baltimore and London.

Kidd, K. K. and Cavalli-Sforza, L. L. (1973). *Soc. Biol.* **20**, 254–265.

Kimble, D. P., Bagshaw, M. H. and Pribram, K. H. (1965). *Neuropsychol.* **3**, 121–128.

Klee, G. D., Spiro, E., Bahn, A. K. and Gorwitz, K. (1967). *In* "Psychiatric Epidemiology and Mental Health Planning" (Eds Montoe, R. P., Klee, G. D. and Brody, E. G.), Psychiatric Research Report No. 22. American Psychiatric Association Washington.

Klein, D. F. and Davis, J. M. (1969). "Diagnosis and Drug Treatment of Psychiatric Disorder". Williams and Wilkins, Baltimore.

Kluver, H. and Bucy, P. C. (1939). *Archs Neurol. Psychiat.* **42**, 979–1000.

Koepke, J. E. and Pribram, K. H. (1966). *J. comp. physiol. Psychol.* **61**, 442–448.

Kohler, W. and Dinnerstein, D. (1947). *In* "Miscellanea Psychologia" (Ed. Michotte, A.) 196–220. Vrin, Paris.

Kohn, M. L. (1969). *In* "Social Psychiatry" (Ed. Kiev, A.) Vol. 1. Science House, New York.

Kohn, M. L. (1976). *Am. J. Psychiat.* **133**, 177.

Kohn, M. L. and Clausen, J. A. (1955). *Am. Sociol. Rev.* **20**, 265.

Kolvin, I. (1971). *Br. J. Psychiat.* **118**, 381–384.

Kolvin, I. Ounsted, C., Richardson, L. M. and Garside, R. F. (1971). *Br. J. Psychiat.* **118**, 396–402.

Kopell, B. S. and Wittner, W. K. (1968). *J. nerv. ment. Dis.* **147**, 4, 418–424.

Kraepelin, E. (1919). "Dementia Praecox and Paraphrenia" (Trans. R. M. Barclay, from 8th edn of "Psychiatrie". Barth, Leipzig). Livingstone, Edinburgh.

Kraepelin, E. (1921). "Manic-Depressive Insanity and Paranoia" (Trans. R. M. Barclay, from 8th edn of "Psychiatrie". Barth, Leipzig). Livingstone, Edinburgh.

Kramer, M. (1963). *Proc. 3rd Wld Congr. Psychiat.* **3**. McGill University Press, Montreal.

Kramer, M. (1969). "Applications of Mental Health Statistics". World Health Organisation, Geneva.

Kretschmer, E. (1942). "Körperbau und Charakter". Springer, Berlin.

Kringlen, E. (1967). "Heredity, and Environment in the Functional Psychoses. An Epidemiological-Clinical Twin Study". University Press, Oslo; Heinemann, London.

Kringlen, E. (1976). *Schiz. Bull.* **2**, 429–433.

Kuwabara, H. (1976). *Int. J. ment. Hlth* **5**, 95–108.

Laduron, P. M., Gommeren, W. R. and Leysen, J. E. (1974). *Biochem. Pharmac.* **23**, 1599–1608.

Laing, R. D. (1960). "The Divided Self: a Study of Sanity and Madness". Quadrangle Books, Chicago.

Laing, R. D. and Esterson, D. (1964). "Sanity, Madness and the Family". Tavistock Publications, London.

Landau, S. G., Buchsbaum, M. S., Carpenter, W., Strauss, J. and Sacks, M. (1975). *Archs gen. Psychiat.* **32**, 1239–1245.

Lang, P. J. and Buss, A. H. (1965). *J. abnorm. Psychol.* **70**, 77—106.

Langer, G., Sachar, E. J., Gruen, P. H. and Halpern, F. S. (1977). *Nature* **266**, 639.

Langfeldt, G. (1937). "The Prognosis, in Schizophrenia and the Factors Influencing the Course of the Disease". Levin and Munksgaard, Copenhagen.

Langfeldt, G. (1960). *Proc. R. Soc. Mod.* **53**, 1047–1051.

Langner, T. S. and Michael, S. T. (1963). "Life Stress and Mental Health: the Midtown Manhattan Study", Vol. 2. Free Press, New York.

Larson, C. A. and Nyman, G. E. (1970). *Hum. Hered.* **20**, 241–247.

Larson, C. A. and Nyman, G. E. (1973). *Acta psychiat. scand.* **49**, 272–280.

Lazarus, T., Locke, B. Z. and Thomas, D. S. (1963). *Millbank Mem. Fund Q.* **41**, 249.

Leach, J. and Wing, J. K. (1979). "Helping Destitute Men". Tavistock Publications, London. In preparation.

Lee, E. S. (1963). *Millbank Mem. Fund Q.* **41**, 249.

Leff, J. P. (1972). *Br. J. hosp. Med.* **8**, 377–380.

Leff, J. P. (1976). *Br. J. clin. Pharmac.* Suppl., 75–78.

Leff, J. P. and Vaughn, C. (1972). *In* "Evaluating a Community Psychiatric Service" (Eds Wing, J. K. and Hailey, A. M.). Oxford University Press, London.

Leff, J. P. and Wing, J. K. (1971). *Br. med. J.* **3**, 599–604.

Leff, J. P., Hirsch, S. R., Gaird, R., Rohde, P. D. and Stevens, B. C. (1973). *Br. J. Psychiat.* **123**, 659–660.

Lehmann, H. (1966). *In* "Psychopathology of Schizophrenia" (Eds Hoch, P. and Zubin, J.). Grune and Stratton, New York.

Letmendia, F. J. and Harris, A. D. (1967). *Br. J. Psychiat.* **113**, 950–968.

Levine, F. M. and Whitney, N. (1970). *J. abnorm. Psych.* **75**, 1, 74–77.

Levit, V. G. (1977). *In* "New Dimensions in Psychiatry: A World View" (Eds Arieti, S. and Chrzanowski, G.) Vol. 2. Wiley, New York.

Levy, D. L. and Weinreb, H. J. (1976). *Science* **194**, 448–450.

Lewis, A. J. (1955). *Proc. Millbank Mem. Fund Ann. Conf.*, 196–206.

Leysen, J. E., Gommeren, W. and Laduron, P. M. (1978). *Biochem. Pharmac.* **27**, 307.

Liberman, R. P. (1970). *J. chron. Dis.* **23**, 803–812.

Liberman, R. P. (1972). *In* "Advances in Behaviour Therapy" (Eds Rubin, R. D., Feusterheim, H., Henderson, J. D. and Ullman, L. P.). Academic Press, New York and London.

Liberman, R. P., Davis, J., Moon, W. and Moore, J. (1973a). *J. nerv. ment. Dis.* **156**, 432–439.

Liberman, R. P., De Risi, W. J., King, L. W. and Austin, N. (1973b). A clinician's guide to personal effectiveness training. Unpublished manuscript, BAM Project, Dynard Mental Health Center.

Liberman, R. P., Teigen, J. R., Patterson, R. and Baker V. (1973c). *J. appl. behav. Anal.* **6**, 57–64.

Liberman, R. P., Wallace, C., Teigen, J. and David, J. (1974). *In* "Innovative Treatment Methods in Psychopathology" (Eds Calloun, K. S., Adams, H. D. and Mitchell, K. M.) 323–412.. Wiley, New York.

Lidz, T., Cornelison, A. R., Fleck, S. and Terry, D. (1957). *Am. J. Psychiat.* **114**, 241–248.

Lidz, T., Cornelison, A. R., Terry, D. and Fleck, S. (1958). *Archs Neurol. Psychiat.* **79**, 305–316.

Lilienfeld, A. M. (1957). *Publ. Hlth. Rept (Wash.)* **11**, 216.

Lindelius, R. (Ed.) (1970). *Acta psychiat. scand.* Suppl. 216.

Lindsey, C. R., Pound, A. and Radford, M. D. (1977). A co-operative playgroup in a psychiatric day hospital (to be published).

Lindsley, O. R. (1956). *Psychiat. Res. Rep.* **5**, 118–139.

Lindvall, O. and Bjorklund, A. (1974). *Acta. Physiol. scand.* Suppl. **412**.

Lindvall, O. and Bjorklund, A. (In press). In "Handbook of Psychopharmacology" (Eds Iversen, L. L., Iversen, S. D. and Snyder ,S. H.). Plenum Press, New York.

Lishman, W. A. and McMeekan, E. R. L. (1976). *Br. J. Psychiat.* **129**, 158–166.

Lobstein, T. J. (1974). Heart rate and skin conductance activity in schizophrenia. Unpublished PhD thesis, University of London.

Locke, B. Z. and Duvall, H. J. (1964). *Eugen. Q.* **11**, 216.

Lovibond, S. H. (1954). *Aust. J. Psychiat.* **6**, 52–70.

Ludwig, A. M., Wood, B. S. and Downs, M. P. (1962). *Am. J. Psychiat.* **119**, 122–127.

Luxenburger, H. (1928). *Z. ges. Neurol. Psychiat.* **116**, 297–326.

MacDonald, N. (1960). *Can. med. Ass. J.* **82**, 218–221.

MacMahon, B. and Pugh, J. F. (1970). "Epidemiology: Principles and Methods". Brown, Little, Boston.

MacMahon, B. and Sawa, J. M. (1961). In "Causes of Mental Distorders: a Review of Epidemilogical Knowledge" (Eds Gruenberg, E. M. and Huxley, M.). Millbank Memorial Fund, New York.

Maher, B. (1972). *Br. J. Psychiat.* **120**, 3–17.

Mahoney, M. J. (1974). "Cognition and Behaviour Modification". Ballinger, Cambridge, Mass.

Mahoney, M. J. (1977). *Am. Psychol.* **32**, No. 1, 5–13.

Main, T. F. (1946). *Bull. Menninger Clin.* **10**, 66.

Malzberg, B. (1963). *Acta psychiat. scand.* **39**, 19.

Malzberg, B. (1964a). *Int. J. soc. Psychiat.* **10**, 19.

Malzberg, B. (1964b). *Am. J. Psychiat.* **120**, 971.

Malzberg, B. and Lee, E. S. (1956). "Migration and mental disease: a study of first admission to hospitals for mental disease, New York, 1939–41". Social Science Research Council, New York.

Mandell, A. J. and Morgan, M. (1971). *Nature* N.B. **230**, 85–87.

Mann, S. and Cree, W. (1976). *Psychol. Med.* **6**, 603–616.

Markowe, M., Steinert, J. and Heyworth-Davis, F. (1967). *Br. J. Psychiat.* **113**, 1101–1106.

Marsden, C. D. (1976). *Lancet* ii, 1079 (Corr.).

Mathers, J. (1972). *Lancet* i, 894–895.

Matthysse, S. (1973). *Fed. Proc.* **32**, 200–214.

Matthysse, S. W. and Kety, S. S. (1974) (Eds). *J. Psychiat. Res.* **11**, 1–364. (Also published 1975 by Pergamon, Oxford.)

Matthysse, S. W. and Kidd, K. K. (1976). *Am. J. Psychiat.* **133**, 185–191.

Matthysse, S. and Lipinski, J. (1975). *Ann. Rev. Med.* **26**, 551–565.

May, A. R. (1976a). "Mental Health Services in Europe". W.H.O. Offset Publications No. 3. W.H.O., Geneva.

May, P. R. A. (1976b). *Am. J. Psychiat.* **133**, 1008–1012.

Mayer-Gross, W. (1932). *In* "Handbuch der Geisteskrankenheiten" Band I X(Ed. Bumke, O.). Springer, Berlin.

McCabe, M. S. (1975). *Acta psychiat. scand.* Suppl. **259**.

McCabe, M. S., Fowler, R. C., Cadoret, R. J. and Winokur, G. (1971). *Psychol. Med.* **1**, 326–332.

McCabe, M. S., Fowler, R. C., Cadoret, R. J. and Winokur, G. (1972). *Br. J. Psychiat.* **120**, 91–94.

McConaghy, N. (1959). *J. Neurol. Neurosurg. Psychiat.* **22**, 243–246.

McConaghy, N. and Clancy, N. (1968). *Br. J. Psychiat.* **114**, 1079–1087.

McGhie, A. (1970). "Pathology of Attention". Penguin, Harmondsworth.

McGhie, A. and Chapman, J. (1961). *Br. J. med. Psychol.* **24**, 103–116.

McGhie, A., Chapman, J. and Lawson, J. S. (1965). *Br. J. Psychiat.* **111**. 383–390.

McNeil, T. F. and Kaij, L. (1976). *Second Int. Conf. Schizophrenia.* Rochester, New York. (In press.)

McPherson, F. M., Antram, M. C., Bagshaw, V. E. and Carmichael, S. K. (1977). *Br. J. Psychiat.* **131**, 56–58.

Mechanic, D. (1968). "Medical Sociology: A Selective View". Free Press, New York.

Mechanic, D. (1970). *In* "Social and Psychological Factors in Stress" (Ed. McGrath, J. E.). Holt, Rinehart and Winston, New York.

Mednick, S. A. (1962). *In* "Clinical Psychology. Proceedings of the XIV International Congress of Applied Psychology" (Ed. Nielson, G. S.), Vol. 4. Munksgaard, Copenhagen.

Mednick, S. A. and Schulsinger, F. (1968). *In* "The Transmission of Schizophrenia" (Eds Rosenthal, D. and Kety, S.). Pergamon Press, Oxford.

Mednick, S. A., Schulsinger, F., Higgins, J. and Bell, B. (Eds) (1974). "Genetics, Environment and Psychopathology". North-Holland, Amsterdam.

Mednick, S. A., Schulsinger, F. and Schulsinger, H. (1975). *In* "Childhood Personality and Psychopathology: Current Topics (Ed. Davids, A.), Vol. 2. Wiley, New York.

Mednick, S. A., Schulsinger, F., Teasdale, T. W., Schulsinger, H., Venables P. H. and Rock, D. R. (1977). Schizophrenia in High Risk Children. Sex differences and predisposing factors. Paper presented to Kittay Scientific Foundation 5th International Symposium, New York.

Meehl, P. E. (1962). *Am. Psychol.* **17**, 827–838.

Meichenbaum, D. H. (1969). *Behav. Res. Ther.* **8**, 147–152.

Meichenbaum, D. H. and Cameron, R. (1973). *Behav. Ther.* **4**, 515–534.

Meltzer, H. Y. and Stahl, S. M. (1974). *Res. Commun. Chem. Pathol. Pharmoc.* **7**, 419–422.

Meltzer, H. Y., Sachar, E. J. and Frantz, A. G. (1974). *Archs gen. Psychiat.* **31**, 564–572.

Middlemiss, D. N., Blakeborough, L. and Leather, S. R. (1977). *Nature* **267**, 289–290.

Milby, J. B. (1970). *J. appl. behav. Anal.* **3**, 149–152.

Miles, A. (1971). *Br. J. Psychiat.* **119**, 611–620.

Miller, E. J. and Gwynne, G. V. (1972). "A Life Apart". Tavistock Publications London.

Miller, R. J. and Hiley, C. R. (1974). *Nature* **248**, 596–597.

Mirsky, A. F. (1969). *A. Rev. Psychol.* **20**, 321–348.

Mischel, W. (1973). *Psychol. Rev.* **80**, 252–283.

Mishler, E. G. and Waxler, N. E. (1965). *Merrill-Palmer Q.* **2**, 269.

Morgan, R. (1974). *Br. J. hosp. Med.* **12**, 231–242.

Morgan, R. and Cheadle, J. (1974). *Acta. psychiat. scand.* **50**, 78–85.

Mosher, L. R., Pollin, W. and Stabenau, J. R. (1971). *Br. J. Psychiat.* **118**, 29–42.

Murphy, H. B. M. (1959). *In* "Culture and Mental Health" (Ed. K. Marin). Macmillan, New York.

Murphy, H. B. M. (1968). *In* "The Transmission of Schizophrenia" (Eds Rosenthal, D. and Kety, S. S.). Pergamon, New York.

Murphy, H. B. M. and Raman, A. C. (1971). *Br. J. Psychiat.* **119**, 489–497.

Murphy, D. and Weiss, R. (1972). *Am. J. Psychiat.* **128**, 1351–1357.

Murphy, D. and Wyatt, R. (1972). *Nature* **238**, 225–226.

Myers, J. K. and Roberts, B. H. (1959). "Family and Class Dynamics in Mental Illness". Wiley, New York.

Myers, S., Caldwell, D. and Purcell, G. (1973). *Biol. Psychiat.* **7**, **3**, 255–261.

Myerson, A. (1939). *Am. J. Psychiat.* **95**, 1197–1204.

Narasimhachari, N., Plant, J. M. and Leiner, K. U. (1971). *Biochem. Med.* **5**, 304–310.

Narasimhachari, N., Avalos, J., Fujimori, M. and Himwich, H. E. (1972a). *Biol. Psychiat.* **5**, 311–318.

Narasimhachari, N., Plaut, J. M. and Himwich, H. E. (1972b). *Life Sci.*, **11**, 221–227.

National Association for Mental Health (1977). Home from hospital: progress and results. MIND Report, London.

National Institute of Mental Health (1964). *Archs gen. Psychiat.* **10**, 246–261.

Neisser, V. (1967). "Cognitive Psychology". Appleton-Century-Crofts, New York.

Nies, A., Robinson, D. S., Lambon, K. R. and Lampert, R. P. (1973). *Archs gen. Psychiat.* **28**, 834–837.

O'Connor, N. and Rawnsley, K. (1959). *Br. J. med. Psychol.* **32**, 133–143.

O'Connor, N., Heron, A. and Carstairs, G. M. (1956). *Occup. Psychol.* **30**, 1–12.

Ødegaard, Ø. (1946). *Psychiat. Q.* **20**, 381.

Ødegaard, Ø, (1952). *Psychiat. Q.* **26**, 212.

Ødegaard, Ø. (1956). *Int. J. soc. Psychiat.* **2**, 85.

Ødegaard, Ø. (1963). *Acta psychiat. scand.* Suppl. **169**, 39, 94–104.

Ødegaard, Ø. (1971). *Soc. Psychiat.* **6**, 53.

Ødegaard, Ø (1972). *In* "Genetic Factors in 'Schizophrenia' " (Ed. Kaplan, A. R.) 256–275. Thomas, Springfield, Illinois.

Oltman, J. E. and Friedman, S. (1965). *Archs gen. Psychiat.* **12**, 46.

O'Neal, P. and Robins, L. N. (1958). *Am. J. Psychiat.* **115**, 385–391.

Oon, M. C., Muray, R. M., Brockinton, I. F. (1975). *Lancet* **2**, 1146–1147.

Ornitz, E. A. (1970). *Compreh. Psychiat.* **11**, 159–173.

Osmond, H., Smythies, J. R. and Harley-Mason, J. (1952). *J. ment. Sci.* **98**, 309–315.

Owen, F., Bourne, R., Crow, T. J., Johnstone, E. C., Bailey, A. R. and Hershon, H. I. (1976). *Archs gen. Psychiat.* **33**, 1370–1373.

Paffenbarger, R. S. (1964). *Br. J. prev. soc. Med.* **18**, 189.

Park, L. C., Baldessarini, R. J. and Kety, S. S. (1965). *Archs gen. Psychiat.* **12**, 346–351.

Parker, N. (1964). *Br. J. Psychiat.* **110**, 496–504.

Parsons, T. and Fox, R. C. (1952). *J. soc. Issues* **8**, 31–44.

Pasamanick, B. (1961). *In* "Comparative Epidemiology of the Mental Disorders" (Eds Hoch, P. H. and Zubin, J.). New York.

Pasamanick, B. and Lilenfeld, A. (1955). *J. Am. med. Ass.* **159**, 155–160.

Patterson, R. L. and Teigen, J. R. (1973). *J. app. behav. Anal.* **6**, 65–70.

Patterson, T. and Venables, P. H. (1977). (In preparation.)

Pavlov, I. (1927). "Conditional Reflexes: an Investigation of Physiological Activity in the Cerebral Cortex" (Trans. G. V. Antrep). Oxford University Press, New York.

Pavy, D. (1968). *Psychol. Bull.* **70**, 3, 164–178.

Paykel, E. S. (1974). *In* "Stressful Life Events" (Eds Dohrenwend, B. S. and Dohrenwend, B. P.). Wiley, New York.

Paykel, E. S. (1977). Contribution of life-events to causation of psychiatric illness. Unpublished MS.

Payne, R. W. (1962). *Br. J. soc. clin. Psychol.* **1**, 213–221.

Payne, R. W. and Caird, W. K. (1967). *J. abnorm. Psychol.* **72**, 112–121.

Peroutka, S. J., U'Prichard, D. C., Greenburg, D. A. and Snyder, S. H. (1977). *Neuropharmac.* **16**, 549–556.

Perris, C. (1974). *Acta psychiat. scand. Suppl.* 253.

Petrie, A. (1960). *Ann. N. Y. Acad. Sci.* **86**, 13–27.

Phillips, J. E., Jacobson, N. and Turner, W. J. (1965). *Br. J. Psychiat.* **iii**, 823.

Phillips, L. (1953). *J. nerv. ment. Dis.* **117**, 515.

Phillips, L. (1968). "Human Adaptation and its Failures". Academic Press, New York and London.

Pinder, R. M., Brogden, R. N., Sawyer, P. R., Speight, T. M., Spencer, R. and Avery, G. S. (1976). *Drugs* (NZ) **12**, 1–40.

Plank, R. (1959). *Am. J. Orthopsychiat.* **28**, 819.

Pletscher, A. and Kyburg, E. (1976). *In* "Schizophrenia Today" (Eds Kemali, D., Bartholine, G. and Richter, D.) 183–200. Pergamon Press, Oxford.

Plum, F. (1972). *Bull. Neurosci. Res. Prog.* **10**, 384.

Pollin, W. and Stabenau, J. R. (1968). *In* "The Transmission of Schizophrenia" (Eds Rosenthal, D. and Kety, S. S.) 317–332. Pergamon Press, Oxford.

Pollin, W., Cardon, P. V. and Kety, S. S. (1961). *Science* **133**, 104–105.

Pollin, W., Stabenau, J. R., Mosher, L. and Tupin, J. (1966). *Am. J. Orthopsychiat.* **36**, 492.

Pollin, W., Allen, M. G., Hoffer, A., Stabenau, J. R. and Hrubec, Z. (1969). *Am. J. Psychiat.* **126**, 597–609.

Post, F. (1966). "Persistent Persecutory States of the Elderly". Pergamon Press, Oxford.

Post, R. M., Fink, E., Carpenter, W. T. and Goodwin, F. K. (1975). *Archs gen. Psychiat.* **32**, 1063–1069.

Prien, R. F. and Klett, C. J. (1970). An appraisal of the long-term use of tranquillizing medication with hospitalised chronic schizophrenics. Pre-publication Report No. 85. Central Neuro-Psychiatric Research Laboratory, Perry Point, Maryland.

Prien, R. F., Cole, J. O. and Belkin, N. F. (1968). *Br. J. Psychiat.* **115**, 679–686.

Pugh, T. F., Jerath, B. K., Schmidt, W. M. and Reed, R. B. (1963). *New Engl. J. Med.* **268**, 1224.

Randrup, A. and Munkvad, I. (1974). *J. Psychiat. Res.* **11**, 1–10.

Rapoport, R. N. (1960). "Community as Doctor". Tavistock Publications, London.

Rappaport, M., Silverman, J., Hopkins, H. K. and Hall, K. (1971). *Science* **174**, 723–725.

Rappaport, M., Hopkins, H. K. and Hall, K. (1972). *Archs gen. Psychiat.* **27**, 747–752.

Reed, S. C., Hartley, C., Anderson, V. E., Phillips, V. P. and Johnson, N. A. (1973). "They Psychoses: Family Studies". Saunders, Philadelphia.

Reich, T., Cloninger, C. R. and Guze, S. B. (1975). *Br. J. Psychiat.* **127**, 1–10.

Reid, D. D. (1960). "Epidemiological Methods in the Study of Mental Disorders". Public Health Papers No. 2. Geneva, WHO.

Reiss, D. (1968). *In* "The Transmission of Schizophrenia" (Eds Rosenthal, D. and Kety, S. S.). Pergamon Press, New York.

Renton, C. A., Affleck, J. W., Carstairs, M. and Forrest, A. D. (1963). *Acta psychiat. scand.* **39**, 548–600.

Reybee, J. and Kinch, B. R. (1973). Treatment of auditory hallucinations using "focussing". Unpublished study.

Reynolds, E. H. (1968). *Lancet* **1**, 398–401.

Reynolds, E. H. (1975). *Lancet* **2**, 189–190.

Richter, D. (1970). *Biol. Psychiat.* **2**, 153–164.

Richter, D. (1976). *In* "Schizophrenia Today" (Eds Kemali, D., Bartholini, G. and Richter, D.) 71–83. Pergamon Press, Oxford.

Ricks, D. M. and Wing, L. (1975). *J. Autism Childhood Schiz.* **5**, 191–221.

Ridges, A. P. (1973). *In* "Biochemistry and Mental Illness" (Eds Iversen, L. L. and Rose, S. P. R.). *Biochem. Soc. Special Publ.* **1**, 175–188.

Riding, J. and Munro, A. (1975). *Acta psychiat. scand.* **52**, 23–30.

Ringuette, E. and Kennedy, T. (1966). *J. abnorm. Psychol.* **71**, 136–141.

Rin, H. and Lin, T. Y. (1962). *J. ment. Sci.* **108**, 134.

Ritzler, B. and Rosenbaum, G. (1974). *J. abnorm. Psychol.* **83**, 2, 106–111.

Robers, J. A. Fraser (1965). *In* "Genetics and the Epidemiology of Chronic Diseases" (Eds Neel, J. V., Shaw, M. W. and Schull, W. J.) 77–86. Public Health Service Publication No. 1163. U.S. Dept Health, Education, and Welfare, Public Health Service, Washington, D.C.

Roberts, J. A. Fraser (1973). "An Introduction to Medical Genetics". Oxford University Press, London.

Robins, L. N. (1970). *In* "Psychiatric Epidemiology" (Eds Haer, E. H. and Wing, J. K.). Oxford University Press, London.

Rodnight, R., Murray, R. M., Oon, M. C. H., Brockington, I. F., Nicholls, P. and Birley, J. L. T. (1977). *Psychol. Med.* **6**, 649–657.

Rogers, C. R., Gendlin, E. T., Kiesler, D. and Truax, C. B. (1967). "The Therapeutic Relationship and its Impact: a Study of Psychotherapy with Schizophrenics". University Wisconsin Press, Madison.

Rogler, X. and Hollingshead, A. B. (1965). "Trapped: Families and Schizophrenia". Wiley, New York.

Rollin, H. R. (1963). *Br. med. J.* **1**, 786–788.

Rosenbaum, G., Cohen, B., Luby, E., Gotleib, J. and Yelen, D. (1959). *Archs gen. Psychiat.* **1** 651–656.

Rosenbaum, G., Fleming, F. and Rosen, H. (1965). *J. abnorm. Psychol.* **70**, 446–450.

Rosenhan, D. L. (1973). *Science* **179**, 250–258.

Rosanoff, A. J., Handy, L. M., Plesset, I. R. and Brush, S. (1934). *Am. J. Psychiat.* **91**, 247–286.

Rosenthal, D. (1970). "Genetic Theory and Abnormal Behavior". McGraw-Hill, New York.

Rosenthal D. (1971). *Behav. Sci.* **16**, 191–201.

Rosenthal, D. (1972). *Int. J. ment. Health* **1**, No. 1–2, 63–75.

Rosenthal, D. and Kety, S. S. (Eds) (1968). "The Transmission of Schizophrenia". Pergamon Press, Oxford.

Rosenthal, D. and Van Dyke, J. (1970). *Acta psychiat. scand. Suppl.* 219, **46**, 183–189.

Rosenthal, D., Wender, P. H., Kety, S. S., Schulsinger, F., Welner, J. and Østergaard, L. (1968). *In* "The Transmission of Schizophrenia" (Eds Rosenthal, D. and Kety, S. S.) 377–391. Pergamon Press, Oxford.

Rosenthal, G., Ineson, H. and Andrews, P. (1972). *Nursing Times* **68**, 1182–1185.

Rosman, B., Wild, C., Ricci, J., Flech, S. and Lidz, T. (1964). *J. psychiat. Res.* **2**, 211–221.

Rowitz, L. and Levy, L. (1968). *Archs gen. Psychiat.* **19**, 571.

Rutner, I. T. and Bugle, C. (1969). *J. consult. clin. Psychol.* **33**, 651–663.

Rutter, M. (1972). "Maternal Deprivation". Penguin Books, London.

Rutter, M. and Brown, G. W. (1966). *Soc. Psychiat.* **1**, 38–53.

Saavedra, J. M. and Axelrod, J. (1972a). *Science* **75**, 1365–1366.

Saavedra, J. M. and Axelrod, J. (1972b). *J. pharmac. exp. Ther.* **182**, 363–369.

Saavedra, J. M., Coyle, J. T. and Axelrod, J. (1973). *J. Neurochem.* **20**, 743–752.

Sachs, O. W. (1973). "Awakenings". Duckworth, London.

Salzinger, K., Portnoy, G., Pisoni, D. B. and Feldman, R. S. (1970). *J. abnorm. Psychol.* **75**, 258–264.

Sandler, M. and Reynolds, G, P. (1976). *Lancet* **1**, 70–71.

Sartorius, N. (1976). *Psychiat. Ann.* **6**, 24–35.

Scarr, S. (1968). *Eugen. Q.* **15**, 34–40.

Scharfetter, C., Moerbt, H. and Wing, J. K. *Arch. Psychiat. Nervenkr.* **222**, 61–67.

Scheff, T. J. (1966). "Being Mentally Ill". Aldine, Chicago.

Schildkraut, J., Herzog, J. M., Orsulak, P. J., Edelman, S. E., Shein, H. M. and Frazier, S. H. (1976). *Am. J. Psychiat.* **133**, 438–443.

Schizophrenia Bulletin (1976). Vol. 2, No. 3.

Schneider, K. (1971). "Klinische Psychopathologie", 9th edn. Thieme, Stuttgart.

Schooler, C. (1961). *Archs gen. Psychiat.* **4**, 91.

Schroeder, C. W. (1942). *Am. J. Sociol.* **48**, 40.

Schwartz, M. A., Aikens, A. M. and Wyatt, R. J. (1974a). *Psychopharmacol.* **38**, 319–328.

Schwartz, M. A., Wyatt, R. J., Yang, H. Y. T. and Neff, N. H. (1974b). *Archs gen. Psychiat.* **31**, 557–560.

Seeman, P. (1972). *Pharmac. Rev.* **24**, 583–655.

Seeman, P., Lee, T., Chau-Wong, M. and Wong, K. (1976). *Nature* **261**, 717–719.

Shagass, C., Amadeo, M. and Overton, D. A. (1974). *Biol. Psychiat.* **9**, 245–260.

Shagass, C., Roemer, R. A. and Amadeo, M. (1976). *Archs gen. Psychiat.* **33**, 121–125.

Shakow, D. (1962). *Archs gen. Psychiat.* **6**, 1–17.

Shapiro, M. B. (1966). *J. gen. Psychol.* **74**, 3–23.

Sharan, S. N. (1966). *J. abnorm. Psychol.* **71**, 345–353.

Shaskan, E. G. and Becker, R. E. (1975). *Nature* **253**, 659–660.

Shepherd, G. (1977). *Behav. Ther.* (in press).

Sherman, J. A. (1965). *J. abnorm. soc. Psychol.* **70**, 155–164.

Shields, J. (1954). *Eugen. Rev.* **45**, 213–246.

Shields, J. (1962). "Monozygotic Twins Brought up Apart and Brought Up Together". Oxford University Press, London.

Shields, J. (1968). *In* "The Transmission of Schizophrenia" (Eds Rosenthal, D. and Kety, S. S.) 95–126. Pergamon Press, Oxford.

Shields, J. (1973). *In* "Handbook of Abnormal Psychology" (Ed. Eysenck, H. J.) 2nd edn, 540–603. Pitman Medical, London.

Shields, J. (1977). *Psychol. Med.* **7**, 7–01.

Shields, J. and Gottesman, I. I. (1972). *Archs gen. Psychiat.* **27**, 725–730.

Shields, T. and Slater, E. (1975). *In* "Contemporary Psychiatry "(Eds Silverstone, J. and Barraclough, B.) *Br. J. Psychiat. Spec. Publ. No.* 9. Headley Bros., Ashford, Kent.

Shields, J., Gottesman, I. I. and Slater, E. (1967). *Acta psychiat. scand.* **43**, 385–396.

Shields, J., Heston, L. L. and Gottesman, I. I. (1975). *In* "Genetic Research in Psychiatry" (Eds Fieve, R. R., Rosenthal, D. and Brill, H.) 167–197. Johns Hopkins University Press, Baltimore and London.

Siegler, M., Osmond, H. and Mann, H. (1969). *Br. J. Psychiat.* **115**, 947–958.

Silverman, J. (1964). *Psychol. Rev.* **71**, 352–379.

Silverman, J. (1967). *Psychosom. Med.* **29**, 225–251.

Silverman, J., Buchsbaum, M. and Henkin, R. (1969). *Percept. Mot. Skills* **28**, 71–78.

Simpson, G. M. and Angus, J. W. S. (1970). *Acta psychiat. scand. Suppl.* 212.

Sims, A., Salmons, P. and Humphreys, P. (1977). *Br. J. Psychiat.* **130**, 134–136.

Singer, M. T. and Wynne, L. C. (1966a). *Psychiatry* **29**, 260–288.

Singer, M. T. and Wynne, L. C. (1966b). *Psychiat. Res. Rep.* **20**, 25–38.

Singh, M. M. and Kay, S. R. (1976). *Science* **191**, 401–402.

Skinner, B. F. (1938). "The Behaviour of Organisms". Appleton-Century-Crofts, New York.

Skynner, A. C. R. (1975). *In* "The Large Group" (Ed. Kreeger, L.) Chapter 8. Constable, London.

Slade, P. D. (1972). *Behav. Res. Ther.* **10**, 85–91.

Slater, E. (1958). *Acta genet. Statist. med.* **8**, 50—56.

Slater, E. (1966). *J. med. Genet.* **3**, 159–161.

Slater, E. (1968). *In* "The Transmission of Schizophrenia" (Eds Rosenthal, D. and Kety, S. S.). Pergamon Press, New York.

Slater, E. (1972). *In* "Genetic Factors in 'Schizophrenia' " (Ed. Kaplan, A. R.) 173–180. Thomas, Springfield, Illinois.

Slater, E. and Cowie, V. (1971). "The Genetics of Mental Disorders". Oxford University Press, London.

Slater, E. and Roth, M. (1969). "Clinical Psychiatry" 3rd edn. Cassell, London.

Slater, E., Beard, A. W. and Glithero, E. (1963). *Br. J. Psychiat.* **109**, 95–150.

Smith, C. (1971a). *Am. J. hum. Genet.* **23**, 578–588.

Smith, C. (1971b). *Clin. Genet.* **2**, 303–314.

Smith, J. M. (1976). *Science* **194**, 448.

Smith, T. C., Bower, W. H. and Wignall, C. M. (1965). *Archs gen. Psychiat.* **21**, 352–362.

Smythies, J. R. (1976). *Lancet* ii, 136–139.

Snodgrass, S. R. and Horn, A. S. (1973). *J. Neurochem.* **21**, 687–696.

Snyder, S. H. (1973a). "The Neurosciences. Third Study Program" (Eds Schmitt, F. O. and Worden, F. C.) 721–732. Rockefeller Press, New York.

Snyder, S. H. (1973b). *Am. J. Psychiat.* **130**, 61–67.

Snyder, S. H., Banerjee, S. P., Yamamura, H. I. and Greenberg, D. (1974a). *Science* **184**, 1243–1253.

Snyder, S. H., Greenberg, D. and Yamamura, H. (1974b). *Archs gen. Psychiat.* **31**, 58–61.

Sokolov, E. N. (1963). "Perception and the Conditioned Reflex". Macmillan, New York.

Sommer, R. (1969). "Personal Space". Prentice-Hall, New Jersey.

Sommer, R. and Osmond, H. (1960). *J. ment. Sci.* **106**, 648–662. (Also addendum: *J. ment. Sci.* 1961, **107**, 1030–1032).

Spitzer, R. (1977). *In* "Psychiatric Diagnosis" (Eds Rackoff, V., Stancer, H. C. and Kedward, H.). Brunner Mazel, New York.

Srole, L., Langner, T. S., Michael, S. T. *et al.* (1962). "Mental Health in the Metropolis: the Midtown Manhattan study", Vol. 1. McGraw-Hill, New York.

Steinberg, H. R. and Durell, J. (1968). *Br. J. Psychiat.* **114**, 1097.

Steinberg, H. R. and Robinson, J. (1968). *Nature* **217**, 1054–1055.

Stengel, E. (1960). *Proc. R. Soc. Med.* **53**, 1052.

Stephens, D. A., Atkinson, M. W., Kay, D. W. K., Roth, M. and Garside, R. F. (1975). *Br. J. Psychiat.* **127**, 97–108.

Stevens, B. C. (1969). "Marriage and Fertility of Women suffering from Schizophrenia or Affective Distorders". Maudsley Monographs No. 19. Oxford Universiy Press, London.

Stevens, B. C. (1973a). *Acta psychiat. scand.* **49**, 169–180.

Stevens, B. C. (1973b). *Psychol. Med.* **3**, 141–158.

Stilson, D. W. and Kopell, B. S. (1964). *J. nerv. ment. Dis.* **139**, 3, 209–221.

Stilson, D. W., Kopell, B. S., Vandenbergh, R. and Downs, M. P. (1966). *J. nerv. ment. Dis.* **142**, 235–274.

Stone, A. A. and Eldred, S. H. (1959). *Archs gen. Psychiat.* **1**, 177–179.

Strauss, J. S. and Carpenter, W. T. (1972). *Archs gen. Psychiat.* **27**, 739–746.

Strauss, J. S. and Carpenter, W. T. (1973). The prediction of outome in schizophrenia, II. A.P.A. Ann. Meeting, Honolulu (mimeo).

Strömgren, E. (1950). Statistical and genetical population studies within psychiatry. Methods and principal results. Congrès Internationale de Psychiatrie, Paris, 1950, Rapports VI, Génétique et Eugénique, 155–188. Hermann, Paris.

Sundby, P. and Nyhus, P. (1963). *Acta psychiat. scand.* **39**, 519.

Susser, M. (1973). "Causal Research in the Health Sciences". Oxford University Press, London.

Szara, S. (1961). *Fed. Proc.* **20**, 885–888.

Tarrier, N., Vaughn, C., Lader, M. H. and Leff, J. P. (1977). Bodily reactions to people and events in schizophrenia. To be published.

Taylor, F. R. (1963). *J. clin. Psychol.* **19**, 130–131.

Terris, M. (1965). *Archs gen. Psychiat.* **12**, 420

Thudichum, H. (1884). "A Treatise on the Chemical Constitution of the Brain". Bailliere, Tindall and Cox, London.

Tidmarsh, D. and Wood, S. (1972). *In* "Evaluating a Community Psychiatric Service" (Eds Wing, J. K. and Hailey, A. M.) 327–340. Oxford University Press, London.

Tienari, P. (1963). *Acta psychiat. scand. Suppl.* 171.

Tienari, P. (1968). *In* "The Transmission of Schizophrenia" (Eds Rosenthal, D. and Kety, S. S.) 27–36. Pergamon Press, Oxford.

Tienari, P. (1971). *Psychiat. Fennica* 97–104.

Tietze, C., Lemkau, P. V. and Cooper, M. (1941). *Am. J. Sociol.* **47**, 167.

Tooth, G. C. and Brook, E. M. (1961). *Lancet* **i**, 710–713.

Travis, L. E. (1924). *J. abnorm. soc. Psychol.* **18**, 350–368.

Travis, R. C. (1926). *Psychol. Monogr.* **36**, 18–37.

Tsuang, M. T. (1975). *Biol. Psychiat.* **10**, 465–474.

Tsuang, M. T., Fowler, R. C., Cadoret, R. J. and Monnelly, E. (1974). *Compreh. Psychiat.* **15**, 295–302.

Ullman, L. and Krasner, L. (1969). "A Psycholological Approach to Abnormal Behaviour". Prentice-Hall, Englewood Cliffs, New Jersey.

Ungerstedt, U. (1971). *Acta physiol. scand. Suppl.* 367.

Utena, H., Kanamura, H., Suda, S., Nakamura, R., Machiyama, Y. and Takahashi, R. (1968). *Proc. Japan Acad.* **44**, 1078–1083.

Van Krevelen, D. A. (1971). *J. Autism Childhood Schiz.* **1**, 82–86.

Van Praag, H. M. (1977). *Br. J. Psychiat.* **130**, 463–474.

Varga (1966). "Changes in the Symptomatology of Psychiatric Patterns". Budapest Akademiai Kiado.

Vaughn, C. E. and Leff, J. P. (1976a). *Br. J. Psychiat.* **129**, 125–137.

Venables, P. H. (1957). *J. ment. Sci.* **103**, 197.

Venables, P. H. (1964). *In* "Advances in Experimental Personality Research I" (Ed. Maher, B.) Chapter 1. Academic Press, New York and London.

Venables, P. H. (1967). *In* "Origins of Schizophrenia" (Ed. Romano, J.). Excerpta Medica, Amsterdam.

Venables, P. H. (1973). *In* "Psychopathology" (Eds Hammer, M., Salzinger and Sutton, S.) Chapter 14. Wiley, New York.

Venables, P. H. (1975). *In* "Clinical Applications of Psychophysiology (Ed. Fowler, D. C.). Columbia University Press, New York.

Venables, P. H. and O'Connor, N. (1959). *Q. J. exp. Psychol.* **11**, 175–179.

Venables, P. H. and Tizard, J. (1956). *J. abnorm. soc. Psychol.* **33**, 2, 220–224.

Venables, P. H. and Tizard, J. (1958). *J. ment. Science* **104**, **437**, 1160–1163.

Venables, P. H. and Wing, J. K. (1962). *Archs gen. Psychiat.* **7**, 114–119.

Venables, P. H., Mednick, S. A., Schulsinger, F., Raman, A. C., Bell, B., Dalais, J. C. and Fletcher, R. P. (1977). Screening for risk of mental illness. Paper presented to Kittay Scientific Foundation 5th International Symposium, New York.

Vogt, M. (1974). *J. Psychiat. Res.* **11**, 183–184.

Wadsworth, W. V., Scott, R. F. and Tonge, W. L. (1958). *Lancet* **2**, 896–897.

Wadsworth, W. V., Wells, B. W. P. and Scott, R. F. (1962). A comparative study of chronic schizophrenics and normal subjects on a work task involving sequential operations.

Walsh, D. (1969). *Br. J. Psychiat.* **115**, 449.

Wansbrough, S. N. (1971). Contract and pay questions in industrial therapy units. King Edward VII's Hospital Fund for London.

Wansbrough, S. N. and Miles, A. (1968). Industrial therapy in psychiatric hospitals. King Edward VII's Hospital Fund for London.

Waring, M. and Rocks, D. (1965). *J. nerv. ment. Dis.* **140**, 351–364.

Watt, D. C. (1975). *Psychol. Med.* **5**, 222–226.

Watt, N. F. and Lubensky, A. W. (1976). *J. consult. clin. Psychol.* **44**, 363–375.

Watt, N. F., Stolorow, R. D., Lubensky, A. W. and McLelland, D. C. (1970). *Am. J. Ortho-psychiat.* **40**, 637–657.

Watts, F. N. (1974). *In* "Social Treatments in a Textbook of Human Psychology" (Eds Eysenck, H. J. and Wilson, G. D.). Academic Press, London and New York.

Watts, F. N. (1977). *Br. J. soc. clin. Psych.* (in press).

Watts, F. N. and Bennett, D. H. (1977). *Psych. Med.* (in press).

Watzlawick, P., Beavin, J. H. and Jackson, D. D. (1968). "Pragmatics of Human Communications". Faber, London.

Weakland, J. H. (1960). *In* "The Etiology of Schizophrenia" (Ed. Jackson, D.). Basic Books, New York.

Wells, F. L. and Kelley, C. M. (1922). *Am. J. Psychiat.* **2**, 53–59.

Wender, P. H., Rosenthal, D., Kety, S. S., Schulsinger, F. and Welner, J. (1973). *Archs gen. Psychiat.* **28**, 318–325.

Wender, P. H., Rosenthal, D., Kety, S. S., Schulsinger, F. and Welner, J. (1974). *Archs gen. Psychiat.* **30**, 121–128.

Willcox, D. R. C., Gillan, R. and Hare, F. H. (1965). *Br. med. J.* **ii**, 790–792.

Williams, A. R. T. and Blackler, F. H. M. (1971). *In* "Psychology at Work" (Ed. Warr, P. B.) Chapter 14. Penguin Education, London.

Williams, M. (1966). *Br. J. soc. clin. Psychol.* **5**, 161–171.

Wilson, F. S. and Walters, R. H. (1966). *Behav. Res. Ther.* **4**, 59–67.

Wincze, J. P., Leitenberg, H. and Agras, W. S. (1972). *J. Appl. Behav. Anal.* **25**, 47–262.

Wing, J. K. (1961). *J. ment. Sci.* **107**, 862.

Wing, J. K. (1963). *Br. J. Psychiat.* **109**, 635–641.

Wing, J. K. (1966). *Soc. Psychiat.* **1**, 21–28.

Wing, J. K. (Ed.) (1975). "Schizophrenia from Within". National Schizophrenia Fellowship, 78 Victoria Road, Surbiton, Surrey.

Wing, J. K. (1976). *In* "Early Childhood Autism" (Ed. Wing, L.). Pergamon Press Oxford and New York.

Wing, J. K. (1977). *In* "Psychiatric Diagnosis" (Eds Rackoff, V, Stancer, H. C. and Kedward, H. B.). Brunner Mazel, New York.

Wing, J. K. (1978). "Reasoning about Madness". Oxford University Press, London and New York.

Wing, J. K. and Brown, G. W. (1961). *J. ment. Sci.* **107**, 847–861.

Wing, J. K. and Brown, G. W. (1970). "Institutionalism and Schizophrenia". Cambridge University Press, London.

Wing, J. K. and Freudenberg, R. K. (1961). *Am. J. Psychiat.* **118**, 311.

Wing, J. K. and Fryers, T. (1976). "Psychiatric Services in Camberwell, and Salford". MRC Social Psychiatry Unit, Institute of Psychiatry, London.

Wing, J. K. and Hailey, A. M. (1972) (Eds) "Evaluating a Community Psychiatric Service: The Camberwell Register 1964–71". Oxford University Press, London.

Wing, J. K. and Nixon, J. (1975). *Archs gen. Psychiat.* **32**, 853–859.

Wing, J. K., Bennett, D. H. and Denham, J. (1964). The industrial rehabilitation of long-stay schizophrenic patients. Medical Research Council Memo. No. 42. H.M.S.O., London.

Wing, J. K., Leff, J. and Hirsch, S. H. (1973). *In* "Psychopathology and Psychopharmacology" (Eds Cole, J. O., Freedman, A. M. and Friedhoff, A. J.). Johns Hopkins University Press, Baltimore.

Wing, J. K., Cooper, J. E. and Sartorius, N. (1974). "The Description and Classification of Psychiatric Symptoms: An Instruction Manual for the PSE and Catego System". Cambridge University Press, London.

Wing, J. K., Nixon, J., von Cranach, M. and Strauss, A. (1978). *Arch. Psychiat. Neurol. Sci.* **224**.

Wing, L. (Ed.) (1976). "Early Childhood Autism", 2nd edn. Pergamon Press, Oxford and New York.

Wing, L., Wing, J. K., Stevens, B. and Griffiths, D. (1972). *In* "Evaluating a Community Psychiatric Service: The Camberwell Register 1964–71" (Eds Wing, J. K. and Hailey, A. M.) 283–308. Oxford University Press, London.

Winokur, G., Morrison, J., Clancy, J. and Crowe, R. (1974). *J. nerv. ment. Dis.* **159**, 12–19.

Winter, W. and Feirreira, A. (1967). *Family Process* **6**, 155–172.

Wise, C. D. and Stein, L. (1973). *Science* **181**, 344–346.

Wise, C. D., Baden, M. M. and Stein, L. (1974). *J. Psychiat. Res.* **11**, 185–198.

Wood, S. M. (1976). *J. soc. Pol.* **5**, 389–399.

World Health Organization (1973). "International Pilot Study of Schizophrenia". WHO, Geneva.

World Health Organization (1974). "Glossary of Mental Disorders and Guide to their Classification". WHO, Geneva.

World Health Organization (1978). "Schizophrenia. A two-year follow-up of patients included in the IPSS". Wiley, London.

Wright, S. L. (1966). *Publ. Hlth.* **80**, 164.

Wyatt, R. J., Termini, B. A. and Davis J. (1971). *Schizophrenia Bull.* **4**, 10–66.

Wyatt, R. J., Murphy, D. L., Belmaker, R., Cohen, S., Donnelly, C. H. and Pollin, W. (1973a). *Science* **179**, 916–198.

Wyatt, R. J., Saavedra, J. M. and Axelrod, J. (1973b). *Am. J. Psychiat.* **130**, 754–760.

Wyatt, R. J., Schwartz, M. A., Erdelyi, E. and Barchas, J. D. (1975). *Science* **187**, 368–370.

Wynne, L. C. (1967). *In* "The Origins of Schizophrenia". Excerpta Medica International Congress Ser. No. 151.

Wynne, L. C., Ryckoff, I., Day, J. and Hirsch, S. (1958). *Psychiatry* **21**, 205–220.

Yates, A. J. (1966). *Aust. J. Psychol.* **18**, 2, 103–117.

Yates, A. J. (1970). "Behaviour Therapy". Wiley, New York.

Yolles, S. F. and Kramer, M. (1969). *In* "The Schizophrenic Syndrome" (Eds Bellak, L. and Loeb, L.). Grune and Stratton, New York.

Yorkston, N. J., Zaki, S. A., Thermen, J. F. A. and Havard, C. W. H. (1974). *Br. med. J.* **IV**, 633–635.

Yorkston, N. J., Gruzelier, J. H., Zaki, S. A., Hollander, D., Pitcher, D. R. and Sergeant, H. G. S. (1977). *Lancet* (Sept. 17) **ii**, 575–578.

Zerbin-Rudin, E. (1965). *Praxis* **54**, 1435–1442.

Zerbin-Rudin, E. (1967). *In* "Humangenetik, ein kurzes Handbuch" (Ed. Becker, P. E.) Vol. V/2, 446–577. Thieme, Stuttgart.

Zirkle, C. L. and Kaiser, C. (1970). *In* "Medicinal Chemistry" (Ed. Burger, A.) Vol. II, 1410. Wiley Interscience, New York.

Zubin, J. (1967). *A. Rev. Psychol.* **18**, 373–401.

Subject Index